Postcolonial histories have long emphasized the darker side of narratives of historical progress, especially their role in underwriting global and racial hierarchies. Concepts like primitiveness, backwardness, and underdevelopment not only racialized and gendered peoples and regions but also ranked them on a seemingly naturalized timeline – their "present" is our "past" – and reframed the politics of capitalist expansion and colonization as an orderly, natural process of evolution toward modernity. *Our Time Is Now* reveals that modernity particularly appealed to those excluded from power, precisely because of its aspirational and future orientation. In the process, marginalized peoples creatively imagined diverse political futures that redefined the racialized and temporal terms of modernity. Employing a critical reading of a wide variety of previously untapped sources, Julie Gibbings demonstrates how the struggle between indigenous people and settlers to manage contested ideas of time and history as well as practices of modern politics, economics, and social norms were central to the rise of coffee capitalism in Guatemala and to twentieth-century populist dictatorship and revolution.

Julie Gibbings is a lecturer in the School of History, Classics, and Archaeology at the University of Edinburgh.

Cambridge Latin American Studies

General Editors

KRIS LANE, Tulane University
MATTHEW RESTALL, Pennsylvania State University

Editor Emeritus

HERBERT S. KLEIN
Gouverneur Morris Emeritus Professor of History, Columbia University
and Hoover Research Fellow, Stanford University

Other Books in the Series

(continued after index)

Our Time Is Now

Race and Modernity in Postcolonial Guatemala

JULIE GIBBINGS

University of Edinburgh

CAMBRIDGE
UNIVERSITY PRESS

CAMBRIDGE
UNIVERSITY PRESS

University Printing House, Cambridge CB2 8BS, United Kingdom

One Liberty Plaza, 20th Floor, New York, NY 10006, USA

477 Williamstown Road, Port Melbourne, VIC 3207, Australia

314-321, 3rd Floor, Plot 3, Splendor Forum, Jasola District Centre, New Delhi - 110025, India

103 Penang Road, #05-06/07, Visioncrest Commercial, Singapore 238467

Cambridge University Press is part of the University of Cambridge.

It furthers the University's mission by disseminating knowledge in the pursuit of
education, learning and research at the highest international levels of excellence.

www.cambridge.org
Information on this title: www.cambridge.org/9781108733489
DOI: 10.1017/9781108774048

© Julie Gibbings 2020

First published 2020
First paperback edition 2022

A catalogue record for this publication is available from the British Library

ISBN 978-1-108-48914-0 Hardback
ISBN 978-1-108-73348-9 Paperback

*To the Guatemalans who have consistently imagined that a
different, more inclusive world is possible*

Contents

Maps, Figures, and Tables

Maps

Figures

Table

Acknowledgments

This book has taken far longer than I care to admit to complete and in the process it has taken me to reside in eight cities across four countries and two continents. Along the way, I have accumulated far more debts than I can possibly repay. In Guatemala, I would like to thank everyone at the Archivo General de Centro América, the municipalities of Cobán and San Pedro Carchá, the Biblioteca Nacional, Hemeroteca Nacional, as well as the Ministerio de Gobernación, and the Academia de Geografía e Historia in Guatemala City. I would especially like to thank Anna Carla Ericastilla for her tireless work on behalf of Guatemalan archives and for her guidance through the labyrinth of records. Marlon Garcia Arriaga deserves a special acknowledgment for providing invaluable archival expertise in San Pedro Carchá and Cobán, as well as for sharing his sharp insights, keen sense of irony, his stirring art, and above all his love of Alta Verapaz. This work would not be the same without them. I would also like to thank Anaïs García at CIRMA's fototeca for generous support and guidance. In the United States, I would also like to thank David Dressing at Tulane University's Latin American Library for his guidance in working in the Dieseldorff Collection and with Central American records. In addition, Juan Carlos Sarazua provided instrumental research assistance at a crucial juncture that helped to turn the dissertation into a book manuscript.

Outside the archives, there were many Guatemalans whose friendship made my time pleasurable and whose probing questions and lived experiences sharpened my understanding of Guatemalan history and society. I owe special thanks to Matilde González Izás and Gustavo Palma for many lively conversations that shaped this project in innumerable ways.

In Guatemala City, José Manuel Mayorga not only provided a place to live, but shared his incomparable lens into the multiplicity of life in Guatemala City. In Alta Verapaz, I owe a special debt to Juan José Guerrero for his many conversations and historical insights and to Carlos Albino Choc for inviting me to participate in *los costumbres* and for enriching my perspective on Q'eqchi' political ontologies. Juan Moncada deserves special mention for opening his photographic library and for believing in this project. Nan Cuz, who has since the writing passed, also deserves special mention, along with her son Thomas Schafer for supplying the cover image and sharing much more. I would also like to thank Paulina Aguilar Bol, Fernando Arias, Christiane Berth, David Carey Dillon, Ricardo Fagoaga, Alejandro Flores, Amie Kiddle, Michael Kirkpatrick, Selvin Garcia, María Victoria Garcia Vettorazzi, Lisa Munro, Catherine Nolan-Ferrell, Argentina Ponce, Sylvia Reyes Morales, Ingrid Sánchez, Helene Schleehauf, Robert Scott, Sylvia Sellers-Garcia, Alfredo and Manuela Tzi, Regina Wagner, Megan Ybarra, and Albertina Yoj Caal. I would especially like to thank *mis monjas*: Esther Sedano and family, Ana Lucia Grajeda, Hilda Victoria González, and Isai Coello Valladeres.

This book began as a dissertation at the University of Wisconsin-Madison, where I had the good fortune of working with Florencia E. Mallon, Steve J. Stern, and Francisco Scarano. I wish to especially thank Florencia and Steve for providing a model for politically engaged scholarship and collaborative mentorship and for showing me how to ground historical theory in deep empirical research. I would also like to thank Franco for constantly reminding me of the material realities and struggles of marginalized peoples. Though the community of Latin American scholars coming out of UW-Madison is large, I especially want single out Gabi Kuezlni, Jaymie Heilman, Gladys McCormick, Marc Hertzman, Molly Todd, Tamara Feinstein, Yesenia Purmada-Cruz, Andres Matias Ortíz, Geneviéve Dorais, Elena Clare McGrath, Debbie Sharnak, Bridgette Werner, Ponciano del Pino, Jessica Kirstein, and Nancy Appelbaum for a special thank you.

This project was also reconceived during a year at Yale's Agrarian Studies Program. I would especially like to thank Agrarian Studies' co-directors James C. Scott and K. Sivaramakrishnan for making my year so intellectually productive. I would also like to thank Guntra Aistara, Jennifer Lee Johnson, José Martínez, Alba Díaz Gaeda, and Daniel Tubb and everyone who attended the weekly Agrarian Studies seminar for such an intellectually enriching journey. At Yale, I also thank Gilbert Joseph for welcoming me into the community of Latin American historians and for providing crucial mentorship even after I had left. In addition, various people have read drafts of chapters. I would like to thank James C. Scott, Anne Eller, Barbara Weinstein, Vikram Tamboli, Karin Rosemblatt, Jessica Kirstein, Jim Handy, Marcela Echeverria, Owen Jones, Rachel Nolan, Todd Scarth, Alan Shane Dillingham, the Latin American Research cluster at the University of Manitoba, and everyone at Yale's Agrarian Studies Program for providing critical insights. I would also like to thank H. Glenn Penny for our many conversations about Germans abroad and for reading and commenting on the dissertation and book chapters. At the University of Manitoba, I would also like to thank Greg Bak, Jarvis Brownlie, Annette Desmarais, Danielle Dubois, Greg Flemming, Esyllt Jones, Fabiana Li, Adele Perry, Jono Peyton, Joy Stacey, Jocelyn Thorpe, David Watt, and the community at St. John's College for crucial support and friendship. As this project was coming to a close, I welcomed the opportunity to join the School of History, Classics, and Archaeology at the University of Edinburgh. I would like to thank Jake Blanc and Kate Ballantyne for making that transition smooth and friendly. I would especially like to thank Adam Budd for helping make Edinburgh a home.

Several institutions and programs have provided financial and other support that made the research of this book manuscript possible including the Social Sciences and Humanities Research Council of Canada, the University of Wisconsin-Madison, the University of Manitoba, as well as Yale's Agrarian Studies Program. Karen Carroll and Jessica Kirstein provided help with the manuscript preparation. I would also like to thank the editors Deborah Gershenowitz, Kris Lane, and Matthew Restall for believing in this project and bringing it into the world. I am deeply indebted to the two anonymous readers who provided many insightful comments and sharpened the final product. Chapter 3 of this book was originally published (in revised form) as "The Shadow of Slavery: Historical Time, Labor, and Citizenship in Nineteenth-Century Alta Verapaz, Guatemala," in *Hispanic American Historical Review* 96, no. 1 (2016): 73–108, © 2016, Duke University Press. All rights reserved. Republished by permission of the publisher. www.dukeupress.edu. Parts of Chapters 6 and 7 were originally published as "Mestizaje in the Age of Fascism: German and Q'eqchi' Maya Interracial Unions in Alta Verapaz, Guatemala" *German History*, Volume 34, Issue 2, June 2016, Pages 214–236. 2016 Oxford University Press. All Rights reserved. Republished by permission of the publisher.

A core of strong, beautiful, and brilliant people shaped this project in incalculable ways. I would especially like to thank Florencia Mallon for teaching me to be intellectually daring and to not shy away from the big ideas and even bigger projects, no matter how daunting. I would also like to thank Dillon/Heather Vrana for being an incomparable intellectual interlocutor, friend, and co-conspirator, and Laura-Zoë Humphreys for her careful readings, insightful questions, and beautiful friendship. I would like to thank Carrie Ryan for sharing so much over the past years and thinking through this project with me in *all* its incarnations. Finally, I would like to thank Sheri Gibbings for always being there as a friend, a sister, and intellectual interlocutor.

Last but not least, I owe special thanks to my family, particularly my parents, Edith and Neil, whose support is as deep as it is enduring. Not only did they model the hard work and raw determination required to complete this project, but their spirits of ineffable idealism and striving for a better world are at the core of this book. I also especially want to thank my siblings, Sheri, Derrick, and Anita, and their spouses, Rob, Karine, and Guillaume, for teaching me so much over the years about the beauty of familial bonds. My steadfast companions Clio and Iggy showed me how to be more fully in the present and provided a reprieve when I needed it most. Finally, I would like to thank Paul Jenkins for being with me through this project from its conception to its conclusion, and for shaping it and me indelibly along the way.

Introduction

History Will Write Our Names

In the first months of 1920, an unlikely coalition of university students, coffee planters, army officers, urban laborers, and clerical and lay supporters of the Catholic Church organized to overthrow the brutal twenty-two-year dictatorship of Manuel Estrada Cabrera (1898–1920). Multiplying across the country through a loosely knit network of Unionist Party branches and clubs, the diverse movement electrified the country with a unified call for democracy. As the movement swelled in early April 1920, participants suffered violent attacks by the National Police in Guatemala City's streets, which enlivened the resistance and expanded the Unionists' base of support.

Only five days before the dictator's hand-picked National Assembly declared President Estrada Cabrera insane and removed him from office, a group of more than a hundred Q'eqchi' Mayas (hereafter Q'eqchi') from the Unionist Club "Freedom of the Indian" seized the national spotlight. Spearheaded by José Ángel Icó, a relentless Q'eqchi' patriarch, the movement grew from the long-neglected, northern department of Alta Verapaz and sparked fear in the hearts of Guatemala's wealthy landowning classes. Driven by demands that far exceeded the ousting of an aged and corrupt president, these Q'eqchi's sought nothing short of a political revolution in the name of Maya rights and freedoms. Before the all-ladino (non-Maya) National Assembly, the Q'eqchi's delegates announced: "We are knocking on the door of our political emancipation."[1] They demanded Maya rights as citizens and an end to coerced

---

[1] Archivo General de Centro América (hereafter AGCA) B, Legajo (hereafter Leg.) 29466, "Club Unionista 'La Libertad del Indio' a la Asamblea," Cobán, April 3, 1920.

I

labor. Their petition, likely penned with the collaboration of a lawyer, invoked the constitutional articles that granted full rights to all citizens and pointed out the contradictions in the state's historical practices, ranging from a lack of primary schools in rural Maya communities and exclusion of Mayas from local governance to coerced labor and obligatory military service. Evoking the nation's upcoming centenary celebration of independence, the Q'eqchi' Unionist Club maintained: "We believe that if Guatemala wants to take its place among the civilized nations of the world so as to celebrate the centenary of its independence with dignity, before anything else it needs to give the Indian complete freedom." These radical Q'eqchi's concluded their missive by requesting that the assembly "honor our humble petition and take into account that an entire PUEBLO is looking upon Us, as the only ones to resolve their situation of FREEDOM OR SLAVERY" and remember that "History will collect our names in its pages, writing them with gold letters."[2] Evoking the structured binaries of slavery and freedom that framed nearly all nineteenth-century movements for political emancipation, Q'eqchi's pushed the National Assembly, and the nascent Unionist movement, toward broader definitions of the nation, citizenship, and Maya historical agency than previously conceived and demanded inclusion in the present. This book argues that, against state and others' efforts to continually render Mayas as anachronistic subjects who were out of step with progress, Q'eqchi's in Alta Verapaz continually built innovative political modernities and claimed agency as historic actors in the present.

Q'eqchi' Unionists sought to upend nearly a century of state practices toward Mayas in the western and northern coffee-growing regions that were at the heart of the nation's economy. Beginning in the mid-nineteenth century, coffee entrepreneurs drove a rapid political and economic transformation. Prior to the rise of coffee production, Alta Verapaz was largely a political and economic periphery. It neither possessed lucrative resources nor was geographically situated on a route to anywhere: beyond the Verapaz lived the largely autonomous indigenous populations in present-day Petén, Chiapas, and the Yucatán. Beginning in the 1860s, the promise of lucrative coffee production brought not only coffee trees, but also new settlers including ladinos, Germans and other Europeans, and North Americans. By the turn of the century, Alta

[2] Ibid.

Verapaz was transformed from a marginal region into a new center of the nation's political and economic production and power (see Map o.1).

Across the late nineteenth century, indigenous–state relations also changed as the Conservative government of President Rafael Carrera addressed burgeoning demands for indigenous land and labor by eroding colonial-era institutions that protected communal landholding and indigenous local political power, and by expanding and reinstituting the use

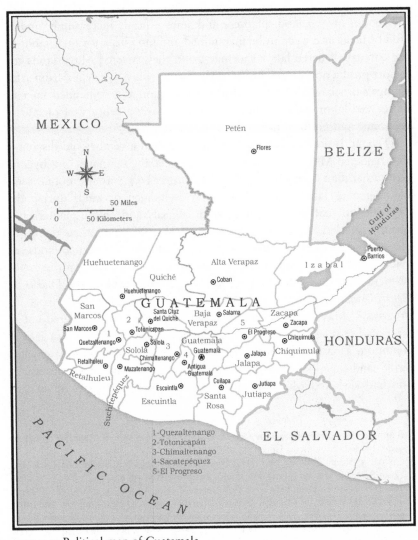

MAP o.1 Political map of Guatemala.
University of Wisconsin-Madison, Cartography Lab

of *mandamientos*, a state-operated system of forced wage labor. As a result of land dispossession and mandamientos, coffee production and export expanded rapidly, and state revenues derived from coffee jumped from less than 1 percent of total exports in 1852 to half of the nation's exports by the end of Conservative rule in 1871.[3] These processes accelerated after 1871 when the new Liberal government institutionalized mandamiento labor, formalized land privatization, and dissolved Maya-controlled town councils in favor of mixed town councils headed by ladinos. Since coffee production in Alta Verapaz overlapped with indigenous-owned land, planters and state officials increasingly understood Mayas as a caste to be maintained and mobilized for their labor in the context of fierce labor shortages, and they coveted Maya lands for export-production crops. In the early 1920s, when Q'eqchi's from Alta Verapaz proclaimed their political emancipation and demanded the end of coerced labor, they sought to overturn nearly a century of racialized economic and political practices.

Q'eqchi' Unionists also challenged more than a century-old discourse that rendered Mayas as anachronistic subjects, the remnants of a bygone past rather than agents of a progressive future. To justify the mobilization of indigenous labor and dispossession of indigenous lands during the expansion of coffee production, state officials and coffee planters frequently recoded Maya resistance to capitalism, including their refusal to labor for meager wages and their fierce hold on subsistence lands, as evidence of an inherent cultural backwardness. Remarking on the coffee planters' difficulties in obtaining labor, one editorialist in the *Diario de Centro-América* asserted that Mayas stood "immobile on the road to progress."[4] Maya opposition to coerced labor, then, was rendered not as a rational response to political and economic coercion but as a racialized condition: a natural indolence that supposedly arose from Guatemala's fertile landscape, which required little effort to produce basic necessities and had sheltered Mayas from the civilizing influences of commerce.[5]

---

[3] Ralph Lee Woodward Jr., *Rafael Carrera and the Emergence of the Republic of Guatemala, 1821–1871* (Athens: University of Georgia Press, 1993), 383.

[4] Quoted in Steven Palmer, "A Liberal Discipline: Inventing Nations in Guatemala and Costa Rica, 1870–1900" (PhD diss., Columbia University, 1990), 179.

[5] This perspective is attributed to the Colombian Mariano Ospina, who was for a time a diplomat in Guatemala. This analysis can be found in various editorials, reports, and coffee planter complaints. See, for example, Antonio Batres Jáuregui, *Los indios su historia y su civilización* (Guatemala: Tipografía La Unión, 1894), 158–9. See also David McCreery, *Rural Guatemala, 1760–1940* (Stanford, CA: Stanford University Press, 1994), 174–6.

A report from the Ministry of Development explained the solution to this supposed lack of drive: "It is necessary to make the Indian work for his own good, for the good of business and for the country because as a result of his apathetic and stationary character and his few needs, he is satisfied with practically nothing."[6] At other times, Maya practices, including their religious and spiritual traditions, were lambasted as problematic legacies of colonialism or as barbaric and superstitious traditions that should have been replaced by science and reason. Together, these discourses represented Mayas as temporal anomalies who needed special kinds of intervention or who threatened the progressive march of the nation.

In response to the Unionist Club "Freedom of the Indian" petition to the National Assembly in April 1920, Guatemalan intellectuals and coffee planters offered familiar, and trenchant, opposition. In the country's foremost newspaper, *El Diario de Centro-América*, an editorialist responded directly to the Freedom of the Indian Club's petition. He argued that Mayas were lazy and superstitious, opposed to all forms of progress and thus not yet ready for self-governance and citizenship. Instead, Mayas required state tutelage, "so that in the future, as soon as possible, *el indio* may constitute a true citizen capable of exercising their rights and fulfilling their obligations to themselves, without any special imposition or regulation."[7] This dynamic of contemporaneity and anachronism also constituted a strategy of temporal containment. State officials, coffee planters, and others often attempted to manage a recalcitrant difference by presuming a totalizing historical movement that applied to all peoples and cultures, labeling certain forms of difference as primitive or anachronistic.[8] The charge of anachronism – the claim that something is out of kilter with the present and really belongs to a superseded past – amounted to "somebody's way of saying 'not yet' to somebody else," of postponing the acquisition of sovereignty and self-government for those "not yet" advanced enough along the course of modernity.[9] This out-of-time argument repeated a refrain that had long been the cornerstone of what I call the *politics of postponement*. In this political strategy, Mayas' full participation as citizens in the nation was

---

[6] Cited in McCreery, *Rural Guatemala*, 175.

[7] Jorge García Salas, "Comentarios a la iniciativa del Club 'La Libertad del Indio,'" *Diario de Centro-América*, May 1, 1920.

[8] Reinhart Koselleck, *The Practice of Conceptual History: Timing History, Spacing Concepts*, trans. Todd Samuel Presner (Stanford, CA: Stanford University Press, 2002).

[9] Dipesh Chakrabarty, *Provincializing Europe: Postcolonial Thought and Historical Difference* (Princeton, NJ: Princeton University Press, 2001), 8.

postponed until an undisclosed time in the future when they had finally shed their uncivilized ways and become modern, thereby allowing the state and coffee planters to set limits to democratic participation and deploy practices largely regarded as antiquated remnants of colonialism and feudalism, such as coerced labor.

The Q'eqchi's of the Unionist Club, however, directly inverted the politics of postponement and made their emancipation a linchpin in Guatemala's final liberation from colonialism and entrance into the modern world of independent nation-states. Q'eqchi' Unionists also claimed the ability to act in historical time, to overcome circumstances, and to create history.[10] As with so many other early twentieth-century national democratic and revolutionary movements, Q'eqchi' Unionists envisioned themselves as historical actors who would finally put an end to the purgatory of history's waiting room. As the potential of a new future appeared on the horizon, Q'eqchi' Unionists, along with many other Guatemalans, also envisioned themselves as agents of revolutionary change, indeed history itself, even as some Q'eqchi's upended the modern notion of a universal, singular time altogether and spoke of times that included the enchanted worlds of gods and nonhumans. For some Q'eqchi's, other-than-human actors, including mountain spirits known as Tzuultaq'as, were also historical agents that directed the pace and quality of change.

Throughout the 1920s, rural Q'eqchi's in Alta Verapaz also took up the promise of a different world in ways that frequently exceeded the demands of the Q'eqchi' Unionists in Guatemala City. Rural Q'eqchi's invaded coffee plantations, uprooted coffee trees, and replaced them with subsistence crops, and they tore up labor contracts and declared themselves free. In doing so, they blended liberal ideas of virtue, autonomy, and self-determination with Q'eqchi' principles of solidarity, reciprocity, and subsistence production, ideas that derived from entirely different sets of principles, including notions of Maya spirit worlds. Through their varied actions, Q'eqchi's lived in a revolutionary time that was something akin to Walter Benjamin's *Jetzt-Zeit* (Now-Time) – that is, a time that diverged from nineteenth-century teleological and linear history. Instead,

---

[10] See, for example, "El Comercio" *El Norte*, April 3, 1889. Historians of Latin America have argued that liberalism "privileged individuals who had attained an independence that depended upon financial means, age, and gender." Sueann Caulfield, Sarah C. Chambers, and Lara Putnam, "Introduction," in *Honor, Status, and Law in Modern Latin America*, ed. Sueann Caulfield, Sarah C. Chambers, and Lara Putnam (Durham, NC: Duke University Press, 2005), 18.

these actors embraced a time that was disruptive and discontinuous with the state's practices of coerced labor and land dispossession and with liberal ideas of human agency. Most significantly, they refused to be relegated to an ahistoric passivity. Their efforts to bring into being other political modalities, however, were frequently met with violence and material retribution. When rural Q'eqchi's took matters into their own hands, the state and coffee planters squashed labor strikes and land invasions with brutal military force, foreshadowing Guatemala's bloody counterinsurgency war in the twentieth century.

This book is a history of how Alta Verapaz, and Guatemala more generally, came into being through the state and coffee planters' active disavowal of Maya political ontologies and the privileging of coffee capitalism and German settler immigration in the nineteenth century. While historians of Guatemala have been quick to identify the prevalence of exclusionary racism at the heart of Guatemalan history, often they have been less willing to uncover the many political projects and futures erased by their own insistent focus on liberalism's exclusions.[11] While attending to the potency of exclusionary liberalism and capitalist exploitation, this book centers the struggles among Altaverapacences over different political projects and imagined futures in the late nineteenth and early twentieth centuries. These struggles reveal that Q'eqchi's continually unsettled and recast the dominant histories of liberal modernity. In this book, I use the term *unsettling* to refer to practices of unfixing, unfastening, and loosening, or depriving of fixity or quiet. In their efforts to upend the politics of postponement with calls for rights and freedom in the present, Mayas unfastened *who*, *when*, and *where* modernity was located. Q'eqchi's in Alta Verapaz continually unfixed the geographical and temporal location of modernity in the North Atlantic corridor or in the hands of a small class of local elites. Instead, they situated it in a distant and largely indigenous frontier region of a peripheral nation and in Q'eqchi's' own hands. By highlighting ongoing practices of exclusion, violence, and coerced labor, Q'eqchi's also unfastened the historical myth that Guatemala's modernity had successfully left behind colonialism. Q'eqchi's reveal instead how the Guatemalan state reproduced colonial practices of coerced labor, racial hierarchy, and land dispossession long after the formal end of colonialism with Spain. When they brought together liberal

---

[11] The exceptions are Greg Grandin, *The Last Colonial Massacre: Latin America in the Cold War* (Chicago: University of Chicago Press, 2011), and Greg Grandin, *The Blood of Guatemala: A History of Race and Nation* (Durham, NC: Duke University Press, 2000).

principles and Maya spirit worlds, they also unsettled disenchanted modernities that erased the agency of nonhuman actors and spirit worlds. By the mid-twentieth century, these dynamics culminated with unsettling modernity in another way: the literal removal of settlers, including the deportation of German citizens to concentration camps in the United States, the nationalization of German-owned properties, and the partial and temporary redistribution of these properties among rural laborers. Q'eqchi's thus challenged many commonly received narratives among historians then and now: the transition from slavery to freedom, the realization of state sovereignty over territorial space, the establishment of liberal democracy through representative government, and the disenchantment of political life. Through these multiple moments, Q'eqchi's demonstrated how the history of modernity braided the liberal promises of emancipation, free labor, and representative government with the heterogeneous pasts of conquest, coerced labor, dominion, and violent exclusion. However, these interwoven and hybrid modernities also grew out of local and specific textured histories and other Maya ontologies and practices.

FORGING KNOTS OF TIME: ALTA VERAPAZ

Alta Verapaz is often understood as an exceptional region that stood outside received Guatemalan narratives for its sixteenth-century history of "peaceful conquest" by the famous protector of the Indians, the Dominican friar Bartolomé de las Casas, and for its exceptional nineteenth-century history of German immigration and modernization through coffee production. Because of its history of peaceful pacification, Alta Verapaz was often seen as lacking the stains of colonialism and thus better positioned to uplift the nation in the journey toward progress. In the early twentieth century, some Guatemalan intellectuals, including Nobel Laurate Miguel Ángel Asturias, imagined Alta Verapaz as a laboratory for national development via coffee production and interracial unions between Germans and Q'eqchi's.[12] For others, however, Alta Verapaz's dual histories of peaceful conquest and German settlement

---

[12] In this sense, Alta Verapaz, like other exceptional regions such as São Paulo in Brazil or the Antioquia in Colombia, reveals a lot about how some Guatemalans imagined the nation. Yet, unlike São Paulo or Antioquia, Alta Verapaz never fulfilled its promise of racial whitening and national progress. Instead, Alta Verapaz remained a site of Guatemalan hopes and desires of a future yet to come. Barbara Weinstein, *The Color of Modernity: São Paulo and the Making of Race and Nation in Brazil* (Durham, NC: Duke

illustrated the importance of understanding the region's nineteenth-century, post-independence histories of conquest and colonization as well as how these histories shaped Guatemala's descent into a bloody, genocidal civil war in the twentieth century. For example, Alfredo Cucul, José Angel Icó's great-nephew, argues that the peaceful conquest was a mere prelude to the real colonial story, which centered on nineteenth-century German settlers and the rise of coffee plantations.[13] This other colonialism, Cucul argued, helps to explain Guatemala's extreme land inequality and racism. Like Cucul, this book asks us to consider the multiplicity of colonialisms, their historical specificity, and the nonlinear entanglements across time and space they helped to produce. From these varied and multivocal pasts, this book aims to narrate Alta Verapaz's history as marked by the uneven, unsettled, contingent histories that fold back on themselves forming knots of time.[14] These "time-knots" are entanglements of life in time that defy linear sequences of modernity in which the past is fully overcome and consigned to history.[15] These are stories filled not with rupture or continuity, but partial reinscriptions and modified displacements.

Alta Verapaz's experience of nineteenth-century capitalist expansion also differed from Guatemala's western highlands, which historical studies have tended to emphasize. In much of the western highlands, coffee production occurred on lands that were at a great distance from indigenous communities, whose lands were more suitable to corn than coffee. Thus, indigenous communities in the western highlands maintained their subsistence lands and were integrated into the world market in a different way. Mayas from the western highlands became migrant laborers who traveled to the coffee coast during planting and harvesting seasons. In contrast, Altaverapacense indigenous lands were often ideal for coffee production. For that reason, coffee expansion in Alta Verapaz occurred through the dispossession of some subsistence lands and labor was mobilized over much shorter distances. As a result, plantation worlds swallowed up entire indigenous communities. In Alta Verapaz, a sexual

University Press, 2015), and Nancy Appelbaum, *Muddied Waters: Race, Region, and Local History in Colombia, 1846–1948* (Durham, NC: Duke University Press, 2003).

[13] Interview with the author, May 17, 2008.

[14] Ann Laura Stoler, *Duress: Imperial Durabilities in Our Times* (Durham, NC: Duke University Press, 2016).

[15] On time-knots, see Chakrabarty, *Provincializing Europe*; Florencia E. Mallon, *Courage Tastes of Blood: The Mapuche Community of Nicolás Ailío and the Chilean State, 1906–2001* (Durham, NC: Duke University Press, 2005).

labor economy also emerged alongside the coffee economy in which elite Q'eqchi' women served as both cooks and concubines on plantations. Here, labor patterns more closely resembled the colonial hacienda or even sharecroppers in the American South. In addition, immigrant German coffee planters quickly established economic predominance in the late nineteenth century and forged a tightly knit diasporic community, even as they established intimate bonds with Q'eqchi' women and produced interracial families. Together, these factors ensured that Alta Verapaz had a different matrix of indigenous, state, and coffee planter relations than the western highlands region. K'iche Maya elites in western highlands city of Quetzaltenango, for example, positioned themselves as promoters of racial regeneration among the lower-class K'iches and distinguished themselves as modern through photography and urban associations. As with their K'iche counterparts, some Q'eqchi' patriarchs in Alta Verapaz positioned themselves as leaders of racial regeneration, but they also frequently sought to reproduce their positions as communal leaders by becoming coffee planters themselves and defending the lower classes from the worst effects of plantation capitalism, coerced labor, and land dispossession. Individuals such as José Ángel Icó and the Unionist Club emerged from Alta Verapaz's specific regional context of Q'eqchi' patriarchy and histories of coerced labor and land dispossession, and helps us to understand Guatemala's regional diversity.

As Altaverapacences struggled over distinct futures during the rise of coffee production in the second half of the nineteenth century, their historical struggles also shaped Guatemala's turbulent and important period between 1898 and 1954. As a result of their conflicting visions and dreams for modernity yet to come, many Altaverapacences experienced the early twentieth century as one of awaiting modernity's arrival.[16] These deep desires for modernity and for the end of the politics of postponement also made postcolonial nations such as Guatemala particularly ripe for populism and revolution – modalities of governance that offered to end for the first time, if only temporarily, the purgatory of history's waiting room and to incorporate those who had long been excluded from modernity's present. When political and economic

---

[16] Michel-Rolph Trouillot, "The Otherwise Modern: Caribbean Lessons from the Savage Slot," in *Critically Modern: Alternatives, Alterities, Anthropologies*, ed. Bruce M. Knauft (Bloomington: Indiana University Press, 2002), 220–40; Michael Kirkpatrick, "Optics and the Culture of Modernity in Guatemala City since the Liberal Reforms" (PhD diss., University of Saskatchewan, 2013).

upheavals such as the 1898 coffee crisis and the 1929 stock market crash rocked the nation, aspirational Altaverapacences supported populists. Manuel Estrada Cabrera (1898–1920) ended marginalized and social-climbing Altaverapacences' waiting by incorporating the entire nation into elaborate state festivals that celebrated the highest symbols of so-called Western civilization, notably the Greco-Roman goddess, Minerva. If these festivals were seemingly impositions from above, many middle-class ladinos and Q'eqchi's nevertheless took up the promise of Western civilization that such festivals afforded and enthusiastically participated in them as a means of staging their own social ambitions or erasing the racial stain of indigeneity. For his part, President Jorge Ubico (1931–44) appealed to middle- and lower-class desires for modernity by building new roads, intervening in domestic affairs, and promising a new future based on sanitation and eugenics. As populists fulfilled plebeian and middle-class aspirations for modernity, many Altaverapacences blamed the region's woes on outsiders or agents of the existing social order, especially German settlers and other "aristocrats". At times, these populisms from above and below inverted who counted as agents of progress and denounced Germans and other wealthy coffee planters as feudal lords.

Alta Verapaz's nineteenth- and twentieth-century histories also reveal new interpretations of Guatemala's famed October Revolution (1944–54). During this revolutionary decade, Guatemalan reformers brought into being a series of democratic social and labor reforms, in addition to the widely recognized 1952 agrarian reform. While the revolution has long been overshadowed by the fateful CIA-supported military coup of 1954, scholars are now beginning to emphasize new transnational connections and the many different revolutions that took place between 1944 and 1954.[17] This book also demonstrates the importance of placing the revolution in the broader global context of World War II. While Altaverapacences harbored simmering anti-German nationalism, these nationalist sentiments took on new anti-imperialist and anti-fascist dimensions with the rise of German National Socialism in the mid-1930s, and then with Guatemala's entrance into World War II on the side of the Allied forces. While almost entirely neglected by historians, the nationalization of German properties on the eve of Guatemala's October

[17] Julie Gibbings and Heather Vrana, eds., *Out of the Shadow: Revisiting the Revolution in Post-Peace Guatemala* (Austin: University of Texas Press, 2020), and Kirsten Weld, "The Other Door: Spain and the Guatemalan Counterrevolution, 1944–54," *Journal of Latin American Studies* 51, no. 2 (2019): 307–31.

Revolution unleashed rural Q'eqchi' expectations that these properties would be distributed among rural workers and the land-poor. For rural Q'eqchi's, the nationalization of German properties was a historic reckoning that rendered the nineteenth-century processes of violent enclosure, dispossession, sexual conquest, and forced labor vividly present. These historic reckonings and expectations, alongside state ownership of nationalized properties, helps us to understand why Guatemala's 1952 agrarian reform generated such anxieties among Guatemalan elites and mass mobilization from below. These histories, however, have been obscured by the exclusion of German settlers from Guatemalan national narratives and the concomitant myth of German social and political insularity.[18]

THE GRAMMAR OF MODERNITY: RACE, COERCED LABOR, AND THE POLITICS OF POSTPONEMENT

At the heart of this book lie the elusive concepts of modernity and time. Since the nineteenth century, scholars have often understood modernity as a product of tying together a triple process that spanned the sixteenth through eighteenth centuries: colonialism and European expansion, the national democratic revolutions of the late eighteenth and early nineteenth centuries, and a set of technological, cultural, and social changes brought about by capitalism, the Reformation, and the Scientific Revolution.[19] Modernity was commonly understood as a set of political and economic processes associated with the rise of the nation-state, the secularization of religion, and the spread of capitalism.

Beginning in the nineteenth century, despite dissenting voices and evidence to the contrary, many statesmen, intellectuals, and others understood these political, economic, and cultural facets of modernity as the product of a largely endogenous European process, or at least one rooted in Europe and then spread across the globe as various others fashioned themselves in the likeness of European or Western society. This version of modernity is what Dipesh Chakrabarty has so forcefully termed "the first in Europe and then elsewhere structure of time."[20] By the late nineteenth

---

[18] Julie Gibbings, "Mestizaje in the Age of Fascism: German and Q'eqchi' Maya Interracial Unions in Alta Verapaz, Guatemala," *German History* 34, no 2. (2016): 214–36.

[19] For these broad definitions of modernity, see the classic Max Weber, *The Protestant Ethic and the Spirit of Capitalism* (New York: Routledge, 2005); Anthony Giddens, *The Consequences of Modernity* (New York: John Wiley & Sons, 2013).

[20] Chakrabarty, *Provincializing Europe*, 8.

century, other countries, such as the United States, had joined the club of modern nations and shifted the location of modernity from Europe to what is colloquially known as the West or, somewhat more accurately, the North Atlantic world, spanning Northern Europe and the United States, along with regional centers that also claimed their own modernity, such as São Paulo, Mexico City, and Buenos Aires. Latin American elites expressed anxieties and wrote tragic narratives about the failures to achieve modernity; some were so uncertain about liberal rights and democracy that they did not believe self-rule was feasible at all.[21] Above all, many Latin American nations argued that their indigenous populations, remnants of an archaic and colonial past, held them back from becoming modern.[22] In Guatemala, this led both Conservative and Liberal statesmen to decry the deleterious effects of Maya political participation and limit the acquisition of citizenship.

In Guatemala by the first half of the nineteenth century, a variety of elite and nonelite actors, including state officials, intellectuals, and marginalized laborers, often narrated the political and economic dimensions of modernity through a combination of liberal-democratic and civilizing metanarratives. The liberal-democratic metanarrative presented capitalism and democracy as inevitably triumphing over feudalism and slavery. In late nineteenth-century Guatemala, Liberal Party elites used the liberal-democratic narrative and its promise of citizenship and emancipation to attack the previous Conservative regime for upholding the colonial order's caste hierarchies. Q'eqchi's, on the other hand, drew on the liberal-democratic metanarrative to denounce coerced labor as anti-modern. Liberal intellectuals also often defined modernity via a civilizing metanarrative that emphasized secularism, scientific reason, and, most significantly, a belief in progress that emphasized shedding the past and inaugurating new futures. This civilizing metanarrative made Western civilization the highest cultural form and defined it as the triumph of reason and science over fanaticism and superstition. Guatemalan statesmen and intellectuals deployed this civilizing metanarrative to promote European immigration and coerced labor as the antidote to Maya backwardness.

---

[21] Angel Rama and John Charles Chasteen, *The Lettered City* (Durham, NC: Duke University Press, 1996); Erika Pani, *Nación, constitución y reforma, 1821–1908* (México: Fondo de Cultura Economica, 2010); Anne Eller, *We Dream Together: Dominican Independence, Haiti, and the Fight for Caribbean Freedom* (Durham, NC: Duke University Press, 2016).

[22] Rebecca Earle, *The Return of the Native: Indians and Myth-Making in Spanish America, 1810–1930* (Durham, NC: Duke University Press, 2007).

These liberal-democratic and civilizing metanarratives of Eurocentric modernity were unthinkable without a new conception of historical time. Historical time featured in the making of modernity in two central ways. First, through a new obsession with progress, modernity was conceived as the forward movement of people and places through time toward civilization. Both apologists and critics of the notion of modernity agree that society becomes quintessentially modern when it becomes consumed by the notion of interminable development and the "restless forward movement of time and history."[23] This notion of historical time was made possible by what Walter Benjamin called homogeneous empty space-time as exemplified by the clock.[24] Under the rule of the clock, time is governed by a standard instantaneous present (it's 6 p.m.); the clock graphically represents time as a spatial and measurable number grafted onto a radial face so that progress in the space of the clock hand coincides with the passage of time. The past has elapsed and thus ceases to exist, while the future awaits as a predictable, empty, uniform series of recurring measured intervals, waiting to be filled with experience. By establishing time as something unified and measurable, in which the past is irrevocably left behind as all of (civilized) humanity moves toward the future, modern time underwrites a linear and developmental notion of progress. The process of modernization naturalized time as linear (the past is completed), universal (experienced by everyone in the same way), quantifiable and commodifiable (time is money), and contemporaneous (newer is better). As Michel Foucault further argued, modernity represents not only a particular temporality, but also an ethical imperative to change – modernity anticipates an imminent future as both a task and an obligation.[25]

Historical time figures prominently in modernity through the notion's emphasis on periodization. By periodization, I am referring to what Kathleen Davis defines as a "complex process of conceptualizing categories, which are posited as homogenous and retroactively validated by the

---

[23] Stuart Hall, *Modernity: An Introduction to Modern Societies* (New York: Wiley, 1996), 17.

[24] Walter Benjamin, "Theses on the Philosophy of History," in *Illuminations: Essays and Reflections*, ed. Hannah Arendt, trans. Harry E. Zohn (New York: Schocken Books, 1969). See also Vanessa Ogle, *The Global Transformation of Time: 1870–1950* (Cambridge, MA: Harvard University Press, 2015).

[25] Michel Foucault, "What Is Enlightenment?," in *The Foucault Reader*, ed. Paul Rabinow (New York: Pantheon Books, 1984), 32–50.

designation of a period divide."[26] The modern is implicitly and explicitly defined by its supposed opposite: the nonmodern, which is rendered as another period in historical time. Modern time consciousness developed through the perceived "non-contemporaneousness of diverse, but in the chronological sense, simultaneous histories" that arose from imperialist global expansion.[27] The problem is that such categories exercise an exclusionary force, and they require that those who are not modern adopt particular cultural, economic, and political forms, such as electoral politics and private property, in order to gain access to an ostensibly global modernity. Indeed, some nineteenth-century Latin American intellectuals and statesmen declared the region to be "the vanguard of the Atlantic World" due to its robust history of liberal democracy.[28]

These two aspects of historical time within modernity – progress and periodization – are both elements that made modernity seem both universal and singular, as both belonging to Europe and awaiting the rest of the world in the future. Historical time, in other words, functioned as the grammar of modernity, giving structure and meaning to otherwise loose concepts and processes. The modern renderings of time also demonstrate that the perception of time – while seemingly neutral and objective – is actually a social construction. As such, modern time is not a neutral designation, but already defined by particular histories, interests, and institutions. As Mark Rifkin has argued, it is insufficient to include indigenous peoples in more expansive histories of shared modernities. Rather, we need to understand how these histories can also implicitly cast non-indigenous political categories, periodization, and conceptions of causality as given.[29] Moving beyond the notion of singular time, and following post-Einstein theorists, time can be understood as variable and dependent on subjective location.[30] Within post-Einsteinian notions of time, there is no concept of absolute or singular time. Instead, the experience and measurements of time are contingent. While in physics, this shift in

---

[26] Kathleen Davis, *Periodization and Sovereignty: How Ideas of Feudalism and Secularization Govern the Politics of Time* (Philadelphia: University of Pennsylvania Press, 2012), 3.

[27] Koselleck, *The Practice of Conceptual History*, 114.

[28] James C. Sanders, *The Vanguard of the Atlantic World: Creating Modernity, Nation, and Democracy in Nineteenth-Century Latin America.* (Durham, NC: Duke University Press, 2014).

[29] Mark Rifkin, *Beyond Settler Time: Temporal Sovereignty and Indigenous Self-Determination* (Durham, NC: Duke University Press, 2017).

[30] Ibid.

experience of time depends on relative motion, Mark Rifklin has theorized it can just easily be applied to collective frames such as collective and personal experiences, patterns of memory, and historical legacies. Just as one's viewpoint shifts depending on subjective location, so too does an individual's experience of time. There are, in other words, many different times, and time itself is embedded in a social and historical context.

In Alta Verapaz, Q'eqchi's conceived of time as guided not only by the homogeneous empty time of modernity but also by ancient Maya calendars and the ethics of mountain spirits. With great accuracy, ancient Mayas measured the lunar cycle and solar year, lunar and solar eclipses, and the risings of Venus and Mars. Their calendar rests on a cycle of 260 named and numbered days and is composed of overlays of cycles of differing lengths. Despite conquest and colonization, Mayas, especially in frontier regions such as Alta Verapaz, continued to keep Maya calendars with some variation across regions and linguistic groups.[31] In the Maya calendar, the day represented the most important qualitative unit. The word "day" means "sun," referring not only to the sun's cycle but also to a longer period of time that takes on the sense of timeliness. Where we might say, "the time has come," a Maya says, "the day has come." Each day has an identity and character that influence events. A person's luck, or fate, is called "the face of his day." Someone who attends to the Maya calendar is qualified as a shaman and called a "daykeeper" or "timekeeper." For Mayas, days are both quantitative and qualitative, and days are themselves historical agents that determine events and define destinies. Days were subjects and selves in interactional ritual, and they constitute other-than-human beings in a cooperative cosmic order.[32] Similarly, Q'eqchi's also believed that mountain spirits known as Tzuultaq'as directed events, ensured bountiful harvests, and avenged violations of

---

[31] For an analysis of Maya calendars across Guatemala, see, for example, Suzanne Whitelaw Miles, "A Comparative Analysis of the Survivals of the Ancient Maya Calendar" (PhD diss., University of Chicago, Department of Anthropology, 1948). For Alta Verapaz specifically, see Eric Thompson, "A Maya Calendar from the Alta Vera Paz, Guatemala," *American Anthropologist* 34 (1932): 449–54.

[32] My understanding of the Maya calendar and divination is derived from Barbara Tedlock, *Time and the Highland Maya* (Albuquerque: University of New Mexico Press, 1992); P. van den Akker, "Time, History and Ritual in a K'iche' Community: Contemporary Maya Calendar Knowledge and Practices in the Highlands of Guatemala" (PhD diss., Leiden University, 2018); Bradley Scott Graupner, "The Epistemology of Understanding: Revisiting Highland Maya Daykeeping" (MA thesis, University of Chicago, n.d.); John M. Weeks, *Maya Daykeeping: Three Calendars from Highland Guatemala* (Boulder: University Press of Colorado, 2009).

ethical practices and order. These Q'eqchi' times, however, were not isolated or unchanging; rather, they interacted with an emergent modern reckoning of time over the centuries and generations. Time, then, depended on subjective location; it was not a neutral and natural order and it shifted and changed as Q'eqchi' were more deeply integrated into the coffee-growing economy.

The marking of modern historical time as a natural and neutral order rested on the construction of space as an objective stage upon which teleological narratives could be written. In the late nineteenth century, Guatemala, as elsewhere in Latin America, engaged in an active process of generating scientific maps of the entire country and land-tenure arrangements.[33] Through these cartographic enterprises, space was actively relieved of its contingent and messy histories and practices, and made into a kind of passive backdrop against which historical agents could take action.[34] "Our gaze," Paul Carter writes, "sees through the space of history, as if it was never there."[35] This vision of objective space denies human agency, the way that people transform space into place. Instead, staged space seems preordained and detached from meaning and experience. Agency, when it appears, belongs to the heroic agent of modernity, who makes history on space. The ambiguities of, and struggles over, alternative visions of a better life and different ways of organizing space are actively denied and erased. What remains are the visions of space as a neutral object and history as a teleology of modernization.

As with the emergence of the homogeneous empty time of history, the idea of space as a stage has a history, too. This past is intimately linked to abstractions: the social abstraction of commodity exchange and labor and the political abstraction of the modern territorial state. This objective, neutral, and measurable space was produced and perpetuated through the grids, plans, and schedules employed in capitalist systems and the production of state territorial sovereignty. In Alta Verapaz, however, the state had never reached far into the countryside, and so Mayas often maintained territorial sovereignty and autonomy well into the nineteenth century. With the rise of coffee capitalism, coffee planters, especially

---

[33] See, for example, Raymond B. Craib, *Cartographic Mexico: A History of State Fixations and Fugitive Landscapes* (Durham, NC: Duke University Press, 2004); Nancy P. Appelbaum, *Mapping the Country of Regions: The Chorographic Commission of Nineteenth-Century Colombia* (Chapel Hill: University of North Carolina Press, 2016).

[34] See especially Henri Lefebvre, *The Production of Space* (New York: Wiley, 1992).

[35] Paul Carter, *The Road to Botany Bay: An Exploration of Landscape and History* (Minneapolis: University of Minnesota Press, 2010), xiv.

German settlers, generated their own territorial sovereignty over the space of the plantation by manipulating opaque legal terms of jurisdiction and rights to intervene in the intimate spaces of people's lives and by producing new cartographic grids.[36] Q'eqchi's and other subaltern actors, however, both participated in the making of this abstract space and re-embedded other meanings in it, including the markers of the Tzuultaq'a mountain spirits. When Q'eqchi's were required by new state regulations to scientifically map and fix boundary markers for their land claims, many appear to have used place markers such as crosses and hermitages that may have also indicated the location of Tzuultaq'as.

In Guatemala, these new metanarratives of modernity and related notions of historical time were also intimately linked to state and coffee planter efforts to limit political participation and manage perceived differences in levels of civilization.[37] The notion of modernity rests upon excluding whole cultures, regions, and peoples as nonmodern and, as such, temporal anomalies or anachronisms. For many Guatemalan elites, Mayas existed in the present only as holdovers from a bygone era.[38] Historical periodization – labeling others as medieval relics, feudal lords, or barbaric tribes – served to control and order difference.[39] Proponents of homogeneous time consistently employed the rhetoric of anachronism whenever they encountered a stubborn heterogeneity, as when, for example, Q'eqchi's such as José Angel Icó imagined a political future that included Mayas as citizens. The charge of anachronism amounted to postponing the acquisition of sovereignty and self-government for those who had "not yet" advanced enough along the course of modernity.[40] For this same reason, Francisco Miranda, the nineteenth-century Venezuelan independence leader, retreated from revolutionary independence when he confronted royalist armies. As Jeremy Adelman notes, "The nation he sought to free from its chains was not, in his opinion, a nation at all. While Venezuelans yearned for 'Civil Liberty,' they did not know how to grasp and protect it. They needed a liberation that would tutor

[36] Lauren Benton, *Law and Colonial Cultures: Legal Regimes in World History, 1400–1900* (Cambridge: Cambridge University Press, 2004); Lauren Benton, *A Search for Sovereignty: Law and Geography in European Empires, 1400–1900* (Cambridge: Cambridge University Press, 2010); Stoler, *Duress.*
[37] Johannes Fabian, *Time and the Other: How Anthropology Makes Its Object* (New York: Columbia University Press, 2002).
[38] Zvi Ben-Dor Benite, "The Sphinx and the Historian," *The American Historical Review* 116, no. 3 (2011): 638–52.
[39] Davis, *Periodization and Sovereignty.*   [40] Chakrabarty, *Provincializing Europe*, 8.

them in the ways of liberty and fraternity, to create a nation of virtuous citizens out of a colony of subjects."[41] As Adelman reminds us, these very preoccupations, alongside flexible and shifting meanings and practices of imperial sovereignty, shaped both independence and the enduring legacies of colonialism in Latin America.

State officials, intellectuals, and other elites often relied on racial discourses to resolve the contradictions between the promise of formal equality and the practices of limited citizenship and coerced labor in the late nineteenth century. The Lamarckian understanding of race, which prevailed at this time in Guatemala and Latin America more generally, claimed that difference derived from historical immaturity rather than biological immutability.[42] This emphasis allowed for racial improvement through class and social mobility *over time*, while also enabling elites to justify coerced labor based on the idea that certain groups were not yet ready for free wage labor. Guatemalan coffee planters and state officials, for example, used newly reinvigorated racial language to argue that Mayas had to be forced to work because they had not yet developed wants and needs that would lead them to sell their labor freely on the market. State officials and plantation managers *produced* difference as a tool of labor management.[43] As a result, race often indexed different kinds and degrees of humanity, which accorded different kinds of freedom.[44] In turn, class mobility allowed for indigenous people, Afro-Latin Americans, and people of mixed race to change their racial status by acquiring a new set of social and cultural attributes associated with different kinds of labor, social networks, and cultural performances.[45]

---

[41] Jeremy Adelman, "An Age of Imperial Revolutions," *The American Historical Review* 113, no. 2 (2008): 319.

[42] On race and historicism, see David Theo Goldberg, *The Racial State* (New York: Wiley-Blackwell, 2002). In Latin America more specifically, see also Marisol de la Cadena, "Introducción," in *Formaciones de indianidad: Articulaciones raciales, mestizaje, y nación en América Latina*, ed. Marisol de la Cadena (Bogotá: Envión, 2007), 7–35.

[43] David R. Roediger and Elizabeth D. Esch, *The Production of Difference: Race and the Management of Labor in U.S. History* (Oxford: Oxford University Press, 2014); David Roediger, *Class, Race and Marxism* (New York: Verso Books, 2017).

[44] Thomas C. Holt, *The Problem of Freedom: Race, Labor, and Politics in Jamaica and Britain, 1832–1938* (Baltimore, MD: Johns Hopkins University Press, 1992).

[45] Aníbal Quijano described the invention of race in Latin America as shifting and flexible classifications of difference devised for governing different peoples for labor extraction within the colonial divisions of labor: plantation slavery, various forms of coerced cash-crop labor (*repartimiento, mita*, peonage), indentured labor (*enganche*), and so on. Aníbal Quijano, "Colonialidad del poder y clasificación social," *Contextualizaciones Latinoamericanas* 3, no. 5 (July 20, 2015). For a global perspective on racial capitalism,

This book argues that Guatemalan elites' rendering of difference as anachronism had deep, exclusionary political consequences that effectively postponed self-governance, while also justifying the use of violence to dispossess, enclose, and force others to labor. The efforts of statesmen and elites to postpone the acquisition of citizenship was rarely just a strategic calculation or hypocrisy. Rather, the politics of postponement also permitted disavowing the fact that in the shadow of coerced labor, colonialism, and racism, a different way of doing politics was also taking shape. In Alta Verapaz, Q'eqchi's built a diverse politics grounded in practices of solidarity and reciprocity, subsistence production, and the ethics of mountain spirits and daykeepers. Q'eqchi' ways of imagining and building futures and pasts were often dangerous to ladinos and German settlers, however, because they were not sufficiently or recognizably North Atlantic or they posed perceived threats to the onward march of modernity.[46] Indigenous subsistence production as well as indigenous spiritualities, then, erupted as a temporal anomaly at the very moment when indigenous peoples were building another kind of politics.

Viewing modernity from Latin America, and especially from Alta Verapaz, also throws into sharp relief the problem of racialized exclusion and colonialism. As a largely Maya region that received German immigrants beginning in the mid-nineteenth century, Alta Verapaz became a laboratory for, as well as a space for contesting, the possibility of a Europeanizing modernity based on racial whitening and coffee capitalism. As such, Alta Verapaz does not fit within the binary logics of colonial empire, which suggests the need not only to provincialize Europe but also to provincialize notions of British India as embodying the quintessential colony.[47] As a periphery in the world of modernity, a nation that was understood by much of the world as "not yet" modern, Alta Verapaz did not fit easily within the civilizing or liberal-democratic metanarratives. Nonetheless, aspirations for modernity shaped both state policy and everyday actions in the region, and subaltern actors made

---

see Cedric J. Robinson, *Black Marxism: The Making of the Black Radical Tradition* (Chapel Hill: University of North Carolina Press, 2005). On class and racial mobility, Marisol de la Cadena, *Indigenous Mestizos: The Politics of Race and Culture in Cuzco, Peru, 1919–1991* (Durham, NC: Duke University Press, 2000); Ann Twinam, *Purchasing Whiteness: Pardos, Mulattos, and the Quest for Social Mobility in the Spanish Indies* (Stanford, CA: Stanford University Press, 2015).

[46] Sibylle Fischer, *Modernity Disavowed: Haiti and the Cultures of Slavery in the Age of Revolution* (Durham, NC: Duke University Press, 2004); Rifkin, *Beyond Settler Time*.

[47] On the need to provincialize India, see Stoler, *Duress*.

modernity their own in order to claim a place within the nation.[48] As Carol Gluck writes, "Our sensitivity to the flaws of the one-size-fits-all Western-based conceit of modernity should not obscure the appeal of the modern to the peoples around the world who co-produced it."[49] These subaltern actors did not always use the language of modernity (*modernidad*), but they frequently referenced a set of concepts such as progress (*progreso*), civilization (*civilización*), and development (*fomento*). And in this sense, modernity, more than an empirical referent or even a set of characteristics, was articulated in what Raymond Williams has called a "structure of feelings" about the future.[50] These feelings were also powerful: individuals mobilized and were mobilized by fantasies, desires, and expectations. When José Ángel Icó and a hundred other Q'eqchi's from Alta Verapaz marched to the capital in 1920, they were driven by hope for change and a belief that they were participants in the inauguration of a new era of democracy.

Subaltern actors offer another way of reconceiving modernity. As they took up the promise and expectation of modernity, they often imagined futures and freedoms that did not bear much resemblance to the fractured and limited liberalism of a fictive and largely imagined Europe. Thus, these Q'eqchi's reveal that political modernity is both necessary and inadequate for the task of understanding non-Western histories.[51] Political modernity was necessary because it provided the basis for so much of their nineteenth- and twentieth-century struggles. But political modernity is also insufficient because the very terms of modernity fail to fully grasp the political projects that Q'eqchi's sought to create.[52] Indeed, if we focus only on Maya efforts to forge modern worlds through discernibly modern technologies, such as photography and railroads or even free wage labor, we can easily lose sight of the ways their modernities also reflected entirely different worldviews governed not by modern, secular time but by the times of mountain spirits who were active participants in the making of political and social life. Therefore, Q'eqchi's expose the very limits of

---

[48] On modernity as desire, see Trouillot, "The Otherwise Modern: Caribbean Lessons from the Savage Slot."

[49] Carol Gluck, "The End of Elsewhere: Writing Modernity Now," *The American Historical Review* 116, no. 3 (2011): 687.

[50] Raymond Williams, *Marxism and Literature* (Oxford: Oxford University Press, 1977).

[51] Chakrabarty has also argued that political modernity is both necessary and inadequate; see *Provincializing Europe*.

[52] This is one of the shortcomings of Greg Grandin's *The Blood of Guatemala*, which largely fails to account for Maya cosmologies.

writing disenchanted histories that actively exclude and erase other ways of narrating history, attending to causality, and rendering time. These Q'eqchi's thus challenge the notion that there are more or less pure cases of modernity, that modernities can be judged based on what is more original or authentically modern.[53]

By interrogating the multiplicity of modernities, including Q'eqchi' political ontologies, this book argues that modernity was not just a trope, theory, project, or destination, but rather a series of contested historical processes that were produced over three centuries around the globe. While modernities are neither unitary nor universal, the modern possesses commonalities across time and space, however differently it was experienced in various places. Nor is modernity a disposable fiction from which we can simply walk away; rather, it is a historical process and representation. It is thus necessary to separate struggles over the meaning of modernity (who counted as citizen-agents and who did not, for example) from the processes of modernization themselves – by which I mean some form of the nation-state and capitalism – which were in fact messy and nonlinear, complicated by different histories, geographies, and political struggles. As Florencia Mallon insisted more than two decades ago, there was never any single, real version of the categories of political modernity, such as nationalism, citizenship, or democracy.[54]

THE PRACTICES OF TRANSLATION AND THE POLITICS OF TIME AND SPACE: A NOTE ON METHODOLOGY

While it is easy to acknowledge modernity's multiplicity and hybridity, excavating different worlds from the historical record requires attention to cultural translations and the instrumental role of native intermediaries in those translations. The making of modernities, including abstract time-space, frequently required translations between different cultures and politics, even as these translations forged new ways of existing in the world. The historical process of translation did not, however, begin in the mid-nineteenth century in Alta Verapaz, or anywhere else, but was instead part of a longer, ongoing dialogue across differences that

---

[53] Fischer, *Modernity Disavowed*, 22.

[54] In addition to Florencia E. Mallon, *Peasant and Nation: The Making of Postcolonial Mexico and Peru* (Berkeley: University of California Press, 1995), see also Peter F. Guardino, *Peasants, Politics, and the Formation of Mexico's National State: Guerrero, 1800–1857* (Stanford, CA: Stanford University Press, 1996), and Grandin, *The Blood of Guatemala.*

continually produced new forms. With colonization, various Amerindian groups translated between their cultural practices and those of the conquistadores, as the conquistadores likewise adapted and translated their cultures and political institutions to local contexts. As Jeremy Ravi Mumford has illustrated in the Andes, the General Resettlement of the Indians in the sixteenth century, while a wholesale effort to transform indigenous society by forming *reducciones* (congregations of Indians), nonetheless preserved many aspects of indigenous culture and strengthened the social position of indigenous lords.[55] These intercultural translations occurred within extreme power differentials. In his chronicles of intercultural prcesses in the Andes, Thomas Abercrombie has demonstrated how tensions between creative Andean heterodoxies and colonial drives to extirpate heresies produced a newly bifurcated cosmos and forms of social memory wherein colonial binaries between indigenous and nonindigenous worlds were reproduced, reconciled, and unraveled. While colonialism produced and rested upon defining indigenous and nonindigenous worlds, the binary separation of these worlds then was the subject of constant negotiation and transgression. Therefore, as Abercrombie has argued, the historical task of native intermediaries was not so much to keep "incompatible 'Andean' [indigenous] and 'Western' orders apart as to bring two kinds of powers within a single cosmic order into controlled contact with one another."[56] As a result, the distinctions between indigenous and nonindigenous worlds themselves constitute a product of colonialism, even as they produced new hybrid forms. This long history of intercultural worlds makes the question of defining Western versus non-Western, modern and nonmodern subjectivities, life worlds, and histories problematic and highlights the need to attend to the ongoing politics of cultural translation between different worlds.[57]

In this book, I also maintain that indigenous patriarchs, as native intermediaries, played a crucial role in forging these new, hybrid, intercultural worlds. Their centrality implies rethinking concepts of rural

[55] Jeremy Ravi Mumford, *Vertical Empire: The General Resettlement of Indians in the Colonial Andes* (Durham, NC: Duke University Press, 2012).

[56] Thomas Alan Abercrombie, *Pathways of Memory and Power: Ethnography and History among an Andean People* (Madison: University of Wisconsin Press, 1998), 113.

[57] Such histories also demonstrate the limits of the so-called ontological turn, which first set out to avoid the overdetermined dualism of nature–culture, but in fact often "reif[ies] the most modern binary of all: the radical incommensurability of modern and nonmodern worlds." Bessire Lucas and Bond David, "Ontological Anthropology and the Deferral of Critique," *American Ethnologist* 41, no. 3 (August 14, 2014): 442.

communities so that they are no longer just historical givens but rather understood as the result of the processes of political and cultural imagination. This might be something akin to what Florencia Mallon has called "communal hegemony" – the idea that, through complex hierarchies of communal social and political ties, these native intermediaries continually forged a tenuous communal consensus across racial and gendered differences by defining and redefining communal boundaries of inclusion and exclusion.[58] These intermediaries played a critical role in stabilizing social relations during the transition to capitalism.[59] When communal consensus broke down, these native elites themselves became subject to backlash, which, as we will see, happened in Alta Verapaz at various moments across the nineteenth and early twentieth centuries. Nor were these forms of mediation stable. Rather, as Chapters 4, 6, and 8 demonstrate, Q'eqchi' forms of mediation underwent profound changes with the rise of new kinds of plantations and intermediaries, as well as during moments of democracy and the rise of political parties. Taking these forms of communal mediation seriously also requires understanding native intermediaries as intellectuals who used the law and state policies to pursue their own agendas and to participate in the reimagining of liberal philosophy and practice.[60] Doing so requires not only breaking down the artificial division between scholar as intellectual and indigenous peasant as subject, but also reading archival records, including the everyday disputes of local actors and their letters, as philosophical texts.[61]

Excavating these historical processes, however, requires a careful reading of the power embedded in archival sources, which frequently served to reproduce state power and particular truths. Some aspects of Maya culture, such as Q'eqchi' use of the Maya calendar and the figure of El Q'eq, are virtually absent from the extant archival record. When they do appear in ethnographic accounts, often they are narrated from the contingent perspective of non-Maya ethnographers, some of whom believed that such practices were better left behind. This problem has led me to make use of a wide variety of previously untapped archival sources. These sources include municipal archives, which offer more frequently access to Q'eqchi' patriarchs' efforts to mediate local politics, and plantation

---

[58] Mallon, *Peasant and Nation*.

[59] John Tutino, *Making a New World: Founding Capitalism in the Bajío and Spanish North America* (Durham, NC: Duke University Press, 2011).

[60] See Mallon, *Peasant and Nation*; Mallon, *Courage Tastes of Blood*.

[61] David Kazanjian, *The Brink of Freedom: Improvising Life in the Nineteenth-Century Atlantic World* (Durham, NC: Duke University Press, 2016).

records, which can reveal laborers' agency and actions as well as plantation administrators' efforts to recast laborers' self-representations and manage racial difference.

The archive's powerful partial truths and absences have led me to read both against the archival grain and alongside it. Reading "along the archival grain," as Ann Laura Stoler has championed, has led me to analyze state archives as historical forces in and of themselves that leave traces of how the state ordered knowledge and exerted power. As Stoler has explored, the colonial archive is "a supreme technology of the ... imperial state, a repository of codified beliefs that clustered (and bore witness to) connections between secrecy, the law, and power."[62] As native intermediaries, Q'eqchi' patriarchs frequently learned Spanish as well as the legal and administrative norms of the state. But they did not always represent the interests of Q'eqchi' women and commoners transparently. In reading against the archival grain, then, I scour the archive for traces of what is not said. As Sybille Fisher has noted, "There are layers of signification in the cultural records that cannot be grasped as long as we pay attention only to events and causality in the strict sense."[63] Rather, we need to develop a methodology for excavating the silences and gaps that punctuate the historical record by working from symptomatic fragments. At times, these lacunae also require a speculative reading of subaltern actions, since words often were not left about what might have motivated Q'eqchi' commoners and women to act and which principles guided them. Such readings also seek symbolic truths that stretch beyond the facticity of specific events. Likewise, other ways of imagining history, time, and agency did not emerge only through archival practices. These other ways of rendering history were also embedded in material worlds and landscapes and arose from practices of labor reciprocity and cosmologies of mountain deities that can be traced through a critical dialogue among archival, oral, and visual texts.

By engaging these intertwined histories and hybrid formations of modernity, this book illustrates that different times and spaces coexisted, even if state officials disavowed indigenous political projects. As a result of these diverse and contingent processes, modernities in Alta Verapaz

---

[62] Ann Laura Stoler, "Colonial Archives and the Arts of Governance: On the Content in the Form," in *Refiguring the Archive*, ed. Carolyn Hamilton, Verne Harris, Michèle Pickover, Graeme Reid, Razia Saleh, and Jane Taylor (Boston: Springer, 2002), 83–102; see also Ann Laura Stoler, *Along the Archival Grain: Epistemic Anxieties and Colonial Common Sense* (Princeton: Princeton University Press, 2009).

[63] Fischer, *Modernity Disavowed*, 2.

were emergent and multivocal. An emergent social formation does not necessarily require completely new subjectivities or constituencies, but can also comprise elements of residual ongoing conditions, such as coerced labor, that are rearticulated through new practices. Indeed, the efforts of state officials to render time and space into abstract entities – measurable and unified – were never complete, nor entirely successful. Instead, they helped produce messy "time-knots" that defy the linear notion of time in which the past is fully overcome and consigned to history.[64] We do not move through "homogenous empty time"; rather, we live in deep entanglements where the past is continually made present. Time does not so much pass as *accumulate* most often out of the violent wreckage of conquest, colonialism, and capitalism.[65] The sediments of the past remain latent in the present until subaltern actors activate them through their demands for justice and restitution. Florencia E. Mallon has referred to this process as a "postcolonial palimpsest," in which "racial struggles are reburied in a widening palimpsest of memory, only to be disinterred once again in another historical moment, reconstructed yet again and redeployed."[66] In order to attend to the sedimentation of past colonial and capitalist practices in the present, I retain the "post" in "postcolonial" to emphasize the present violence of primitive accumulation and colonialism in its tangible and intangible forms. Likewise, I examine the multiple temporalities in which people lived that have shaped the contours of this book's narrative. Various chapters illustrate the ways in which the past is not over, and how the articulation of the past and present resurfaces in unexpected forms.

Throughout this book, I have tried to understand the making of Alta Verapaz from the contingent perspectives of a variety of participants, including middle-class ladinos, Q'eqchi' patriarchs, rural Q'eqchi' laborers, German coffee planters, urban working classes, and state officials. I assess their asymmetric information, expectations, and power to uncover their mutual misunderstandings and distinct worldviews. These divergent perspectives also help to reveal what different actors had at

---

[64] On time-knots, see Chakrabarty, *Provincializing Europe*; Mallon, *Courage Tastes of Blood.*

[65] Ian Baucom, *Specters of the Atlantic: Finance Capital, Slavery, and the Philosophy of History* (Durham, NC: Duke University Press, 2005), 311.

[66] Florencia E. Mallon, "A Postcolonial Palimpsest: The Work Race Does in Latin America," in *Histories of Race and Racism: The Andes and Mesoamerica from Colonial Times to the Present*, ed. Laura Gotkowitz (Durham, NC: Duke University Press, 2011), 322.

stake in the making of modernity in Alta Verapaz, and how each tried to shape contigent outcomes.

This book thus offers a multivocal narrative that reflects the deep imbrications of power and perspective that shaped the making of the region and the nation.[67] I maintain these separate perspectives on the making of modernity throughout the book, especially in the accounts of the harsh experiences of coerced labor and life on the plantations. This can make for difficult reading. But it was through the clash of these conflicting perspectives that history was daily made. German coffee planters self-consciously understood themselves as playing a part in a historical project of making manifest the destiny of progress as well as their personal fortunes. For their part, Q'eqchi' laborers might have framed the rise of capitalism in terms of the sinfulness of the German and ladino planters, who had disrupted the moral codes that governed the use of natural resources, and their own providential hopes for salvation. Many modernities, many versions of what was happening, met and were contested in everyday interactions.

ORGANIZATION OF THE BOOK

I have divided the book into two parts. Part I, "Translating Modernities," examines the rise of coffee capitalism and the consolidation of new forms of plantation labor management between the 1860s and the onset of World War I in 1914. This section highlights the gradual and uneven process of transition to capitalism and explores how this process first built on Q'eqchi' political and economic structures, thereby strengthening caste hierarchy and the position of Q'qechi' patriarchs as intermediaries. Chapter 1, "To Live without King or Castle," opens with the 1865 rebellion led by the elderly Q'eqchi' commoner, Jorge Yat, who was charged with wanting to return to an era of republican democracy and dissolve caste hierarchy. This chapter uses that event as a window into nineteenth-century Alta Verapaz's social, economic, and cultural worlds on the eve of coffee production and the 1871 Liberal revolution. It especially demonstrates how indigenous communities far removed from the centers of state power in Cobán and San Pedro Carchá maintained a great deal of autonomy from the state, how Q'eqchi' society was composed of tensions between republican values of representative government and caste

[67] On multivocal narratives, I am drawn especially to Mallon, *Courage Tastes of Blood*.

hierarchy, between solidarity and individualism, and the ways in which Q'eqchi' patriarchs faced democratic challenges from below. Chapter 2, "Possessing Sentiments and Ideas of Progress," examines how Q'eqchi' patriarchs addressed the challenges posed by pressures from below and new state efforts to privatize property, increase coerced wage labor, and expand state authority after the 1871 Liberal Revolution. The efforts of Q'eqchi' patriarchs to become coffee planters who protected rural Mayas from mandamiento labor, however, ultimately failed.

In Chapter 3, "Indolence Is the Death of Character," a frost unleashed by the region's most powerful mountain deity, Tzuultaq'a Xucaneb in 1886, to seek revenge for coffee production and private property, set off a millennial revolt. In the wake of this moral and spiritual crisis, not only did Q'eqchi's express another kind of time, deeply inflected by the belief that mountain spirits were themselves historical agents, but they also opened a national debate over the place of slavery in a modernizing nation. Despite the temporary abolition of coerced labor, however, a political and economic crisis in 1898 drove the return to coerced labor and set the stage for a new kind of plantation economy, which is explored in Chapter 4, "El Q'eq Roams at Night." The 1898 crisis enabled the rapid growth of German-owned plantations and *fincas de mozos*, or plantations whose purpose was to provide residences and subsistence lands for seasonal laborers. There, German planters carved out a partial territorial sovereignty. They established their own judicial systems, appointed representatives before the state authorities, and combined violence and patriarchal affection to bind workers to place. Q'eqchi's expressed their interpretation of this new economy through the figure of El Q'eq, a half-man, half-cow, produced from the sexual union between a German coffee planter and a cow, who policed the plantation at night and stole from those he encountered to enrich German coffee planters. As a hypersexualized beast charged with protecting German plantations and ensuring order, El Q'eq also revealed the territorial limits of state sovereignty and unsettled claims of a linear march toward a liberal nation-state. In short, El Q'eq lays bare Q'eqchi' interpretations of plantation life and racial capitalism in late nineteenth-century Alta Verapaz.

As Part I demonstrates, the consolidation of racial capitalism in Alta Verapaz was contested and violent, but it did not proceed linearly. The abolition of forced wage labor, for example, was shortly followed by its reinstatement and then reform. Free wage labor emerged alongside new forms of debt and dependency. The division of communal properties into small, individually titled plots was not the product of a top-down privatization law, but rather the result of growing tensions within indigenous communities that frayed communal solidarity. By the early decades of the twentieth century, coffee planters also began to purchase the small, individual plots of erstwhile communal properties and reconstituted the individual titles into larger plantations of resident workers. Despite the messiness of these processes, the kinds of social and political plantation worlds that had emerged by 1914 endured, with ongoing variations, until the nationalization of German plantations after World War II and on the eve of Guatemala's famed October Revolution.

Part II of this book, "Aspirations and Anxieties of Unfulfilled Modernities," examines the political, economic, and social consequences of the kind of postponed modernity that took hold in Alta Verapaz. Chapter 5, "On the Throne of Minerva," examines urban beautification efforts, welfare associations, Liberal clubs, and staged state theater during the regime of Manuel Estrada Cabrera (1898–1920). If coffee planters circumscribed state sovereignty in the countryside, in the city of Cobán President Estrada Cabrera responded to popular demands for access to civilization by staging elaborate festivals that provided all Guatemalans access to the highest levels of culture, civilization, and learning, if only temporarily. A series of national and global events – earthquakes, World War I, the Mexican and Russian Revolutions, and the 1919 influenza pandemic – upended these efforts and transformed the Minerva festivals from symbols of national inclusion and modern belonging into ciphers of the corruption and political discontent that erupted in 1920, culminating with the overthrow of Estrada Cabrera.

The democratic experiment that emerged in the aftermath of this political upheaval is the subject of Chapter 6, "Freedom of the Indian." A group of radicalized Q'eqchi's formed the branch of the Unionista Party, with which this introduction opened, that demanded an end to forced wage labor, the abolition of debt contracts, and citizenship for all Mayas. For the next decade, Q'eqchi's engaged in labor strikes and land invasions, which articulated another history of time and space based on prior histories of possession. At the same time, urban reformers and intellectuals, including Miguel Ángel Asturias, increasingly sought to move beyond the failed ladino nation-state that had taken power in 1871. Now, they looked to Alta Verapaz as a model for imagining a new nation. The region embodied their hopes for modernization through prosperous coffee plantations and European immigration, and gave rise to an alternative national *mestizaje* project based on interracial mixing between German immigrants and Mayas.

Guatemala's democratic experiment of the 1920s came to an end with the Great Depression and Central America's Red Scare of 1932. Chapter 7, "Possessing Tezulutlán," examines how General Jorge Ubico, a strong-arm dictator, rapidly expanded the state's reach into the countryside, thereby challenging planter sovereignty and patriarchy. Ubico replaced forced wage labor with vagrancy laws and instituted sanitation and militarized rural education programs. Even as he expanded the repressive end of the state apparatus, Ubico also appealed to the masses through direct intervention in local affairs, particularly on behalf of poor women, and by promising access to civilization in the future via sanitation and eugenic programs. However, Ubico's efforts at state centralization were countered by the consolidation of regional identities in Alta Verapaz around "Tezulutlán" (Land of War), the name that the Nahua allies of Pedro Alvarado had given to the region. This anti-imperialist regional identity expressed growing anti-German nationalism. Ladinos and Germans also appropriated and sought to possess Maya culture as a source of authenticity and timeless tradition as they competed over claims to the region. These new celebrations of Maya authenticity provided a place for Maya patriarchs to reassert their authority as representatives of rural Mayas.

By the time World War II reached full force, these anti-imperialist nationalisms found further expression in anti-fascism, helping to overthrow Ubico and inaugurate Guatemala's renowned "ten years of spring," the subject of Chapter 8, "Now Owners of Our Land." This chapter illustrates how Guatemala's entrance into World War II, the expropriation of German properties, and the internment of German citizens ruptured power relations in the region and nation. As a result, the global conjuncture of World War II also generated the expectations for land redistribution that subsequently shaped Guatemala's 1952 agrarian reform. In this chapter, I examine how, as Q'eqchi' workers and peasants sought land, they articulated long and conflictual Maya histories and memories of possession and dispossession. These Q'eqchi' memories of land use were also shaped by the politics of postponement and meta-narratives of modernity, and the eruption of these rebellious memories in the midst of capitalist agrarian reform unsettled received conceptions of Guatemala's most important social and democratic experiment. The sum of their efforts in wartime, revolution, and neoliberal democracy did not bring an end to the flattened visions of modernity forged in the crucible of Alta Verapaz. To the contrary, the notion that Mayas were aliens to modernity, and the equation of Maya culture with a threat to the nation, resurfaced with particularly horrific consequences during Guatemala's thirty-six-year civil war (1960–96). Nevertheless, Maya struggles to reclaim land during the October revolution represented their attempts to do nothing less than make past injustices present and to refuse strategies of temporal dispossession and containment once and for all.

PART I

TRANSLATING MODERNITIES

I

To Live without King or Castle

Maya Patriarchal Liberalism on the Eve of a New Era, 1860–1871

Continually preaching liberty, equality, and sovereignty to them ... is to drive them towards insurrection, it is to give them arms that they can use against us, putting into practice and affirming the doctrines that we have incautiously taught them.

—La Gaceta de Guatemala, 1850

In 1865 San Pedro Carchá's annual patron saint's day (June 29) began with festivities and ended in blood. Following a ritual dance depicting the Spanish conquest and a Catholic mass, a ninety-nine-year-old illiterate Q'eqchi' named Jorge Yat, along with an estimated 300 followers, marched into the town council office. Before the magistrates and town councilors, they declared Yat – by order of the president and the will of the *pueblo* – the new *alcalde primero* (first mayor). The governing alcalde, Juan Choc, however, refused to pass Yat the alcalde's *vara* (staff of office). Instead, Choc gripped the vara, lifted it high in the air, and drew it forcefully across the elderly patriarch's back, launching Yat's supporters into attack. When the parish priest burst onto the scene moments later, he too became subject to the angry mob. As an altercation ensued, some town councilmen joined Yat's faction and revolted against tyranny. Word spread quickly across the small town, already teeming with rural Q'eqchi's, who had traveled from the surrounding area for the annual saint's day celebrations. Animated by *boj* (maize liquor) and festivities, many rural Q'eqchi's quickly joined the revolt centered in the town's plaza. Revolutionaries also burst into the homes of retired Q'eqchi' and ladino town officials and marched the shackled ex-officials to the local jail. Within hours twenty soldiers arrived from neighboring Cobán, opened fire, and put an end to the short-lived revolution. According to official reports, the soldiers had killed eight Q'eqchi's before the sun set on Carchá's patron saint day. Q'eqchi' witnesses, however, testified that the victims tallied "closer to one hundred ... Children were run into the ground, injured men and women died fleeing to the mountainside."[1]

While the revolutionaries targeted Q'eqchi' authorities (only three ladinos were detained in the raids), official reports evoked the specter of race war. Some state officials and ladino witnesses declared that the revolutionaries intended to "kill the priest and all the ladinos."[2] Historians, often inclined to view ladino–Maya conflict as the principal antagonism in Guatemalan history, have also interpreted the 1865 rebellion as a Maya revolt against ladinos.[3] Such interpretations flatten Maya and ladino social worlds and neglect relations of power and hierarchy within Maya communities. These readings also largely ignore the reasons the Maya patriarchs were attacked in the first place: they were local intermediaries, who mediated between the conflicting interests of indigenous commoners and the state; when they failed to act in the interests of their communities, they often were confronted with angry violence. In the previous months, Jorge Yat and his followers had complained that Q'eqchi' and ladino state officials had engaged in political corruption, persecuted boj producers, and forced Mayas to labor on communal coffee plantations.

Native mediators, such as the Q'eqchi' alcalde Juan Choc, played a crucial role in local governance during three centuries of colonial and postcolonial history, by virtue of their legitimacy and authority among indigenous peoples and their knowledge of Spanish and the legal and administrative system. Q'eqchi' patriarchs' roles as go-betweens varied in meaning and form across time and space, as they negotiated between the competing interests and shifting practices of colonial state officials, ecclesiastical authorities, and indigenous communities. Through their functions as mediators, Q'eqchi' patriarchs held the political, social, and economic order in a fragile balance and helped produce and limit state sovereignty. Most often, they successfully diffused tensions, but on occasion, such as during Yat's rebellion, the pressures were such that native

---

[1] AGCA B Leg. 28601 Expediente (hereafter Exp.) 151 1865; AGCA Juicios-Baja Verapaz (hereafter J-BV) 113 Leg. 26 Exp. 24 1865.

[2] AGCA J-BV 113 Leg. 26 Exp. 24 1865.

[3] Grandin, *The Last Colonial Massacre*, 65; Arden King, *Cobán and the Verapaz: History and Cultural Process in Northern Guatemala* (New Orleans: Middle American Research Institute, 1974), 29.

intermediaries abandoned the middle ground and violence erupted with long-term repercussions.[4]

Jorge Yat's revolution, however, was more than just an episode in archaic colonial politics in a postcolonial age. Yat's revolution condensed the histories of colonial mediation and liberal republicanism into densely woven time-knots. In contrast to modernity's privileging of linear sequence, wherein the past is consigned to a bygone era, time-knots entangle multiple histories together and demonstrate the enduring presence of the past. Jorge Yat had himself lived through the layered transition Mayas experienced, from being subjects in a colonial state to citizens in a new republic. When Jorge Yat and his followers charged the local alcaldes with corruption and exploiting the masses, they also argued that town officials had failed to act as their representatives in local political matters. According to his supporters, Yat's aim was to "restrict the abuses committed by the Alcaldes against the children and *naturales* [Mayas] of the town." When Maya commoners demanded that Yat replace the existing alcaldes, they acted on the democratic belief that people have the right to choose their own representatives and to demand responsiveness from those officials. Indeed, Yat's supporters contended not only that Yat was elected by Sanpedranos but that he would better serve the community as someone who "attended to the needs of the entire pueblo." While the archival record makes the veracity of Yat's election difficult to discern, Yat's supporters' actions and testimonies reveal how colonial and postcolonial histories coexisted and overlapped. In these time-knots, history is defined not by rupture and cause-and-effect flows, but by the weaving together of pasts in the present. Yat's revolution brought together colonial histories of native mediation and postcolonial histories of democratic institutions into a conflictual present.

European settlers, ladinos, and state officials often articulated a different metanarrative, which emphasized the value of civilization and capitalist expansion rather than liberal democracy. They envisioned the Verapaz as a future capitalist space for European settlers and entrepreneurs. Only four years before Yat's revolution, the Tribunal of Commerce commissioned the French immigrant Julio Rossignon to compose a pamphlet about the Department of Verapaz. Entitled *El Porvenir de la Verapaz*, Rossignon described the Verapaz's potential to become Central America's "premier coffee zone." Rather than erasing Maya presence, he

---

[4] See Yanna Yannakakis, *The Art of Being in-between: Native Intermediaries, Indian Identity, and Local Rule in Colonial Oaxaca* (Durham, NC: Duke University Press, 2008).

painted an image of the region's Maya inhabitants as "hardworking" and "peaceful," ready to become a productive labor force for future settlers. Still, however, Rossignon proclaimed: "We will not discuss the history of the natives."[5] For Rossignon, Q'eqchi' history belonged to a bygone past: archaeology, folklore, and ancient traditions. Rossignon disavowed Yat's vision of engaged republican citizenship and Maya political agency. This contrast captures the tension between desires for democratic politics and liberal ideals of equality, on the one hand, and the yearnings for economic wealth and European civilization, on the other.

In this chapter, I use Jorge Yat's revolution to provide a window into mid-nineteenth-century Alta Verapaz. First, this chapter argues that Jorge Yat's revolution illuminates the temporally compressed political histories of native intermediaries in Alta Verapaz. In the late eighteenth and early nineteenth centuries, administrative reforms and new democratic constitutions empowered rural Mayas and radically changed native mediation. Second, this chapter demonstrates how Yat's revolution also revealed another postcolonial time-knot: the merged anxieties projecting a coffee-driven capitalist future, and the longer colonial and postcolonial histories of Maya peasant economies grounded in reciprocal labor obligations, shifting land tenure arrangements, and seasonal migration. Finally, this chapter argues Yat's revolution anticipated two other profound historical dynamics: the settlement of European (principally German) and North American immigrants and the 1871 Liberal revolution.

POSTCOLONIAL TIME-KNOTS I: POLITICS AND MAYA INTERMEDIARIES

Seven months before Jorge Yat stormed San Pedro Carchá's town council, the elderly Yat petitioned President Rafael Carrera on behalf of rural Q'eqchi's. With the help of a *tinterillo* (unofficial lawyer), Venacio Chiquin, Yat asked the president – as "father of the towns" – to remove corrupted local authorities.[6] In subsequent letters, Yat and his supporters outlined how the *corregidor* (chief magistrate), Pablo Sierra, had prevented elected officials from taking office. Instead, Sierra placed his own allies in power. The Q'eqchi' patriarchs of Carchá's municipal council replied that not only were Jorge Yat's accusations false, but Yat could not

[5] Julio Rossignon, *Porvenir de la Verapaz en la república de Guatemala. Memoria dedicada al Consulado de Comercio de Guatemala* (Guatemala: Imprenta de Luna, 1861), 31.

[6] AGCA B Leg. 28601 Exp. 151 1865.

represent the "popular voice" of Carchá.[7] Yat and his followers, the municipal officials retorted, were among Carchá's most "insignificant" people, who simply "wished to live without King or Castle."[8] By invoking Europe's ancien régime, the municipal councilmen equated Yat's followers with "Savagery" and their appeal to the "will of the pueblo" with a range of revolutionary actors who threatened social order in the name of democracy. In conjuring the colonial order of kings and castles against the popular sovereignty of the "will of the pueblo," Carchá's Q'eqchi' patriarchs placed Yat's localized demands in the global history of the Atlantic revolutions. Q'eqchi' patriarchs strategically mobilized the pasts of independence struggles in the present. The battles between ancien régime caste orders and republicanism resonated in the present, because the Conservative government restored some colonial practices and Q'eqchi' patriarchs' authority as intermediaries. Indeed, as liaisons between the state and indigenous communities, Q'eqchi' patriarchs maintained and sometimes challenged Spain's sovereignty.[9]

Immediately after conquest, the Catholic Church and the colonial state identified the native nobility as a class of colonial mediators, who by virtue of their legitimacy among the native peoples could help administer colonial society. Indigenous intermediaries played particularly important roles at the edges of the Spanish Empire, such as the Verapaz, where sovereignty and territorial control were subject to frequent dispute. Native go-betweens derived status from their positions as hereditary patriarchs of ethnic clans.[10] Through the conquest and conversion of outlying areas, ethnic clans and their nobles were consolidated spatially into towns. This settling process, or *reducción*, centralized state authority in two principal municipalities: Cobán (the *cabecera*, or seat of government) and San Pedro Carchá (see Map 1.1).

While Cobán was the seat of colonial authority in the Verapaz, the Spanish crown's sovereignty receded in favor of local actors in the peripheral Verapaz as a whole.[11] After nearly two centuries of Spanish governance, few of the district's indigenous pueblos had parish priests,

[7] Ibid.   [8] Ibid.

[9] See Jordana Dym, *From Sovereign Villages to National States: City, State, and Federation in Central America, 1759–1839* (Albuquerque: University of New Mexico Press, 2006).

[10] Laura E. Matthew and Michel R. Oudijk, eds., *Indian Conquistadors: Indigenous Allies in the Conquest of Mesoamerica* (Norman: University of Oklahoma Press, 2007), and Matthew Restall, *Maya Conquistador* (Boston: Beacon, 1998).

[11] Sylvia Sellers-García, *Distance and Documents at the Spanish Empire's Periphery* (Stanford, CA: Stanford University Press, 2014).

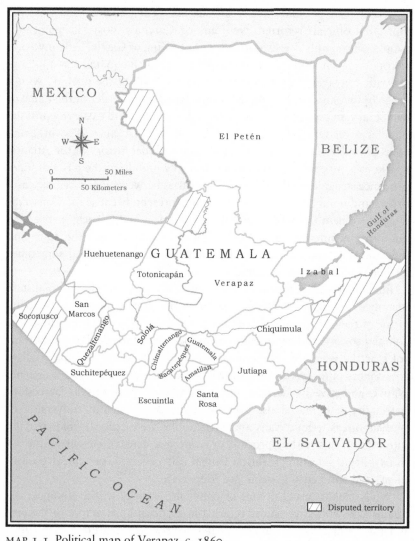

MAP I.I Political map of Verapaz, c. 1860.
University of Wisconsin-Madison, Cartography Lab

and Spaniards were clustered in Cobán. This handful of Spaniards lived in a sea of an estimated 34,000 native peoples.[12] From Cobán, state authority dwindled northward to the more arid lowlands of the departments of El Quiche and the Petén, and to the southeast from Carchá into the

---

[12] King, *Cobán and the Verapaz*, 285.

lowlands of the Polochic River valley, where scattered houses dotted the landscape. The region's rugged terrain made travel difficult; thus, distance served as a barrier to authority, and villagers residing on the margins maintained greater autonomy.[13] Spanish priests, by necessity, relied on local Q'eqchi' patriarchs to facilitate the region's colonial order. In turn, these Maya intermediaries won the reluctant consent of the region's Maya subjects and secured political legitimacy for themselves.

In each of their towns, Q'eqchi' patriarchal elders of the most powerful ethnic clans occupied roles in four central colonial institutions: the *cabildo* (town council), the repartimiento (the Spanish system of forced labor and production), the Catholic Church, and the legal system that divided peoples into two republics: Spanish and Indigenous. Q'eqchi' patriarchs occupied central positions on the town council. Likewise, each ethnic clan and neighborhood possessed a titular saint and *cofradías* (confraternities) modeled on Iberian burial and mutual aid societies. Elders known as *principales* and *chinames* held positions of importance in the cofradías. As town councilmen and elders in the cofradía, Q'eqchi' patriarchs administered repartimiento duties and collected taxes. As town judges, scribes, translators, and *tinterillos* (unofficial lawyers), Q'eqchi' patriarchs such as Venacio Chiquin also played a crucial role in the Spanish justice system.[14]

As intermediaries, Q'eqchi' patriarchs performed essential functions in the state and thus helped generate the archive itself. Learning legal procedures and Spanish, they became notaries, scribes, and tinterillos. Spaniards often called them *indios ladinos*, bicultural figures about whom the Spanish were deeply ambivalent, but on whom the empire also rested. As did other indigenous notaries in Mesoamerica, they recorded wills, land sales, and other transactions in Q'eqchi' Maya. By the mid-nineteenth century, Q'eqchi' intermediaries largely wrote in Spanish, and formed part of the *ciudad letrada*, an elite group of "wielders of pen and paper" who exercised influence far beyond their small numbers.[15] While Q'eqchi' patriarchs used this power to shape philosophical debates and define the meanings of colonial and postcolonial rule over time, they also exercised their power by producing the archive and thus what could be known and

---

[13] Sellers-García, *Distance and Documents*.

[14] Yanna Yannakakis and Martina Schrader-Kniffki, "Between the 'Old Law' and the New: Christian Translation, Indian Jurisdiction, and Criminal Justice in Colonial Oaxaca," *Hispanic American Historical Review* 96, no. 3 (2016): 517–48.

[15] Angel Rama and John Charles Chasteen, *The Lettered City* (Durham, NC: Duke University Press, 1996).

said about the past. Q'eqchi' commoners recognized the potency of patriarchs' literacy and sometimes sought to upend the patriarchs' power over paper. Jorge Yat, for example, claimed to possess presidential correspondence appointing him alcalde primero. When the president's letter went missing, Yat accused the Q'eqchi' alcaldes and corregidor of "hiding important papers." Even these lost papers wielded an incredible influence.[16]

Through their roles in colonial state and ecclesiastical institutions, Q'eqchi' patriarchs mediated between the competing demands of the colonial state and indigenous commoners. They made colonial systems function and created a hybrid colonial culture. Native intermediaries made the colonial economy function through the collection of tribute and oversight of the repartimiento. At times, however, they stood up to abusive Spanish officials and shielded their towns from the kinds of violence and coercion that might provoke a rebellion. Indigenous elders instructed their fellow villagers in the Christian doctrine, but discretely led communities in native rituals. The authority of the Q'eqchi' patriarchs was also intimately connected to the Tzuultaq'a mountain spirits and the practice of keeping the Maya calendar. Appearing in their dreams, mountain spirits counseled Q'eqchi' patriarchs on setting the dates for rituals and planting and on making appointments to religious offices. Some Q'eqchi' patriarchs were also Maya shamans charged with the special role of keeping the Maya calendar, and thus foretelling the character of days and years to come. This dual rule facilitated translations between Catholicism and Maya religion, forging new hybrid cultures. Q'eqchi' patriarchs and commoners united also around a common dress, language, and food culture centered on corn that distinguished them from non-Mayas. Native legal agents also petitioned higher royal authorities to censure Spanish priests and magistrates for interfering in town governance, all the while pursuing the interests of their own political factions. Through these practices, Q'eqchi' patriarchs secured the political power of their lineages, but also made their villages dependent on the Spanish legal system.

The strong bonds of reciprocity between the indigenous nobility and commoners limited the nature of colonial exploitation. Q'eqchi' patriarchs had to answer not only to the Spanish state officials and priests but

---

[16] On indigenous archives, see Joanne Rappaport and Tom Cummins, *Beyond the Lettered City: Indigenous Alphabetic Literacy and Visuality in the Andes, 16th to 18th Centuries* (Durham, NC: Duke University Press, 2011).

also to the commoners who legitimated their authority within indigenous society. Over centuries of negotiation and mediation, Q'eqchi' patriarchs' legitimacy as elders thus rested on their ability to mediate between the demands of colonial officials and those of Q'eqchi' commoners. Q'eqchi' patriarchs were respected as "good fathers" and fulfilled their end of a set of Q'eqchi' reciprocal norms and obligations. On the town council, in the church, and in the legal system, Q'eqchi' patriarchs ensured that they represented the interests of commoners in public matters. They also resolved disputes between individuals and distributed access to subsistence lands as well as forests. In return, Q'eqchi' commoners labored in communal projects and paid taxes. As community leaders and cabildo officers, Q'eqchi' patriarchs defended commoners, delivered tribute to the crown, and maintained reciprocal relations between their communities. Fulfilling these competing demands enhanced political legitimacy, social status, and material wealth. As intermediaries between Q'eqchi' commoners, the Church, and the colonial state, Q'eqchi' patriarchs negotiated a balance between competing interests. When commoners called native intermediaries to account, as happened during Jorge Yat's rebellion, Q'eqchi' patriarchs found their political options limited and their intermediary role imperiled. In such instances, Maya patriarchs often could not hold violence at bay, and they faced two options: position themselves as leaders in moments of violent resistance or become primary targets of those confrontations.

In the late eighteenth century, a colonial crisis tested the enduring balance of Q'eqchi' mediation that had maintained the colonial system. The Bourbon Spanish crown, confronting imperial competition from France and Great Britain after strategic losses following the Seven Years' War (1756–63), sought to strengthen defense and to promote commercial development and administrative efficiency.[17] The Bourbon administration implemented cultural, political, and economic reforms designed to subordinate and Hispanicize native officeholders, squeeze more revenue from indigenous pueblos, and subject indigenous peoples to new labor regimes. The Bourbon Reforms, thus, had significant effects on indigenous society. In the Verapaz, the reforms, including a dramatic 104 percent

---

[17] On late colonial transformations in Central America, see especially Dym, *From Sovereign Villages*; Miles L. Wortman, *Government and Society in Central America, 1680–1840* (New York: Columbia University Press, 1982); Jordana Dym and Christopher Belaubre, eds., *Politics, Economy, and Society in Bourbon Central America, 1759–1821* (Boulder: University of Colorado Press, 2007); Catherine Komisaruk, *Labor and Love in Guatemala: The Eve of Independence* (Stanford, CA: Stanford University Press, 2013).

increase in tribute, coincided with the economic disruption caused by war, locusts, and the decline of the dye industry. Together, these historical processes touched off a storm of protests leading to a major riot in Cobán in 1803.[18] In this instance, as during Yat's 1865 rebellion, Q'eqchi' patriarchs, including the *alcalde mayor* (equivalent to *alcalde primero*) and the indigenous *gobernador*, did not become leaders of the rebellion, but rather its principal victims. By the time Napoleon Bonaparte invaded Spain in 1808 – provoking military resistance and the drafting of Spain's first constitution in 1812 – Q'eqchi' commoners were ready for a new definition of local political power that shifted sovereignty to the people. In the memorable words of the Q'eqchi' patriarchs of San Pedro Carchá, they were ready for a world without king and castle.

The Spanish constitution of 1812 introduced major institutional changes, including universal male suffrage, popular elections, and the elimination of legal distinctions between different groups of citizens. By formally ending the 300-year-old legal distinction between indigenous peoples and Spaniards, the constitutional system altered the social and institutional worlds in which rural Central Americans lived, and made elections central to political governance. Once differentiated subjects of an absolutist regime, indigenous villagers first became equal members of a constitutional monarchy, and then, after 1821, citizens of a liberal Central American republic with the right to vote and participate in local government and beyond. The new laws also abolished any distinctively indigenous local authority and introduced new relationships with non-indigenous people, who were also gaining new rights. Liberal reforms provided opportunities for self-government and autonomy, while curtailing privileges. For Cobaneros and Sanpedranos, liberal reforms also altered the dynamics of native mediation. New ideas of democratic governance blended into older notions of communal reciprocity.[19]

For Q'eqchi' villagers, the most transformative institutions of the 1812 Spanish constitution were those involving town government. Town councils were replaced with constitutional *ayuntamientos* (municipal councils). In ayuntamientos, officials were elected not by the indigenous communities but by the population of the town as a whole. For

---

[18] Manuel Fernandez Molina, *Los tributos en el reino de Guatemala: 1786–1821* (Guatemala: IIES, 2000); AGCA A 14.1 Leg. 4072 Exp. 32228.

[19] For an example of such blending, see also David McCreery, "Atanasio Tzul, Lucas Aguilar, and the Indian Kingdom of Totonicapán," in *The Human Tradition in Latin America: The Nineteenth Century*, ed. Judith Ewell and William Beezley (Wilmington, DE: Scholarly Resources, 1989), 39–58.

villagers, the ayuntamientos represented a new way of designating village authority and raised the possibility of indigenous villagers sharing power with or even losing power to local ladinos.[20] In the Verapaz, Q'eqchi's readily adopted the new ayuntamientos. The distinguished liberal, José de Valle, celebrated in his newspaper, *El Amigo de la Patria*, that Cobán had installed a mixed ayuntamiento with ten indigenous members and two ladino ones, who served lesser positions.[21] By contrast, in Quetzaltenango ladinos took advantage of the ayuntamientos to threaten K'iche patriarchal control over local resources. Among K'iches in Quetzaltenango, the ayuntamientos unleashed resistance. In towns such as Cobán and San Pedro Carchá, however, villagers rapidly embraced ayuntamientos as a means to strengthen local autonomy at the expense of the governor.[22] Q'eqchi' authorities in Cobán favored full compliance with the constitution, since the constitutional council could help indigenous communities when it was controlled by its own members. Yet ayuntamientos also altered the dynamics between Q'eqchi' patriarchs and commoners by allowing commoners to exercise greater power in local government.[23]

The 1812 Spanish constitution lasted only two years, yet despite its short duration, it had revolutionary implications. After the Allied powers restored Ferdinand VII to the Spanish throne in March 1814, Ferdinand sought to restore the Bourbon doctrine that authority resided in the king. In 1820, confronting turmoil within Spain, the king revived the constitutional monarchy to preserve his control over the Iberian Peninsula as well as the remaining overseas territories. In Guatemala, Maya commoners took advantage of the return to constitutionalism to challenge local authorities. In Totonicapan, Maya commoners revolted and whipped patriarchs who collected tribute until they fell unconscious.[24] These Maya

---

[20] Dym, *From Sovereign Villages*, 276. See also Karen D. Caplan, "The Legal Revolution in Town Politics: Oaxaca and Yucatán, 1812–1825," *Hispanic American Historical Review* 83, no. 2 (May 2003): 255–93.

[21] José Cecilio del Valle, *Escritos del Licenciado José Cecilio del Valle* (Guatemala: Editorial José de Pineda Ibarra, 1969), 30–31. For a discussion of this, see Lina E. Barrios, *Tras las huellas del poder local: La alcaldía indígena en Guatemala del siglo XVI al siglo XX* (Guatemala: Universidad Rafael Landívar, Instituto de Investigaciones Económicas y Sociales, 2001).

[22] Grandin, *The Blood of Guatemala*, 71–72; Dym, *From Sovereign Villages*, 132.

[23] For how this took place in Guatemala, see Dym, *From Sovereign Villages*, and Aaron Pollack, *Levantamiento K'iche'en Totonicapán, 1820: Los lugares de las políticas subalternas* (Guatemala: AVANCSO, 2008).

[24] McCreery, "Atanasio Tzul, Lucas Aguilar, and the Indian Kingdom of Totonicapán," 51.

revolts convinced Maya patriarchs and Creoles alike of the need for independence from Spain.[25] In 1821 the colonial Kingdom of Guatemala became the republican United Provinces of Central America.

Battles between republicans and loyalists continued after independence. These ideological conflicts were cemented into two predominant political parties: the Conservatives, who were associated with the colonial social order, the Church, and centralism; and the Liberals, who were associated with formal legal equality, anticlericalism, and federalism. Guatemala's Liberal chief of state, Dr. Mariano Gálvez, attempted, for example, to dismantle archaic Spanish institutions, including the corporate protections afforded to the Catholic Church and indigenous communities. He also reorganized town councils along the lines established in Spain's 1812 constitution. His most radical reforms, however, were the Livingston Codes. These reforms diminished local autonomy and established legal equality. In an effort to attract European immigrants, Gálvez also awarded vast territories to foreign investors.[26] These liberal reforms upset the fragile balance that Maya intermediaries had negotiated, and an estimated thirty rebellions shook Guatemala between 1831 and 1838.[27] In 1837, when a cholera epidemic further enlivened resistance, Rafael Carrera, a Conservative *caudillo* (strongman leader), led the overthrow of the Liberals, and the Central America federation dissolved.

As president of the Republic of Guatemala, Rafael Carrera restored the colonial-era system of two republics and town councils. Conservatives maintained that the Liberal reforms of the 1830s had been too rapid. While Conservatives, too, aspired to republican values, they also believed in gradual reform in order "to inculcate respect for the constitutive authorities [because] ... working for a living and ... admiring what is foreign are the most sure methods, although slow, to civilize the ignorant masses." Even more, liberal doctrines were dangerous: "Continually preaching liberty, equality, and sovereignty to them ... is to drive them towards insurrection, it gives them arms that they can use against us, putting into practice and affirming the doctrines that we have incautiously

[25] Dym, *From Sovereign Villages*, 65.

[26] Mario Rodríguez, "The Livingston Codes in the Guatemalan Crisis of 1837–38," in *Applied Enlightenment: 19th-Century Liberalism* (New Orleans: Middle American Research Institute, Tulane University, 1972), 1–32.

[27] Mario Rodríguez, *The Cádiz Experiment in Central America, 1808 to 1826* (Berkeley: University of California Press, 1978), 42.

taught them."[28] Conservatives argued that Mayas were not yet ready for full citizenship, and sought to postpone Maya emancipation. When Maya patriarchs in Carchá declared that Yat wanted to "live without King or Castle," they too referred to the dangers of liberalism when applied to Mayas. When Yat revolted against tyranny, he conjured the memory of a time when Q'eqchi' lower classes were citizens and could hold their local officials accountable.

By the mid-nineteenth century, the Conservative-restored republic joined the civil and religious hierarchies and reestablished the place of Q'eqchi' patriarchs as central intermediary figures.[29] The new, merged, civil–religious hierarchy brought town councils and cofradías into a single system. In the process, the civil–religious hierarchy reinvigorated indigenous hierarchies and mediation, while also reducing the local political power of Q'eqchi' commoners. By the time of Jorge Yat's rebellion, voting for local authorities was restricted to Maya patriarchs who had already served on the town council. Jorge Yat, who had not served in the combined civil–religious hierarchy, was thus ineligible to vote in local elections. Voting regulations also excluded illiterate and unpropertied commoners.[30]

While the restored republic supposedly reinstated the colonial-era municipal governments, the historical experiences of early liberal–democratic experiments had imprinted the notion that town officials were representatives of the pueblo and were ultimately responsible to them. As a Q'eqchi' who had lived through the constitutional ayuntamientos and the early republican period, Jorge Yat remembered a time when commoners voted in elections, challenged Maya hierarchies, and called Q'eqchi' patriarchs to respond to them. Q'eqchi' commoners likely believed their disenfranchisement violated Q'eqchi' norms. With the help of the

---

[28] *La Gaceta de Guatemala*, February 21, 1850.
[29] See Adriaan C. Van Oss, *Catholic Colonialism: A Parish History of Guatemala, 1524–1821* (Cambridge: Cambridge University Press, 1986), and John K. Chance and William B. Taylor, "Cofradías and Cargos: An Historical Perspective on the Mesoamerican Civil-Religious Hierarchy," *American Ethnologist* 12, no. 1 (1985): 1–26.
[30] In 1845, the government briefly reestablished the right for all citizens, but it lasted only until 1847. See Sonia Alda Mejías, *La participación indígena en la construcción de la república de Guatemala, s. XIX* (Madrid: Universidad Autónoma de Madrid, 2000), 217. In 1851, the National Assembly also established a system of indirect vote for elections of the president and judges of the Superior Court, who would be selected by representatives in the National Assembly. Conservatives believed that a system of indirect vote would prohibit the kinds of "intrigues" that had supposedly tainted prior elections, see ibid., 215.

tinterillo Venacio Chiquin, a group of Q'eqchi' commoners, for example, forged a letter to the president, allegedly written by the principales and chinames of Carchá, demanding the release of Jorge Yat from prison and his instatement as Carchá's alcalde. The Q'eqchi' patriarchs of Carchá quickly discovered the forgery and denounced the appropriation of their authority by what they called "frauds."[31]

The civil–religious hierarchy worked, to some degree, to resolve tensions between Q'eqchi' commoners and patriarchs by creating opportunities for social mobility among Q'eqchi's. By amalgamating positions in cofradías and town councils, the restored republic allowed both men from the hereditary elite (who claimed descent from pre-Hispanic ruling families) and men who had worked their way up by *cargos* (contributions, duties, and communal sacrifices) to occupy all the important positions in the community. Villagers also gained authority and prestige within their communities through service in the civil–religious hierarchy, particularly through the more influential and wealthier cofradías located in Cobán and Carchá. Some Q'eqchi' commoners might become patriarchs whose authority derived not from hereditary status but from their service in the civil–religious hierarchy. Through this service, Q'eqchi's social climbers demonstrated that they were benevolent father figures who dutifully fulfilled their obligations to the community.

Despite Q'eqchi' commoners' disenfranchisement, the Q'eqchi' patriarchs who occupied positions in the civil–religious hierarchy were obliged to represent the commoners' interests. While town councilmen acted as intermediaries, the villagers regarded them as community guardians in local political conflicts. Q'eqchi' patriarchs were "good fathers" within a system of familial-like reciprocal bonds of mutual responsibility and obligation. If the patriarchs ignored pressures from below, their integrity as community representatives could erode, and, Maya commoners reasoned, they could be removed from office. Q'eqchi' communities united adherence to the traditions and hierarchies of the civil–religious system, on the one hand, and a liberal notion that townspeople had the right to elect their representatives who would in turn be responsible to the communities, on the other.[32] When Jorge Yat's supporters wrote to

[31] AGCA J-BV 113 Leg. 26 Exp. 24 1865.

[32] On the emergence of democratic tendencies in Latin American indigenous communities around the turn of the nineteenth century, see Sinclair Thomson, *We Alone Will Rule: Native Andean Politics in the Age of Insurgency* (Madison: University of Wisconsin Press, 2002); Florencia E. Mallon, *Peasant and Nation: The Making of Postcolonial Mexico and Peru* (Berkeley: University of California Press, 1995); Peter Guardino, *The Time of*

the departmental corregidor demanding Yat's release from prison, they described Yat as "a good man (hombre de bien)," who was "most concerned for el pueblo." Another argued that Yat was "a man who loved the pueblo, and we love him. He would not be a tyrant and all his public acts are honorable, we very much want him to be freed before the new year so that he can receive the first alcalde's vara."[33] As a virtuous patriarch to the townspeople, these Q'eqchi' commoners selected Yat to represent them in local matters.

By the late 1850s, Q'eqchi' commoners were increasingly frustrated with Conservative legislation that undermined their access to communal resources, increased demands on their labor, and imposed state monopolies on alcohol production that undercut local economies. As a result, Q'eqchi' commoners felt that the Q'eqchi' patriarchs did not represent their interests, and revolts directed at Q'eqchi' patriarchs became frequent.[34] In the months prior to his revolution, Yat had expressed discontent over the collection of taxes "even from the most poor." Yat accused the alcaldes of "lighting fire to our sugar cane" and preventing them from "alleviating ourselves with the making of boj." After Yat's rebellion, Q'eqchi' town councilors sought to purge the municipality of troublemakers. In 1867, for example, a dozen Q'eqchi' commoners wrote to the president, claiming that the indigenous alcaldes of San Pedro Carchá had "expelled them off their native soil" and "forced them to settle in the towns Cajabon, San Agustin, Panzós and San Juan [Chamelco]."[35] Yat's short-lived revolution was rooted in a blend of Q'eqchi' liberal–democratic norms and enduring forms of Maya hierarchy and mediation, and articulated colonial and republican pasts with the Conservative-era present. Yat's revolution also spoke to how the Atlantic revolutions reverberated and were remade in specific cultural and historical contexts. While the notion that Q'eqchi' patriarchs were responsible to their villages had origins in colonial mediation, Q'eqchi' democratic ideologies were dramatically transformed during the liberal experiments of the early nineteenth century.

Liberty: Popular Political Culture in Oaxaca, 1750–1850 (Durham, NC: Duke University Press, 2005).

[33] AGCA Ministerio de Gobernación (hereafter MG) B Leg. 28602 Exp. 268 1865.

[34] AGCA Jefatura Político de Alta Verapaz (hereafter JP-AV) 1861, "Al Sr. Tentinte de Corregidor de AV, de Juan Valdez," Salamá, September 20, 1861.

[35] AGCA B Leg. 28611 Exp. 385. See also AGCA MG B Leg. 28576 Exp. 147 Fol. 8; and AGCA MG B Leg. 2877 Exp. 26 Fol. 185.

POSTCOLONIAL TIME-KNOTS II: PEASANT SUBSISTENCE
ECONOMIES AND GEOGRAPHY

When asked by the town judge why Yat had fomented a rebellion, several Q'eqchi' patriarchs remarked that Q'eqchi' commoners were angered by the town council's planting of coffee in the town's *ejidos* (town's commonlands), normally reserved for *milpa*, fields that combined maize and other crops such as beans and squash.[36] While none of the rebels mentioned coffee planting among their grievances, Q'eqchi' patriarchs pointed to coffee as a source of popular discontent. State officials repeatedly prophesized that coffee production would inevitably produce violent Maya uprisings. In 1860 the corregidor Pablo Sierra wrote to his superior in Salamá, warning him of the dangers of coffee production.[37] Others such as Julio Rossignon believed coffee could be harvested without disrupting the existing order, and thus promised the region extraordinary prosperity. Rossignon's call for the colonization of the Verapaz also circulated in the widely read official newspaper, *La Gaceta de Guatemala*, where he declared that "Verapaz is truly, without an exaggeration, comparable in its combination of resources to the island of Saint Domingue [Haiti]: that it will produce more [coffee] than all of the Republic of Costa Rica; and that the development of its riches, intimately linked to the state, can be obtained without upheavals, without upsetting public order, peace, nor religious institutions."[38] Even the ex-president of Colombia, Dr. Mariano Ospina, visited the Verapaz to explore the prospect of coffee planting.[39] Unlike the political time-knot of liberal republicanism and caste hierarchy, this economic time-knot of subsistence economies and coffee production prompted fears of a seemingly inevitable future wherein progress through export production violently encountered and overthrew indigenous producers and transformed them into a landless proletariat.

For Mayas, however, this romantic coffee future was also embedded in longer histories of indigenous peasant economies with its seasonal time and the region's mountain spirit–inflected geography. State officials and would-be coffee planters systematically presented Maya subsistence and

---

[36] AGCA J-BV 113 Leg. 26 Exp. 24 1865.
[37] AGCA, "Corregidor al sub-corregidor Pablo Sierra," September 21, 1860; AGCA JP-AV 1865.
[38] Rossignon, *Porvenir de la Verapaz*, 37.
[39] AGCA JP-AV 1860 Paq. 1, "Juan E. Valdez a Sr. Teniente Corregidor de la Alta Verapaz," June 25, 1860.

commercial production, seasonal migration, and reciprocal labor obligations as backward and barbarous, and thus lacking in the fullness of humanity. Within civilizing narratives of the rise of coffee production, state officials and others disavowed rural Mayas such as Yat, politically excluding them as anachronistic. From a Q'eqchi' perspective, this economic postcolonial time-knot reveals how Q'eqchi' commoners also articulated an ethics of communal solidarity and reciprocal obligations, as well as individualism and competition. Q'eqchi' social and economic worlds depended on an intraregional dispersion of power and on seasonal migration to different ecological zones, with different productive capacities and different temporal rhythms of production. Through interregional trade, kinship networks, and the civil–religious hierarchy, Q'eqchi' commoners formed a relatively autonomous peasant economy. Q'eqchi' economies represented a dangerous counterpart to Yat's political calls for democracy: the Q'eqchi' self-sufficient peasant economy of small producers destabilized romanticized futures of rows of coffee trees cut into the jagged mountains and readily available Maya laborers tirelessly tilling, pruning, and harvesting coffee beans. To understand Q'eqchi' alternatives, it is necessary to unpack rural Mayas' social, cultural, and ecological worlds.

Alta Verapaz's Mayas resided in three ecological zones: the cold highland mountain ridges, the temperate valley floors, and the lowland plains (see Map 1.2). These different ecological zones were connected by indigenous commercial traders and the seasonal migration of many families from the highlands to the lowlands during the dry season. Geologically part of the Antillean structure, Alta Verapaz is defined by sharp hills and valleys and, as a result of the prevalence of karst formations, very few rivers and superficial water sources but many caves and underground rivers.[40] These two factors – rugged terrain with a great deal of

---

[40] For the region's human geography, Karl Sapper, "Die Alta Verapaz (Guatemala): Eine Landeskundliche Skizze Mit Fünf Originalkarten," *Mittheilungen Der Geographischen Gesellschaft in Hamburg* 61 (1901): 78–224; Michael Robert Wilson, "A Highland Maya People and Their Habitat: The Natural History, Demography and Economy of the K'ekchi" (PhD diss., University of Oregon, 1972); William E. Carter, *New Lands and Old Traditions: Kekchi Cultivators in the Guatemalan Lowlands* (Gainesville: University of Florida Press, 1969); Liza Grandia, *Enclosed: Conservation, Cattle, and Commerce among the Q'eqchi' Maya Lowlanders* (Seattle: University of Washington Press, 2012). For the environment and physical geography, I also draw on King, *Cobán and the Verapaz*, 10–12; Anthony G. Coates, "The Forging of Central America," in *Central America: A Natural and Cultural History*, ed. Antony G. Coates (New Haven, CT: Yale University Press, 1997), 32–33; David Rains Wallace, "Central American Landscapes,"

MAP 1.2 Map of Alta Verapaz.
University of Wisconsin-Madison, Cartography Lab

microclimatic diversity and variable access to water – shaped different
productive land uses, population distribution, and commercial networks.
The same rugged terrain, underground rivers, and caves were also sacred
places and home to powerful mountain deities, or Tzuultaq'as.

The highest peaks of the Verapaz reach 3,000 meters above sea level
and were ill-suited to agriculture, due to the risk of frost, the rocky
exposed terrain, and poor-quality limestone soils that were vulnerable

in *Central America: A Natural and Cultural History*, ed. Anthony G. Coates (New
Haven, CT: Yale University Press, 1997), 77–81; Sapper, "Die Alta Verapaz
(Guatemala)."

to erosion with the near-steady rainfall experienced in these regions. In these densely wooded oak–conifer forests, villagers collected a variety of wild products such as rubber, vanilla, and maguey (fiber for making ropes), as well as firewood, construction materials, and game. Many of these forest products were crucial for Maya subsistence as well as the local and regional commercial economy. Mahogany and cedar, for example, were sold to local carpenters in Cobán and San Pedro Carchá, while maguey was used to create a wide variety of goods including satchels, ropes, and hammocks. From Cobán and San Pedro Carchá, Q'eqchi' merchants carried these products to more distant markets including Guatemala City and Queztaltenango.[41]

In the southwestern-highlands basins surrounding Cobán, where volcanic deposits produced rich soils for agricultural development, indigenous settlement was concentrated during colonial conversion and resettlement. The soils of valley floors needed no more fallowing than the two or three months between harvest in late July through September and the next year's clearing in the months of January through late April.[42] Intricate variations in slope and soil created a series of tiny microclimates where fertility, humidity, and access to sunlight could change radically from one part of a slope, hill, or valley to another. Cultivation thus was a complex task, requiring specialized knowledge of the terrain and crops. Maya peasants took advantage of these conditions by planting in two or three different microclimate zones, making use of even the slightest change in angle or quality of soil to maximize productivity.[43] Within each unit, Q'eqchi's also planted different varieties of maize, fitting the needs of the maize to the characteristics of the soil on the smallest scale. Maize was interspersed with a diversity of secondary food crops such as nitrogen-fixing beans, which replenished the soil organically, as well as a variety of wild plants from the secondary forest that grew alongside the milpa. In areas where water was scarce, Q'eqchi's migrated from the highlands to the lowland river valleys where they planted a second, winter crop of maize in riverside plots that flooded annually with silt.[44] In this central region, wealthier Q'eqchi's raised the region's cattle in soils deemed too rocky or compact for maize.

---

[41] Sapper, "Die Alta Verapaz (Guatemala)."

[42] Wilson, "A Highland Maya People and Their Habitat," 38.

[43] Carter, *New Lands and Old Traditions*; Wilson, "A Highland Maya People and Their Habitat"; Grandia, *Enclosed*.

[44] See AGCA Sección de Tierras – Alta Verapaz (herafter ST-AV) Paq. 23 Exp. 2; AGCA ST-AV Paq. 7 Exp. 17; AGCA MG B Leg. 28576 Exp. 147; AGCA B Leg. 28576 Exp. 147.

Moving away from the rich volcanic soils deposited around Cobán and San Pedro Carchá, the region's soils were more often limestone and clay-based and would dry out or erode easily. As a result, villagers living beyond the southwestern core region were required to rotate cultivation, leaving a field fallow for at least four years following one season of maize production.[45] These regions thus supported a much lower population density as individuals required a greater area for annual cultivation. Nineteenth-century travelers tended to describe lowland landscapes and people as more barbaric due to the hot and humid climate, the threat of illnesses like malaria and yellow fever, and Mayas' semi-nomadic practices and dispersed settlements. Since migratory Mayas lacked fixed residences and practiced shifting cultivation, many nineteenth-century commentators believed such seasonally nomadic life was antithetical to the time-space of modern private property, annual cultivation, and fixed village settlements.[46] Yet because most non-Maya landownership was concentrated in central valleys of Cobán, Q'eqchi's migration across ecological zones cemented their political and social autonomy.

Throughout the 1860s, Q'eqchi' and ladino authorities complained about the savagery of rural Sanpedranos who, like Jorge Yat and many of his followers, resided within the mountainous terrain descending southeast toward Lake Izabal and the Polochic River valley, like those who populated the northern arid lowlands of Cahabón. The mid-nineteenth-century travel writer Arthur Morelet, for example, described arriving in Cobán's temperate highlands from the northern lowlands: "The 'tierra templada': that is to say the most salubrious and interesting zone of equatorial America ... inaugurated for me a new era, in which health and a sense of security were to succeed languor, annoyance and peril. At the same time, I saw a change in the whole face of nature, in the appearance of the sky, the character of the plants and animals, and in the morals and aptitudes of the people. It was almost like visiting a new country."[47] In contrast to the Cahabón natives residing in the northern lowlands, Cobaneros were "active, enterprising, and industrious," and they "possess[ed] the essential elements of civilization."[48] Through such descriptions, travel writers like Morelet translated Maya agricultural and social practices into

---

[45] Wilson, "A Highland Maya People and Their Habitat," 38.

[46] Rossignon, *Porvenir de La Verapaz*; Sapper, "Die Alta Verapaz (Guatemala)."

[47] Arthur Morelet, *Travels in Central America, Including Accounts of Some Regions Unexplored since the Conquest*, ed. Mariano Florence Squier (New York: Leypoldt, Holt & Williams, 1871), 329.

[48] Ibid., 331–2.

the civilizing metanarrative and expressed their anxieties about spaces that were haunted by disease, uncivilized practices, and limited state territorial sovereignty.

More distant barbaric villages, however, were crucial to the region's commercial economy. Not only did lowland populations provide a second crop of maize at a moment of scarcity, but they also provided goods for local consumption and regional trade, especially chiles, cacao, tobacco, and cotton.[49] Likewise, in the northeastern corner of the department, a salt mine furnished salt for the region and for trade across Guatemala.[50] These lowland products, especially cotton, were crucial for the regional economy. Lowland villagers sold cotton to artisans in Cobán and Carchá, who manufactured them into textiles for sale to merchants, who carried them to distant markets.

The central god in Q'eqchi' cosmography, the figure of Tzuultaq'a defined another ontological framing of the relationship between highlands/lowlands and center/periphery. Tzuultaq'as, often translated as the Gods of the Hill and Valley, resided in the mountains and the region's numerous caves, known as "stone houses." Q'eqchi's built some churches and chapels atop agrarian shrines to the Tzuultaq'as. Perched on top of a hill, the Calvary church in Cobán, for example, is explicitly treated as Tzuultaq'a. Throughout Maya Mesoamerica, sacred buildings are considered mountains.[51] Each village identified its own sacred spot where the Tzuultaq'as lived; typically, these spots were named after nearby bodies of water, animals, crops, people, and Catholic saints. Likewise, Tzuultaq'as were often marked by crosses along footpaths, so when villagers passed through different territories they prayed to crosses along the way. Maya crosses symbolized and demarcated distinct territories and resident villagers, while also uniting disparate villagers through travel.[52] In addition to ceremonies surrounding the harvest and planting, Q'eqchi's also made regular pilgrimages to more powerful sacred sites. Tzuultaq'as, in other words, articulate concepts of center and periphery, since the principal mountains and strongest Tzuultaq'as are located around Cobán. The hills close to lowland villages are believed

---

[49] Sapper, "Die Alta Verapaz (Guatemala)."   [50] Rossignon, *Porvenir de La Verapaz.*

[51] Robert M. Hill, *Colonial Cakchiqueles: Highland Maya Adaptation to Spanish Rule, 1600–1700* (Fort Worth, TX: Harcourt Brace Jovanovich, 1992), 8.

[52] See, especially, Abigail E. Adams, "The Transformation of the Tzuultaq'a: Jorge Ubico, Protestants and Other Verapaz Maya at the Crossroads of Community, State and Transnational Interests," *Journal of Latin American Anthropology* 6, no. 2 (2001): 198–233.

to have less powerful Tzuultaq'as. Like the kinship and commercial networks that articulate hierarchy and connection between the highlands and lowlands, lowland Tzuultaq'as communicate with the more powerful mountains around Cobán.

While some contemporary Q'eqchi's conceptualize Tzuultaq'as as one facet of a monotheistic god, perhaps akin to the Holy Spirit, others understand Tzuultaq'as as a separate force alongside a Christian God, something akin to the concept of Mother Nature. Tzuultaq'as possessed all of nature's abundance, and thus Q'eqchi's were required to ask permission to harvest and hunt in the Tzuultaq'as' territory. Tzuultaq'as also act as an ethical barometer for Q'eqchi's; they can become revengeful and mean when communal norms are breached, while they can also be kind and generous by providing bountiful harvests.[53]

Jorge Yat's village, Tzamali, occupied a strategic ecological, commercial, and cultural transition zone between the wealthy, powerful, and fertile lands of Cobán and San Pedro Carchá and the sparsely populated, weaker, and torrid zones surrounding Panzós. His village was located along the commercial routes linking the lowlands and the highlands and contained elements of both places. Villagers likely lived in scattered huts, possessed a greater degree of autonomy, and practiced shifting cultivation. However, they were not so distant from Carchá that they could be entirely free from the state, especially since state officials cracked down on clandestine boj production, enforced contributions, and rounded up laborers for work on emerging coffee plantations. Even still, the Q'eqhi' patriarchs of San Pedro Carchá referred to the revolutionaries as "a multitude of 'unknown' Indians," suggesting that they had few direct interactions with Sanpedranos from Tzamali. Unlike Panzós, Tzamali was also too distant from other departments to threaten to leave the Verapaz, when authorities made excessive demands for labor and taxes. Yat lived in a hybrid, boundary zone between the two different types of places – it straddled the autonomous and yet less powerful lowlands and the rich valleys of Cobán and Carchá. From his place between these two regions, Yat gained strategic power as an intermediary for Q'eqchi' commoners from the lowland regions.

[53] On Tzuultaq'as, see ibid.; Grandia, *Enclosed*, Karl Sapper, "Religious Customs and Beliefs of the Q'eqchi' Indians," in *Early Scholars' Visits to Central America: Reports by Karl Sapper, Walter Lehmann, and Franz Termer*, ed. Marilyn Beaudry-Corbett and Ellen T. Hardy (Los Angeles: Costen Institute of Archaeology, University of California, 2000); Carlos Rafael J. Cabarrús, *La cosmovisión K'ekchi' en proceso de cambio* (San Salvador: Universidad Centroamericana, 1979).

Beyond these regional interdependencies, hierarchies, and conflicts, individual Q'eqchi' villages were also highly complex social worlds with their own tensions between solidarity and conflict across emergent class divides.[54] The precarious nature of rotating subsistence agriculture increased conflicts among villagers over access to lands in the best micro-environments and available labor. Q'eqchi' patriarchs played a crucial role in distributing land and resolving conflicts. For villagers, variable access to land and labor made cooperation equally important, since individual households could not regularly meet their needs without the support of their neighbors. Solidarity thus was also cemented through labor sharing. Especially during planting, villagers tended to work together in a group, moving from one person's plot to another. The farmer benefiting from his neighbors' help was expected to make ceremonial arrangements (*mayek*) for the planting of the maize, as well as provide breakfast and lunch along with traditional boj.[55] This system of labor sharing produced solidarities and was based on mutual reciprocity and obligation that mirrored the ethics of Tzuultaq'as. Labor sharing, while expedient, was also difficult to organize since it had to be timed with the moon cycle and the start of the rainy season. Time, thus, was governed not by the mechanized clock and the universal calendar, but by lunar and seasonal time, by labor exchanges and relations of solidarity. In good years, the overall balance of different activities meant that each family was able to meet its subsistence needs and to market a small crop surplus and a few extra commodities in San Pedro Carchá or Cobán. In a bad year, however, villagers would often plant a second maize crop or increase their nonagricultural activities by producing more artisan crafts and, if they had any, selling some cattle. Villagers sought to balance the precarious nature of subsistence agriculture by diversifying their household economies along gendered lines. While men generally were in charge of tending to fields, women and children brewed boj, made candles, weaved fabric for clothing, and molded pottery for sale. In good years, the overall balance of different activities meant that each family was able to meet its subsistence needs and to market a small crop surplus and a few extra commodities in San Pedro Carchá or Cobán. In a bad year,

---

[54] On solidarity as cemented in peasant economies, see especially Florencia E. Mallon, *The Defense of Community in Peru's Central Highlands: Peasant Struggle and Capitalist Transition, 1860–1940* (Princeton: Princeton University Press, 1983).

[55] Carter, *New Lands and Old Traditions*; Wilson, "A Highland Maya People and Their Habitat"; Richard Wilson, *Maya Resurgence in Guatemala: Q'eqchi' Experiences* (Norman: University of Oklahoma Press, 1999); Grandia, *Enclosed*.

however, villagers would often plant a second crop of maize or increase their proportion of nonagricultural activities by producing more artisan crafts and, if they had any, selling some cattle. While precarious, rural Mayas could strengthen their autonomy by participating in the civil-religious hierarchy in more powerful towns.

Individual Q'eqchi' households protected their autonomy and cemented their inclusion in the broader Maya society through cofradías. These religious lay brotherhoods organized the annual fiestas, rituals, and masses through which the village honored its saints. Cofradías were crucial sources of credit, access to land, and the provision of labor. Cofradías funded their activities – burials for members, charity for the poor, masses for souls, as well as food, music, and drink for their annual fiesta – through membership fees, obligatory contributions, interest on money lent, rent on lands, and bequests. Q'eqchi's donated money and property to cofradías in the stated belief that by honoring saints with processions, fiestas, and masses, they were placing themselves under the divine protection of heavenly beings. Individuals often posted a given amount of capital for loan, and the interest then went to the assigned cofradía. Each year, the cofradía membership selected a *mayordomo*, who was responsible for organizing the annual *paab'ank* (the fiesta for the patron saint), ensuring the good will of the Tzuultaq'a mountain deities, curing the ill, and providing credit, prayer, and counsel when necessary. The mayordomo organized cofradía work parties to plant the church lands they owned; arranged for the necessary masses, processions, meals, and drink; and paid for any excess expense out of his own pocket.

For Q'eqchi's, rituals required that those wishing to move up the ladder of community prestige spend large sums of money on fiestas. Maya rituals have thus often been seen as a way of redistributing wealth in Maya communities, and transforming representations of class difference into genuine expressions of communal solidarity. The goal of participating in cofradías was to earn recognition and veneration in the historical memory of the town.[56] Reflecting the economic status of its members, village brotherhoods were usually quite poor when compared with the more powerful cofradías in the area's towns such as San Pedro Carchá and Cobán, where wealthy cofradías had access to the richest and most

---

[56] S. Ashley Kistler, *Maya Market Women: Power and Tradition in San Juan Chamelco, Guatemala* (Urbana: University of Illinois Press, 2014), 6.

productive lands and owned several urban properties.[57] On the day of Yat's revolt, many Q'eqchi' patriarchs reported avoiding the wrath of the event, since they were attending to preparations in the cofradías of San Pablo and San Pedro. Like the cyclical time of Maya agricultural production, the ritual time of Maya cofradía life helped reproduce the norms of reciprocity and solidarity.

The Maya peasant economy rested on three different and frequently overlapping types of property: *ejidos*, *parcialidades*, and private property. Under Spanish colonial law, each Maya town held in common title one league (roughly equal to thirty-nine *caballerías*, a caballería being equal to 44.66 hectares) of *ejidal* (common) land, usually comprising pasture, agricultural, and wooded lands. In practice, most towns actually claimed and used much more land than was actually granted by colonial law, although they generally did possess title for these additional lands. In Cobán and San Pedro Carchá, in what was commonly called the town's ejidos, a complex mixture of private and communal land tenure use existed.[58] Q'eqchi's could acquire land in usufruct, that is, by working the land or improving it, and often these usufructary land rights resembled something akin to private property. Without formal title, Mayas with usufructary land rights needed to respect Q'eqchi' patriarchs' governance of land disputes and distribution. Access to common lands for planting milpa, grazing cattle, or harvesting wood, however, was still governed by the indigenous elders. Q'eqchi' hereditary elites protected woodlands from deforestation and pastures from overgrazing, oversaw communal planting, and regulated when the town's harvest was to begin.[59] Likewise, ethnic clan lands, known as *parcialidades*, occupied large swaths of territory within and outside those towns.

Land also mediated concepts of time, ancestry, collective identity, and the sacred. In the voluminous documentation of land disputes in Alta Verapaz, the intimacy of Maya knowledge of and relationship to the land is readily apparent. Each parcel had a name, recognized by at least the town's patriarchs and by neighboring patriarchs. Elites and perhaps some commoners knew the land intimately and could narrate its contours, rises,

---

[57] AGCA ST-AV Paq. 1 Exp. 6; AGCA ST-AV Paq. 1 Exp. 13; AGCA ST-AV Paq. 2 Exp. 10; AGCA ST-AV Paq. 4 Exp. 8; and on the sale of cofradía properties, AGCA Jucios-Alta Verapaz (hereafter J-AV) 108 Leg. 6 Exp. 426 1882; AGCA J-AV 108 Leg. 6 Exp. 428; AGCA J-AV 108 Leg. 6 Exp. 430.

[58] David McCreery, *Rural Guatemala: 1760–1940* (Stanford: Stanford University Press, 1994), 45.

[59] See also Grandin, *The Blood of Guatemala*, 49–53.

dips, textures, boundaries, stone features, and how it was situated with respect to other parcels. In locating land use and ownership in space, indigenous witnesses and litigants also made territorial claims through reference to deep historical time and lineage, invoking possessions "since time immemorial" by virtue of the labor of their ancestors, who could be real or mythical, and often divine. Litigants made land, historical time, and lineage – all elements of the sacred – central to their conception of property rights and demonstrated a positive invocation of tradition.[60]

The prevalence of usufructary land rights within communal regimes meant that families claimed and retained plots of land over generations in ways that resembled private property. The buying, selling, inheritance, and exchange of land, however, also tended to generate an extremely fragmented pattern of land tenure, where boundary conflicts among and within families were a constant occurrence. These land tenure arrangements guaranteed that usufructary rights would not coincide with the political–administrative boundaries of municipalities, nor at times with any boundaries at all.[61] Rather, usufructary land use and shifting cultivation ensured that boundaries would remain fluid. As late as the mid-eighteenth century, Q'eqchi' elders claimed that the lands surrounding their towns did not have fixed boundaries, nor did anyone own land.[62] In 1785 a Q'eqchi' principal attempted to title as individual property a tract of land called Chichen; the Q'eqchi' patriarchs resisted, claiming that Chichen was part of their common lands. Although acknowledging that the applicant had possessed the land in question "from time immemorial," no one in the municipality had "bought land from the king." Rather, Cobaneros were accustomed to buying and selling among themselves land they had acquired through usufruct. To purchase land from the state would go against their system of governance, which had long resolved conflicts within the framework of indigenous customs.[63] Usufruct also

---

[60] See, for example, AGCA JP-AV 1866–1869, "Expediente de limites entre Cobán and Santa Cruz 1866," August 24, 1866. On new conceptions of custom in the eighteenth century, see Bianca Premo, "Custom Today: Temporality, Customary Law, and Indigenous Enlightenment," *Hispanic American Historical Review* 94, no. 3 (2014): 355–79.

[61] AGCA JP-AV 1866–1869, "Expediente de limites entre Cobán and Santa Cruz 1866," August 24, 1866.

[62] On the lack of boundaries, see AGCA A1 Leg. 6036 Exp. 53239 and AGCA A1 Leg. 6033 Exp. 53213. On the distribution of lands, McCreery, *Rural Guatemala*, especially chapter 2; Francisco de Solano, *Tierra y sociedad en el reino de Guatemala* (Guatemala: Editorial Universitaria, Guatemala, 1977).

[63] AGCA B Leg. 6033 Exp. 53213; AGCA B Leg. 6036 Exp. 53239.

made state governance difficult and safeguarded the relative autonomy of Q'eqchi's peasants.

Q'eqchi' patriarchs' central role in governing the distribution of land, credit, and labor, however, also left them well situated to use their position to accumulate capital.[64] As Maya patriarchs, they had privileged access to the labor of Q'eqchi' commoners, women, and children. Q'eqchi' patriarchs could use this labor to subsidize their commercial activities, such as textile manufacturing. As principales, they could apply communal resources to their private enterprises, and as political elites in the town council they could use their connections to gain access to credit and markets not available to most commoners or women, and then to supply loans to these same people. Traditionally, principales used their access to credit and capital to fund the manufacture of textiles. In the final decades of the eighteenth century, Sebastian Bol, for example, loaned villagers money to pay tribute generally at a rate of 5 percent, in addition to funds available directly through the cofradías. He was also able to make money from the principal held by the cofradía, which was often invested in the manufacture of cotton goods. For every 100 pesos invested in raw cotton, individuals like Bol could realize a profit of about 6 pesos from the sale of finished textiles. Through this system, Q'eqchi' hereditary elites accumulated wealth. Bol owned cotton worth 64 pesos, as well as pepper, salt, tobacco, and cotton thread. His tile-roofed house was valued at 105 pesos, and he owned an additional eleven urban plots.[65] In return for their accumulation of wealth, Q'eqchi' patriarchs were required to represent the interests of the pueblo in local politics and to guarantee the salvation of their people through their patronage of cofradía saint's days.

In the late 1850s, however, Q'eqchi' patriarchs discovered a new source of wealth: coffee. By 1859 Q'eqchi' alcaldes from the municipalities of Cobán and San Pedro Carchá, in alliance with the corregidor in Cobán, began to provide favorable loans of up to 500 pesos at a 6 percent annual interest rate and granted access to municipal land at reduced rates for those who were willing to plant coffee. By providing both land and capital for development, the corregidor claimed the region was opening the way for "the poor classes" to become coffee planters.[66] By March

---

[64] See also Grandin, *The Blood of Guatemala*; Steve J. Stern, *Peru's Indian Peoples and the Challenge of Spanish Conquest: Huamanga to 1640* (Madison: University of Wisconsin Press, 1993), 158–83.

[65] On Bol, see AGCA A1 Leg. 99 Exp. 2123, folios 6–9. On cofradía capital and loans, see Van Oss, *Catholic Colonialism*, 112.

[66] *La Gaceta de Guatemala*, June 4, 1859, 1–2.

1862, thirty-nine coffee plantations were in operation in Cobán, with thirty-two more in nearby San Pedro Carchá, almost all of them planted by Q'eqchi's. The corregidor reported nearly 70,000 mature coffee plants in the department, with two million more in various stages of establishment.[67] In total, the corregidor tallied seventy-five coffee plantations with some two million coffee plants and seedlings. The Verapaz planted nearly twice as many coffee plants as any other department.[68]

Unlike the western highlands, coffee entrepreneurs in Alta Verapaz were overwhelmingly Q'eqchi' patriarchs. Likewise, Q'eqchi' patriarchs began to plant municipal properties, once used for maize production, with coffee. The expansion of coffee production, however, also met with challenges. A series of frosts in the early 1860s ruined seedlings, and the region's high humidity caused difficulties. The most significant deterrents to the expansion of coffee growing by Q'eqchi' communities were conflict over the appropriate use and distribution of the fertile land surrounding Cobán, the settlement of foreigners and ladinos who wished to begin production themselves, and growing resistance to mandamientos, a system of forced wage labor derived from the reinstitution of colonial-era repartimientos.[69]

The expansion of coffee production not only created new economic opportunities for Q'eqchi' patriarchs, but also enticed immigrants and set off unprecedented demands for Q'eqchi' land and labor. Few areas of Q'eqchi' social and political life were left untouched by the expansion of coffee across the region, giving rise to unprecedented tensions. Likewise, settlers had an interest in expanding the reach of the state and consolidating ladino control over the region. Within months of the 1865 revolt, ladinos from across the region wrote to the president requesting that the Verapaz department be divided into upper and lower halves (Baja Verapaz and Alta Verapaz). Alta Verapaz's expansive territory, the ladinos argued, could not be adequately governed from Salamá. As a novel source of wealth and state revenue, the region, the ladinos believed, would be better administered from Cobán. Notably, these ladinos were also supported by many Q'eqchi' patriarchs, who presumably understood state expansion as increasing rather than diminishing their own power.[70]

---

[67] *La Gaceta de Guatemala*, April 13, 1862, 2; *El Noticioso*, December 28, 1861, 2–3.

[68] Suchitepéquez with 1,087,006 coffee plants and seedlings spread across 86 plantations. Regina Wagner, *Historia del café de Guatemala* (Bogotá: Villegas Editores, 2001), 45; see also *La Gaceta de Guatemala*, May 23, June 12, July 14 and 22, and October 18, 1862.

[69] *La Gaceta de Guatemala*, July 6 and 18, 1860; and *El Noticioso*, November 25, 1861.

[70] AGCA MG B Leg. 28602 Exp. 258.

The Q'eqchi' Maya region of Alta Verapaz was thus a network of tensions between cooperation and competition, solidarity and conflict, communal reciprocity and liberal individualism, patriarchal forms of caste hierarchy and a belief in democratic representation, all within a hierarchically ordered spatial division of the region into highlands and lowlands. During moments of state expansion and economic change, the delicate balance between these opposing tendencies could unravel, leading to political movements such as Yat's revolution and the retaliation that followed. These conflicts, while normal aspects of Q'eqchi' social worlds, were also expressions of broader Conservative state policies as well as changing commercial and social relations in the region. As the state and commerce reached into the more distant, lowland regions of the countryside, lowland Q'eqchi's lost some autonomy, and the delicate balance between opposing forces within Q'eqchi' society was bound to falter. While the Q'eqchi' subsistence economy and indigenous social organization were understood as backward and immobile on the road to progress, encroachment on Maya subsistence production, the alienation of Maya land, and the appropriation of Maya labor were also nonetheless indispensable to settler visions of progress and freedom.

EARLY FRONTIER COLONIZATION, CONSERVATIVE MODERNIZATION, AND CAPITALIST EXPANSION

Jorge Yat was still on trial for sedition when Heinrich Rudolf Dieseldorff (1831–1918) of Hamburg arrived in Cobán at the end of 1865. Dieseldorff had been preceded by a generation of foreign settlers, including the French citizen Julio Rossignon, the British Charles Meany and John Carter, and the Swiss Carl Rudolf Klée, many of whom had been involved in Guatemala's failed foreign colonization concessions of the 1830s and 1840s.[71] Dieseldorff, unlike Rossignon, had not participated in the state-directed wilderness empires of the 1830s and 1840s. Dieseldorff was among the first of a new generation of settlers following familial and economic networks across oceans and national borders. In addition to German settler colonists, Alta Verapaz became home to North American, British, French, Central American, Mexican, and Colombian settlers seeking wealth and opportunity, transforming the

---

[71] William J. Griffith, *Empires in the Wilderness* (Chapel Hill: University of North Carolina Press, 1965), 32.

region from a largely indigenous frontier, distant and peripheral to
Guatemala society, into a growing cosmopolitan hub. According to
available statistics, the historian Arden King estimated the population
of the entire Verapaz (Alta and Baja) at 70,000 in 1851. By 1880 the
population of Alta Verapaz alone had reached 86,943 including
82,770 Mayas, 3,999 ladinos, and 174 foreign settlers.[72] These settlers
represented the civilizing vision embodied in Rossignon's *Porvenir de la
Verapaz.* This section details how these settlers sought prosperous
futures by reinvigorating the colonial-era institutions of coerced labor
and appropriating communal property. By strengthening these colonial
conventions, the settlers also fortified the role of Q'eqchi' patriarchs as
native intermediaries through the 1850s and 1860s.

    While most settlers hoped to build a coffee plantation, few were able to
purchase land immediately due to Conservative restrictions on land
privatization and lack of capital. Many followed the path of Dieseldorff.
Before arriving in Cobán, Dieseldorff worked for his brother in an English
commercial house in Belize and then, wanting to find his own way, sought
to establish a cotton plantation in the department of Zacapa. This venture
failed, however, when the first crop was destroyed by locusts.[73] In the
meantime, Dieseldorff heard rumors that Alta Verapaz was meagerly
supplied with manufactured goods, imported through Guatemala City.
Direct import of European goods to Cobán seemed to offer a good
opportunity. Settling in Cobán, Dieseldorff opened a small store, which
he stocked with imported merchandise purchased with a minimum
amount of credit that he obtained from his brother's English firm. Drawing on the capital and contacts Dieseldorff had made through his import–
export business, he also began to build his capital by loaning money at
high interest rates. With the profits he gained from his store and loans,
Dieseldorff acquired land for a coffee plantation near Cobán.[74] In more
than a few instances, moreover, merchant creditors, like Dieseldorff,

---

[72] King, *Cobán and the Verapaz,* 285.

[73] Martin Frey, *Deutschtum in Der Alta Verapaz; Herausgegeben Analässlich des 50 Jährigen Bestehens des Deutschen Vereins zu Cobán, Guatemala, 1888–1938* (Stuttgart:
Deutschen Verlagsanstalt, 1938), 14–15; Guillermo Náñez Falcón, "Erwin Paul Dieseldorff, German Entrepreneur in the Alta Verapaz of Guatemala, 1889–1937" (PhD diss.,
Tulane University, 1970).

[74] Frey, *Deutschtum in Der Alta Verapaz*; Regina Wagner, *Los alemanes en Guatemala,
1828–1944* (Guatemala: Editorial IDEA, Universidad en Su Casa, Universidad Francisco
Marroquín, 2007), 174–5.

ended up as owners of property when debtors were no longer able to meet their payments.[75]

Eventually, merchants like Dieseldorff might also gain access to properties through *censo* (rent) in the ejidos in the fertile and well-watered basin surrounding Cobán, San Pedro Carchá, San Cristobal, and San Juan Chamelco. State officials like Pablo Sierra, for example, advocated on behalf of new settlers in their petitions to the Q'eqchi-controlled municipality. Conservative authorities like Sierra cajoled and coerced indigenous officials into renting desirable parcels of land – like those controlled by Julio Rossignon – from the municipalities to grow coffee.[76] This procedure, called *censo enfiteusis*, in effect replicated what had long been standard practice in the cochineal districts of Antigua and Amatitlán, where cochineal growers obtained long-term leases on municipal lands in return for the payment of an annual fee equivalent to a small percentage of the estimated value of the land.[77] Normally, censo properties were relatively small, approximately 200 cuerdas, and thus the capital investment required was minimal and the limited production could be sold on local markets or to larger producers.[78] Sometimes the state granted censo lands that were already occupied by Q'eqchi' villagers who claimed rights to plant milpa.[79] The labor demands were also less intensive and could be met through a combination of family labor and small amounts of seasonal hired labor.

---

[75] AGCA Protocolos Originales (hereafter PO), Buenaventura Polanco, 1861–65, No. 25, folio 76, "En la ciudad de Cobán a 4 de agosto de 1863, comparecen Don Luis Torres, deudor de referido Don Molina Sierra."

[76] See, for example, Cobán Archivo Municipal (hereafter CM) 1873 "Coacción del terreno de Cux-ha concedido a Don José Barahona," April 5, 1873, and May 31, 1859. A list of names of individuals who received loans from the Municipalities of the Verapaz to begin coffee or sugar plantations contain only Ladino names. See AGCA B Leg. 28602 Exp. 258.

[77] David McCreery, "State Power, Indigenous Communities, and Land in Nineteenth-Century Guatemala, 1820–1920," in *Guatemalan Indians and the State, 1540–1988*, ed. Carol A. Smith (Austin: University of Texas Press, 1990), 100.

[78] Two hundred cuerdas is around half a caballería, or 22 hectares. Based on Charles Wagely's study of Chimbal, 200 cuerdas was likely sufficient, depending on the quality of the land awarded, for an average family to produce close to enough food for their own subsistence. See Wagely, *Economics of a Guatemalan Village*, Memoirs of the American Anthropological Association, no. 58 (Menasha, WI: American Anthropological Association, 1941), 55. AGCA JP-AV 1866-69 P1, "Al Teniente Corregidor del Municipalidad de Cobán," October 25, 1860.

[79] AGCA JP-AV 1866-69 P1, "Teniente Corregidor al Municipalidad de Cobán," July 26, 1860.

Still, landowners often had a hard time paying back their loans to the municipality, and defaults were frequent.[80]

Once non-Mayas held the land in censo lease, they often ceased to pay the rental fee and treated the land as *tierras baldías* (unoccupied public lands owned by the state), and thus sold the lands without going through the municipality. At times, Conservative authorities simply refused to enforce indigenous communal property rights in the face of settler incursions. When Cobán's patriarchs wrote to the president, contesting Julio Rossignon's appropriation of commonly held lands, the Conservative government did virtually nothing.[81] Despite these protests, ladino and Maya state officials granted small loans and censo land to coffee planters beginning in 1859. Within a year, Cobán's officials had awarded 1,850 cuerdas to ten different individuals, including the British investor José Carter.[82] Renting lands in censo reduced the initial capital cost of getting started in coffee production and was almost the only way for most settlers to gain access to valuable ejido land.

As a result, by 1860 the corregidor Pablo Sierra wrote to his superior in Salamá of the "very delicate and dangerous situation" surrounding the granting of censo in the region's ejidos. The Mayas of Alta Verapaz, he argued, had been spared these "unhappy and capricious questions" that the Mayas of Los Altos had long since suffered, and it was necessary to protect them by establishing firm boundaries to properties and awarding title to individuals.[83] Q'eqchi's responded to these encroachments by migrating to the lowlands, raising fears of an impending moral decline. In April 1867, the vicar of the Verapaz responded to a complaint lodged by the region's corregidor that Mayas in Cobán and Carchá "lacked morals," by which he meant their tendency to live dispersed throughout the countryside rather than in the towns. While the corregidor had blamed this moral decline on the lack of priests, the vicar blamed it on the sale and renting of censo land to settlers for coffee growing. The vicar charged that the corregidor permitted coffee planters to take over not only the communities' ejidos but also the *barrios'* (neighborhoods') and cofradías' land. This practice forced Mayas to move deeper into the mountains. In some neighborhoods, the vicar lamented, you could now find only coffee, and if the trend was not stopped soon, the entire town of Cobán

---

[80] AGCA JP-AV 1861, "Juan E. Valdez al Pablo Sierra Salama," December 20, 1861.
[81] AGCA B Leg. 28579 Exp. 160.
[82] AGCA JP-AV 1860, "Juan E. Valdez al Pablo Sierra Salama," October 25, 1860.
[83] AGCA JP-AV 1865, "Juan E. Valdez al Pablo Sierra," September 15, 1860.

would shortly be nothing but a coffee field. The loss of Maya communal lands was also occurring in Tactic and in Tucuru.[84]

While the vicar likely exaggerated the situation, Mayas also resisted the loss of communal lands directly through petitions and appeals. When Don Manuel Meza attempted to clear land in Cobán's ejidos, Serapio and Apolinario Pop ripped out his coffee plants and complained that "they had never given any kind of consent because the authorities had to favor them, since they, along with many others, planted annual milpas there." A municipal investigation determined that no one possessed titles to the properties, "since they were known as ejidos and it was not necessary to have a title."[85] Seeking to profit from the burgeoning land market, some Q'eqchi's sold their plots within the town's ejidos.[86] Even though non-Mayas utilized censo to gain access to land, Q'eqchi's likewise continued to rent censo lands, and in Carchá, the majority of censo land awarded went to Q'eqchi's.[87]

In the outskirts of Cobán, with rich volcanic soil, larger plantations gradually developed. In the early nineteenth century, some Q'eqchi' patriarchs had taken advantage of Liberal land privatization laws to purchase land as private property. Privatized properties laid the foundations for well-connected and wealthy settlers to gain a larger foothold in the region, sometimes through marriage or concubinage with elite Q'eqchi' women. Such transactions could be complicated, however, since land was often purchased where no title existed and where Q'eqchi's had long resided in an agreement with the previous owner.[88] The formal boundaries were sometimes quite extensive and unclear, but landowners used only a small portion of the land at any given time for planting coffee or pasturing animals. In 1866 Carlos Meany owned four caballerías of land planted with 90,000 coffee trees. These plantation owners used labor from resident Maya families, supplemented by occasional mandamiento levies from neighboring villages, to tend to coffee plants. Resident households, or *colonos*, received a subsistence plot, the right to pasture their own animals on plantation lands, and a limited number of subsistence items such as clothes. In exchange, they were obliged to work a

[84] AGCA MG 28587 33.

[85] AGCA JP-AV 1860, "Pablo Sierra al Corregidor," July 26, 1860.

[86] AGCA JP-AV 1866-69, "Corregidor al Pablo Sierra," July 18, 1867.

[87] These census records are found in San Pedro Carchá Archivo Municipal (hereafter SPCM) 1882 in an untitled book.

[88] AGCA JP- AV 1866-69 Paq. 1, "Ambriocio Molinero sobre finca Chimax," October 28, 1866.

certain amount of time per month as agricultural laborers in the plantation owners' fields. By the turn of the century, these *fincas de mozos*
(plantations housing a labor force), as they were called, were greatly
expanded and became the principal mechanism for coffee planters to
obtain laborers.

In addition to a scarcity of domestic capital and loans to purchase
larger plots of land and equipment and to invest in coffee trees, coffee
planters also faced labor shortages. Labor was required for a wide variety
of tasks during every stage of the process: from planting and pruning
coffee trees to harvesting, sorting, and processing the beans and even
carrying coffee and other goods by foot from plantation to port. Since
the peasants had a vibrant subsistence economy, coffee planters had
difficulty in making them work outside their communities. Landowners
faced three choices: purchase all the land, leaving Maya peasants with no
alternative but to sell their labor; import already indentured laborers; or
have the state directly compel laborers to work on their plantations.
Given the abundance of land and the strength of the village economies,
the first alternative was impossible in the short run, and the second option
required significant capital. The only viable choice was the third option.
Likewise, coffee planters needed laborers for only part of the year, which
roughly corresponded with the off-season in highlands corn cultivation.
This convergence facilitated a situation in which subsistence production
could occur alongside, and subsidize, labor on coffee plantations. Coffee
production, as a result, could not swallow up the entire region, and
subsistence agricultural land would be needed to maintain the reserve of
coffee laborers and to subsidize wages.[89]

Coerced labor in Guatemala, known as mandamiento, was derived
from the colonial-era repartimientos, a system of forced wage advances
for public works and labor on haciendas that began following the epidemics of the 1570s and became a prominent feature of seventeenth-
century Guatemala.[90] Unlike colonial Mexico where large numbers of
Indians lived in debt peonage on haciendas, Central American Creoles
relied on repartimiento as the chief manner of gaining labor from the

---

[89] See David McCreery, "'An Odious Feudalism': Mandamiento Labor and Commercial
Agriculture in Guatemala, 1858–1920," *Latin American Perspectives* 13, no. 1 (1986):
99–117.
[90] Murdo MacLeod reports that repartimientos were much more widespread in Guatemala
than in Mexico; see MacLeod, *Spanish Central America*, 3rd edition (Austin: University
of Texas Press, 2008), 295–6.

Mayas who lived in the highlands of Guatemala, Chiapas, and the Verapaz.[91] Despite efforts by the Bourbon reformers to ban repartimientos as part of a general effort to create an agricultural, wage-earning proletariat and a free peasantry in the mid-eighteenth century, the forced labor drafts continued and even increased as labor shortages abounded in mining and indigo-growing regions. For a brief moment, the state even expanded repartimientos to *castas* (mixed-race groups) in the 1780s, but by the first decades of the nineteenth century this practice of coerced labor had largely disappeared. Half a century later, however, the repartimiento was reintroduced as mandamientos in order to address labor shortages on emergent coffee plantations.

Like colonial-era repartimientos, mandamiento labor drafts were also administered by Q'eqchi' patriarchs from within the institutions of the civil–religious hierarchy. Mandamientos involved a system of wage advances, wherein a coffee planter requested a certain number of laborers for a set period of time from the Maya town council. The *regidores* (low-level town councilors) deposited the cash advances with the cofradía for fiestas, repayment of loans, and even for bail for its members.[92] The regidores then rounded up Q'eqchi' commoners to provide their labor for a set number of days in exchange for the religious and other services provided by the cofradía. The regidores themselves were often rewarded by satisfied landowners. In 1867 the corregidor attempted to put a stop to this system, arguing that an absolute separation between the town council and the cofradías was needed; however, he was unsuccessful.[93] Likewise, when non-Maya settlers needed access to land, they would turn to the Q'eqchi' authorities, who profited from the rent or sale of communal property. By working within and through the combined civil–religious hierarchy, coffee planters and Q'eqchi' patriarchs ensured that this nascent capitalism was grafted onto Maya norms of reciprocity and solidarity. While at first Maya mediation and institutions stabilized capital accumulation, eventually this emergent capitalism generated a moral crisis in Maya society.

While mandamientos strengthened the position of Q'eqchi' patriarchs and funded cofradías, they also had strategic benefits for coffee planters, in comparison with other labor regimes. Mandamientos satisfied their

---

[91] See Wortman, *Government and Society in Central America*, xiii–xiv.

[92] AGCA JP-AV 1871, "Al JP de Alcalde municipal de Cobán," August 10, 1871.

[93] CM Estantería (hereafter Est.) 1 Paq. 16, "Corregidor al alcalde municipal de Cobán," February 15, 1867.

need for a temporary labor force available for seasonal work and prevented the dramatic rise in wages that would occur in a free labor market with a sudden growth in demand for workers.[94] Mandamiento labor was also an expression of the scarcity of capital for the payment of wage advances. Mandamientos, in contrast to direct labor contracts, required only partial payment, and wages were also generally lower. Drawing on connections to the departmental governor and town council, wealthy ladinos and European planters benefited from mandamientos.[95]

Despite the coffee planters' reliance on mandamientos, this form of coerced labor was not formally reinstituted by the Conservative government. Conservatives generally favored a free wage labor market. Recognizing the importance of the labor question, the Economic Society set up a commission in 1868 to draft new national labor regulations. The members contended that worker shortages arose from the poor customs of Mayas, who accepted money for work, spent it on alcohol, and then plotted to escape their obligations. Even worse, growing numbers of vagrants and swindlers were corrupting the rest of the indigenous population. To remedy the situation, the committee detailed fifty-four articles of a revised labor law. The law divided the workforce into two categories: *protejidos* (Mayas) and *independientes* (ladinos and whites). The law provided for the enforcement of voluntary labor debt agreements but rejected direct coercion by the state: "The worker ought to be free to agree to a contract or not and to stipulate the conditions and price of his labor."[96] Julio Rossignon maintained that the system of wage advances forced employers to tie up significant amounts of capital in advances, and yet the system created few incentives to work efficiently. Since workers tended to accept more than they could repay and were always working, they had very little incentive to work hard. Drawing on the liberal–democratic metanarrative, Rossignon warned that Guatemala risked creating a feudal system of perpetually indebted serfs. The society eventually

---

[94] McCreery, "An Odious Feudalism," 104.

[95] Of the 208 mandamiento requests I located in the archives, there was not one request from a Q'eqchi'. The vast majority were from individuals with familial connections to the Liberal authorities or from the wealthy European, primarily German, immigrant population. See also René Reeves, *Ladinos with Ladinos, Indians with Indians: Land, Labor, and Regional Ethnic Conflict in the Making of Guatemala* (Stanford, CA: Stanford University Press, 2006), 98.

[96] *La Sociedad Económica*, April 13, 1868, and August 9, 1869. The draft law appears in *La Sociedad Económica*, September 30, October 15, November 30, December 15 and 31, 1870, and February 19, 1871.

agreed that wage advances were a "vicious custom," but ultimately believed that it could not be abandoned immediately. Conservatives in general believed that, even if Mayas were only semi-civilized and given to laziness and drunkenness, they should nevertheless be protected from themselves and others who would exploit them. As a result, Conservatives tended to argue that Mayas should not be "forced ... to perform wage labor" against their will.[97] Of course, under the laws of 1847 and 1851, not to mention dozens of vagrancy statutes, Mayas could be forced to do precisely that, and by the 1860s mandamiento drafts had already made a considerable resurgence. From the perspective of most would-be coffee entrepreneurs, Conservatives were overconcerned with protecting Mayas and not nearly enough so with the growers' need for cheap and readily available labor.[98]

Even with mandamientos, ambitious coffee planters confronted significant challenges to acquiring sufficient labor. When Dieseldorff, for example, advanced money to the town mayor to collect twelve laborers to clear his newly purchased land so he could plant coffee, the alcalde wrote to the *teniente* (lieutenant) *corregidor* to return the funds. According to the alcalde, Astancio Xol, "There are no people in the entire town since everyone is clearing their fields in the outskirts of town, and it is not possible to get them to work."[99] In 1861 the corregidor of the Verapaz, Juan Valdez, also wrote to Pablo Sierra in Cobán, demanding that he bring in laborers who were away working in their fields. "Unquestionable are the advantages coffee plantations in this region provide and will provide," the corregidor explained, "and I have spoken with you personally about the protection that coffee entrepreneurs must be given and the laborers that they need." Speaking of the delays facing the plantations in the area as a result of an insufficient workforce, Pablo Sierra argued that coffee planters should be supplied with laborers, regardless of the milpa harvest.[100]

Coffee capitalists established plantations by grafting their need for land and labor onto Maya institutions and mediation, which helped stabilize Maya social relations in a moment of change. As colonial histories suggest, Maya patriarchs, however, could operate only within certain

[97] This is from a series of articles in the *La Gaceta de Guatemala* arguing for a more aggressive approach to mobilizing Maya labor dated February 7, 16, and 24, 1867, also JP-AV 1866–69, "Corregidor-Sub Correigdor," August 27, 1867.

[98] McCreery, *Rural Guatemala*, 168–9.

[99] CM Est. 1 Paq. 16, "Alcalde primero al teniente corregidor," March 10, 1867.

[100] AGCA JP-AV, "Juan Valdez a Pablo Sierra," Salamá, June 18, 1861.

parameters or face potent backlash from commoners. As coffee planters appropriated Maya lands and demanded Maya labor, they undermined the delicate balance between Maya patriarchs and commoners. Moreover, coffee planters grew frustrated by the need for close personal connections to Maya patriarchs, and how Maya caste hierarchy placed limitations on local ladino political power, as well as on access to land and labor. These competing demands set the stage for a new Liberal government that would systematically erode Q'eqchi' political power, institutionalize coerced labor, and promote a land market and privatization.

CONCLUSION

Yat's short-lived rebellion was recorded not as an attempted revolution against local Maya authority but as a barbaric Maya revolt against ladinos and the economic progress represented by coffee production. Maya witnesses themselves portray a very different story of grievances about taxes and representation that fits within the broader narratives of the Atlantic revolutions. Maya patriarchs, victims of the supposed riot, recognized this when they declared that Yat simply wanted to live without king and castle. Yet the actions of Yat's followers and their testimonies – whom they attacked and how, the reasons they provided, and the way they described Yat's motives – were rendered silent by the violence of the archive itself. The archival erasure also tells us a great deal about the fantasies and fears of ladino state officials who rendered Yat's revolution as a caste war in the making, and the assumptions of historians who subsequently wrote about it as if those statements were, indeed, accurate.

Jorge Yat's revolution also illuminates the social, political, and economic tensions embedded in Q'eqchi' caste hierarchy and the dynamic exchanges between the highland and lowland regions of the northern Verapaz. Reading along and against the archival grain, Yat's attempted revolution also reveals the interplay between Q'eqchi' notions of reciprocity and liberal individualism, between communal obligations and democratic governance. The revolution also pointed to a deep fear, among some Q'eqchi' patriarchs, of liberalism's promise of equality and democracy. Indeed, republicanism represented a threat in Alta Verapaz for Q'eqchi' patriarchs not because it threatened their autonomy but because it challenged the basis of the caste hierarchy and shifted the weight in favor of those rural lower classes who "simply wished to live without King or Castle."[101] While Yat's revolution was the result of the Q'eqchi' patriarchs' failure to negotiate the precarious balance between communal norms of reciprocity and the duty to act as representatives of villagers, the balance was not restored in the immediate aftermath of Yat's failed revolution. The final half of the 1860s witnessed the further expansion of the state, commerce, and coffee as well as the growth of a settler immigrant community, which further eroded the volatile equilibrium negotiated between highland Q'eqchi' patriarchs and lowland Q'eqchi's commoners. As the German settler Franz Sarg recalled in 1870: "The demands on the Indian population are increasing steadily. Coffee planters expect them to work in their plantations, export firms demand that they transport coffee, and the government requests that they build roads. All this creates a listlessness among the Indians, which becomes more and more evident when the difficulties of their tasks increase."[102] As Mayas resisted, their insolence was recast as indolence; and Sarg's simple formula – growth in demands for Maya labor equaled increasing Maya laziness – became a maxim of ladino and German coffee planters' politics of postponement in the following decades.

Yat's failed revolt, local in nature and quick in its demise, also stood on the precipice of a more pivotal and enduring event of national significance: the 1871 Liberal revolution. According to court testimonies from Yat's trial, two weeks prior to San Pedro Carchá's fateful saint day, Yat traveled to Guatemala City and met with the Liberal rebel Serapio de la Cruz, who was already plotting against President Vicente Cerna, the recently appointed successor to Rafael Carrera. While Yat admitted to meeting Cerna, he did not disclose any details about their meeting to the court. Yat's accusers may have wished to paint Yat's revolution as a dangerous threat, and perhaps Yat, too, saw value in projecting a national meaning onto these local events. Yet even if this court testimony was more fiction than fact, the meeting between two revolutionaries was plausible enough to grant broader national implications to rural discontent and the Liberal leanings of Mayas in Alta Verapaz. It may also help to explain why, when Liberal rebels marched into Cobán in the first months of 1871, they discovered a squadron of armed Q'eqchi's

---

[101] Grandin, *The Blood of Guatemala*, 77–81, 101–3.
[102] Frey, *Deutschtum in der Alta Verapaz*, 6.

ready to join the revolutionary forces.[103] Perhaps the Maya patriarchs recognized that, on this occasion, they were better off joining the uprising coming from western highlands centered in Quetzaltenango. The ladinos from Guatemala's rich western highlands who led the 1871 Liberal revolution, however, had a different idea altogether of what constituted the new Liberal order.

[103] Much of the documentation for the months leading up to and after the revolution is no longer available. See AGCA JP-AV 1870–2 Paq. 1, "Sr. Comandante General de la Verapaz del Sub-JP," April 21, 26, and May 6, 1871. For reactions, see especially "Al Sub-JP del Alcalde de Senaju," September 11 and 16, 1871. Franz Sarg also claims in his memoirs that the Liberal Revolution was an indigenous revolt in Alta Verapaz; see Frey, *Deutschtum in der Alta Verapaz*, 7.

2

Possessing Sentiments and Ideas of Progress

Coffee Planting, Land Privatization, and the Liberal Reform, 1871–1886

In all our history the incessant battle between the present and the past dominates; between the men who held us back in the Middle Ages and the men who drive us forward.... In those nations where the light of civilization does not yet penetrate, the destruction is far greater and its consequences far more tragic.

—Lorenzo Montúfar, *Reseña Histórica de Centro América* (1879)

Opening his monumental, multivolume history of Central America with the ominous warning above, the Guatemalan historian Lorenzo Montúfar averred that, while Liberals had successfully taken state power from Conservatives in 1871, the nation's battle was far from over. This other national struggle, he argued, was not simply between Liberal and Conservative partisan factions, but between the men of the present and the men of the past, between the agents of civilization and progress and those of barbarism and stagnation. Montúfar's words echoed those of the Argentine historian Domingo Faustino Sarmiento, who had famously argued that for the nation to become civilized, it had to destroy the barbarism within its breast.[1] Like Sarmiento, Montúfar applied temporal metaphors to classify, order, and define the nation's population and its territory – to demarcate its enemies, the barbarous others, and its allies, the true citizens in the nation's uncertain march toward modernity. Civilization, as Rebecca Earle has explored, functioned as a metaphor for the

[1] Domingo F. Sarmiento, *Facundo – Civilización y Barbarie – Vida de Juan Facundo Quiroga* (Santiago: Imprenta del Progreso, 1845).

75

capacity to participate in civic life and thus to be citizens.[2] Seeking to
marginalize threats to national progress, Latin American elites tended to
define citizenship as civilization by the late nineteenth century. Civilizing
metanarratives, as stories of the experience of reaching the great goal of
civilization, illustrated how Mayas and others trapped in the past could
eventually become citizens. In this understanding of citizenship, historical
time and periodization served as forms for managing the threat of
difference.[3]

The Liberal patriots from the western highlands who took power in
1871 were no different. As a set of mixed-race individuals, the ladino
Liberals who ousted Conservatives in 1871 viewed the principal antagonism of Guatemala as one between progressive ladinos and uncivilized
Mayas, as ladino interpretations of Jorge Yat's rebellion illustrated.[4] This
was a vision based in their historical experiences as economically ascend-
ant coffee planters who believed their prosperity was thwarted by Mayas
and Conservative state policies that limited ladino access to Maya land
and labor. These ladino Liberals from the western highlands uniquely
viewed Mayas as a problem: Mayas' lack of civilization, they believed,
weakened the state and undermined the coffee economy. They associated
the characteristics of citizens – including literacy, property ownership,
individual autonomy, and patriotism – with civilized men. Only cultured
men were deemed to have "civic virtue"; only they were capable of self-
government; and only they were worthy of equal rights. In legal terms,
Liberals stipulated the requirements for citizenship in nonracial terms, in
line with the official abandonment of racial categories common in post-
independence Latin America. The 1879 Liberal constitution reduced the
property and literacy requirements instituted by the Conservatives. Yet,
despite legal clarity and formal equality, most Liberals, like Montúfar,
doubted the capacity of indigenous peoples for citizenship. Rather, they
reasoned that indigenous sentiments and lifestyles harkened to a barbaric
past.[5] Unlike the Conservatives, Liberals believed the historic task of
civilizing Mayas could best be undertaken through formal, legal equality,
and thus ended the Conservative-era restored republic that had granted
Mayas control over town councils. Seeking to promote modernization,

---

[2] Earle, *The Return of the Native*, 163.   [3] Ibid., 174–81.
[4] Grandin, *The Blood of Guatemala*; Arturo Taracena Arriola, *Etnicidad, estado, nación en
Guatemala, 1808–1944* (Guatemala: CIRMA, 2002), 103–5.
[5] Mallon, *Peasant and Nation*; Taracena Arriola, *Etnicidad, estado, nación en Guatemala*;
and Mejías, *La participación indígena*.

Liberals also introduced legislation to privatize land and formally institutionalize mandimentos. They recognized that such a battle against a large sector of its population required a strong and ladino-controlled state apparatus that could rein in the barbarous practices of the past and eradicate old caste hierarchies, that could implement policies which would increase the nation's riches, promote progress and commerce, and civilize the uncivilized.

Like so many of his Liberal contemporaries, Victoriano Pop, the Maya Q'eqchi' first alcalde of San Pedro Carchá, was deeply preoccupied with the idea of national progress as a struggle of civilization against barbarism. His vision of the place of Mayas in the nation, however, was radically different. "Possessing sentiments and ideas of mutual progress, with true patriotism and at the mercy of our present Liberal system," Pop began his annual report to the national government, "we [the municipal council and departmental governor] were resolved to protect agriculture, commerce, and communication routes ... as the only true sources that constitute the elevation and welfare of the Nations that, today, we see in the apogee of their prosperity."[6] Embracing the moral virtues of "honor, work, wisdom and peace," Pop contended that the largely indigenous municipality of San Pedro Carchá was on its way to "completely possessing the delightful and expansive field of Liberty that when properly understood produces true harmony and fraternal union." Victoriano Pop, and others like him, claimed to be national citizens, but in doing so, his account of what that belonging would mean, and the significance of Maya presence, represented a noteworthy shift from contemporary accounts of Guatemalan history. Through this Liberal patriotism, Victoriano Pop of San Pedro Carchá unsettled notions of modernity that represented all Mayas as backward and uncivilized, as impediments to national progress. Instead, Pop, along with other Maya patriarchs, claimed an equal place in the nation for Mayas like himself. Only fifteen years earlier, Pop's predecessors had argued against Jorge Yat's liberal and republican discourses by declaring that Yat was an unimportant person, who wished only to live without the colonial caste order. Where Q'eqchi' patriarchs like Pop had once championed the bygone colonial order to reassert their caste authority in the face of challenges from rural Maya commoners, in the aftermath of the 1871 Liberal revolution, they adopted liberal discourses to reassert their place in the new order and strengthen Maya

[6] SPCM Memorias del año 1881.

social and political worlds. Many Q'eqchi' patriarchs also sought to
become coffee entrepeneurs, and thus to claim a place in the present
and future of the nation. The new Liberal state, however, abolished the
restored republic and reduced Q'eqchi' patriarchs' role as cultural and
political intermediaries, thus also undermining Q'eqchi' principles of
reciprocity and mutual obligation. In the 1870s and 1880s, the region
witnessed a widening gulf between the liberal principles articulated by
Q'eqchi' patriarchs and the practice of state governance.

In this chapter, I examine Liberal modernization efforts in Guatemala, and how Liberal lawmakers encoded a racialized scheme of
national progress, a struggle between civilization and barbarism, in laws
that promoted European immigration and ownership of land, while
politically marginalizing Mayas and rendering them into a stable labor
force for coffee production. They aimed to gradually convert the region
from a largely Maya frontier of migratory subsistence producers into a
nation of capitalist investors and productive laborers with fixed residences. Guided by interwoven notions of racial difference and progress,
state officials sought to constitute a modern nation by rendering Mayas
as threats to national progress. These ideas were guided by preconceived
ideas about what counted as modernity, ideas that were derived from
their reading of global histories, and Central America's own historical
struggle to defeat regressive forces that held these nations back from
achieving modernity. State efforts to promote a modern nation were also
writ large across space through various state-building efforts for the
better regulation of mandamiento labor, the realization of public works
projects, and the collection of taxes. State officials sought to make
different regions of the nation modern, governable, and profitable by
fixing boundaries and people in place, by bringing a halt to migratory
patterns of agricultural production, and by privatizing property and
defining municipal and administrative boundaries.[7] Such practices were
designed to render place as abstract space, that is, something that is
unified, measurable, and ready for commodification and the projection
of teleological narratives of modernity.

Such attempts at top-down modernization, or what James C. Scott
called "state simplifications," were naive. Q'eqchi's had long relied on

---

[7] See also Raymond B. Craib, *Cartographic Mexico: A History of State Fixations and
Fugitive Landscapes* (Durham, NC: Duke University Press, 2004); James C. Scott, *Seeing
like a State: How Certain Schemes to Improve the Human Condition Have Failed* (New
Haven, CT: Yale University Press, 1998).

shifting cultivation in ways that rendered both land and jurisdictional boundaries of municipalities fluid; existing land titles were notoriously imprecise and multiple land claims already plagued the entire region. These proposals unsurprisingly produced conflict – especially when they sought an absolute synchronicity between agricultural property and jurisdictional boundaries. Indeed, while the acts of measuring, mapping, and titling properties have often been seen as merely a technical backdrop, these processes were critical not only to the division of land but also to the problem of labor acquisition for coffee plantations and the renegotiation of local political power within and between municipalities. Thus not only did state officials confront challenges in their attempts to render a culturally and ecologically diverse region into legible and uniform space, but the implementation of their policies depended on local knowledges and practices.[8] Q'eqchi' political projects and ontologies shaped the attempted modernization of Q'eqchi' territories. Because state efforts to map the landscape were contingent on Q'eqchi' knowledge, the resulting maps at once incorporated and erased the Maya cosmological landscapes of Tzuultaq'as. As a result, Liberal reforms generated unexpected contradictions and new social tensions that manifested in competing understandings of property as Mayas attempted to render communal properties into privatized coffee plantations with resident labor forces. Likewise, ladinos, Mayas, and German settlers all contested who counted as agents of history and progress, and who were, as Lorenzo Montúfar avowed, men of the past.

THE LIBERAL REFORM

After the 1871 Liberal revolution, Guatemala's new Liberal statesmen wasted little time enacting their modernization project by expanding the state apparatus. Reflecting on the period known as the Liberal Reform, one spokesperson declared only seven years after the revolution that President Justo Rufino Barrios had "realized a reform more complete than nations much more advanced."[9] Recent historiography has challenged a "reform-as-revolution" perspective, demonstrating instead continuities between Conservative and Liberal policies surrounding the

---

[8] See, especially, Scott, *Seeing like a State*.
[9] A. V. García, *Guatemala y sus progresos en presencia de la reacción, 1878* (Guatemala: Tipografía La Unión, 1878), 10.

privatization of Maya communal properties and forced labor on coffee plantations.[10] What did change with the Liberal revolution, however, was the extension of the state and the institutionalization of many informal practices, such as mandamiento labor and the privatization of indigenous land, that under Conservatives had largely taken place through Maya patriarchs and the civil–religious hierarchy. In other words, while Conservatives and Liberals shared the same goal of acquiring Maya lands and mobilizing Maya labor, Conservatives pursued this goal by seeking to co-opt traditional Maya leadership structures (grafting capitalism onto Maya patriarchy), while Liberals pursued it by swelling a ladino-controlled state based on formal, legal equality.[11] Most significantly, governance via a ladino state rather than Maya hierarchy required fixing municipal and departmental boundaries, reigning in shifting cultivation and migratory patterns of agriculture, and mapping the landscape.

The first crucial piece of state reform occurred at the local level in the dismantling of the civil institutions of Maya caste hierarchy, particularly Maya-controlled town councils. Under the conservatives, Mayas were considered a distinct class of citizens and legally were treated as wards of the state under the restored republic. Liberals, by contrast, believed that the Mayas' failure to conform to modernity was a direct result of their implacable resistance to change and their stubborn determination to retain their distinctive culture and identity. Caste hierarchy had to end, then, not simply because liberalism demanded formal equality before the law, but also because caste-based legal distinctions were viewed as tantamount to helping the indigenous majority resist further modernization. As a result, in town after town, Liberals quickly abolished Maya town councils and replaced them with a single governing body, where ladinos occupied all the most important administrative posts. By the time of the annual municipal elections of 1872, for example, Cobán's town council was governed by ladino first and second alcaldes, and Maya patriarchs were relegated to the third alcalde, thus shrinking the spaces of legal pluralism and Maya sovereignty. In San Pedro Carchá, however, widespread protests erupted when the departmental governor attempted to introduce the position of ladino alcalde. A ladino, Sanpedrano Q'eqchi' patriarchs claimed, could not represent the interests of the entire pueblo.

---

[10] Reeves, *Ladinos with Ladinos*; and Gudmundson and Fuentes, *Central America, 1821–1871*.

[11] Reeves, *Ladinos with Ladinos*.

In places like San Pedro Carchá, where Maya caste hierarchy was particularly strong and the ladino presence was small, departmental governors acquiesced to resistance in fear of rebellion and instead appointed a ladino political commissioner to help oversee local affairs.

Second, the state sought to regularize land ownership, promote agricultural export production, and expand its tax base by passing a series of liberal land laws – most infamously, the tierras baldías laws of 1873 and 1874.[12] Following the colonial precedent of reconstituting underused territory as crown lands, the Liberal government defined as idle (tierras baldías) all lands that were not "planted in coffee, sugar, cacao, or hay," and claimed them as national property, to be surveyed, bought, and auctioned off to the highest bidder.[13] Q'eqchi' lands that had been used to plant milpa were designated as idle tierras baldías and were suddenly available for appropriation by land-hungry speculators. While the state did not directly attack communal property, as had occurred in neighboring El Salvador and Mexico, Liberals recognized communal property ownership as a problem and demanded land privatization as the remedy.[14] The result was the gradual conversion of communal lands into private property. For example, the state passed Decree 170 abolishing *censo enfitéutico*, the system of renting municipal lands. After 1877 all censo lands were sold at minimal cost to the renters as private property.[15] Land privatization, however, did not necessarily entail ladino appropriation of Maya lands. For example, in San Pedro Carchá, of the sixty-three individuals who received private title from censo lands between 1880 and 1882, only eleven were ladinos. None of the properties purchased by ladinos was among the largest or most valuable lands awarded.[16] Moreover, much of the property awarded in the first decade after the Liberal reforms went to Mayas. In addition, the state also expropriated what it

---

[12] *Recopilación de leyes agrarias* (Guatemala: Tipografía "La Unión," 1890), July 22, 1873, 85–6, and May 13, 1874, 86; *Recopilación de leyes emitidas por el gobierno democrático de la República de Guatemala*, vol. 1 (Guatemala: Tipografía El Progreso, 1881), October 17, 1873, 201–2.

[13] J. C. Cambranes, *Coffee and Peasants in Guatemala: The Origins of the Modern Plantation Economy in Guatemala, 1853–1897* (Indianapolis: Plumsock Foundation, 1985), 341.

[14] On the reasons why Liberals did not abolish communal property, see McCreery, *Rural Guatemala*, 251.

[15] See David McCreery, "State Power, Indigenous Communities, and Land in Nineteenth-Century Guatemala, 1820–1920," in *Guatemalan Indians and the State, 1540–1988*, ed. Carol A. Smith (Austin: University of Texas Press, 1990), 106.

[16] These censo records are found in SPCM 1882 in an untitled book.

considered to be the remaining church properties: the urban properties of
Maya cofradías. While seemingly insignificant, these expropriations were
a blow to the capital and credit systems of cofradías and seriously limited
the ability of Q'eqchi's to secure loans often necessary for the payment of
rural land measuring and titling.[17]

Third, the Liberal state legalized and institutionalized mandamiento
labor in 1877.[18] Liberal mandamientos largely replicated Conservative
practices. As they had since the 1850s, mandamientos were used to secure
laborers for work on coffee plantations and for public works projects
such as building churches, bridges, or roads. In the context of coffee
plantations, planters sent requests to town officials or, in the case of Alta
Verapaz, the agricultural commission, to supply a certain number of
laborers (legally up to sixty people, but often requests were for twice as
many) and for a period of fifteen to thirty days. Town mayors or the
agricultural commission would then send planters' requests to members
of the town council, usually Maya regidores, who would then distribute
wage advances and round up workers. Once a laborer accepted an
advance, often by force, they were legally bound to work. Q'eqchi's
regularly complained that mandamientos were resulting in food shortages
and other hardships. As early as 1875, local officials in San Juan Chamelco reported that, because of the "incessant" demands for labor during
the past year, the town had lost much of its crop and was suffering a food
shortage. Unless they received at least a month's relief now, they said, they
would lose their harvest again.[19]

Liberals also viewed coerced labor as one step in the civilizing
metanarrative toward modernity and wage labor, wherein extra-
economic coercion and gradual loss of access to subsistence land would
lead to a fully realized labor force that did not have to be compelled to
work for wages by the state. Guatemalan Liberals were in step with their
Caribbean counterparts who imagined indentured and tenant projects as
steps on the path to a free labor force in the aftermath of slavery's end.[20]
Like Caribbean elites, Guatemalan intellectuals continued to harbor nag-
ging racist doubts that Mayas would ever become fully civilized; free
wage labor remained a distant promise. Liberals introduced new legal

---

[17] On the expropriation of cofradía capital, see AGCA J-AV 108 Leg. 6 A 1882–4.
[18] CM Box 1, July 28, 1853, "Solicitud por mozos del JP al alcalde municipal."
[19] AGCA JP-AV 1875, "Juez Municipal Chamelco-JP," April 15, 1875.
[20] Thomas C. Holt, *The Problem of Freedom: Race, Labor, and Politics in Jamaica and Britain, 1832–1938* (Baltimore: Johns Hopkins University Press, 1992).

codes that enabled Mayas to avoid mandamiento labor, as well as military service, if they had sufficient land or income or if they already possessed a debt for goods or money advanced for agricultural labor in an export sector. State institutions of forced labor existed alongside, and supported the growth of, debt peonage as laborers often preferred to accept debt with a plantation owner known for their good treatment of laborers than be subject to state-run road gangs. Mandamientos and debt peonage also facilitated the transfer of land possession from rural Q'eqchi' subsistence producers to coffee planters and investors, who frequently purchased lands with the purpose of mobilizing the residents for labor on their plantations. For example, when Manuel Maria Sierra petitioned the land known as Saxcoc, located north of Cobán, he noted that while "various indigenous families inhabited the area," his intention "was nothing other than to work the land and conserve in it those inhabitants who will undoubtedly be useful for the business that I propose to create."[21] As a result of these codes, the workforce of mandamientos was exclusively Maya. In 1888 there were 18,587 Mayas subject to mandamiento labor in Alta Verapaz, or approximately 20.5 percent of the Maya population. The percentage of the population recruited for mandamientos varied greatly from town to town, depending on both the racial demographics of the town (since only Mayas were subject to forced labor) and the number of plantations that relied on either direct debt contracts or a resident labor force. For example, fully 43.7 percent of the population in the largely indigenous municipality of San Cristobal were drafted for mandamientos, while only 3.2 percent were in Cobán, where most of the country's ladinos and Europeans resided.[22] Likewise, the planters who benefited from mandamientos were not Q'eqchi' patriarchs, but rather wealthy ladinos and European settlers who maintained connections with the departmental governor and town council.[23]

Over the course of the next half-century, the mobilization of labor through mandamientos, the marginalization of Mayas from local political power, and the privatization of communal lands became ideological

---

[21] AGCA ST-AV P4 E9.

[22] "Mandamientos en el año 1888," *El Porvenir*, January 27, 1889. The total Maya population in Alta Verapaz, based on an average of the 1880 and 1893 census data, was 90,852.

[23] Of the 208 mandamientos requests I located in the archives, there was not one request from a Q'eqchi'. The vast majority were from individuals with familial connections to the Liberal authorities or from the wealthy European, primarily German, immigrant population. See also Reeves, *Ladinos with Ladinos*, 98.

obsessions among Guatemalan Liberals, who saw these laws as the solution to a host of social, economic, and political problems that articulated the national struggle against the men of the past. Socially, these laws sought to break down "indigenous isolation" and bring Mayas into contact with ladinos. As the nineteenth-century Guatemalan historian Antonio Batres Jáuregui contended, "History has demonstrated that it is dangerous enough to leave the *indios* to form a *status* in *statu*, perpetuating their separation, the vulgarity of their customs, their misery and all the motives for hating the castas [system]."[24] These social ills could be resolved if Mayas lived in proximity to ladinos, learned Spanish, and adopted Western clothing.[25] The privatization of communal lands, Liberals believed, would halt migratory agricultural practices and fix people to stable individual plots, instill the indigenous population with the proper sentiments of individualism, and stimulate economic activity – all fundamental steps in the progressive march toward civilization. Economically, these laws would create a stable and relatively inexpensive labor force and facilitate the creation of a property cadastre and rising revenue from property taxes.

Through the civilizing metanarrative of capitalist expansion, state-building, and racial whitening embodied and articulated in Liberal laws, state practices inscribed onto the landscape a set of different meanings and temporalities about who and what counted as agents of the past and agents of the present. The marginalization of Mayas from local political power facilitated the acquisition of both lands and labor, and land privatization resolved thorny questions over municipal and state limits through the creation of authoritative maps. Land privatization and mandamiento labor, however, also racialized certain landscapes, particularly those dedicated to subsistence production, as indigenous, backward, and unproductive, while valuing cattle ranches and coffee plantations as productive, commercial, and modern – therefore, racially white. As the Guatemalan surveyor Cayetano Batres explained in his manual *Tratado de Agrimensura Legal*, private property was central to the supposedly universal evolution of societies and marked the distance between the "savage hunter whose only property is that of the bow and arrow" and the agriculturalist who cultivates the countryside in order to leave it to their inheritors. "Property results first from instinct," continued Batres,

[24] Antonio Batres Jáuregui, *Los indios, su historia y su civilización* (Guatemala: Tipografía la Unión, 1893), 2.
[25] Ibid., 184–91.

"and then from social convention and ultimately for the right ... consummated in the constitutions of all cultured nations."[26]

For state administrators, such as departmental governors, preoccupations with building a functional, ladino-controlled state apparatus and a modern nation of citizens coalesced around the need to firm up boundaries and create reliable maps that could be used to adequately assess taxes, determine who was subject to labor obligations in which municipality, promote a market in the purchase and sale of property that would facilitate capitalist expansion, and generally administer the population. In early 1873, Cobán's municipal council called all the municipality's property owners to bring their documents into the town offices so that town officials could assess who owned what. It was an incredibly naive proposition, given the poor documentation and multiple claims that already plagued the entire region. Indeed, there were no large-scale topographic maps of the area; no cadastral maps had been or would ever be made; no exploration commissions or survey teams had traversed the terrain; and before the town council's optimistic call, no systematic attempts had been made to gather and order local documents, land titles, or other information.

While they have often been seen as merely a technical backdrop, the acts of measuring, mapping, and titling properties were critical not only to the division of land but also to the problem of labor acquisition for coffee plantations and the renegotiation of political power within municipalities. This was especially true in the context of migratory patterns of agricultural production and the confusion and conflicts that resulted when Q'eqchi's migrated, seasonally or permanently, into new municipal jurisdictions. The desire to fix territorial and jurisdictional boundaries was combined with the desire to fix people to places, to turn them into smallholders and laborers. This process was easier said than done. The mountainous terrain of Alta Verapaz was neither easily traversable nor fully surveyed. It was not, as we have seen, a blank slate awaiting topographic inscription. Alta Verapaz was, rather, an inhabited and fertile land dense with meaning and history; it was, in other words, a series of places. Q'eqchi's and ladinos had studiously woven together the dense places of Alta Verapaz through experience and practice, fragmented it with conflict, and shaped it by centuries of migration between the highlands and lowlands.

[26] Cayetano Batres, *Tratado de agrimensura legal* (New York: Imprenta de las Novedades, 1884), 6.

The mapping and privatization of land – the Liberal state's attempt to simplify and codify the territory it governed – ran up against overlapping jurisdiction and land use rights, with ambiguous and shifting borders and place names. State officials also had to reconcile contradictory and competing claims embedded within a set of social, political, and economic struggles over labor, sovereignty, and visions of progress that were seldom documented in writing. Archival power operated both by its presences and by its absences. As Raymond Craib has stated, Mexican Liberal efforts to create fixed land surveys and render lived places defined by migration and social conflict into abstract space ensured that "measurements competed with memories of land use, inscription with inheritance, and technical abstraction with social experience as arbiters of reality."[27] The process of mapping the landscape thus would also conflict with the different meanings of property and place. Indeed, the greatest complication confronted by Liberals occurred not because of Maya resistance to land privatization and mapping, but precisely because Maya patriarchs and communities actively sought to translate Q'eqchi' cosmographies into the fixed terms of the map, to transform communally owned properties into private ones, and to construct coffee plantations. Q'eqchi' patriarchs faced a difficult conundrum as ladinos sought to wrestle governance from them. If Yat's failed 1865 revolution highlighted what could happen when the delicate balance between solidarity and individualism, communal obligations and republican forms of representation, in Maya social worlds was upset, then Q'eqchi' patriarchs' efforts to participate in the expansion of coffee production and the mapping of the landscape were an attempt to renegotiate the fragile equilibrium that held together a socially stratified Maya society, divided between Maya patriarchs and lower classes. Liberal programs, however, also opened the door for Conservatives to adapt a proindigenous stance and seek alliances with disgruntled Q'eqchi' patriarchs.

Q'EQCHI' COFFEE PLANTERS

In August 1875, Ramon Sierra, a ladino resident of San Pedro Carchá, notified authorities that more than 300 Mayas, armed with rifles, were organizing in the village of Saxcoc with a "vision of forming a rebellion

[27] Craib, *Cartographic Mexico*, 57.

against the authorities and ladinos."[28] Court records unearthed from remaining municipal archives speak to how rumors like these traveled through partially overheard conversations and sideways glances from the countryside into the marketplace and up the corridors to the town council offices and finally were inscribed, recorded, and archived. First to face questioning was the *alcalde auxiliar* of Saxcoc, who likewise testified that a "multitude of armed Indians" had met to "form a plan to attack the authorities and ladinos of this city." Yet he also insisted that villagers had gathered a contribution of 400 pesos to initiate a claim for the village's common lands. By the time that local authorities had summoned the Q'eqchi' patriarchs of Saxcoc to the city, the plans for an armed uprising, if such plans had ever existed, had dissipated. The evidence for sedition, principally rumors, was insufficient for conviction. The testimonies nonetheless made clear the intention of these Q'eqchi's to purchase Saxcoc's common lands from the government. While we may never know what went on in Saxcoc, the incident is deeply suggestive of the ongoing social anxieties and tensions surrounding land titling. In a nearby village, a Q'eqchi' patriarch responded to the attempts of a French immigrant to title their land by petitioning President Barrios: "For many years we have occupied the lands called Chacán-Xalama-Zacrap, lands which are today *baldíos*.... José Balsells has petitioned these same lands and despite our rights as ancient and first possessors he wants to remove us from our properties reducing us to poverty."[29]

The process of titling land for Maya villagers was fraught with risks that could jeopardize rather than secure landownership. First, the process of petitioning lands required villagers to hand over to the state their closely guarded colonial-era titles. Even though state officials often regarded these titles and their corresponding maps as inaccurate and of limited value, Q'eqchi's recognized the authoritative value of archival records, and giving them to the state often signaled a loss of power. Second, measuring and titling lands was expensive, and purchasing land itself even more so. Finally, once villagers had gained a title, they were well aware that the title did not guarantee security of ownership. As had happened frequently in the past, villagers later confronted others who laid claim to ownership of the property, sometimes themselves in possession of an overlapping title.

[28] SPCM 1873, "Ramón Sierra al Alcalde Municipal de San Pedro Carchá," August 18, 1875.
[29] AGCA ST-AV Paq. 5 Exp. 13.

In other instances, villagers faced boundary intrusions and usurpations as boundary markers were moved or destroyed.[30]

Despite these dangers, difficulties, and costs, however, many villagers, including those rumored to be rebels in Saxcoc, did seek and secure title to their land. Village common lands known as ejidos were among the first to be titled, because, as one Cobanero town official explained, "Every day it becomes more palpable the difficulty in obtaining [wood] as a result of the increase in petitions for tierras baldías."[31] Village lands had long served as sources of water, wood, herbs, and other essentials. San Pedro Carchá's town council approved petitions for the town's watering hole in May 1879, for "various communal uses."[32] Yet even more prevalent than the petitioning of ejidos were the efforts of Q'eqchi' patriarchs to seek individual title to both commonly held lands of ethnic clans (parcialidades) and private properties, often with an eye to planting coffee.

Q'eqchi' patriarchs sought to become coffee planters through two distinct strategies. First, Q'eqchi' hereditary patriarchs of communal properties petitioned for title as a way to affirm ethnic identity and communal memory grounded in space and territory as well as to expand their prestige and protect lower-class Q'eqchi's from the demands of mandamiento labor.[33] Having secured legitimate title and planted coffee, Q'eqchi' hereditary patriarchs then petitioned the state for an exemption from mandamiento labor on behalf of Q'eqchi' commoners who resided on the land. For state purposes, patriarchs translated Q'eqchi' commoners into resident laborers and labor contracts subsumed the reciprocal norms governing communal obligations. For example, Pedro Coc and Fabian Tiul of Tanchi-Raxaha in San Pedro Carchá requested labor exemptions from the municipal government. Tanchi-Raxaha had long been a communal property and was titled under the name of Salvador Coc, Pedro's recently deceased father, in 1879. By the early 1880s, Pedro Coc and Fabian Tuil claimed to be "coffee planters," who were "in possession of fifty-six

---

[30] The departmental governor records are replete with such cases. See, for example, AGCA JP-AV 1884 Paq. 2, "José María Cu 'Panaxpel' al JP," August 8, 1884; AGCA JP-AV 1884 Paq. 5, "Florencia Sep. Denuncia un terreno China Chulm," n.d.

[31] AGCA ST-AV Paq. 7 Exp. 17 1880.   [32] AGCA ST-AV Paq. 7 Exp. 16 1879.

[33] On the importance of place and territory to Q'eqchi' identity, see Richard Wilson, *Maya Resurgence in Guatemala: Q'eqchi' Experiences* (Norman: University of Oklahoma Press, 1999); Abigail E. Adams, "The Transformation of Tzuultaq'a: Jorge Ubico, Protestants and Other Verapaz Maya at the Crossroads of Community, State and Transnational Interests," *Journal of Latin American Anthropology* 6, no. 2 (2001): 198–233; and Carlos Rafael Cabarrús, *La cosmovisión Q'eqchi' en proceso de cambio* (San Salvador: Universidad Centroamericana, 1979).

caballerías of land planted with coffee, sugar cane, corn, and beans." Tiul and Coc attested to state authorities that they had seventy *colonos* (resident laborers) under their dominion. These colonos "freely give us the fields that they occupy in our property and we also pay them the customary wages," Tiul and Coc declared. As coffee planters, Tiul and Coc had simply translated the hereditary rights of Q'eqchi' patriarchs into the legal rights of coffee planters with resident labor forces.

As a second strategy, Q'eqchi' patriarchs measured and titled tierras baldías. By purchasing and titling new lands for coffee production and cattle grazing, they also took advantage of land privatization to expand their sphere of influence and class position.[34] Between 1871 and 1884, Q'eqchi' patriarchs titled 912 out of 2,058 caballerías as representatives of ethnic clans as well as individual property owners.[35] Until 1882, more Q'eqchi' patriarchs sought to title tierras baldías in Alta Verapaz than ladino and foreign settlers combined.[36] As landowners, they had secured their rights to represent Q'eqchi's by virtue of their citizenship within liberal political frameworks that made occupation or property ownership the basis for exemption from forced wage labor duties and citizenship. As patriarchs, they secured their positions as village elders by representing villagers in local affairs and fulfilling their obligation to provide access to the means of subsistence production.

While sometimes Q'eqchi' patriarchs, such as the modernizing coffee planters Fabian Tiul and Pedro Coc of Tanchi-Raxaha, claimed to be agents of modernity in order to legitimize their ownership, at other times patriarchs used indigenous custom and tradition to claim rights to do the same. Q'eqchi' patriarchs, even those who would later claim to be agents of progress and to be establishing coffee plantations, sought to justify their holdings, in writing, by blending discourses of use rights since time immemorial with a discourse of proprietary rights gained from colonial grants. These letters tended to stress an early foundational moment by indigenous ancestors beyond the annals of history, followed thereafter by official recognition from the Spanish authorities and the granting of lands to the pueblo. For example, Marcos Choc wrote to the minister of the interior, as a Q'eqchi' patriarch and representative of commoners, that

[34] On liberal land laws, see Reeves, *Ladinos with Ladinos*; McCreery, "State Power, Indigenous Communities, and Land."

[35] See *Memoria presentada a la lejislatura de 1884 por la Secretaría de Estado en el Despacho de Gobernación i Justicia, de la República de Guatemala* (Guatemala: Tipografía Nacional, 1884), appendix 5. One caballería is approximately equal to 45 hectares.

[36] This is based on the admittedly incomplete records of the Sección de Tierras at the AGCA.

"since ancient times and in favor of the tolerance of our customs according to ancient legislation, we, the *naturales*, went about acquiring claim [*fincando de hecho*] to our residence in the places that offered us the most obvious comfort and cultivation of agriculture, and from this fortune and without contradiction we have cared for and cultivated the land of this area since the time of our fathers." The area that Choc had titled on behalf of some 887 Q'eqchi' families stretched from the "height of the mountain 'Tolom-quiej'" and passed along the margins of the Cahabón River, which "bathed and fertilized the fields that we have extended through its fertile valleys." Choc condensed his claim into what he considered to be the essentials for an official audience. His history moved with little hesitation from a time immemorial – when the villagers' ancestors performed foundational acts of improvement that conferred customary claim – to the present, when their descendants continued to work the same lands. At any given moment between these two poles, the villagers had purportedly enjoyed a peaceful possession and, as such, had natural rights to it. The shrinking of time in Choc's narrative painted a portrait of uninterrupted possession, untouched by the conflicts that plagued the countryside. Drawing on the authority conferred to tradition and unchanging essences within modern discourse, Q'eqchi' patriarchs like Choc sought to render what were often conflicted histories of land use into a basis for claims to land title. In this way, Q'eqchi' patriarchs often appealed to both the authenticity of tradition and the newness and agency of modernity. In the era of Liberal reforms, however, custom and tradition could also become symbols of stagnation and the past.

While the Liberal state theoretically recognized Mayas' customary rights to land by requiring petitioners and claimants to recognize ancient titles and notify inhabitants when they intended to seek title, in practice few state officials recognized indigenous customary land use as granting priority in making a claim. Many individuals seeking to title a tierra baldía, including Q'eqchi' patriarchs, readily dismissed customary land rights, reducing inhabitants to occupants lacking legal rights. When state officials asked Gabriel Xó if the tierra baldía his friend and neighbor, Sebastian Choc, was formally petitioning had any inhabitants, Gabriel Xó declared, "It is true that the land is inhabited by a few indigenous families from Carchá, but they do not have any title and they possessed it only for the custom that there is to occupy the land."[37] Others seeking title argued

[37] AGCA ST-AV Paq. 3 Exp.10.

that the law did not recognize customary use, even if Mayas believed it should. For example, the British settler John Carter maintained in his petition that "certainly there are a few indigenous families that live disseminated in the property and that possess [the land] without any title and only for their own will, since it is well known that the Indians always consider themselves the only owners of all the lands and they empower themselves without having the faculty to do so."[38] Still, the state sometimes intervened on behalf of Q'eqchi' claimants, particularly if the residents could produce an earlier title. In addition, as David McCreery has explored, the greater a region's agricultural potential and the greater the importance of the ladino or European settler who wished to exploit it, the greater the likelihood the state would intervene to weaken or dismantle the autonomy of its indigenous communities.[39]

Q'EQCHI' CARTOGRAPHIES

In order to successfully petition and claim title to land, Q'eqchi's were required by law to engage the scientific practices of measuring landscapes, of fixing onto a blank slate – and with measurable quadrants – territories that had long been shaped by migration and subsistence economies. The acts of measuring and titling served to reinforce or rewrite the historical memory of land use and redraw the boundaries separating communities. Such land claims often served to reinforce the connective bonds between patriarchal elites and commoners. Old land titles, often dating from the late sixteenth century, surfaced from dusty village patriarchs' personal or communal archives in demonstration of existing claims, and the boundary markers inscribed in those documents were repeated, revised, and inscribed anew. These ancient maps and titles formed part of a lineage's archive, passed down from generation to generation. Gabriel Xó, for example, responding to rumors that the ladino José María Coronado planned to petition lands known as "Chamal" or "Chiquib," initiated his own petition. Xó provided a "memoir that his ancestors had left him" (dating from 1588) that the court had recently translated from Q'eqchi' to Spanish, demonstrating the ancestral limits, markers, and place names. Declaring that Xó "was obliged to measure the land scientifically in order to know the areas that correspond to it and definitively recognize its limits," the departmental governor insisted that Xó pay for a new measurement and title.[40]

---

[38] AGCA ST-AV Paq. 4 Exp. 9.   [39] McCreery, *Rural Guatemala*, 251.
[40] AGCA ST-AV Paq. 5 Exp. 15; see also AGCA ST-AV Paq 5. Exp. 11.

Thus not only did the new title secure existing land rights, but the process of measuring and petitioning drew on indigenous memories and archives, reinforcing the value and power of both indigenous memory and state power. Combining the science of cartography with indigenous knowledge and spiritual places, Q'eqchi' patriarchal elites solidified their control over the distribution of subsistence lands and their access to lands suitable for coffee and other commercial production. In doing so, they also reaffirmed and remade the Maya spirits, Tzuultaq'as, who resided in caves but were symbolized by mountainous landscapes; boundary markers such as crosses, stones and trees; and footpaths and roads. As one anthropologist has noted, Tzuultaq'a "marks the crossroads and transitions between Verapaz communities, and between competing interests at stake in the Verapaz."[41]

Even as Q'eqchi's adapted to the requirements of scientific measurement, scientific practices of mapping the landscape also had to be adapted to and translated from existing Maya practices of measuring distance and marking borders. Since many Q'eqchi' patriarchs and villagers were keen to claim the entire territory that they considered to be part of their customary rights, memories and what were commonly termed "ancient markers" were crucial to defining new boundaries. When Marcos Choc and the residents of Sillab set out to remeasure the property they sought to title, they declared, through interpreters, that the new survey must extend beyond what the surveyor, Francisco Vela, had suggested since it was crucial that they "always have their ancient markers." As Vela traveled by foot accompanied by a few representatives of Sillab, he noted how they pointed out different crosses, hermitages, and mountain tops, often with multiple names, such as the cross known as "Chirital" or "Cecasis."

Q'eqchi' patriarchal elites used the surveying and titling of land to meld the marking of property boundaries together with indigenous spiritual norms and worldviews, and thus legitimize new property regimes for rural Q'eqchi's. More than just neutral and abstract markers of property boundaries, one might also read these as markers from the cultural world of Q'eqchi's whose vision of rural space was governed by Tzuultaq'as. These mountain spirits were more important than any other factor in the Q'eqchi' cosmographical world – they governed the fertility of the landscape and the community, and demarcated filial bonds. They were guardians of plants, people, and forest animals and

---

[41] Adams, "The Transformation of the Tzuultaq'a," 202.

were related by filial ties. The Q'eqchi' elders and residents who guided the land surveyors through the footpaths that demarcated the boundaries of their ethnic lineages selected Tzuultaq'as' crosses, altars, and shrines as the surveyor's markers, differentiating one property from another.[42] As Q'eqchi' patriarchal elites melded the marking of property boundaries together with indigenous spiritual norms and worldviews, they acted as native intermediaries who translated and mediated between state practices and indigenous communities. In the process, they made the exercise of land titling meaningful to Maya villagers, while satisfying new state regulations. Old titles that had been passed on from generation to generation were rewritten, archived with the state bureaucracy, and given new legal potency.

Q'eqchi' knowledge and memory also shaped the petitions made by ladino and European settlers. Surveyors and petitioners lacked sufficient knowledge of the region and required the support of local Q'eqchi's. Even more, rarely were properties entirely uninhabited, and thus local residents were often called on to participate in the acts of measuring as witnesses, although they acted more as local guides. As a result, ladinos and European properties frequently relied on both Maya knowledge and sacred landmarks to delimit territories. For example, when José Lino Cordón measured Yaxbatz in 1874, the surveyor began, along with his "assistant witnesses," who were the Maya inhabitants of the property, at the road called Choctum, three leagues north of Cobán. "We crossed the highest point on the Yaxbatz mountain," the agronomist wrote, "where the interested party showed us a cross that the Indians call Cuxmaz as it is the marker that points towards the North." As the surveyor continued along the path guided by the witnesses and Cordón, they selected points and markers, such as the home of Martin Xun, roads, and hermitages.[43]

These cartographic practices blended the science of making the landscape and its communities legible, fixed, and available for state governance and capitalist expansion with the well-worn footpaths and crosses that symbolized the cosmographical lives of the Q'eqchi' and the spirits

---

[42] For examples of cases where these spiritual aspects of boundary marking are evident in the references to indigenous crosses, see AGCA ST-AV Paq. 3 Exp. 2; AGCA ST-AV Paq. 3 Exp. 3; AGCA ST-AV Paq. 3 Exp. 6; AGCA ST-AV Paq. 5 Exp. 1; AGCA ST-AV Paq. 5 Exp. 10. Just because these cartographic processes drew on indigenous cosmography does not mean that the process was without conflict. See, for example, AGCA ST-AV Paq. 4 Exp. 9 and AGCA ST-AV Paq. 1 Exp. 13.

[43] AGCA ST-AV Paq. 3 Exp. 3.

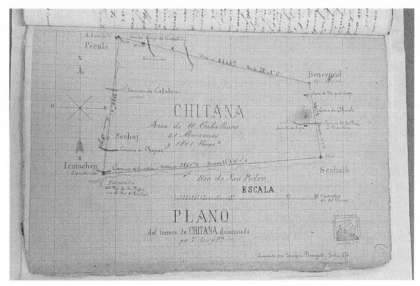

FIGURE 2.1 Sketch of Chitaña.
AGCA ST-AV Paq. 3 Exp. 13. Photograph by author

who demarcated the geographical limits of communities.[44] The land
survey map shown in Figure 2.1, often referred to as a *plano* (plan) or
croquis (sketch), was produced by the surveyor Enrique Bourgeois on
behalf of Tomas Icó, Antonio Tiul, and Agustin Choc.[45] The map illustrates the combination of scientific measurements, natural landscape
features (such as rivers and hills), roads leading to town, and local
hermitages. An emphasis is placed – in both the map and the narration
of its measurement – on a small mountain or hill called Abinal and the
hermitage located next to it. These natural features, most especially the
mountain Abinal and its hermitage, are infused with double meanings as
both scientific boundary markers and spiritual places. Likewise, when
José Coc petitioned for the lands known as "Setoc," the Q'eqchi's witnesses who measured the property defined its principal boundaries by a
series of crosses (Cruz Ichab and Cruz de Chiritisaj) and a hill (Cumbre de

---

[44] Raymond Craib has explored mapping as a process of "state fixation" – attempts to
define, stabilize, and make legible landscapes so as to control resources such as communal
lands and to appropriate them for national narratives. See Craib, *Cartographic Mexico*.
Thongchai Winichakul discusses how scientific maps erase "other" histories and geographies, replacing them with new national ones; see *Siam Mapped: A History of the Geo-
Body of a Nation* (Honolulu: University of Hawai'i Press, 1994).

[45] AGCA ST-AV Paq. 3 Exp. 13.

Chisanac), which for Q'eqchi's served not only as territorial boundary markers but as symbols of Tzuultaq'as.[46] Maps thus serve to validate property boundaries and state power, but they also allow for multiple interpretations. As with other survey maps conducted during this time, villages and homes are absent; milpa fields and coffee plants are erased; and the property is made to appear empty and awaiting cultivation. While these land-tenure maps provided a graphic inventory, a codification of information about ownership, tenancy, value, and agricultural potential, they also emptied and erased other histories and geographies.

These performative acts of land surveying similarly translated Q'eqchi' ritual pilgrimages to local landmarks into cadastral maps and legal documents. Just as these spiritual journeys brought together neighboring communities in a symbolic act that revalidated political boundaries, cadastral maps made public and official, measurable and fixed, the boundaries that separated one community or ethnic lineage from another. As part of a land survey, these ritual acts were carefully documented in a narrative form that erased any evidence of their spiritual meanings and instead rendered them as scientific practice, archived and objective. The translation of Q'eqchi' vernacular landscapes that were multiple, conflictual, and shifting into cartographic maps that were empty, homogenous, and linear was, however, an arduous process that was never fully completed because maps were always open to multiple interpretations and uses that exceeded the map itself.

In addition to the limited knowledge of surveyors, problems also arose because many supposed boundaries had often been quite fluid, and the Q'eqchi' experience of space was not defined by universal, measurable distance, but more often based on travel time between places. The provisions of land division required that any territorial ambiguities – coincident use rights, empty spaces, zonal boundaries, or natural and imprecise border markers – be reconciled in order to give borders a vertical precision. As we have seen, villagers had long lived with territorial ambiguities, negotiating usufructal tenure relationships via the system of caste hierarchy and rooted in Maya norms of reciprocity and communal solidarity. As the state attempted to render such regimes precise and fixed, old mechanisms of negotiation and agreement were to be replaced by vertical lines and precise markers, arbitrated by the state.

[46] AGCA ST-AV Paq. 4 Exp. 4.

Sometimes land surveyors, whose payment depended on the size of the territory requested, took advantage of such ambiguities. For example, when Victoriano Pop, the prominent Q'eqchi' patriarch who exalted Maya contributions to national progress, petitioned for the land known as Chanjmacan in 1881, he believed the property to be approximately four caballerías in size. Another witness suggested that the property extended across two or three caballerías. When the surveyor, Jesús Ordoñez, measured the land with the aid of Pop and some Q'eqchi' witnesses, however, the size of the property exceeded Pop's estimate by twenty-three caballerías. When Odroñez was questioned about the magnitude of the discrepancy, he responded, "The measurement was done for the markers that the land petitioner had assured him marked the territory that Pop had possessed through his ancestors since time immemorial.... I understand that in this there was nothing more than a mistake since these Indians, and still many people who are not, believe that a caballería encloses an area much larger than in reality it does."[47]

Such errors, whether produced out of malice or ignorance, were common. No formal land survey training was available in Guatemala until the early 1870s, and the few land titles produced before then were often inaccurate, with unclear boundary markers, multiple place names, and overlapping boundaries.[48] Such practices and memories bled into liberal land practices, confounding attempts to fix a single meaning to space. As one surveyor gingerly expressed to the Ministry of Government, "Even the surveyors use interchangeably the names Chirrity y Saj o Satul y Statut," and such practices had the effect of undermining the law so that "buyers will not be able to have security in their acquisitions and even more dangerous, if these omissions are not noted, there could follow transcendental harm (*perjuicios*)."[49]

As a result of the problems produced by the rugged terrain and ambiguously defined borders, surveyors also often took shortcuts. When Marcos Choc purchased the petition rights to Sillab from Juan Prado and Fernando Chévez, he believed that the petition would include the entire territory known as "Sillab" – an incredible 190 caballerías, or nearly 85 square kilometers. According to Choc, the surveyor, the French immigrant Enrique Bourgeois, who did much of the early land titling in the

---

[47] AGCA ST-AV Paq. 12 Exp 6.
[48] See McCreery *Rural Guatemala*, 59; and AGCA B80.1 3563 81259 F.2.
[49] AGCA ST-AV Paq. 4 Exp. 8.

region, made many errors. Perhaps Choc was right – due to the "impass-ability" of the terrain, Bourgeois conducted the survey without witnesses and provided no details about the perimeter, extension, available area, boundaries, or even the name of the land.[50] Such errors and omissions could be quite problematic. Yet, somehow, the survey had passed the revision process in Guatemala City. At times, these same revisionist surveyors expressed their horror at the technical errors they encountered and declared that such errors endangered peace and progress and drained the nation's public riches and private capital.[51]

Yet despite all these ambiguities and errors, there were relatively few protracted or violent conflicts over land. In part, this was because Alta Verapaz remained an open frontier with a broad expanse of available land. Some conflicts, however, did arise as Maya villagers and patriarchs, ladinos and foreign settlers, struggled to gain access to the most fertile lands. The region's diversity of microclimates and varied elevation and temperature across small distances meant that soil fertility and suitability to cultivation were also quite varied. As a result, more than one person or village often claimed the same territory. For example, when Sebastian Choc from the Barrio de Santiago in San Pedro Carchá attempted to title Chitaña in 1876, it was discovered that another Q'eqchi' patriarch, Candelaria Ba, had also petitioned and measured part of the property: "Like all of these places, one cannot determine the boundaries based on a name since one doesn't know how far a property that has such-and-such a name goes."[52] Tiburcio Caal and the residents of Xucaneb also fought over territorial boundaries. According to Caal, the most prominent Q'eq-chi' patriarch in Cobán, villagers in Xucaneb had "removed the old markers to advance another fixed line that marked their property as much greater than its neighboring *baldíos* [*tierras baldías*]."[53] Likewise, Gabriel Xó of San Pedro Carchá was incensed to discover that Manuel Lucas petitioned, measured, and purchased a piece of land within Xó's own already existing title.[54] As surveyors had warned, difficulties in surveying landscapes translated into a proliferation of overlapping claims, the con-stant need to update and remeasure properties, and land demarcations that defied dreams of linear order.

In contested fertile terrain, however, conflicts emerged and revealed old divisions. At times, villagers disagreed over whether they should or could

---

[50] AGCA ST-AV Paq. 23 Exp. 2.   [51] AGCA ST-AV Paq. 10 Exp. 4.
[52] AGCA ST-AV Paq. 3 Exp. 10.   [53] AGCA ST-AV Paq. 16 Exp. 8.
[54] AGCA ST-AV Paq. 6 Exp. 13.

undertake the expense of petitioning for ownership of the property or whether they should allow the property to be purchased and titled by someone else. For example, when Manuel María Sierra petitioned for Saxcoc in Cobán, the surveyor noted, "First, we did the required citation to the families of indigenous inhabitants of the land Saxcoc, according to the superior order and just once we brought together the majority of them and let them know the objective of my commission which they understood and told me that they did not oppose it at all and that although they had their plants and their possessions in the property however they were in agreement with the measurement since they were fine in the service of Srs. Sierra and Ponce. Although there persisted a few protesters [*mugieres*] making opposition, it was not for the opportune advice they were given."[55] At other times, there were conflicts in the village over who was the rightful Q'eqchi' patriarch in a petition.[56]

The most protracted conflicts, however, occurred not simply over territorial boundaries between different villagers, patriarchs, ladinos, and European settlers over the same piece of land. New prolonged battles flourished as the state tried to redefine and reorganize property and achieve a simple but absolute synchronicity between agricultural land-holdings and the administrative territory of municipalities. Conflicts over borders between individuals could generally be resolved without undue conflict, because, while not all land was equally fertile, there was no scarcity of land in general. Where problems became acute was over the administrative boundaries of municipalities, where the stakes were about control over taxation and laboring bodies made complicated by decades of migration.

DEFINING BORDERS, ADMINISTERING LABOR

In late nineteenth-century Alta Verapaz, state officials obsessed over borders. One cannot open a departmental governor's report without encountering repeated references to the need to fix (*fijar*) boundaries. Migration, both seasonal and permanent, meant that municipal and departmental political jurisdictions did not overlap with territory. As many state officials complained, it was indigenous "custom" to go to the district in which "they were recognized to be born" to register births, deaths, baptisms, and other matters, even though they resided in different

[55] AGCA ST-AV Paq. 4 Exp. 9.   [56] AGCA ST-AV Paq. 4 Exp. 8.

municipalities or even in other departments.[57] As anthropologists have illustrated, Q'eqchi's have a strong connection to their place of birth, the place where, according to Q'eqchi' custom, their umbilical cord is buried.[58] Ambiguously defined municipal and state limits, however, hindered the rationalization for property taxation and raised repeated jurisdictional questions over land claimed by two (or more) municipalities. Even more, they enabled Q'eqchi's to escape mandamiento labor obligations by claiming to owe service to another jurisdiction, but sometimes providing service in neither.

By the 1880s, as a result of growing demands for mandamiento labor and Q'eqchi's fleeing the same, nearly every municipality was in a dispute with its neighboring municipalities. At times those disputes became violent, such that the departmental governor even advocated giving away, at zero cost, ejidos located on municipal boundaries in order to fix boundaries and reduce conflicts.[59] These disputes, however, could not be resolved based on natural boundaries or even on historical land use, since boundaries had never been fixed and were instead subject to migration. As such, struggles over determining borders were struggles over stabilizing definitions of who counted as barbaric men of the past or as civilized men of the present, how historical time and racial ascriptions were distributed, and which metanarratives and visions of progress won the day.

In 1877 ladino state officials and their Q'eqchi' patriarch allies succeeded in separating the lower and upper halves of the Verapaz into two separate departments. While few records documenting this process remain within national or regional archives, we know that Cobaneros had fought for this outcome since at least the 1860s. However, the delimitation of a new boundary between Alta and Baja Verapaz, on the one hand, and the neighboring departments of El Quiche, Izabal, and El Petén, on the other, failed to settle once and for all the administrative boundary lines that defined these departments. For the next few decades, administrators and Maya laborers and subsistence producers would continue to fight over how to delineate the space that constituted the imagined and legal–administrative world of Alta Verapaz.

The most protracted and frequent conflicts occurred over the administration of mandamiento labor. Since Q'eqchi' social and political worlds

---

[57] See, for example, AGCA JP-AV Paq. 4 1884, "Sr JP del Registro Civil San Cristobal," August 24, 1884.
[58] Kistler, *Maya Market Women*.   [59] AGCA ST-AV Paq. 7 Exp. 17 1880.

were rooted in the municipality of birth by tightly woven extended familial and ethnic bonds, Q'eqchi's born in one jurisdiction but residing in another often refused to pay taxes or contribute services to the jurisdiction of their current residence, traveling instead to their native jurisdiction for all those matters. Some traveled great distances, including to the neighboring departments of Izabal and El Quiché, to participate in annual saint's day festivals and other affairs. State officials, meanwhile, furiously chased migrant Q'eqchi's from their jurisdictions. Sanpedrano officials were particularly notorious for hunting down migrant villagers. For example, Martin Pop, Santiago Tzi, and Santiago Tzuil, who resided in Lanquín but were born in San Pedro Carchá, appeared before the departmental governor complaining about how officials from Carchá would invade the jurisdiction of Lanquín and force them to carry coffee to Panzos.[60] In 1880 the departmental governor wrote to the Ministry of the Interior complaining about how Sanpedrano authorities "had the custom of requiring services and payment of the community funds wherever Sanpedranos live and they break into other jurisdictions annoying the respective authorities. In these towns, there is the need for laborers for the agricultural businesses that are of importance. To remedy this inconvenience, it is indispensable that Sanpedranos pay their labor obligations and taxes in the jurisdiction where they live and not in their town of origin."[61]

While decades of seasonal and permanent migration rendered property boundaries distinct from administrative boundaries of municipalities, the process of titling properties also generated more jurisdictional conflicts than it resolved. In some instances, lands were petitioned that crossed jurisdictional boundaries, forcing new property owners to make strategic decisions about which jurisdiction they would like to reside in.[62] Eduardo Felice, for example, purchased a property that was in both Cahabón and Carchá and made a request to the departmental governor that the municipal boundary be redrawn so the property was in Cahabón. This, however, drew the anger of Sanpedrano officials, who declared that all the inhabitants were from Carchá and should pay their taxes and services in their native jurisdiction.[63] In another instance, Felice tried to have a property moved from the jurisdiction of Chisec to Cobán, since the

---

[60] SPCM 1878, "Martin Pop, Santiago Tzi, y Santiago Tzuil"; see also SPCM 1883, "Pedro Chub."
[61] AGCA B Leg. 28674 Exp. 158 1880.   [62] AGCA ST-AV Paq. 4 Exp. 9.
[63] SPCM "Informe al JP (hereafter JP) de la Comisión Recaudadora," 1893.

authorities in Chisec refused to help him discipline his labor force and were undermining his efforts to bring civilization to a rural region. "You, Señor Departmental Governor, know how the race that lives in those places is," explained Felice.

> Worse than their neighbors the Lacadones, the *indios* from there do not have a fixed residence. Without houses and without a legal plot of subsistence land they flee to the most impassable mountains, they do not know patrones and authority, and they are repulsed by whatever kind of work.... I have brought them together and I make them work, I always pay them, and above what they earn, I have given them ideas of civilization and I am going to create a school for the children, but not all of them are convinced and some have fled, breaking the contract and bringing disorder. Against these factors, which do not penalize me much financially, but destroy the advances I have made in discipline and order on the plantation, I have appealed to the authorities in Chisec who have done nothing.[64]

In turn, Felice asked Cobanero officials for special treatment and considerations, "because in a few years all of this rich zone of Alta Verapaz as far as the Petén, until now unpopulated and ours, will be a new agricultural center and a new source of national riches for all."[65] Rarely, in other words, was the question of drawing a boundary simply about the natural territorial boundaries that might exist; rather, it was cast as a matter of defending civilization against barbarism.

Against such narratives, some Q'eqchi' patriarchs challenged municipal boundaries on the opposite basis – to protect residents from the barbarism of foreigners and their greed. In 1875 José Coc Delgado, a prominent Q'eqchi' patriarch from San Pedro Carchá, petitioned the government to sell part of Cobán's ejidos, known as Setoc. In his petition, Coc Delgado maintained that the six caballerías of land he petitioned were apt for cattle ranching, subsistence farming, and coffee production. He sought the lands, he wrote, "to plant and raise cattle and to leave something forever in the peaceful possession of my children." As did many of Carchá's Q'eqchi' elite, he had also begun to purchase lands both within the municipal boundaries of Carchá and in adjacent municipalities as part of a general strategy of accumulating wealth and expanding his influence. After the land had been mapped and measured, the Q'eqchi' men and women inhabiting the area complained to the departmental governor that they had possessed the land from "time immemorial" and wished to contest its sale. Shortly thereafter, Cobán's municipal council stepped in and declared its resolve to protect Cobán's

---

[64] AGCA JP-AV Paq. 4 1884, "Eduardo Felice al JP," September 25, 1884. [65] Ibid.

ejidos. Just as it appeared that Cobán had won the battle to retain Setoc, in September 1878, for unstated reasons, the residents of Setoc suddenly relinquished their claims to Coc Delgado, and the departmental governor declared Coc Delgado "the sole legitimate owner of the entire property [who] ... was obliged to protect these Cobaneros as *colonos* of his land."[66] Since Coc Delgado was a prominent Sanpedrano Q'eqchi' patriarch who would serve as first alcalde of San Pedro Carchá the following year, a new municipal boundary was drawn to incorporate the area into Carchá despite the protests of Cobán's municipal authorities.

Faced with labor shortages for the coffee harvest and public works projects, Cobán's municipal authorities ignored the new municipal boundary and, by 1879, were demanding that the residents of Setoc provide labor for the plantations in Cobán's jurisdiction. In early 1884, with the support of a new departmental governor, Cobán's authorities had the municipal line redrawn in order to include the inhabitants of Setoc.[67] In response, José Coc Delgado demanded that the municipal government of Cobán leave his colonos in peace. Speaking for the residents, he argued that his colonos wished to remain part of Carchá, "not because they flee from work, not because they would like [their work obligations] to be moderate and justly compensated but that the Cobanero landowners, mostly foreigners, always abuse the ignorance and naiveté of the Indians, obliging them to work for nine reales a month, such a scant salary that it was not sufficient even for their most urgent needs over the course of a week; and this does not happen in the jurisdiction of Carchá." While the Cobán officials Juan Noriega and Domingo Paz dismissed Coc Delgado's claims, and the boundary conflict between Carchá and Cobán would remain largely unsettled for decades to come, José Coc Delgado continued to pursue his efforts to protect his colonos and other rural Q'eqchi's from the clutches of foreign coffee plantation owners. María Antonietta de Felice, an Italian immigrant infamous for

---

[66] AGCA ST-AV Paq. 4 Exp. 4.

[67] AGCA ST-AV Paq. 20 Exp. 1 1884. See also AGCA JP-AV Paq. 3 1884, "Carta al JP de Adrián Vidaurre," September 3, 1884; AGCA JP-AV 1884 Paq. 4, "Carta de la Comisión Política de Carchá a don Enrique Carranza," August 23, 1884; AGCA JP-AV 1884 Paq. 4, "Carta al JP de Juan Coronado," April 26, 1884; AGCA JP-AV 1885 Paq. 1, "Carta al JP de Marcos Choc y compañeros," May 18, 1885; AGCA JP-AV 1885 Paq. 3, "Carta al JP de Juan Cucul y compañeros," August 8, 1885; AGCA JP-AV 1885 Paq. 5, "Carta al JP del alcalde 1° de Carchá," July 19, 1885; AGCA JP-AV 1885 Paq. 6 "Carta al JP de José Coc Delgado," November 20, 1885; CM Est. 3 Paq. 18, "Correspondencia del mes de junio d1884"; CM Est. 3 Paq. 19, "Correspondencia del mes de junio de 1904."

her poor treatment of laborers, complained that Coc Delgado "has conquered many of my *colonos*, so that they pass to live in his lands, telling them that there they will receive exemption from public service duties."[68] Disputes over who counted as agents of progress would continue to grow in the following years as the demands of mandamiento labor increased, raising the specter of slavery.

These examples illustrate how the sharp lines of political boundaries and property demarcation were neither timeless nor natural, as well as how the requirement to fix borders often spurred as many conflicts as it resolved. Late nineteenth-century disputes over boundaries were not necessarily simple manifestations of age-old antagonisms that could be resolved by the formalization of borders – the rationale put forward by contemporary intellectuals and officials, who sought to put villagers outside history. Indeed, the opposite appears to have been the case: boundary conflicts proliferated in the final decades of the nineteenth century as villagers were forced to define village boundaries that previously had been fluid and ambiguous.[69] The disputes that arose were often waged, as we have seen, through the metanarrative of civilization defeating barbarism, progress overcoming retrogression, and in the process that metanarrative shaped the definition of territorial and jurisdictional boundaries. Indeed, these temporal categorizations of peoples and places as barbarous or civilized increasingly became a bone of contention as immigration to the region and the use of mandamiento labor expanded beginning in the early 1880s.

RACE, CLASS, AND CITIZENSHIP: THE POLITICS OF STATE RECOGNITION

By the mid-1880s, as coffee prices skyrocketed and Alta Verapaz was increasingly recognized as a supplier of quality coffee in European markets, Q'eqchi' patriarchs faced growing competition for lands and labor from an expanding sector of immigrant settlers who increasingly demanded privileged access to land and labor due to their civilized status and their ability and desire to promote commerce and stimulate national progress. With the consolidation of the German state in 1871, Germans,

---

[68] See AGCA JP-AV 1886 Paq. 2, "Carta al JP de María Felice," October 9, 1886.

[69] See also Craib, *Cartographic Mexico*, and Peter Sahlins, *Boundaries: The Making of France and Spain in the Pyrenees* (Berkeley: University of California Press, 1989), chapter 4.

especially from the commercial centers of Hamburg and Bremen, likewise were emboldened to venture into new places where they might find profitable enterprises. For example, the German settler Richard Sapper proposed to the Ministry of Development (Ministerio de Fomento) that the national government grant him an astounding 400 caballerías of land located in northeastern Carchá, more than ten times the limit of petition-able land established by law. If granted "favorable circumstances," Sapper promised to develop the frontier and increase the nation's riches.[70] At the same time that European settlers like Sapper claimed privileged access to land and labor, the local press and state officials increasingly decried the monopolization of the most productive lands by Q'eqchi's. Editorialists condemned the inefficient use of land by Q'eqchi' patriarchs, whose properties were "only used for the cultivation of corn and beans, in small areas, harming active entrepreneurs, who see that these are fertile lands."[71] In rare instances, these racist complaints entered the documen-tary record, illustrating how ascriptions of race shaped state policy. For example, when Victoriano Pop requested that the size of his petition be reduced, the land surveyor Jesús Ordoñez reminded state officials that it was "in the interests of the nation that the petitioner's denunciation remain for the full twenty-seven caballerías, since the petitioner is not always the person who is awarded the property, but he who offers the most in the auction, and I have reason to believe that he [Pop] will not be able to pay." As long as the petition remained large, Ordoñez reasoned not only that its sale would swell the state's coffers, but that the land was also more likely to be awarded to a "wealthy town ladino or a foreigner," who would not leave it "empty and vacant."[72] As coffee prices rose and competition for land and labor grew, racialized distinctions between civilized men and uncivilized others also shaped the state officials' deci-sions about the implementation of state policy, particularly decisions about who would and would not be subject to forced labor. Ladinos, immigrants, and Q'eqchi's thus articulated competing ideas about who the real agents of history were and who held the nation back.

---

[70] AGCA ST-AV Paq. 24 Exp. 3. When the property was finally measured, Sapper appealed to "the good intentions of the government to protect agricultural enterprises and above all those formed for agriculture by immigrants" in order to prevent the property from being auctioned publicly. Archivo Histórico del Ministerio de Gobernación (hereafter AHMG) C-102, Interesado Ricardo Sapper 1889.

[71] "Medida importante," *El Demócrata*, December 19, 1886; "Ministro de Gobernación-Luis Molina, JP de Alta Verapaz," May 29, 1880 AGCA B. Leg. 28674 Exp. 238.

[72] AGCA ST-AV Paq. 12 Exp 6.

Q'eqchi's and ladinos alike adopted anti-European language and frequently challenged the rights of European settlers like Richard Sapper to Guatemalan territory via nationalist discourse. Even the departmental governor, General Manuel Aguilar, opposed Richard Sapper's petition, arguing that it foreshadowed the monopolization of the land market by foreign investment houses. If foreigners were permitted such large and favorable concessions, he argued, "many other citizens would be excluded from the possibility of acquiring small properties, and would have to become *colonos* of those who possess these tracts of land."[73] A group of middle-class ladinos from Cobán also wrote to the Ministry of the Interior petitioning that they be granted part of the lands solicited by Sapper. "Approximately eight leagues north of Cobán and San Pedro Carchá there is a magnificent agricultural region, especially apt for coffee cultivation, which is about to be monopolized by Don Richard Sapper, with a petition for four hundred caballerías of land," they noted. Along with his associates Oscar Nostiz and William E. Dieseldorff, Sapper, they claimed, already owned more than 150 caballerías of land in the region to the north and northeast of Cobán. They appealed to the minister: "The nation does not gain any advantage by granting to only one person or one company these large extensions of land that form the wealth of the nation and are the key to its aggrandizement." Even more, the ladinos claimed that the region's ills – poverty, conflict, and dependency – arose from the land's concentration in the hands of a few. Based on this reasoning, they asked the minister to grant them individual titles to the lands that Sapper had already petitioned for and measured.[74] The government, responding to such complaints, cited laws regarding the size of petitionable properties and forced Sapper to divide the lands among some of his German friends.

Q'eqchi's, too, adopted anti-immigrant discourses as they sought to strategically position themselves within the temporalities and metanarratives of liberalism as a new commercial class of landowners. "The indigenous class to which we belong, at the mercy of philanthropists and the liberal tendencies of our benevolent General Justo Rufino Barrios, enjoys the same guarantees and rights conceded previously only to the ladino class. In this favorable situation in which the fundamental charter of the Republic has placed us, we have the right to possess and enjoy all of that

---

[73] AGCA ST-AV Paq. 24 Exp. 3.
[74] Achivo Histórico del Ministerio de Gobernación (hereafter AHMG) C102-Interesado Sapper.

which we own with just title," noted Fabian Tiul and Pedro Coc of Tanchi-Raxaha. "Before the law we are equals to whatever national or foreigner," they concluded.[75] These rights included not only the owner-ship of property as true citizens, but, as Tiul and Coc argued, their right to employ their colonos in the harvesting of coffee without the intervention of state authorities. At stake, they claimed, was not only their coffee harvest but also the wealth and happiness of the nation.

Just as Q'eqchi' patriarchs moved strategically between occupying the past as bearers of customary land rights and laying claim to the future as a new class of landowners, their patriarchal duties to protect the indi-genous classes and their love for progress positioned them as the reso-lution to the antagonistic metanarratives of civilization and liberal democracy. This resolution – civilization with emancipation – also contained the dual promises to end exploitation and racial degeneration. When José Coc Delgado protected his colonos from the avarice, ambi-tion, and brutality of wayward Europeans and ladinos, he protected them not only from exploitation but also from racial degeneration. The ubiquitous phrase "our degenerate race" increasingly became a call to end exploitation at the hands of foreigners and ladinos. In 1885 Fabian Tiul of Tanchi-Raxaha wrote to the departmental governor pleading that his colonos not be forced to work on the plantation of María Antonietta de Felice, to avoid the abuses that exacerbate "our miserable and unfavorable way of living ... that unfortunately falls upon our almost reprobate and degenerate race."[76] If exploitation brought degeneration, then the end of exploitation could also initiate racial regeneration. Just as occupation and public conduct were indicators of degrees of civilization, improvements in living conditions, habits, and customs could lead to racial regeneration by enhancing bodily health and function, morality and sentiments.[77] Guatemalan intellectuals also increasingly asserted that the "Indian problem" grew out of colonialism and exploitation, and that an end to the abuses of landlords would usher in racial improvement.[78]

---

[75] AGCA JP-AV 1885, Paq. 3, "Carta al JP de Pedro Coc y Fabian Tiul," March 18, 1885.
[76] AGCA JP-AV 1885 Paq. 3, "Carta al JP de Fabian Tiul y compañeros," February 5, 1885.
[77] See, for example, Luis Lazo Arriaga, *Elementos de anatomía, fisiología é higiene: Para uso de los institutos y escuelas de Centro-América* (Paris: Garnier, 1888).
[78] This movement is discussed in greater detail in the following chapter. For Guatemalan intellectuals, see, especially, the periodical *El Educacionista* and Antonio Batres Jáuregui, *Los indios, su historia y su civilización* (Guatemala: Tipografía la Unión, 1893).

The Q'eqchi'patriarchs' unique position both as protectors of the indigenous class and as agents of progress enabled them to proclaim their superior morality and to question the privileges often granted to foreign settlers like Sapper and Felice. "The foreigners lack all justice, without recognizing that they have come to *our* country, under the protection of the progressive laws of the Government," Salvador Pacay protested to the departmental government. "If they want they can make and gain a fortune, but not content with the products that our fertile soils offer them in superabundance, they try, like Señor [Eduardo] Felice to place upon us greater, much greater work than what corresponds to the pay we receive." The foreigners, complained Pacay, "unjustly dismiss us, passing above the universal laws of reason and justice."[79] By claiming that Europeans, with their unbridled desire for wealth, tended toward the sort of greed and exploitation that contravened Enlightenment ideals of reason, the Q'eqchi' elite also positioned themselves as morally superior, the true bearers of the civilizing effects of commerce and progress. Their manliness – including their manners, virtues, and self-restraint – was more civilized than that of the Europeans and ladinos who, seduced by the desire for wealth, exploited the indigenous masses. By engaging the first-in-Europe-then-elsewhere structure of time, the Q'eqchi' elite both contested the universality of Europeans as apostles of modernity and claimed a privileged position within the civilizing metanarrative of progress and racial improvement.

Despite Q'eqchi' patriarchs' efforts to appeal to liberal discourse and metanarratives and to establish coffee plantations, state officials disregarded Q'eqchi' patriarchs' requests for mandamiento exemptions for their laborers. As labor demands grew in the mid-1880s, the ladino-controlled agricultural commissions in Cobán and San Pedro Carchá began drafting the colonos on the plantations of the hereditary Q'eqchi' elite. When Fabian Tiul of Tanchi-Raxaha complained to the departmental governor that the agricultural commission was violating their rights as landowners by forcing "his" colonos to work on the plantations of ladinos and foreigners, the agricultural commissioner, Sebastian Bailon, scoffed in response; he had no knowledge of a property of fifty-six caballerías owned by Tiul. Rather, the commissioner noted that Tiul and Coc were "only representatives of the co-owners." How could it be, queried the commissioner, that "individuals of this town, being

---

[79] AGCA JP-AV 1885 Paq. 5, "Carta de Salvador Pacay al JP," January 18, 1886.

members of the proletariat class, would claim such a large number of *colonos*?" Tiul and Coc, he concluded, must be liars and impostors.[80] The colonos of Tiul's properties would, in fact, be obliged to work on other plantations because the land was distributed among the residents as smallholders who were not exempt from the state's forced labor requirements. As far as the agriculture commission was concerned, in other words, no plantation existed. When Sebastian Tzuil of San Pedro Carchá similarly wrote to the departmental governor that he was expanding his coffee plantation of "already more than a thousand plants," and needed to be sure his colonos would not be obliged to work on other plantations, the commissioner again responded that the plantation of eleven caballerías was divided among many Q'eqchi's. Tzuil, the commissioner disputed, "just wants to have the inhabitants exonerated from the demands of agricultural work by falsely calling them his colonos."[81]

Narratives abound in both the historical record and scholarship that portray Mayas as concerned principally with subsistence production, erasing their active engagement as coffee planters and their desires to forge a different kind of regional economy and a different kind of modernity. Yet the fact that Q'eqchi' patriarchs attempting to establish coffee plantations were unable to secure a labor force for the coffee harvest suggests that not even the greatest "entrepreneurial spirit" could have made such plantations viable from the start. It is difficult to quantify the enduring impact of state opposition to such efforts, but it was significant, especially as Q'eqchi' patriarchs could no longer fulfill their patriarchal obligations to protect lower-class Q'eqchi's from excessive state intervention and forced labor duties, undermining the delicate balance between reciprocal obligations and duties in Q'eqchi' social life.

CONCLUSION

Guatemala's 1871 Liberal revolution was first and foremost a state-building project built on the contradictory foundations of private property, forced wage labor, and formal, legal equality in a liberal constitution. It sought to shift control over local affairs from the institutions and social

---

[80] AGCA JP-AV 1885, Paq. 1, "Carta al JP de la Comisión de Agricultura de Carchá," May 5, 1885; see also AGCA JP-AV 1885, Paq. 1, "Carta al JP de Fabian Tiul," April 2, 1885; AGCA JP-AV 1885 Paq. 5, "Carta al JP de Fabian Tiul," May 18, 1885; AGCA JP-AV 1885 Paq. 5, "Carta al JP de Fabian Tiul," April 8, 1885.

[81] Emphasis my own. See AGCA JP-AV 1885 Paq. 5, "Carta al JP de Sebastian Tzuil," March 5, 1885.

worlds of Maya caste hierarchy to a ladino-controlled state apparatus, and to expand state sovereignty into the countryside by marginalizing Maya patriarchs as intermediaries. A central component of this state-building project was the delineation of administrative and private property boundaries and related efforts to fix migratory Q'eqchi's to place. Not only did state officials confront difficulties in rendering ecologically and socially complex landscapes with multiple place names and shifting boundaries into linear forms with fixed edges, but their mapping efforts required local, indigenous knowledge of place.

Q'eqchi's were not passive vectors of knowledge in an otherwise top-down state-building affair, but actively participated in surveying the landscape and thus helped produce new scientific geographies and histories that incorporated, reshaped, and rendered invisible Q'eqchi' spiritual ones. Surveys at once reaffirmed and strengthened Q'eqchi' memories of rights to territory, while also rupturing and remaking them. The remapping of space also opened the door for Q'eqchi' patriarchs to transform communal properties they once governed as village elders into private coffee plantations they governed as coffee planters. Q'eqchi' patriarchs-cum-coffee planters sought both inclusion within the nation as full citizens and to fulfill their patriarchal obligations to protect the lower classes from the vagaries of the state and particularly excessive demands on their labor. The expansion of coffee production, however, fueled growing demands for labor, and with it battles over administrative boundaries dividing municipalities, villages, and properties. A crucial component of these debates resonated with larger concerns about the meaning of political modernity, particularly who counted as agents of or obstacles to progress. Coffee production grew substantially: between 1862 and 1878, the number of coffee trees planted grew from two to three million and then dramatically increased again after global coffee prices skyrocketed in the 1880s.[82]

As the Liberal state undermined the foundations of Q'eqchi' patriarchal authority while simultaneously increasing demands on the labor of Q'eqchi' commoners, some rural Q'eqchi's did what so many others before them had done: they sought refuge in the mountains beyond the clutches of the state.[83] In the carved-out spaces of the jagged mountain

---

[82] While the number of coffee trees planted was quite high, production was often lower than other departments because of the more difficult climate. See Wagner, *Historia del café de Guatemala*, 105.

[83] For comparative examples, see James C. Scott, *The Art of Not Being Governed: An Anarchist History of Upland Southeast Asia* (New Haven, CT: Yale University Press, 2009).

ranges and in the inhospitable lowlands descending into Panzos to the southeast and Belize to the north, they engaged in shifting agricultural production and turned to the healing power of millennial leaders. For those who remained behind, however, a looming subsistence crisis and excessive demands on their labor upset the careful balance of reciprocal obligations and duties and ushered in a moral crisis. In September of 1885, Domingo Chocoj, Miguel Coy, and Felipe Caal, residents of the neighboring villages of Tontem and Sarranch, wrote to the departmental governor, Luis Molina: "We no longer have even a piece of land to plant milpa.... In our land there is no longer any wood."[84] Four months later, Tzuultaq'a Xucaneb, the most powerful mountain deity in the Verapaz, set the world straight in an event that disrupted the coffee economy and unleashed a moral crisis among rural Mayas. In the process, Tzuultaq'a Xucaneb laid bare the contradictions between the liberal promise of freedom and equality and the slavery of forced wage labor.

[84] AGCA JP-AV 1885 Paq. 4, "Domingo Chocoj, Manuel Coy y Felipe Caal vecinos de Cobán al JP," September 11, 1885. For deforestation, see also CM Municipal, April 30, 1886; AGCA JP-AV 1886 Paq. 5, "Secretaría de Fomento-JP," March 20, 1886; and "La agricultura se hunde en Cobán," in *El Boletín Agrícola*, Cobán, July 1, 1888.

3

Indolence Is the Death of Character

The Making of Race and Labor, 1886–1898

Nations served by slaves carry within them the seeds of their own destruction ... until, ripping out the cancer, the vigorous force of expansion is reborn in the collectivity.

—Antonio Batres Jáuregui, *Los Indios, su civilización y su historia* (1892)

On the night of November 16, 1885, Juan de la Cruz, a humble ladino tailor, led an estimated 200 Maya men along a footpath to a cave called Los Lacandones, situated in rocky terrain governed by Xucaneb, the most powerful Tzuultaq'a in Alta Verapaz.[1] In the cave, they prayed, burned incense, and occasioned the formidable mountain spirit's support.[2] Such pilgrimages were customary rites designed to elicit Tzuultaq'a powers to ensure a bountiful harvest and peaceful social relations. Three months later, however, when a frost destroyed the coffee crop, ladinos and Q'eqchi's alike accused Juan de la Cruz and his followers of inciting Xucaneb to seek revenge for the "evils of coffee production and private property."[3] Calcita Prado, a ladina from one of Cobán's most respected families, testified in de la Cruz's trial for sedition: "It is true, there is news among the Indians that Don Juan de la Cruz went to pray in the cave of

---

[1] A version of this chapter was originally published as "The Shadow of Slavery: Historical Time, Labor, and Citizenship in Nineteenth-Century Alta Verapaz, Guatemala," *Hispanic American Historical Review* 96, no. 1 (2016): 73–108, © 2016, Duke University Press. All rights reserved. Republished by permission of the publisher, www.dukeupress.edu.

[2] According to anthropologists, Xucaneb is the most powerful of thirteen Tzuultaq'as in Alta Verapaz. See, especially, Wilson, *Maya Resurgence in Guatemala*; Dieseldorff, "Religión y arte de los mayas."

[3] AGCA J-AV Leg. 16 Exp. 16, "Contra Juan de la Cruz y compañeros por sedición."

Xucaneb called Los Lacandones, and he was able to get the saint of the mountain to send the frost that burned all of the coffee plantations." The frost unleashed a revolutionary millenarianism that prompted many Mayas to abandon their bonded labor status by fleeing as far as Belize and by outsmarting local town officials who rounded up workers to fulfill mandamiento duties.[4] Without apparent warning, Altaverapacence Mayas no longer resigned themselves to inescapable labor on coffee plantations. In response to the Maya flight and resistance, the departmental governor militarized mandamiento labor, jailed delinquent laborers, and limited the rights and freedoms available under the law when applied to Mayas, including habeas corpus. In June 1886, the region's newspapers and town councils erupted in a debate about the essential character of Mayas, their role in the region's progress, and the practice of mandamientos that encapsulated the tensions between the liberal promise of universal freedom and equality and the slavery of mandamientos.

Many Altaverapacences narrated the story of Juan de la Cruz and his appeal to Xucaneb for divine assistance as a revolt not only against coffee production and foreign landowners but against all forms of progress and modernity.[5] This narration was more than a mere description, but an argument about the racial character of Mayas, the meaning of progress and history, and the limits of freedom and citizenship. Writing in the local newspaper *El Demócrata*, Juan Coronado claimed that Xucaneb's revenge demonstrated that Mayas were "indolent and apathetic, afraid of reform, and terrified of progress," and thus, before Mayas could acquire freedom and equality, they needed "the civilizing force of time."[6] Another editorialist noted, "Indolence is the death of character, the atrophy of the soul and the negation of progress."[7] As the state cracked down on rural Mayas, ladinos also sought to fix and stabilize Mayas as racialized laborers by relegating them to the past as anachronisms.

The Xucaneb events not only led to a revolt against mandamientos, but touched off a firestorm of political debate about the intersection of coerced labor, capitalism, and modernity. These debates circulated among Q'eqchi's, ladinos, and German settlers in Alta Verapaz, but also

---

[4] AGCA B Leg. 29735 Exp. 266 and 269, "Los indígenas de Cobán solicitan se les exonera de algunos trabajos que obligan en favor de particulares," August 19, 1886; SPCM 1886 "Correspondencia de la comisión de agricultura"; and CM Est. 4 Paq. 24, "Correspondencia de la comisión de agricultura," August 1886.

[5] "La cuestión palpitante," *El Demócrata*, Cobán, July 25, 1886; "La Junta de Fomento de la Alta Verapaz," *El Demócrata*, Cobán, July 18, 1886.

[6] "La cuestión palpitante."   [7] "El Trabajo," *La Voz de Cobán*, March 31, 1897, 1–2.

nationally among elite Guatemalan intellectuals and statesmen. Q'eqchi' patriarchs, along with sympathetic ladino indigenistas (proindigenous reformers), lambasted mandamiento labor as an archaic form of slavery, advocated free wage labor, and loudly denounced the racial degeneration caused by exploitation at the hands of barbaric European and ladino coffee planters. Q'eqchi' patriarchs drew on the metanarrative charting the rise of modern democracy and capitalism against feudalism and slavery in order to wage a political contest that redrew the boundaries between slavery and freedom, coercion and consent. In the process, they also contested the civilizing metanarrative and the racialized notion that Mayas were uncivilized and belonged to another time.

If we read against the archival grain, however, Xucaneb's revenge also illustrates the efforts of Juan de la Cruz and some Q'eqchi's to force ladinos and foreign settlers to recognize another place in time – to situate themselves in the well-grooved histories of the Tzuultaq'as with their attendant cyclical and rhythmic notions of balance and mutual reciprocity. By examining the actions of Q'eqchi's, including their flight from labor obligations, alongside what we know of Q'eqchi' cosmology and what the archival record inadvertently tells us about Q'eqchi' beliefs about the causes of the frost, the astute reader can grasp how Xucaneb's frost released an insurgent Q'eqchi' ordering of space and time and unsettled the Liberal state's idea of modernity. Against fixed and legible renderings of the landscape and its people, Xucaneb's revenge incited Q'eqchi's to abandon their work contracts on coffee plantations and to seek refuge in the lowlands from the state and coffee planters. Against efforts to create a seamless linear narrative of history as progress and human agency inherent in Eurocentric worldviews, Tzuultaq'as evoked Q'eqchi' conceptions of time as cyclical and history as directed by inanimate moral and spiritual forces, other-than-human beings. Against efforts to fix racial boundaries and hierarchies between ladinos and Mayas, Xucaneb's revenge revealed that racial transgressions produced dangerous alliances between lower-class ladinos like Juan de la Cruz and rural, lower-class Q'eqchi's. The seemingly neutral word revolt, when used by ladino editorialists, thus provided less of a description of the events than an account of one side of a conflict about the meaning of modernity in nineteenth-century Alta Verapaz.

In this chapter, I will first examine how mandamiento labor helped generate the conditions that precipitated Xucaneb's revenge by imperiling Maya subsistence production and disrupting communal norms, and then trace the event's aftermath. In particular, I will highlight how new alliances between Q'eqchi' patriarchs and ladino indigenistas emerged to combat mandamiento labor as a relic of another time, and how those efforts were met by rhetoric that racialized Mayas as indolent and in need of coerced labor. In addition, land reforms designed to prevent land monopolization and provide subsistence plots for Mayas actually hastened the privatization of communal lands. This growing push to privatize land, however, can only be understood in the context of the rupture between Q'eqchi' patriarchs and commoners marked by Xucaneb, and thus was not simply a top-down capitalist reform imposed by the state. The events of Xucaneb also had effects that would last for decades to come. After 1886 the relationships between Maya patriarchs and Q'eqchi' commoners were never the same, and, as we will see in Chapter 4, state reforms that followed in the wake of Xucaneb and national debates helped consolidate a racial capitalism in Guatemala. The events themselves became etched into the popular memory and repeatedly resurfaced in moments of political turmoil for decades to come. Because the frost was seen to have been caused by supernatural forces, it also generated anxieties about the very meaning and possibilities of progress premised on humanity's heroic abilities to direct history. As Bliss Cua Lim has argued, the supernatural "discloses the limits of historical time, the frisson of secular historiography's encounter with temporalities emphatically at odds with and not fully miscible to itself."[8] While environmental historians have recognized how the environment, and especially natural disasters, can be agents of history, Xucaneb's frost also forces us disrupt our own secular understandings of historical causation with the enchanted worlds where nonhumans, including mountain spirits, were also agents of history.[9]

A WORLD OUT OF ORDER: THE ORIGINS AND MEANINGS OF XUCANEB'S REVENGE

Juan de la Cruz's pilgrimage was an ordinary one in many respects – it involved months of prayer, fasting, and sexual abstinence, as well as the collection of monetary and other contributions. The ceremony was unique in other ways. Tzuultaq'a Xucaneb appeared through the voices of Juan de la Cruz and his mother, Albina, during a mass held at the house

---

[8] Bliss Cua Lim, *Translating Time: Cinema, the Fantastic, and Temporal Critique* (Durham, NC: Duke University Press, 2009), 2.

[9] See, for example, Louis A. Pérez Jr., *Winds of Change: Hurricanes and the Transformation of Nineteenth-Century Cuba* (Chapel Hill: University of North Carolina Press, 2001).

of the Q'eqchi' mayordomo Secundario Maas. According to testimonies taken during Juan de la Cruz's trial, Xucaneb had not declared that he would "burn coffee" and "bring an end to private property" as the newspapers and rumors charged, but rather had promised to ensure a bountiful maize harvest.[10] After Xucaneb's unusual apparition, Juan de la Cruz and Q'eqchi' commoners from the towns of Santa Cruz, Cobán, and San Juan Chamelco collected small monetary contributions to pay for candles, incense, boj, and food for the cave ritual. While these events can be easily dismissed as the efforts of a shrewd ladino to swindle money from disaffected Q'eqchi's, the pilgrimage to Xucaneb was, for many Q'eqchi's, a logical response to a growing moral crisis in Q'eqchi' society. This calamity arose from intensifying mandamiento labor demands, privatizing communal land, and expanding coffee production. Together, these forces imperiled Maya autonomy and subsistence production, deepened nascent class divisions between Maya patriarchs and commoners, and allowed for new intermediaries such as Juan de la Cruz to emerge.

While Q'eqchi's had long been accustomed to providing their labor to the state and ethnic kin, Liberal institutionalization of mandamientos undermined Q'eqchi' conceptions of labor obligations as mutual reciprocity. Even under Conservatives, Maya-controlled town councils administered mandamientos and thus kept labor obligations in line with Maya reciprocity practices. After the 1871 Liberal revolution, the departmental governor of Alta Verapaz, Luis Molina, shifted the administration of mandamientos to ladino-controlled town councils in places like Cobán, or to agricultural commissions in indigenous-governed municipalities like San Pedro Carchá. These administrative changes to mandamientos were simple, yet profound. Under the Conservatives' restored republic, income generated from mandamientos was given to Maya town councils and entered the coffers of cofradías to spend on the religious festivals that ensured salvation. Under the new Liberal regime, however, income from mandamientos went to public works projects to support capitalist expansion and modernization. Moreover, Liberal-era mandamiento labor was guided not by the principles of reciprocal obligations but by racial discourses that defined Mayas as lazy and in need of forced labor.[11]

---

[10] Unless otherwise noted, this discussion draws on AGCA J-AV 103 Leg. 16 Exp. 9 1886; AGCA J-AV 103 Leg. 16 Exp. 20 1886; AGCA J-AV 103 Leg. 15 Exp. 29 1886.

[11] To see how cofradía income was generated from the mandamientos, see AGCA J-AV 103 Leg. 1 Exp. 18 1874.

As the role of regulating the exchange of mutual services between Q'eqchi' patriarchs and commoner households moved from the Q'eqchi'-governed town councils to ladino-controlled agricultural commissions, labor ceased to be an expression of mutual reciprocity governed by kin and community ties, and became more directly expressive of race and class hierarchies and the market demand for labor, and more vulnerable to sabotage or rebellion. Mandamiento labor in the post-Liberal period thus increasingly became, in the words of Karl Polanyi, disembedded from social relations, paving the way for the imposition of market relations under capitalism.[12] Q'eqchi' patriarchs' decisions to ally themselves with Liberals, promote communal land privatization, and use the language of slavery and freedom ultimately may have hastened this process.

As we have seen, mandamientos were advantageous for European and ladino coffee planters who largely needed part-time labor (Chapter 1) and threatened Q'eqchi' patriarchs' traditional control over labor (Chapter 2). For the Q'eqchi' lower classes, however, expanding mandamiento labor demands imperiled personal and communal self-sufficiency and autonomy. Long, hard days of work in dangerous conditions pressed in on health. The back-breaking labor of carrying coffee and other goods between the cold and temperate climates of central Alta Verapaz to the hot lowlands of the coast invited diseases.[13] Laboring day and night, Mayas transported heavy bags of coffee from Cobán and San Pedro Carchá to coastal ports. Maya porters frequently returned to their communities exhausted or ill and thus unable to participate fully in their own household subsistence and economic activities, as well as those of their neighbors. Women and children were not necessarily able to make up for a husband's or father's ill health, since they, too, were subject to mandamientos. In the coffee plantations, women and children picked coffee from sunrise to sunset during the crucial harvest season. They complained that plantation administrators did not give them time to

---

[12] Karl Polanyi, *The Great Transformation: The Political and Economic Origins of Our Time* (Boston: Beacon Press, 2001).

[13] There are numerous examples of requests for exemptions from other services due to health problems arising from mandamiento labor. Since the 1860s, state officials and Maya patriarchs complained of the health dangers of heavy transport into the hot lowlands. See, for example, AGCA JP-AV1873–74 P1, "Juez Municipal Carcha-Sub-JP," March 27, 1873; AGCA JP-AV 1885 P5, "Felipe Caal por exención de servicios municipales," August 18, 1885.

gather firewood to dry their clothing from the constant rains, so that many of them came down with colds and the flu.[14]

While indigenous food production subsidized coffee production (coffee planters could pay below-subsistence wages), mandamiento labor encroached on the household and communal labor that made self-sufficiency possible. For the required two to four months of labor every year, a laborer did not earn remuneration sufficient to maintain his or her household's basic needs and pay off taxes and thus needed to produce subsistence agricultural goods. The state's regulation of mandamiento labor provided a modest wage, along with food rations for the duration of the labor time. But from the moment a mandamiento laborer's service began, they contended with pressures to enter commercial transactions, which reduced their net pay. Rations usually consisted of dried tortilla meal, called *totoposte*, which lasted up to two weeks and was usually insufficient to maintain the laborers, and workers were swept up in labor raids so quickly they rarely had time to prepare adequate rations.[15] If rations were insufficient, Maya laborers needed to purchase the remainder from their temporary employer or in the market.[16] Nor were laborers able to ignore traditional religious obligations and other festivities, which had long required Mayas to enter into market transactions. Coffee planters, too, eager to save on wages, sold goods at inflated prices.[17] Under these circumstances, coffee plantation laborers were fortunate if their remuneration, after deductions, was sufficient to support themselves while laboring, let alone compensate for the labor time lost to the household economy. In effect, the work of coffee plantation laborers subsidized ladino and European coffee planters, who were thereby freed from having to pay a salary that could, by itself, sustain and reproduce the labor power of their workforce.

Coffee planters also kept laborers on the plantation for longer than the time specified in the order, thus diminishing workers' pay and pulling them away from their communities for longer periods of time. Mandamiento regulations provided that Mayas were required to work for a set number of days, but coffee planters frequently used tasks (*tareas*) rather than a set number of hours or days to measure the fulfillment of labor requirements. Coffee laborers were given certain tasks such as picking a determined amount of coffee or clearing a specific area of the groves.[18]

---

[14] AGCA JP-AV 1880, "Cahabón-Comisonado Político de Senaju," December 20, 1880.
[15] AGCA B 119.21.0. Leg. 47743 Exp. 179.   [16] McCreery, *Rural Guatemala*, 268.
[17] Ibid.   [18] Ibid., 267.

Each task was supposed to be equivalent to one day's work, but more often than not these tasks took far longer to complete. Mayas thus constantly complained that the tasks assigned to them were far more than they could complete in even a couple of days.[19] The Q'eqchi's on one of William E. Dieseldorff's plantations summed up the dilemma: "Before we finish a week with one owner, another forces money on us, and because the tasks are so large or because there is not enough coffee, we often cannot complete a task in a day and fall behind, keeping us from getting to our plantings, which we have not yet been able to prepare."[20] By relating wages to tasks instead of labor time, coffee planters sought to extract more work from laborers and increase plantation productivity.

Mandamiento labor also undermined Q'eqchi' reciprocal labor obligations. As long as rural Q'eqchi's were tied to a mandamiento, they could not apply their labors to their own fields or to the exchange of reciprocal labors that normally earned them the assistance of other households. Since mandamiento laborers belonged to the poorer segments of Maya society, they also enjoyed a smaller, less-effective network of kin ties that could be mobilized for the care of fields and animals during their absence. Crisanto Saquil complained on behalf of his entire village in 1886 of being "violently separated from their families" in order to work on a plantation.[21] A returning mandamiento laborer frequently encountered deteriorating or unworked fields and an eroding network of relatives to call on for reciprocal labor assistance. More than representing a discrete amount of labor time lost to the household economy during the year, such mandamientos brought with them the corrosion of relationships that the families could not survive without. This crisis, which affected most Maya communities, was particularly acute in regions where traditional communal lands used for planting maize and gathering wood were becoming coffee plantations. The erosion of traditional forms of labor exchange was accompanied by a growing shortage of productive lands. For this reason, Mayas frequently petitioned the departmental governor for exemption from mandamientos so they could tend their own fields.[22] Q'eqchi' patriarchs requested exemptions from obligatory

---

[19] Ibid.   [20] AGCA JP-AV 1885 Paq. 2, "Varios Pueblos Indigenas – JP," April 12, 1885.

[21] AGCA JP-AV 1886 Paq. 3, "Crisanto Saquil al JP," February 9, 1886.

[22] See, for example, AGCA JP-AV 1885 Paq. 3, "José Pop y Domingo Caal al JP," May 26, 1885.

labor services to the city on behalf of their barrios due to mandamiento labor demands.[23]

Q'eqchi' patriarchs, aware of the pressures that mandamientos exerted on Maya communities, had attempted to mitigate these effects by keeping more laborers at home. Efforts to create Q'eqchi'-owned coffee plantations are indicative of the Q'eqchi' patriarchs' desire for both the wealth and prestige offered by coffee production and the security that mandamiento labor exemptions offered Maya communities. Yet, as we have seen, with skyrocketing coffee prices and growing demands for laborers, ladino state officials were unwilling to recognize Q'eqchi' patriarchs' efforts to translate communally owned properties into coffee plantations. Even within town councils, the mechanisms that Q'eqchi' patriarchs used to negotiate mandamiento demands – such as failing to fill planters' requests for laborers and seeking workers in other jurisdictions – had also been undermined by the switch to ladino-controlled labor-acquisition models. Q'eqchi' patriarchs, in other words, were coming up short on their set of obligations to provide protection to Q'eqchi' commoners. As a result of all these factors, Q'eqchi's began to understand mandamiento labor not as simply a political difficulty to be addressed via the courts but as a moral transgression – as a world out of order.

Q'eqchi's understood moral problems within both Christianity and Maya cosmography. As we have seen, the latter was particularly important in relationship to Maya notions of reciprocity, obligation, and resource allocation and use. The Tzuultaq'as regulate the use of resources and other objects within their territories according to a series of prohibitions, moral values, and norms (*awas*).[24] Because the Tzuultaq'as own animals, for example, a hunter must first ask permission from a Tzuultaq'a to hunt, or else face the wrath of the mountain spirit. Awas are also central to Q'eqchi' justice. As one anthropologist has argued, Q'eqchi's rarely partake in acts of revenge; rather, they allow nature to enact justice. Esteban Haeserijn has suggested that "the awas are in charge of putting everything in order. To get rid of the awas would be equivalent to starting a revolution."[25] Indeed, Tzuultaq'as were potent and volatile forces. They could be generous and ensure

[23] AGCA JP-AV 1885 Paq. 4, "Barrios de Cobán al JP," August 8, 1886.

[24] On corn planting, wealth accumulation, and Maya spirituality, see Wilson, *Maya Resurgence in Guatemala*, 77–8.

[25] Esteban Haeserijn, "Filosofía popular de los k'ekchi' de hoy," mimeographed article (Guatemala, 1973), p. 5, cited in Carlos Rafael J. Cabarrús, *La cosmovisión K'ekchi' en proceso de cambio* (San Salvador: Universidad Centroamericana, 1979), 23.

bountiful harvests, but they could also be demanding and vindictive when crossed. When, only a short three months after the rituals in Xucaneb, a serious frost destroyed the region's coffee trees and other crops, many believed the awas were setting the world straight. Given the spiteful character of Tzuultaq'as and their power to deliver or deny bountiful harvests, it is understandable that Q'eqchi's would interpret the frost that destroyed their crops as a moral crisis.

The Xucaneb events at once expressed and deepened a growing class division between Q'eqchi' commoners and patriarchs. As we have seen, Q'eqchi' society in the 1860s and 1870s witnessed a crisis as commoners and patriarchs alike adapted to a growing settler population, the encroachment of increasingly punitive land and labor laws, and the expansion of coffee production. Q'eqchi' commoners' sense that patriarchs were no longer able or willing to represent their interests led to a search for new intermediaries – first in the elderly Q'eqchi' Jorge Yat and then in the ladino artisan Juan de la Cruz. Q'eqchi' patriarchs thus likely viewed Juan de la Cruz's pilgrimage to Xucaneb as a threat to their roles as guardians of Maya spiritual life, much as they had understood Yat's pretensions to be alcalde as a threat to the social order of Maya society. Thus, when the frost struck the region, it also struck fear in the hearts of Q'eqchi' patriarchs such as Tiburcio Caal, who called the authorities to arrest Juan de la Cruz and Q'eqchi's who had participated in the pilgrimage.[26] For those Q'eqchi' patriarchs, these events and the subsequent flight of laborers likely deepened their anxieties about their place in a new era of Liberal progress.

For other Mayas, Xucaneb's revenge validated their fears about the expansion of coffee production and exacerbated the erosion of the subsistence economy. The frost damaged not only coffee plants, but also subsistence and other commercial crops central to Maya household production. In the wake of Xucaneb's frost, 175 Q'eqchi's, headed by the municipal regidores Eugenio Caal Pop and Felix Cú, wrote to the president requesting exemptions from mandamientos and an end to the abuses of town councilmen. They pleaded to the president, "Notorious are the causes that motivated the ruin of the coffee plantations, the estates of the rich of Cobán, as well as the loss of the crops our poor Indians sowed with the frosts of January this year. The frost has left us in a terrible situation, and as a consequence, in a state of utter poverty, lacking

---

[26] Wilson, *Maya Resurgence in Guatemala*, 15–26.

the basic necessities to sustain ourselves and our children."[27] Many Q'eqchi's' flight to the lowlands further undermined the subsistence production of those who remained in Alta Verapaz's central valley.

The desire to flee mandamientos during the coffee boom of the early 1880s was also very understandable as the balance between consent and coercion tipped heavily toward coercion. Local authorities drafted anyone they could find: "When I was twelve the official and a number of policemen arrived at my house, forced my mother to accept 60 reales, and stuck my name in his black book, and I was sentenced."[28] Resisters were jailed. One Sanpedrano recalled, "When a poor man would arrive home [from a mandamiento], he received the awful news from his wife that the officials had left another sixty reales with orders to work again, perhaps this time an even less hospitable area."[29] Once drafted, Q'eqchi's had few opportunities to escape, and if they did they were furiously pursued.

For many Maya laborers, the frost inspired faith that an imminent historical rupture would usher in a new moral order or restore an older one. The belief that this upheaval would re-create their world – purify it of past disparities and ailments – also corresponded to a cyclical view of history. In a moment of crisis, Xucaneb's revenge spoke to Mayas yearning for change and expressed uneasy truths about the changes within Maya society. By the early 1880s, Maya commoners' actions expressed alarm that Q'eqchi' patriarchs were undermining norms of reciprocity and imperiling subsistence production, and therefore were no longer capable of defending their interests. Xucaneb's revenge must have offered hope to many Mayas that they could transcend the present and usher in a new era in which the social and spiritual order would be restored.

Through the aftermath of Xucaneb, Juan de la Cruz and his Maya followers also made ladinos recognize another time and place governed not by the principles of capitalism and progress but by cyclical time, the agency of days, and norms of reciprocity. Revolutionary millenarianism is defined by desires to inaugurate a profound transformation, one initiated by supernatural forces. Once unleashed, these other-than-human powers destroy an existing social order and quickly bring into being a new and

---

[27] AGCA B Leg. 28735 Exp. 266 1886. For a response from the press, see "La Junta de Fomento de la Alta Verapaz," *El Demócrata*, Cobán, July 18, 1886.

[28] AGCA JP-AV 1875, "Indígenas de Carchá – JP," March 6, 1875.

[29] AGCA JP-AV 1880 Paq. 2, "Cofradías de Carchá al JP," n.d. 1880.

more perfect world.[30] Historians have often understood millenarian movements as arising in a moment of crisis among disaffected social groups for whom a direct political or military assault is impossible.[31] These moral crises are also often experienced as a profound divergence between competing ontologies. In Alta Verapaz, the erosion of Maya autonomy and subsistence production stood alongside the continuing allure of coffee expansion and progress and the desire to be included in the present and recognized as citizens. The spiritual crisis of Xucaneb was provoked not only by the burden of mandamiento labor and political disaffection but by the clash between these two different ways of being in the world.

The events of Xucaneb meant that Q'eqchi' patriarchs, in their role as intermediaries, needed to address the growing chasm between patriarchs and commoners as well as mitigate the fears and reprisals unleashed by state officials and coffee planters against recalcitrant laborers. To do so, some Q'eqchi' patriarchs turned to alliances with ladino indigenistas, many of whom had roots in the Conservative Party, to advocate for the end of mandamiento labor. For Q'eqchi' patriarchs and their ladino allies, the resolution to this moral crisis required not a millenarian revolution, but free wage labor and an end to indigenous exploitation.

XUCANEB'S AFTERMATH, THE PROBLEM OF SLAVERY, AND THE RACIALIZATION OF LABOR

The departmental governor, José Villacorta, responded to the flood of petitions for mandamiento exemptions that swamped his office, the looming subsistence crisis, and the widespread flight of laborers by granting temporary exemptions, including the four months requested by Q'eqchi's from Cobán to plant maize.[32] Many of these exemptions, however, were never put into practice by local officials, who continued to pursue Mayas for labor. As a result, when the coffee harvest was about to get under way in October 1886, and the pursuit of laborers came into

[30] This perspective, however, assumes that once democratic processes are in place that allow for the expression of dissatisfaction, millenarian movements would disappear.

[31] See, for example, Stern, *Peru's Indian Peoples*, especially chapter 3. As Jean and John Comaroff have argued, such rituals and practices did not necessarily represent the opposite of modernity but rather were rituals central to modernity's foundations. See Jean Comaroff and John Comaroff, eds., *Modernity and Its Malcontents: Ritual and Power in Postcolonial Africa* (Chicago: University of Chicago Press, 1993).

[32] For a complaint regarding this failure, see AGCA MG B Leg. 28755 Exp. 2742 1887.

full swing, the "Prophet of Xucaneb," as Juan de la Cruz had infamously been titled, was again rumored to be stirring the waters of discontent. One newspaper accused him of seeking "the redemption of the Indians" through his propaganda. Juan de la Cruz supposedly claimed all lands taken from Mayas would be returned.[33] Cobán's upper classes also received word of Juan de la Cruz's purported new conspiracies, and rumors spread of plots to set fire to the houses of foreigners and plans to assassinate ladinos.[34] While it is difficult to know the nature of Juan de la Cruz's political intentions, these rumors themselves are a form of cultural knowledge that not only reveals but also creates a certain reality. As Ann Laura Stoler has argued, such rumors "shape what people thought they knew, blurring the lines between events witnessed and those envisioned, between performed brutality and the potentiality for it."[35] As such, fact was indistinguishable from fiction, and fictions easily shaped emerging facts. In the messy aftermath of Xucaneb's revenge, ladino, German, and Q'eqchi' elites debated a series of reforms that evinced anxiety about the urban racial boundary-crossers like Juan de la Cruz. In the process, they redrew the lines between slavery and freedom, coercion and consent, and sought to reform urban space.

In the face of an "indigenous conspiracy against the ladinos and foreigners of the department," an emergency meeting of the departmental advisory board was called to deal with the matter. The members included Cobán's most upstanding citizens: William E. Dieseldorff, Pablo Sierra, and Mariano Rivera Paz. This coalition of local elites agreed that a civil guard must be formed immediately with the purpose of surveillance. Dieseldorff, echoing the voices of many others, argued that "the instigators of this rebellion are also the tinterillos ... [against whom] it is necessary to apply all the rigor of the law to ensure peace in the region and to benefit the same *indios* whose naiveté they abuse with whatever pretext, only to take their valiant savings from their dedication to agricultural work."[36] But far from simply safeguarding the city, the civil guard raided Q'eqchi' patriarchs' homes, confiscated their hunting weapons, and marched some of them off to jail.

---

[33] "Mesa revuelta," *El Demócrata*, Cobán, October 31, 1886, 3.

[34] AGCA B Leg. 28735 Exp. 2692 1886.

[35] Ann Laura Stoler, "'In Cold Blood': Hieararchies of Credibility and the Politics of Colonial Narratives," *Representations* 37, Special Issue: Imperial Fantasies and Postcolonial Histories (1992): 154.

[36] "Sesión extraordinaria del Consejo Consultivo del Departamento," *El Demócrata*, Cobán, November 7, 1886, 2.

In early July, the departmental governor militarized forced wage labor recruitment, dispatching armed soldiers to round up workers and limiting constitutional guarantees, such as habeas corpus.[37] Alarmed by the prospect of disgruntled Q'eqchi's stirring up racial trouble, local authorities in Cobán moved quickly to reconsider how they administered mandamientos by opening a formal inquiry into the possible abolition of the ladino-controlled agricultural commission and the return to the Conservative-era system of Maya-administered mandamiento labor. While some Q'eqchi' and ladino officials recognized the need to restore Q'eqchi' norms of labor reciprocity by reforming the administration of mandamientos, others boldly declared that the problem resided not with Mayas but with the slavery of mandamientos.[38] The use of the term "slavery" by Q'eqchi' patriarchs and ladino indigenistas here was not just a metaphor that created a sort of universal comparison for disparate injustices. Rather, it expressed their deep concerns about the coercive nature of mandamientos and signaled an awareness of political struggles to end chattel slavery across the continent. In 1886, the year of Xucaneb's revenge, Spain abolished slavery in Cuba and two years later Brazil abolished slavery, signaling the legal death of the institution across the hemisphere.

Among the most vocal opponents of mandamiento labor was Fidel Ponce, a well-respected lawyer from one of the region's wealthiest ladino families. Commissioned to write a report on mandamientos by Cobán's town council, Ponce expressed his unequivocal disdain for the "archaic institution." Mandamientos, he declared, not only violated the individual rights guaranteed to Mayas by the constitution, but were redundant, because "voluntarily, these same Indians in general look for work where they receive good treatment and punctual payment." Advocating free wage labor, Ponce noted that the "time of slavery" had now passed in "the civilized nations of the world."[39] By creating an equivalence between the chattel slavery of Africans and the mandamientos of Mayas, Ponce inserted Alta Verapaz into a global historical

---

[37] "Mesa revuelta," *Demócrata*, October 31, 1886; "Sesión extraordinaria del consejo consultivo del departamento," *El Demócrata*, November 7, 1886; "Habeas corpus," *El Demócrata*, November 25, 1886; and for attempts to regulate saint worship, AGCA B Leg. 28735, Exp. 2691, "Algunos indios de Cobán solicitan que se les nombre autoridades que los protejan y les hagan justicia imparcialmente," December 18, 1886.

[38] The following discussion is drawn from AGCA B Leg. 28735 Exp. 264, "Supresión de la comisión de agricultura," October 8, 1886.

[39] Ibid.

metanarrative charting the end of slavery and feudalism and the rise of capitalism and democracy.

Where Ponce and his allies rendered mandamientos a relic of the past, the proponents of mandamiento labor responded by racializing Mayas as antimodern holdovers. Víctor Sierra, a ladino town councilman, responded to Ponce's report with rage, noting the failure of the labor supply to meet demand. In the aftermath of the frost and the lost coffee harvest, Sierra reasoned, the region should logically have an excess supply of laborers, but planters faced a larger labor shortage than in previous years. Here, Sierra declared, was proof of Maya backwardness.[40] Rather than laboring for the progress of the nation, Mayas, he asserted, "attend to the necessities of their family, dividing their precious time between the hammock, tobacco, some hunting and fishing and the juice of the three or four sugar cane plants that they possess like one of their boorish ancestors." Even more, Sierra questioned whether Mayas would ever be fit for the constitutional guarantees Ponce wanted to attribute to them. "The majority of our Indians, who understand nothing of Spanish, and to say it only once, are totally lacking in everything other than the machete and the *mecapal* [tumpline].... To them, should true liberty be applied?" Sierra asked. Invoking the recent memory of Xucaneb, Sierra averred that, "gifted with the fatal idea of equality, the Indians, blindly determined by their stagnation and vagrancy, ... will agitate against progress ... until they become revolutionary; because this voice is the voice of ignorance, of regression, of fanaticism itself." For Sierra, true citizens were modernizing agents of capitalism, and this necessarily ruled out Mayas, whose barbaric, historically stagnated condition rendered them an outright threat to the nation's progress.

The actions of some Q'eqchi's – flight, labor evasion, and demands for subsistence production – in the aftermath of the events at Xucaneb were understood by many elites as proof that Q'eqchi's lacked the proper desires of the "economic man" – desires for material wealth, self-improvement, and economic well-being. The logic ran as follows: Mayas refused to work on the coffee plantations as needed for the meager wages coffee planters were willing to pay. Therefore, Mayas will not work on the coffee plantations. Therefore, Mayas will not work. Insolence was rendered as indolence, and Mayas were racialized as lazy. It was not

[40] Sierra may also have exaggerated losses due to the frost. According to available statistics, there was only a 10 percent decline in coffee production for the year 1885–6; *Informe de la Dirección General de Estadística* 1885 and 1886.

enough to simply increase wages, argued local officials, because "our Indians do not demand an increase in wages, what they want is to be left alone and to be free."[41]

Many regional and national elites believed that the Mayas' lack of desire to work arose from their limited needs and aspirations, and the ease by which they could satisfy those elementary desires. According to these elites, the abundant and fertile Guatemalan landscape required little effort to produce the basic necessities for primitive Mayan life. As a result, the reasoning went, Mayas had failed to follow the path of modern European nations in the development of habits of vigorous work and aspirations for ever-increasing material wealth. One intellectual observed that "the Indian vegetates in poverty and loathes work."[42] From Mayas' repugnance for work grew labor shortages that hampered ambitious coffee planters' plans for the expansion of coffee and other export crops. What Guatemala lacked was not inhabitants, but hard-working citizens who would work for wages. Since elites tended to believe economic incentives were lost on Mayas, state officials championed forms of coercion and indoctrination to forge a labor force through mandamientos.[43]

Q'eqchi' patriarchs were well aware that mandamientos were justified by Mayas' purported opposition to modernity and the market, and thus attacked precisely these arguments. While ladinos and Q'eqchi's debated mandamientos in Cobán's town council, Mateo Chub, an illiterate first alcalde of neighboring San Pedro Carchá, mobilized the support of the town's Q'eqchi' patriarchs to petition for the abolition of mandamientos. "Capable of entering and leaving contracts on our own will," Chub argued, with the help of a tinterrillo, in a petition to the president, "we should be permitted to adjust the price of our work, a price which should not depend on the customs nor will of the governor but on the abundance or lack of workers [*brazos*] and the personal labors that we have or would

---

[41] "Cuestión de mozos," *El Demócrata*, January 27, 1889.

[42] This perspective has been attributed to the Colombian Mariano Ospina, who was a diplomat in Guatemala for a time. The same general attitude can be found in various editorials, reports, and farmer complaints. See also Batres Jáuregui, *Los indios*, 158–9.

[43] During the Bourbon era, as Ricardo Salvatore has demonstrated, colonial officials viewed forced consumption as a means to integrate Indians into the economy, while in the early independence period officials privileged the role of government as a civilizing force over the economy. By the late nineteenth century in Guatemala, however, the civilizing force of the market reemerged in full swing. See Ricardo Salvatore, "The Normalization of Economic Life: Representations of the Economy in Golden-Age Buenos Aires, 1890–1913," *Hispanic American Historical Review* 81, no. 1 (2001): 2–42.

have to abandon."[44] As did Conservatives in the Economic Society two decades earlier, Chub demanded the end of mandamientos not because they violated Maya rights but because Q'eqchi's possessed economic reason and forced labor contravened the natural economy of supply and demand.

Unfortunately for Chub, the departmental governor, José Villacorta, who was sympathetic to Maya concerns, was forced to resign under pressure from the regional coffee elite.[45] José Villacorta determined to ensure the smooth running of the 1887 coffee harvest and dismissed Mateo Chub's petition, explaining to the president, "The Indian, by nature, is refractory of all progress and since he is not surrounded by needs, would like to give himself over to absolute idleness."[46] He then removed Chub from office and accused him of holding clandestine meetings, telling rural Q'eqchi's that they did not have to work, and, perhaps worst of all – aiding Juan de la Cruz's conspiracies that had led to the pilgrimage to Xucaneb. The German coffee planter Hans von Turkheim brilliantly encapsulated the consensus among the region's coffee-planting ladinos and European settlers, when he wrote later that year: "The time has not yet come for making free men of the Indians, first they need to be instructed how to work." According to von Turkheim, what Mayas needed was "the civilizing force of time rather than the temporary persuasion of reason."[47] That von Turkheim and others who advocated for mandamiento labor relied on the notion of the historical immaturity of Mayas illustrates how historical time was used by elites to say "not yet" to those who desired self-governance and free wage labor.

Coffee planters also reasoned that mandamiento labor was also a civilizing force that improved the race, since it forced Mayas into greater contact with civilized planters. "In the Verapaz," argued one ladino, "demanding orderly work of *el indio* is the surest method of obtaining his civilization."[48] Coffee planters argued that through "good management" on their plantations, Mayas could be civilized. Eduardo Felice, who had been called the "most abusive person in the department [of Alta Verapaz]," claimed that disciplined labor on his plantation furthered national goals because, he said, "I make them work, I always pay them

---

[44] AGCA J-AV Leg. 17 Exp. 35, "Contra Mateo Chub por calumnia," 1887.
[45] "Marchemos," *El Demócrata*, January 12, 1887.   [46] Ibid.
[47] Juan Türkheim to von Bismark, June 1, 1889, cited in Cambranes, *Coffee and Peasants*, 203–4.
[48] "La cuestión de mozos," *El Demócrata*, April 3, 1887, p. 1.

and even more than what they earn in wages, I give them ideas of civilization."[49] Forced labor in public works, planters believed, was also a way to discipline lazy laborers. As Herman Hesse noted in a letter to the alcalde of San Pedro Carchá, "As you have more means, I would like you to summon for your upcoming trip [to Panzós] two lazy *mozos* [resident laborers], Juan Si from Muyha and Juan Caal from Bancab, whom with pleasure we would provide to punish them."[50] According to these arguments, combining social engineering with economic liberalism, forced labor would – *over time* – lead to racial regeneration.

The events of Xucaneb also unleashed racial anxieties as individuals like Juan de la Cruz, who were urban artisans and small merchants, troubled the racial hierarchies on which mandamiento labor, and an emergent racial capitalism, relied. In the immediate aftermath of Xucaneb, Cobaneros complained about "suspicious Indians hanging around the corners day and night" and the "Indians and ladinos who were completely taken over by drunkenness and other vices." Crime and prostitution, according to many, were on the rise. Indians were dirty and, besides selling themselves in the street, did not go to a doctor when they got sick, but let "nature take its course." Juan de la Cruz himself embodied many of these racial anxieties about urban space. We know from court records that he was a ladino tailor who had migrated to Cobán from Salamá. Given the history of African slavery near Salamá, and his distinct religious understandings of mountain deities, de la Cruz may have been a ladino of Afro-descendant origins. Upper-class, racially whitened ladinos feared these new lower classes, whose unclear racial heritage and poverty disrupted racialized class boundaries between wealthy ladino and German coffee planters and poor Maya laborers, and fostered anxieties about the political fallout of these unsavory characters. Within a decade, ladinos in Cobán, with the aid of charitable societies, began a series of urban reforms to address these anxieties. In 1887 a new market was completed. A makeshift hospital was opened in 1889 from funds generated by charitable donations. A few years later, elite Cobaneros founded the Welfare Society. A police force was established in 1890, and in 1893 it was expanded to include a special section

---

[49] AGCA JP-AV 1884 Paq. 4, "Eduardo Felice al JP," Cobán, September 24, 1884; AGCA B 99-7-34 Leg. 13083, "Carta al Sr. Ministro de Relaciones Exteriores del JP de Alta Verapaz," January 22, 1890.

[50] SPCM 1896, "Alcalde 1° de Herman Hesse," n.d.

dedicated to policing children who did not attend school.[51] While these nascent urban reforms might have assuaged ladino elites' racial fears, state officials recognized that their efforts were useless without rural reforms that would stem the tide of rural Q'eqchi's migrating to the cities. Beginning in 1889, the departmental governor, in collaboration with the president, thus undertook special land reforms designed to protect indigenous smallholders and promote land privatization.

For rural Mayas, the failure to end mandamientos was perhaps an indication of the failure of Xucaneb's revenge. In the context of growing disillusionment and moral crisis, some Q'eqchi's continued to find hope in the promise of spiritual reform, and followed Juan de la Cruz's stepfather, Lazaro Medina, to the neighboring department of El Quiché.[52] For the following seven years, Medina baptized Maya children, administered mass, and promised salvation. Claiming to have direct contact with God, he sought contributions from Sanpedranos living in Carchá to ensure abundant crops and prevent illness. Those Mayas unwilling or unable to leave their community and kin often sought refuge as resident laborers in the fincas de mozos of coffee plantation owners known for their decent treatment of laborers or sought to secure their own parcel of private property.[53] The limits of the pilgrimage to Xucaneb to provoke change underscored the impasse of radical disillusionment, political weakness, and moral uncertainty in which Maya commoners found themselves imprisoned in the 1880s. Ladinos and European settlers,

---

[51] See "El mercado," *El Demócrata*, Cobán, July 4, 1886; "El mercado es un foco de corrupción," *El Demócrata*, November 21, 1886; "A la policía," *El Demócrata*, March 27, 1887; "Policía," *El Demócrata*, January 30, 1887; "Policía," *El Demócrata*, May 1, 1887; "Sociedad de caridad i beneficencia," *El Demócrata*, September 26, 1886; "A la policía," *El Demócrata*, March 27, 1887. On the marketplace, see also CM Est. 4 Paq. 13 Actos de la Municipalidad 1887, "A grandes males, grandes remedios," *El Porvenir*, December 8, 1889; "Mejoras necesarias," *El Porvenir*, November 2 and December 14, 1890. For the creation of the hospital, see AGCA MG B Leg. 28734 Exp. 2573 1886; AGCA MG B Leg. 28741 Exp. 249 1887; AGCA MG B Leg. 8754 Exp. 2725 1887; AGCA MG B Leg. 28777 Exp. 1889; AGCA MG B Leg. 28766 Exp. 1906 1888; AGCA MG B Leg. 28769 Exp. 134 1889; "El Hospital," *El Porvenir*, February 3, 1889. For the police force, see AGCA MG B Leg. 28789 Exp. 1125 1890; CM Est. 3 Paq. 1 1891, Partes del Director de la Policía. For the school police, see "República de la policía escolar en Cobán," *El Guatemalteco*, September 7, 1893. In 1895, the Municipality of Cobán also began the practice of nominating alcaldes auxiliares for each barrio and canton in the city. See AGCA MG B Leg. 28896 Exp. 1083.

[52] AGCA J-AV 103 Leg. 27 B Exp. 25 1893.

[53] This phenomenon is mentioned frequently in planter complaints as well as in reports of the departmental governor. See also "Emigración de indígenas," *El Porvenir*, February 10, 1889, 1–2.

however, continued to narrate the events at Xucaneb as a Maya revolt against labor and modernization, thereby privileging the civilizing meta-narratives over liberal–democratic ones. In the following years, cave worship and Maya rituals invoked the specter of Juan de la Cruz's exploits and the danger of Maya "ignorance and fanaticism."[54]

MAYA COMMONERS AND LAND PRIVATIZATION

As the coffee harvests returned to normal levels and demands for labor reached startling new heights for the 1887 harvest, Alta Verapaz's departmental governor decided to solve the labor shortages by annexing parts of the neighboring department of Izabal, where Q'eqchi' communities fleeing mandamientos had taken root over the previous two decades. The departmental governor justified the annexation by arguing that not only were the inhabitants of these new settlements natives of Alta Verapaz, but they would be best governed by authorities from their home pueblo of Carchá. Immoral, diseased, and lawless, the inhabitants required the guiding force of Alta Verapaz's authorities. Altaverapacence state officials, the departmental governor promised, would administer justice, ensure peace and order, and above all else civilize the migrants by requiring them to work. By November the migrant villages in Izabel were annexed to the department of Alta Verapaz, reinforcing the racialized distinctions between highlands and lowlands, expanding the territorial reach of Alta Verapaz's authority, and creating a new reserve of mandamiento laborers.[55] As Nancy Appelbaum has illustrated, in Colombia the territorial boundaries demarcating departments were the product not of natural landscapes but of historical conflicts and racialized representations of people and places.[56]

State efforts to secure a labor force by widening Alta Verapaz's political jurisdiction failed, however, to address the labor problem and the

---

[54] "Consecuencias de la ignorancia y el fanatismo," *El Demócrata*, April 25, 1889.

[55] "Segrega tres aldeas del depto. de Izabal y las anexa al de la Alta Verapaz: 2 noviembre 1887," in *Recopilación de leyes de Guatemala*, vol. 6, (Guatemala: Tipografía La Unión, 1889), 322. For migrations to the new communities, see AGCA B Leg. 285777 1859; AGCA B Leg. 26611 1867; AGCA B Leg. 28612 1867. For the border war, see AGCA B Leg. 28749 Exp. 1872, Exp. 2263, Exp. 2351; AGCA B Leg. 28750 Exp. 2263 1887; AGCA Leg. 28750 Exp. 2351 1887; AGCA B Leg. 28750 Exp. 2710 1887; AGCA B Leg. 28743 Exp. 638 1887; AGCA B Leg. 28754 Exp. 210 1887; AGCA B Leg. 28811 Exp. 2041 1891; AGCA B Leg. 28811 Exp. 2045 1891.

[56] Nancy P. Appelbaum, *Muddied Waters: Race, Region, and Local History in Colombia, 1846–1948* (Durham: Duke University Press, 2003).

specter of Xucaneb. In April 1889, for example, rumors spread that Sanpedranos were meeting in a variety of caves to worship the gods of the mountain and the valley to address grain shortages and the upcoming planting of milpa.[57] This time, rumors spread that the rebellious pilgrims planned to destroy coffee plantations and "to do away with the coffee planters themselves."[58] In referring to these speculations, one columnist noted, "There is a certain repugnance on the part of the indigenous for agricultural work and we have seen cases in which they openly demonstrate hostility toward their *patrones*."[59] As anxieties about food shortages grew, the departmental governor, as well as coffee planters, acknowledged that reforms were needed to protect Maya subsistence production as one of the bedrocks of the region, while continuing to promote the expansion of coffee production.

A short eight months after the grain shortage and rumors of a new uprising, the departmental governor negotiated a new plan with the support of the national assembly and President José María Reina Barrios to address the region's labor and subsistence problems. The government issued a special decree for Alta Verapaz aimed at protecting indigenous smallholders. "The interests of the nation do not coincide with the monopolization of the nation's lands by a few," the new decree began. From an indigenista position, the law ordered that each municipality name a commission to measure 200 cuerdas and 25 varas for each Maya who worked land in communal properties, whether those were ethnic clan lands or ejidos.[60] In essence, the law protected Maya smallholders by privatizing communal properties. Town councils may have silently objected to the new decree, as the mandated municipal commissions are notably absent from the remaining archival record and do not seem to have been created at all. Rural Maya villagers, however, may have perceived the decree differently from the Q'eqchi' patriarchs and ladino town councilmen. Maya commoners petitioned for individual land titles under the decree.[61] Since no boundaries had been officially established within communal lands, Maya commoners' petitions generated conflict and competition among villagers over access to land. These conflicts were especially sharp in places where a Q'eqchi' patriarch already claimed sole

---

[57] "Consecuencias de la ignorancia y el fanatismo," *El Demócrata*, April 25, 1889.
[58] Ibid.   [59] Ibid.
[60] Acuerdo Gubernativo de 3 de diciembre de 1889. Titulación de algunas tierras a favor de indígenas de Alta Verapaz. Jorge Skinner-Klée, *Legislación indigenista de Guatemala* (México: Instituto Indigenista Interamericano, 1954), 44.
[61] See, especially, AGCA JP-AV 1890 Paq. 1.

ownership of the communal property as their private plantation.[62] The
implementation of the decree privatizing communal lands was thus driven
by disgruntled or fearful Maya commoners rather than by state imposition from above.

Conflicts between Maya commoners and patriarchs over land
privatization reveal that rural Maya commoners felt compelled to take
up Alta Verapaz's special decree as a response to the gradual erosion of
communal bonds and labor exchanges, as well as the growing distrust
between some Q'eqchi' patriarchs and rural lower classes. Faced with
uncertainties, some rural Q'eqchi's saw more security in holding private
title to a small piece of land than in being collective owners of a larger
communal property or, even worse, residents on a property owned by a
Q'eqchi' patriarch. As sole owners, these Q'eqchi' patriarchs had the legal
right to sell what had been commonly owned land, even though all the
members of the community contributed to the costs of surveying. These
dangers were real. In 1890 José Ax, patriarch of the village Chimelb, sold
the communal lands titled in his name to the Sierra Prado family, much to
the dismay of the residents.[63] The Q'eqchi's of Chimelb spent the
following thirty years battling the legality of the sale, new land tenure
boundaries, and the relentless efforts by Felipa Sierra de Prado to turn
them into resident laborers of her expanding coffee plantation.[64] News of
José Ax's sale of Chimelb and other similar instances likely made an
impression on Q'eqchi' commoners, who grew skeptical of the village
patriarchs' coffee plantations. In 1896 the residents of Rubejlchaj and
Chanjuc discovered that the Q'eqchi' patriarch of their clan, Santiago
Tiul, had titled their communal property in his name five years earlier.
Angered by Santiago Tiul's personal appropriation of their communal
rights, the residents demanded that "the land be divided among us in
portions proportional to the money each of us contributed [for mapping
and titling]."[65] Q'eqchi' commoners rightly feared that patriarchs were
claiming entire communal properties as their personal plantations.

---

[62] AGCA JP-AV "Carta al JP de José Chub," Carchá, January 26, 1891.

[63] See AGCA J-AV 103 Leg. 25 C Exp. 14 1892; AGCA J-AV 103 Leg. 26 Exp. 18 1892;
    AGCA J-AV Leg. 27 Exp. 11 1893; AGCA J-AV Leg. 17 Exp. 35 1887; AGCA J-AV 103
    Leg. 46 Exp. 9; AGCA B Leg. 28835 Exp. 3457 1892. For other examples, see AGCA J-
    AV 104 Leg. 21 A Exp. 9.

[64] AGCA MG B Leg. 28815 Exp. 2571 1891; AGCA MG B Leg. 28813 Exp. 2299
    "A" 1891.

[65] AGCA ST-AV Paq. 60 Exp. 8 1900, "Santiago Tiul y compañeros, Rubelchaj Chanyuc en
    Carchá."

Q'eqchi's thus took action, including using the 1889 decree, to protect their rights from wayward Q'eqchi' patriarchs who might appropriate communal ownership and even sell communal properties against the wishes of commoners.

For Q'eqchi' patriarchs, the 1889 law exacerbated an already tense and difficult situation as they sought to negotiate between the new promise of coffee production, their desires to protect Maya commoners, and mandamiento labor. This situation could lead to conflict between village patriarchs and distrust, as happened in Tanchi-Raxaha, the communal property that Fabian Tiul and Pedro Coc had sought to turn into a coffee plantation only a few years earlier. Shortly after the passage of Alta Verapaz's special decree, Tiul, along with many villagers, believed that Coc was seeking to "make himself owner of the entire [coffee] enterprise." Fearing the loss of his claims to Tanchi-Raxaha, Tiul then petitioned for sole title to fifteen caballerías in neighboring untitled tierras baldías recognized by locals as part of Tanchi-Raxaha. When Tiul met resistance from Coc and the residents of Tanchi-Raxaha, he sold his rights to the ladino Manuel C. Mendez. As a result, Q'eqchi' commoners petitioned for the breakup of Tanchi-Raxaha into individual plots. Once Coc and Tuil confronted the possibility that the common property would be privatized into small individual plots, they joined forces again to make new appeals to protect the rural inhabitants of Tanchi- Raxaha.[66]

These cases illustrate that land privatization was not solely the result of procapitalist laws imposed from above by the state.[67] Rather, the subdivision of communal lands derived from a combination of internal pressures and dynamics, including the gradual erosion of the bonds between Q'eqchi' patriarchs and commoners and the insecurities generated by mandamiento labor. Land privatization was also protracted and heavily contested. The dismemberment of Q'eqchi' common properties not only

---

[66] AGCA ST-AV Paq. 32 Exp. 7 1889, "Pedro Coc y compañeros, Tanchi-Raxaha en Carchá." See also AGCA B Leg. 28804 Exp. 12454 1891, "Solicitud de Lucas Coc, Sebastián Choc y comp. Vecinos de San Pedro Carchá"; AGCA B Leg. 28808 Exp. 1573, "Lucas Coc y demás compañeros, dueños del terreno nombrado Tanchi-Raxaha: queja contra Balsells"; AGCA ST-AV Paq. 32 Exp. 7.

[67] This is an emerging consensus in the literature broadly speaking about land privatization. See, for example, Emilio Kourí, *A Pueblo Divided: Business, Property, and Community in Papantla, Mexico* (Stanford, CA: Stanford University Press, 2004); Aldo A. Lauria-Santiago, *An Agrarian Republic: Commercial Agriculture and the Politics of Peasant Communities in El Salvador, 1823–1914* (Pittsburgh, PA: University of Pittsburgh Press, 1999); Julie A. Charlip, *Cultivating Coffee: The Farmers of Carazo, Nicaragua, 1880–1930* (Athens: Ohio University Press, 2003).

undermined Q'eqchi' patriarchs' authority and their self-representation as coffee planters and agents of national progress; it also left Q'eqchi' commoners vulnerable to aggressive coffee planters. With individual title, some Q'eqchi's placed their land titles as collateral for small loans in difficult times. When Q'eqchi' smallholders were unable to pay up, they became tenant farmers or landless migrants pushed toward the city or more distant regions.

In response to land privatization and the erosion of their local political power, some Q'eqchi' patriarchs began to reinforce alternative spheres of power and influence by harnessing the power of cofradías and forging new political alliances with ladino indigenistas, who increasingly critiqued the practice of forced labor as cruel and antiquated and sought to protect the indigenous race. Where rural Q'eqchi's had aligned with Juan de la Cruz, a poor urban ladino, Q'eqchi' patriarchs turned to a new group of professional, urban, middle-class ladinos. Yet alliances between Q'eqchi' patriarchs and ladino indigenistas were tenuous, as they were often motivated by different purposes. These cross-racial alliances, however, enabled lower-class Q'eqchi's to contest mandamiento labor that neither Q'eqchi' patriarchs nor ladino indigenistas could fully control. As we will see, Q'eqchi' patriarchs and commoners unsettled both civilizing and liberal–democratic metanarratives of modernity.

ENDING SLAVERY IN THE TIME OF FREEDOM

During the late nineteenth century, local intellectuals were among the most influential advocates of social and political reform, often acting as mediators among communities, regional elites, and the state.[68] Indeed, many of early indigenista liberal groups were local and regional intellectuals, who penned articles in the press, occupied positions as lawyers, and participated in local government. During Reina Barrios's presidency (1892–8), indigenista liberals gained influence nationally and implemented measures to protect indigenous municipalities, abolish forced wage labor, and promote indigenous education.[69] They advocated for

---

[68] Florencia E. Mallon, *Peasant and Nation: The Making of Postcolonial Mexico and Peru* (Berkeley: University of California Press, 1995), 16–17, 294–5.

[69] Acuerdos gubernativos de 16 de julio de 1892, 29 de octubre de 1892, 10 de noviembre de 1892, 15 noviembre 1892, 24 de octubre de 1893, and 27 de enero de 1894 in Jorge Skinner-Klée, *Legislación indigenista de Guatemala*.

recognition of the civil rights and freedoms of Mayas, enshrined in the constitution, as the only way to realize a truly civilized nation.

Among the more radical indigenistas was Rosendo Santa Cruz, a liberal born in Jutiapa who was appointed departmental governor of Alta Verapaz in early 1892. With the support of like-minded indigenistas in Alta Verapaz, Santa Cruz quickly began to implement reforms such as the demilitarization of mandamiento labor, the gathering of statistics on indebted plantation laborers, and the reigning-in of extralegal corporal punishment and confinement. Most infuriating to ladinos and German settlers, he frequently sided with Q'eqchi' laborers in their disputes with the region's coffee planters. In his first report to the Ministry of the Interior as departmental governor, Santa Cruz satirized liberals' acute concerns about indigenous peoples as impediments to progress, arguments that ladinos like Víctor Sierra had used to legitimize the policy of forced wage labor. Santa Cruz labeled European and ladino coffee planters immoral and "opposed to progress."[70] He painted an alarming picture of unruly Europeans and ladinos recklessly pursuing their selfish desires with no regard for their deleterious effects on society, while Q'eqchi's ended up as slaves since "the predominant tendency has been to exploit the indigenous race under the pretext of Government support for agriculture." European settlers and ladino state officials were to be held accountable for paralyzing the improvement of infrastructure and for "the very sad spectacle of seeing justice tossed in the dirt." Santa Cruz disdainfully called these planters "exploiters of the Indian race," "power hungry," "feudal lords," "slave drivers," "monopolists of lands and men," and "criminals." He accused ladinos and European coffee planters and the authorities who had supported them of usurping hundreds of caballerías of Maya land and of refusing to establish rural schools as mandated by the labor law. According to Santa Cruz, mandamientos had made Indians into slaves. Lamenting the sad state of the nation, he argued that if something was not done, the region would remain in a constant state of regress.

In his report, Santa Cruz also wrote of his shock at the application of mandamiento laws to women and expressed discomfort with its inversion of traditional gender norms. Turning civilizing discourse on its head, he lambasted Europeans for morally corrupting Q'eqchi' women, who, when forced to work on plantations, traded in their "white robe of

---

[70] Informe del JP de Alta Verapaz, *El Guatemalteco, Diario Oficial*, August 20, 1892, AGCA B Leg. 28824 Exp. 841 1892.

virginity to wear that of the indecent brothel." The traditional Q'eqchi'
home, once peaceful, had descended into disgrace and discord. The
widow, respected in all "cultured societies," was condemned to live
"under the ferocity of the stick that obliges her to produce riches for the
white, while she and her children suffer hunger and poverty." He pointed
to the rapid spread of venereal disease with the application of mandamiento labor to women, suggesting that European and ladino coffee
planters should examine their own moral shortcomings. Santa Cruz's
linking of gender and nationalism bears out Joane Nagel's observation
that national moral economies "identify desirable and undesirable
members by creating gender, sexual, and ethnic boundaries and hierarchies within nations, establish criteria for judging good and bad performances of nationalist masculinity and femininity, and define threats to
national moral and sexual integrity."[71] Precisely because nationalism
was articulated through its moral economy, references to sex became
endowed with a rhetorical power and political currency that capitalized
on but was not limited to the domain of sex. Such "sex talk," like
references to gender and race, however, gained strategic potency, as Nagel
notes, when it signaled a threat to the nation's march toward civilization
and progress, when it spoke to who counted as agents of history or as
obstacles to it.

Rosendo Santa Cruz also made explicit the racialized representations
of who could and could not be coffee planters that had inhibited the
recognition of Q'eqchi' coffee planters. In his report, he noted that

coffee, whether it is produced by *el indio* or the cobanero Ladino who cultivates
his own land, is worth the same in European markets. And if the intention of the
legislator, when he established the law of mandamientos, was to promote the
growth of national development, multiplying its riches through the exploitation of
its forests and agricultural lands, there is no doubt that I will have fulfilled my
obligation protecting the *indio*, who also throws himself into agricultural enterprises as much as the foreigner; since difference in color does not constitute
difference in principles before the law, where all are judged as equals.[72]

By foregrounding Q'eqchi' perspectives on coffee planting and contrast-
ing it with state practices that favored the coffee plantations of wealthy
ladinos and Germans, Rosendo Santa Cruz unpinned an integral part of

---

[71] Joane Nagel, *Race, Ethnicity, and Sexuality: Intimate Intersections, Forbidden Frontiers*
(New York: Oxford University Press, 2003), 146.
[72] "Informe del JP de Alta Verapaz," *El Guatemalteco*, August 20, 1892; AGCA
B Leg. 28824 Exp. 841 1892.

the civilizing rhetoric of the state. In short, his multilayered argument positioned ladinos and German settlers not as bearers of civilization but as obstacles to it, and elevated Q'eqchi's to a position of equality. Santa Cruz's report, reproduced in Guatemala's official newspaper, provoked the ire of many Altaverapacence landowners and catapulted the region into a national debate about mandamientos and the constitutional rights of Mayas that would eventually, if only temporarily, result in the abolition of mandamientos. Significantly, Santa Cruz's report, alongside the petitions of Q'eqchi' patriarchs, chopped away at the veneer of European and ladino moral superiority by positioning them not as bearers of progress but as obstacles to it.

Q'eqchi' patriarchs also articulated a political vision that gave Q'eqchi's a unique and privileged role in promoting national progress. Many Q'eqchi' patriarchs portrayed themselves as protectors of the indigenous race. "The foreigners lack all justice, without recognizing that they have come to *our* country, under the protection of the progressive laws of the Government," Salvador Pacay, as representative of his village, protested to the departmental government. "If they want they can make a fortune, but not content with the products that our fertile soils offer them in superabundance, they try, like Señor Eduardo Felice, to place upon us greater, much greater work than what corresponds to the pay we receive." The foreigners, he complained, "unjustly dismiss us, passing above the universal laws of reason and justice."[73] Far from simply cheating their pay, Pacay affirmed his own moral superiority and his rights as a citizen of the nation by asserting that Europeans, with their unbridled desire for wealth, were greedy and exploited Mayas. José Coc Delgado similarly assumed a position as a protector of the indigenous race. When town officials from Cobán attempted to round up laborers from Coc Delgado's property, Setoc, he wrote to the departmental governor requesting that Cobán's authorities leave his residents in peace, "not because they flee from work, not because they would like [their work obligations] to be moderate and justly compensated; but that the Cobanero landowners, mostly foreigners, always abuse the ignorance and naiveté of the Indians, obliging them to work for nine reales a month, such a scant salary that it was not sufficient even for their most urgent needs over the course of a week."[74] Painting an image of hungry and exploited Mayas, victims of Cobanero greed, Coc Delgado sought

[73] AGCA JP-AV 1885 Paq. 5 "JP- Salvador Pacay," January 18, 1886.
[74] AGCA ST-AV Paq. 20 Exp. 1.

not only to protect his mozos but to assert his own moral superiority. Some Guatemalan intellectuals similarly argued that the "Indian problem" grew out of exploitation at the hands of landowners. The protection of Indians from greedy landlords would thus usher in a new era of progress.[75]

These petitions and reports provide a decidedly middle- and upper-class male set of perspectives that reflect the predominantly elite male authorship of petitions. Even when the rural lower classes made petitions, they relied on ladino and Q'eqchi' scribes and lawyers to provide translations. Concerns over mandamientos and coffee planting were not, of course, the sole preserve of elite men. Lower-class Q'eqchi's offered through action their own response to mandamiento labor and coffee in the events of Xucaneb: alliances with an outsider ladino, a pilgrimage to ensure bountiful harvests, flight and labor evasions, and eventually land privatization. Moreover, rural Q'eqchi's, through tinterrillos, also endorsed the promise of liberalism that could be measured by the historical movement from slavery to freedom. "The time of slavery has now passed; for us the destitute race an era of liberty is opening, in which we are all equal before the law and he who commits an error must be punished," wrote Diego Che of San Pedro Carchá in 1892.[76] "Since the French Revolution did away with lords and their privilege," forty Q'eqchi' laborers wrote to the government, most likely with the help of a ladino lawyer, "slavery has been abolished everywhere on the planet.... The Indian should not be exploited to the point where he is converted into a slave as in the days of old.... We are made to work for free as it used to be done for the feudal lords."[77] Mayas continued to employ the languages of freedom and slavery through the late nineteenth and early twentieth centuries. "We are not slaves but citizens," wrote 138 Q'eqchi's to the president.[78] That these discourses relied on a metanarrative of the historical movement from feudalism and slavery to democracy and capitalism speaks to the pervasiveness and enduring potency of the liberal–democratic and civilizing metanarratives of progress and modernization.

With the support of radical liberals in Alta Verapaz, Santa Cruz intervened on behalf of Q'eqchi' commoners, especially in the case of the residents of Chimelb. According to court records, José Ax, a Q'eqchi'

---

[75] See especially the periodicals of *El Educacionista* and Batres Jáuregui, *Los indios, su historia y su civilización.*

[76] AGCA J-AV Leg. 25 C Exp. 13.   [77] AGCA J-AV 104 Leg. 13 Exp. 3.

[78] SPCM, 12 de diciembre de 1907, "José Chub y comp.-Presidente."

patriarch, sold Felipa Sierra the communal property Chimelb, inhabited by Ax's own ethnic clan members. However, they did not agree to Ax's sale of Chimelb and thus refused to recognize Felipa Sierra's claim. In turn, Felipa Sierra terrorized the residents of Chimelb. She sent soldiers from the local garrison to burn the Maya residents' houses and crops, threaten the residents with violence, and force them to work on plantations in the lowlands region of Panzós. A long court battle ensued, as the residents of Chimelb charged Sierra with theft, trespassing, slander, and physical violence.[79] The residents of Chimelb likewise charged José Ax with stealing the money he received from the sale of the property. Unlike previous departmental governors, Rosendo Santa Cruz sided with the residents and sought to put an end to the "tyranny exercised over *los indios*" by Felipa Sierra. Beyond this specific case, Santa Cruz also ended the practice of sending soldiers at the request of planters to capture laborers who had escaped their obligations.

In response to Santa Cruz's efforts to protect rural laborers, coffee planters retaliated with vitriolic discourses and a refusal to comply with his orders. Felipa Sierra called Santa Cruz "vile," "barbarous," and "greedy." Outraged by the "lack of protection for agriculture" demonstrated by Santa Cruz, one ladino wrote in the *Diario de Centro-América* that the departmental governors' reforms had, in just a few months, resulted in the abandonment of coffee plantations and the fall of land prices. Worst of all, he wrote, it would be "the false philanthropy that condemns a nation to barbarism, regression and ruin."[80] Coffee planters refused to observe his reforms. When Santa Cruz mandated a rural census in order to better regulate labor, some coffee planters denied the entry of state officials, who were charged with conducting the census, onto their property.[81] Facing opposition and unable to fulfill all Santa Cruz's requests, the director of the police resigned from his position the day before Santa Cruz published his "blasphemous" report.[82]

In Guatemala City, however, a growing consensus among Liberals was emerging: slavery had been abolished everywhere in the hemisphere, and

---

[79] AGCA MG B Leg. 28835 Exp. 3457; AGCA J-AV 103 Leg. 26 C Exp. 12 1891; AGCA J-AV 103 Leg. 25 C Exp. 16; AGCA J-AV 103 Leg. 25 C Exp. 14; AGCA J-AV 103 Leg. 26 Exp. 18; AGCA J-AV 103 Leg. 27 D Exp. 11.

[80] "Brazos," *Diario de Centro-América*, May 24, 1892; AGCA J-AV 103 Leg. C Exp. 5 1892.

[81] See, for example, AGCA MG B Leg. 28857 Exp. 3067 1892.

[82] AGCA JP-AV 1892 Paq. 1, "Carta al JP de Manuel Pellecer, Director de la Policía," August 19, 1892.

mandamientos were a colonial holdover, an anachronism in a modern nation. In April 1892 the Ministry of Development invited coffee planters to provide recommendations on how to reform Guatemala's 1877 Labor Law. Responses coming from Alta Verapaz ranged from Juan von Turkheim's insistence that the abolition of mandamientos would be the "complete ruin of the department" to José Guillen's suggestion that reform was crucial, since the only other method to solve the labor shortage would be to "contract more European immigration." In his "humble opinion," Fidel Soria of San Cristobal wrote that the law was "very wise," but given the obvious difficulties, "we would be much better off" if mandamientos came to an end.[83] Nonetheless, planters' reports in Alta Verapaz made clear that few coffee planters favored abolishing mandamientos. When Santa Cruz published his scathing report four months later, Altaverapacence coffee planters were enraged. In response, prominent coffee planters – including Ernesto Marroquin, Ricardo Sapper, and Max Leipprand – sponsored a meeting, open to all agriculturists in the region, to form an agricultural society.[84] The association quickly became the coffee planters' political engine and voice. They agitated the president, unsuccessfully at first, for the removal of Santa Cruz from office.[85]

As a result of Santa Cruz's public reports and efforts at reform, the region of Alta Verapaz – Guatemala's beacon of progress and racial whitening – was catapulted to the foreground in national debates about forced labor, economic progress, and how best to civilize the Indians. Two months later, the National Assembly seized on the historic moment of the four-hundredth anniversary of the conquest of the Americas to examine the historical origins of the Indian problem, establishing a competition for the best historical analysis addressing how to most efficiently civilize Mayas.[86] While the competition did not directly evoke the issue of mandamientos, the debates that erupted in the National Assembly and national newspapers over the coming months ensured that any entry would have to address the issue.

A year after the initial consultation with coffee planters in April 1893, Francisco Azurdia, a prominent lawyer and national delegate, proposed a

---

[83] AGCA JP-AV 1892 Paq. 1, "Carta al JP de Juan von Turkheim," April 13, 1892; "Carta al JP de José Guillen," April 11, 1892; "Carta al JP de Fidel Soria," April 9, 1892.

[84] See the reprinted circular, "La agricultura en Alta Verapaz," *El Diario de Centro-América*, July 29, 1892.

[85] AGCA B Leg. 28826 Exp 2463.

[86] "Decreto del Ejecutivo No. 451, 10 de octubre de 1892," in Skinner-Klée, *Legislación indigenista*, 45–6.

motion to the National Assembly to abolish mandamientos. The motion sparked a lively debate in the assembly and national newspapers.[87] The central axis of the debate mirrored the discord between the regional, planter-dominant vision articulated in Alta Verapaz and the ideas of radical indigenista liberals like Rosendo Santa Cruz. Newspapers such as *El Diario de Centro-América* and *La Nueva Era* cautioned against reckless actions that would jeopardize the onward march of progress. "If the mandamiento law is not applied," reasoned one editorialist, "the decline of national agriculture will surely ensue, that is to say, the future of the Nation will come to be one of vagrancy, criminality, and the impoverishment of *el indio*; because from the moment in which the unfortunate [Indian] is left abandoned to his desires and tendencies, he will look for the slavery of the most seductive plantation owner or he will fall into the sensuousness of laziness."[88] Their condition could only be alleviated by "their moral perfection" and "a gentle treatment, abundant and nutritious food, and comfortable and sanitary living quarters."[89] On the other hand, the more radical newspaper *La República* argued that mandamientos were nothing more than "an injustice and the absolute negation of freedom for all Indians."[90] In both the National Assembly and the public sphere, an uneasy consensus emerged that blended idealism with pragmatic skepticism. *La Nueva Era* declared, "Mandamientos are an abomination and must be completely outlawed."[91] As a result of coffee planter resistance, state officials forced Rosendo Santa Cruz to resign as departmental governor barely into his second year of tenure in 1893.

In October 1893, the National Assembly announced the winner of the national competition on how best to civilize the Indian: Antonio Batres Jáuregui . A member of one of Guatemala's most prestigious creole families, Batres Jáuregui had penned an elegant argument for the abolition of mandamientos and the implementation of indigenous education. "We must remove them from their state of pariah, so that they can be converted into citizens," he explained.[92] This goal required, above all else, the end of the slavery of mandamientos. In light of Batres's argument and

---

[87] For a more detailed recounting of the debates in the National Assembly, see McCreery, *Rural Guatemala*, 188–93.

[88] "Revista de la Prensa," *La Nueva Era*, April 14, 1893.

[89] Ibid.; "Ley de trabajadores," *Diario de Centro-América*, April 10, 1893.

[90] "En Pro de los Indios," *La República*, April 6, 1893.

[91] "Los mandamientos," *La Nueva Era*, April 21, 1893.

[92] Batres Jáuregui, *Los indios, su civilización e historia*, 172.

the emerging public consensus, President Reina Barrios abolished mandamientos on October 23, 1893. "As a result of the expansion and
development that agricultural enterprises have achieved," he reasoned,
"as well as the love of work and the desire to procure for oneself well-
being that has awoken in all social classes, the reasons behind passing the
law of April 3rd, 1877, that regulates the services of workers, have been
disappearing."[93]

Even though Reina Barrios abolished mandamientos, however, he had
not eradicated extra-economic coercion. Article 3 of the new labor law
stated: "Those who have been obliged to serve in mandamientos may
now be drafted into the detachments of *zapadores*."[94] The new law
merely traded one form of coerced labor for another: persons who
formerly were subject to mandamientos now found themselves
threatened with forced incorporation in the zapadores, labor battalions
organized under military discipline for work on roads and fortifications.
In order to avoid work as a zapador, a rural Maya had to either pay an
annual tax of ten pesos, live as a resident labor on a plantation, owe a
debt of at least thirty pesos for labor, or have a contract for at least three
months' work per year on an export plantation.[95] The newspaper *La
República* explained the logic clearly: "The only indirect coercion forcing
the Indians to work [is the threat] that he will be sent to the battalions of
the zapadores."[96] Indeed, the belief that Mayas needed to be coerced to
labor on coffee plantations remained steadfast: "In a free society work
should not be regulated, but left to individual choice and to conditions of
supply and demand, [however] in a period of transition it is necessary to
issue laws that will remove difficulties and hasten the passage from
coercion to independent action."[97]

By the time Reina Barrios finally brought an end to mandamiento labor
in March 1894, most Guatemalans, including some coffee planters,
agreed that mandamientos were an unsavory vestige of colonial rule, a
kind of slavery in an otherwise modern age. As David McCreery has
suggested, the government may very well have found more persuasive
reasoning in the leveling-off of coffee exports from their peak in the late
1880s and the gradual switch to debt peonage in Guatemala's prosperous

[93] "Decreto Gubernativo No. 471 de 23 de octubre1893," in Skinner-Klée, *Legislación indigenista*, 49–50.
[94] *Recopilación de las leyes emitidas por el gobierno democrático de la República de Guatemala* (Guatemala: La Tipografía La Unión, 1874), 362–3.
[95] "Disposiciones emitidas," *El Republicano*, April 1, 1894.
[96] *La República*, May 9, 1894.   [97] "Decree 486," in *Recopilación de las leyes*, 316–24.

coffee-growing region along the Atlantic coast.[98] Even in Alta Verapaz, a growing number of coffee planters were frustrated with mandamientos and believed that, at the very least, they needed reform. For some, mandamientos were a problem not because coerced labor was a vestige of the past but because the capital necessary for wage advances and bribes to local officials prohibited the entrance of smaller coffee planters.[99] They also often lacked personal and political relations with the ladino town council or agricultural commission that could facilitate the acquisition of labor in a timely manner.

Despite state coercion and regulation, the high coffee prices of the early 1890s helped foster the emergence of a wage labor market in Alta Verapaz. Local officials frequently demanded higher wages than those established by law, leading astute coffee planters to bypass the state altogether and set their own contracts with laborers through privatized mandamientos known as *habilitaciones* (wage advances; literally, financing).[100] Coffee planters hired a *habilitador*, named for the habilitación they gave the workers to seal a work agreement. The habilitador was a labor recruiter who advanced the coffee planters' money to Mayas in promise of future labor, signed Mayas to contracts, rounded up the workers, and dispatched them to the plantation when needed.[101] After the abolition of mandamientos, ladinos from the agricultural commissions became habilitadores. Much like labor recruitment under mandamientos, these habilitadores signed up workers in the villages and surrounding countryside. Habilitadores took advantage of holidays, when Mayas sought money for alcohol, and of cyclical corn shortages and high food prices in June and July. In return for their efforts, habilitadores received a small salary or a flat rate for each worker contracted and a commission based on the number of days worked by the men they recruited.[102] Finally, wealthy coffee planters expanded fincas de mozos: coffee planters purchased an inhabited property in order to establish labor contracts with the residents. Employers with lands suitable to milpa production on their coffee estates also rented those lands to Mayas in exchange for labor. Access to such land could be a powerful draw when a drought hit, and where land shortages were developing.

[98] David McCreery, "'An Odious Feudalism': Mandamiento Labor and Commercial Agriculture in Guatemala, 1858–1920," *Latin American Perspectives* 13, no. 1 (1986): 107.
[99] McCreery, *Rural Guatemala*, 221.
[100] AGCA JP-AV 1890 Paq. 2, "Agricultores de San Cristobal al JP," March 23, 1890.
[101] See McCreery, *Rural Guatemala*, 225.   [102] Ibid.

Finally, coffee planters got another boon when the Guatemalan state, in 1894, passed further land legislation, this time designed, ostensibly, to reduce irregularities in the petitioning of tierras baldías, ensure more accurate surveys and maps, and thwart the growth of large plantations. While the new law seemed to be addressing land monopolization, it actually hastened the process of land privatization among Q'eqchi' villagers by reducing the amount of a baldío that any single person could purchase from thirty to fifteen caballerías. While coffee planters easily evaded the law by adding the names of their relatives to a petition, this law effectively prohibited Q'eqchi' patriarchs from titling whole communal lands as individuals. It thus largely ended the practice of translating communal properties into coffee plantations, and the documentary record evidences a noticeable return to the strategy of titling properties under the names of entire communities as co-owners.

The 1894 land law also created a new set of costs and risks that hastened the process of land privatization and the formation of fincas de mozos. First, the government required a corps of surveyors to check owners' titles and measure and mark all state lands for the sale of baldíos and ejidos. While these surveys were ostensibly designed to reduce future conflicts over boundaries, this requirement also dramatically increased the cost of surveying.[103] Higher costs likely prevented some Mayas from titling their property and pushed others into debt. Second, the new law stipulated that all baldíos were to be sold at public auction with base prices set at 250–500 pesos per caballería, depending on the potential use value of the land. Not only did this represent a fivefold increase in the minimum price, but Q'eqchi' villagers were faced with the terrifying possibility that, after having paid the substantial cost for measurement, they could be outbid at public auction and lose the property altogether. In addition to the internal pressures toward dismemberment of communal landholdings, the 1894 land law thus increased both the risk and costs Q'eqchi' villagers faced in titling land. Villagers nonetheless often felt compelled to retitle their properties according to the new survey standards, which, alongside high coffee prices, resulted in a surge in the number of petitions (see Table 3.1). Thus, even laws such as the new land regulations and the abolition of mandamientos, while seemingly designed to

---

[103] Julio César Méndez Montenegro, *444 años de legislación agraria, 1513–1957* (Guatemala: Revista de la Facultad de Ciencias Jurídicas y Sociales de Guatemala, 1960), 234–45.

TABLE 3.1 *Number of petitions for land in San Pedro Carchá and Cobán*

Years	Number of petitions
1890–4	54
1895–9	102
1900–4	72
1905–9	40
1910–14	40
1915–19	15

Source: Indice seccion de tierras, AGCA.

support smallholders and rural laborers, did little to support Q'eqchi' patriarchs and commoners.

Land privatization following the 1889 special decree for Alta Verapaz and the 1894 national land law was not a linear process with a singular cause. At first, divisions and skepticism between Q'eqchi' patriarchs and commoners, along with the pressures of mandamiento labor on rural lower-class Mayas, seemed to drive the process of privatization. The 1894 land law, however, introduced new financial pressures of high land prices and speculation into the equation. For example, divisions between villagers and Q'eqchi' patriarchs propelled the division of the communal property known as Tanchi-Raxaha into individual land titles by 1890. By 1894 the residents of Tanchi-Raxaha resolved their differences and united once again behind the patriarch Pedro Coc. Together, they sought a new communal title under the revised land laws of 1894.[104] According to new legal requirements, Tanchi-Raxaha was remeasured and put up for public auction.[105] At the sale, two ladinos who were infamous for land speculation, Manuel Mendez and Juan Prado, dramatically inflated the price of Tanchi-Raxaha. Pedro Coc and the villagers of Tanchi-Raxaha agreed to pay an astounding 45,000 pesos, at least double or triple the actual value of the property. Once they had secured ownership, Pedro Coc wrote to the president on behalf of the villagers of Tanchi-Raxaha requesting that the price be reduced. The community, he explained, only agreed to pay such a high price because the residents "wanted to avoid being slaves to the resident foreigners in Cobán that,

---

[104] AHMG C-20 Alta Verapaz, 1890, "Pedro Coc y compañeros: solicitud de amparo contro oros condueños del terreno Tanchi-Raxaha que lo vendieron sito en Carchá," February 20, 1890.

[105] AGCA ST-AV Paq. 32 Exp. 7.

very far from understanding that work and industry are free, make us work by force for the miserable amount of twenty-five centavos a day, without attending to the fact that we too are coffee entrepreneurs." The price was then reduced to 200 pesos per caballería, which the Q'eqchi's of Tanchi-Raxaha paid on March 29, 1895. Nonetheless, the debt required for the purchase of Tanchi-Raxaha ultimately fractured the community, and by the first decade of the twentieth century, the communal holding had been dissolved into individual plots. Breaking up Tanchi-Raxaha into individual plots also paved the way, as we will see in Chapter 4, for the loss of land due to debt as individuals used their land titles to secure loans.[106] As a result, Tanchi-Raxaha itself was gradually reconstructed by Erwin Paul Dieseldorff as a finca de mozos, a coffee plantation with resident laborers obliged to work for him.[107] The 1894 law, thus, hardly offered the great protections against large landholdings that it purported to.

The indigenista laws of the early 1890s, however limited and contradictory, came to an end when revolutionary political exiles invaded Guatemala from Mexico in 1897 and disrupted the export economy. The need to defend the republic against revolution meant that laborers were forced into the army, even as news of a record 1897 global harvest was set to depress world markets.[108] President Reina Barrios responded by reintroducing mandamientos. While he intended for the mandamientos to last for only one harvest, Reina Barrios was assassinated shortly afterward, and his successor, Manuel Estrada Cabrera (1898–1920), faced with external and internal threats and a declining world coffee market, elected to continue the drafts. In 1898 the departmental governor of Alta Verapaz wrote to planters and municipal authorities affirming his "unconditional support for agriculture."[109] By the first months of 1899, President Estrada Cabrera also made known his dissatisfaction with indigenista liberals when Rosendo Santa Cruz was assassinated in the

---

[106] These fears of sale of individual plots drove Tiburcio Caal, one of the preeminent Q'eqchi' patriarchs of Cobán, to distribute Cobán's ejidos known as "Chitu" to 254 of the town's poorest Q'eqchi's with special stipulations that the owners would not sell, rent, or mortgage the property for twenty-five years. AGCA ST-AV P13 E10.

[107] AGCA Departamento de Agrario Nacional (hereafter DAN) Paq. 6 Exp. 6, "Raxaha, Carchá, W. E. Dieseldorff."

[108] Jorge Luján Muñoz, *Las revoluciones de 1897, la muerte de J. M. Reina Barrios y la elección de M. Estrada Cabrera* (Guatemala City: Artemis Editor, 2003).

[109] SPCM 1898, "JP al alcalde 1° Municipal," February 24, 1898, and "JP al alcalde 1° Municipal," February 3, 1898.

small town of Tactic that April.[110] The question of mandamiento labor thus continued to serve as the flash point for the nation's most fundamental contradictions. In 1907 Juan Arzú Batres, a member of one of Guatemala's premier families, synthesized the dilemma of postcolonial liberalism in Guatemala, writing in the newspaper *La República*: "It is indispensable to find a way to obtain the labor of *el indio* in order to increase agricultural production without decaying the sacred rights possessed by men who reside in civilized nations and without exercising a coercion upon him that constitutes slavery."[111]

CONCLUSION

Xucaneb's revenge illustrates the efforts of rural Q'eqchi's and their ladino ally, Juan de la Cruz, to force ladinos, European settlers, and others to recognize another ontology – one grounded not in the linear and historicist models of time and space that guided nineteenth-century obsessions with progress and liberalism but in cyclical rhythms, notions of reciprocity, and mountain deities as historical agents. Q'eqchi' patriarchs, however, recognized the need to engage in an ongoing translation and mediation between Q'eqchi' ontologies and liberal state ones. To this end, they allied with ladino indigenistas who inserted Q'eqchi' experiences of mandamientos into the hemispheric tide of antislavery moments and the metanarratives charting the end of slavery and feudalism and the rise of capitalism and democracy. Q'eqchi's fought over the categorization and containment of the structured oppositions between slavery and freedom, coercion and consent, and the racialization of Q'eqchi' as laborers. Crucial to Q'eqchi' struggles was historical time itself and the battles over how to categorize Q'eqchi's within a linear, temporal scheme from barbarism to civilization.

In the wake of Xucaneb, Q'eqchi's also continued to flee to more distant regions. A traveler in the distant upper reaches of El Quiché department around the turn of the century reported: "There are people living in the woods here and there, though you do not see where until you come upon them; Indians mostly, immigrants from the settled parts of the Alta Verapaz running away from plantation work and the oppressions of the Government or the authorities.... But they do not long escape

[110] Flavio Rojas Lima, ed., *Diccionario histórico biográfico de Guatemala* (Guatemala City: Asociación de Amigos del País, 2004), 830.
[111] "Calamidades sociales: Los indios y los ladinos," *La República*, May 1, 1907.

vexation. Somebody buys the land and puts the inhabitants to work; or else they have to run away further."[112] Q'eqchi's fleeing mandamiento labor also headed south into the uninhabited mountains north of Lake Izabal. By 1897 earlier efforts to annex certain Q'eqchi' villages established in Izabal erupted into yet another border war between Alta Verapaz and Izabal. The departmental governor of Alta Verapaz claimed that his counterpart in Izabal was encouraging emigration; the departmental governor of Izabal countered by blaming the migration on the onerous labor demands of coffee growing in Alta Verapaz and the ladino invasion of Maya lands. The governor of Izabal reported that hundreds of Mayas lived in these mountains and resisted "anything like a wage advance."[113] For Q'eqchi's, however, the territorial borders between nation-states, departments, and even municipalities became important precisely because these borders were not fixed. Rather, territorial boundaries were frequently subject to dispute, and such disputes between vying government authorities granted them a strategic political advantage to escape onerous labor obligations.

Only two years after the events of Xucaneb, the foundations were also being laid for the rapid expansion of German coffee plantations in Alta Verapaz. In 1887 the German and Guatemalan governments had signed a Free Trade Agreement, which guaranteed free trade between the nations and granted German citizens the right to buy and own lands, warehouses, and shops in both nations and to name representatives in Guatemala. In addition, the agreement, which lasted until 1915, guaranteed legal protection for German citizens and their properties, and exonerated Germans from military service in Guatemala. It also protected German nationality by considering as German citizens the legitimate children of German nationals born in Guatemala.[114] That same year, the German diaspora in Alta Verapaz created Central America's first German Club. Unsurprisingly, the consolidation of the trope of Maya "laziness" took place alongside the establishment of a self-described hardworking German race. The binary framework helped give structure and meaning to teleological

---

[112] Robert Burkitt, "Explorations in the Western Highlands of Guatemala," *The Museum Journal, University of Pennsylvania* 21 (1930): 45.

[113] AGCA MG Leg. 28699 Exp. 117; MG Leg. 28873 Exp. 131; MG Leg. 28757 Exp. 225; AGCA Ministerio de Fomento (hereafter MF) No. 14865, November 3, 1897.

[114] On the trade agreement, see Julio Castellanos Cambranes, *El imperialismo alemán en Guatemala: El tratado de comercio de 1887* (Guatemala: Universidad de San Carlos, 1977).

narratives of progress and modernization even as these narratives were increasingly bound to everyday social and economic life. Race was fluid and mobile, but also fixed to deeper and less mobile structures of capitalism. The hardships experienced by Mayas thus were diametrically reflected in what the historian Regina Wagner has termed the "apogee of the coffee economy."[115]

[115] Wagner, *Historia del café en Guatemala*, 119

4

El Q'eq Roams at Night

Plantation Sovereignty and Racial Capitalism, 1898–1914

"El Q'eq roams at night," explained Miguel Yat, an elderly retired *caporal* (foreman) from Richard Sapper's plantation, in an interview.[1] Recounting how he stumbled on el Q'eq (the black one in Q'eqchi) while hunting on an ex-German plantation, Yat's eyes lit up as he relived the fear he had experienced upon seeing the half-man, half-cow. According to popular interpretations, el Q'eq is the product of German sexual encounters with a cow, and each German coffee plantation had their own Q'eq, who was charged with guarding the plantation. Stealing from the poor and consuming copious amounts of eggs, a Maya symbol of fertility, el Q'eq represented an inversion of Q'eqchi' ethics of solidarity and reciprocity. As the product of a sexual encounter between a German man and animal, el Q'eq also challenged dichotomies between culture and nature, human and animal, the civilized and uncivilized, central to Eurocentric modernities and civilizing metanarratives and spoke of the centrality of sexual labor to the plantation economy.[2] As a sexualized beast charged with protecting German plantations and ensuring order, el Q'eq also revealed the territorial limits of the Guatemalan state's sovereignty and unsettled claims of a linear march toward a liberal nation-state. Operating under the cover of darkness, el Q'eq reveals Q'eqchi' interpretations of plantation life and racial capitalism in late nineteenth-century Alta Verapaz.

---

[1] Miguel Yat, interviews with the author, November 24, 26, and December 4, 2007.

[2] For a definition of modernity based on the opposition between humans and the natural and animal world, see Bruno Latour, *We Have Never Been Modern* (Cambridge, MA: Harvard University Press, 2012).

In this chapter, I examine the consolidation of racial capitalism in Alta Verapaz based on the expansion of German-owned properties and, in particular, fincas de mozos. Taking advantage of an economic crisis precipitated by Brazilian coffee overproduction, a few well-positioned German coffee planters purchased the indebted plantations of other Germans, ladinos, and Q'eqchi's. In order to resolve the labor crisis, German planters purchased not only coffee plantations, but also entire rural Q'eqchi' villages and their subsistence plots, creating fincas de mozos. In these new fincas de mozos, Maya families exchanged their labor during coffee harvests for the right to grow subsistence crops. Modeled on Q'eqchi' ethnic clan lands and colonial haciendas, coffee planters used fincas de mozos to translate Maya communal labor reciprocity into contracted labor on plantations and to translate Maya patriarchal protections against coerced labor and abuses into planter protections against the same. As el Q'eq suggests, however, Mayas were also fixed to the cordoned-off space of the plantation and policed by a shadowy figure. As part of the capital value of the plantation, Mayas were also commodified via the purchase and sale of fincas de mozos.

The literal translation of fincas de mozos is "plantations of boys," signaling the biting racial and patriarchal politics of plantation life. Mozos (resident laborers) were mere boys; they were understood as socially and politically immature and thus unable to exercise their rights as citizens, whereas the coffee planter was the citizen and "father" of those boys.[3] On fincas de mozos, German coffee planters consolidated racial ascriptions and hierarchies that distinguished civilized German planters from uncivilized Maya laborers and forged a racial capitalism and modernity based on the perpetual postponement of indebted Maya laborers from free wage labor and citizenship. German capital accumulation in Alta Verapaz, however, combined violence with proclamations of interracial love and harmony. Rather than obliterating difference, Germans sought to maintain Maya culture and made the management of difference central to racial capitalism. Through this racial management, German coffee planters also imagined themselves as civilized and their futures wrung gradually from the racialized bodies of their laborers.

[3] Justin Wolfe, "Those That Live by the Work of Their Hands: Labour, Ethnicity and Nation-State Formation in Nicaragua, 1850–1900," *Journal of Latin American Studies* 36, no. 1 (2004): 57–83.

As plantation patriarchs, coffee planters also founded a partial territorial sovereignty on their plantations. The famed German geographer
Karl Sapper noted that the Guatemalan state granted "some of its sovereign rights" when it awarded land titles for plantations. Since plantation
owners were responsible for appointing state representatives on their
plantations, Sapper explained that the coffee planters were awarded a
"kind of limited self-government." Viewing this system favorably, Sapper
recognized that this partial sovereignty allowed European immigrants to
form "truly patriarchal relations [with] Indians."[4] While German coffee
planters sought to create harmonious and patriarchal relations on their
plantations, the relationship between coffee planters and laborers was
both intimate and violent, and planters' exercise of sovereignty was
always partial, incomplete, and unsettling.[5] As Matilde González-Izás
has argued, the plantation world was not simply defined by economic
relations and commercialization; the plantation was also a cultural and
political space that ordered the countryside and structured racial, class,
and gender hierarchies.[6]

This chapter draws on oral histories of the shadowy figure of el Q'eq to
open windows into Q'eqchi' philosophical interpretations of coffee
capitalism in Alta Verapaz. While Karl Marx analyzed the making of
abstract labor and the commodity fetish as processes that arose from the
measuring and quantifying of labor time and the exchange value of
commodities, Q'eqchi' understandings foreground a different reading of
capitalism. The figure of el Q'eq illustrates the violence of capitalism in
Alta Verapaz not through a Marxist metonymic chain of exchangeable
commodities but through metaphor and allegory of lived experience and
ethics. El Q'eq reveals deeper social truths about the perversion of Q'eqchi' ethics and norms of solidarity and reciprocity, and the violence of the
politics of postponement and primitive capital accumulation. As these

---

[4] See Karl Sapper, "Die Soziale Stellung der Indianer in der Alta Verapaz, Guatemala,"
Petermanns Mitteilungen 37 (1891): 45.

[5] Matilde González Izás also argues that German coffee plantations, in particular, were
composed of a combination of paternalism and violence; *Modernización capitalista,
racismo y violencia: Guatemala (1750–1930)* (Mexico City: El Colegio de México, 201),
390–1. For the conceptualization of sovereignty as detached from the state and as a
localized, tenuous, and incomplete project, I follow Thomas Blom Hansen and Finn
Stepputat, eds., *Sovereign Bodies: Citizens, Migrants, and States in the Postcolonial World*
(Princeton, NJ: Princeton University Press, 2005); Giorgio Agamben, *Homo Sacer: Sovereign Power and Bare Life*, trans. Daniel Heller-Roazen (Stanford, CA: Stanford University
Press, 1998); and Stoler, *Duresss*.

[6] González-Izás, *Modernización capitalista*, 390.

interpretations also reveal, Q'eqchi' laborers constantly pushed back coffee planters' efforts to manage and control plantation life, and forged in those autonomous spaces degrees of freedom. This chapter first examines the economic crisis that helped create the conditions for the expansion of German coffee plantations in Alta Verapaz. Then it assesses how fincas de mozos were created through the translation of Q'eqchi' social forms, and how Q'eqchi's laborers exerted power in their relationship to administrators and planters to better their own lives. Finally, this chapter discusses the brutal combination of patriarchal affection and violence that defined plantation life.

ECONOMIC CRISIS AND THE FORGING OF RACIAL CAPITALISM

According to oral histories, el Q'eq originated at the turn of the twentieth century when a combination of economic and political crises gave rise to new ways of organizing plantation labor. An animal designed to police the space of the plantation, el Q'eq is said to have captured laborers attempting to flee, and thus helped to fix migrant Q'eqchi's to the plantation territory. German desires to immobilize Maya laborers, to locate them indelibly in plantation space and guarantee their labor, emerged alongside the growing mobility of commodities and other peoples through the railway. On the eve of Guatemala's worst economic crisis since independence, Altaverapacences gathered on April 30, 1897, in Cobán's town square to inaugurate the Verapaz railway. Financed by the region's German coffee planters, many Altaverapacences believed the railway announced a new epoch of prosperity, mobility, and greater proximity to European markets. Crying "at long last!," local newspapers avowed that the railway was the "most important achievement" in the region's illustrious history of "peace and progress." "Today," the departmental governor declared, "through the civilizing clarion of the railway, transformed into an enormous trumpet of the age, we announce to the nations of the globe, our doors open for honorable immigrants to settle in an extensive coffee-growing region."[7] The railway symbolized a future prosperity brought by what Marx understood as the annihilation of space by time: the quickening of the movement of people, commodities, and

---

[7] "Alocución," *El Norte*, April 30, 1897.

capital across space, making the world, in effect, a smaller place.[8] In Alta Verapaz, however, state officials' exaggerated proclamations were little more than nineteenth-century propaganda designed to counter long-standing representations of the region as isolated and distant from the centers of modernity. In reality, the railway reached neither the Atlantic port nor the departmental capital of Cobán. Instead, it stretched a mere 35 kilometers from Panzós near the Río Dulce to the small village of La Tinta. Immigrants, as well as goods, were still required to travel via a small steamship from the Atlantic port of Livingston up the Río Dulce to Panzós where the train would carry them on to La Tinta. After having made this arduous journey, weary travelers faced yet another two-day journey by porter and mule to Cobán.[9] Faithful in modernity's relentless march, Altaverapacences believed the railway would shorten travel times between Alta Verapaz and Europe and usher in a new age of mobility and migration. As el Q'eq suggested, while purportedly hailing the mobility of European immigrants and commodities, the railway also enabled coffee planters to reduce Maya mobility and attempt to bind them by debt and dependency to fincas de mozos.

The German investors in the Verapaz railway almost immediately confronted technical, geographical, and political difficulties that increased costs and delayed completion. Railway contractors were forced to blast through the mountainsides in order to sufficiently widen the region's narrow valleys so that even a small train might pass through. Rapid deforestation caused by the need for wood supplies resulted in soil erosion and, along with a small earthquake, resulted in massive landslides that destroyed their progress. Workers and overseers were plagued with malaria, and labor conditions were abysmal.[10] In September 1897, a revolt against President Reyna Barrios interrupted work as the government called on workers to join the military in defeating the revolution.[11] Plagued by high costs and poor and irregular service, the Alta Verapaz–based investors sold the railway in

[8] On railways and modernity, see Michael Matthews, *The Civilizing Machine: A Cultural History of Mexican Railroads, 1876–1910* (Lincoln: University of Nebraska Press, 2013); Wolfgang Schivelbusch, *The Railway Journey: The Industrialization of Time and Space in the Nineteenth Century* (Berkeley: University of California Press, 2014). On railways in Guatemala, see Wayne Anderson, "The Development of Export Transportation in Liberal Guatemala, 1871–1920" (PhD diss., Tulane University, 1986).

[9] See Alfred Maudslay's tales of travel in Ian Graham, *Maudslay and the Maya: A Biography* (Norman: University of Oklahoma Press, 2002), 113.

[10] *Memoria de la superintendencia de la compañía del ferro-carril Verapaz* (Guatemala: Ministerio de Fomento, 1896).

[11] AGCA B 129 Leg. 22187 Exp. 1260.

1909 to a firm in Germany.[12] While service improved, this German company had little interest in keeping tariffs low. By the 1920s, Altaverapacences complained that the cost of passage from Panacheje to Livingston was double the cost of a passage from Livingston to ports in Europe.[13] By then, the railway's economic unviability and poor service became metaphors for the nation's stagnation and the postponement of progress.

Worse than the technical and other difficulties that the railway faced, many Altaverapacences' hopes for growing prosperity were cut short by Brazilian overproduction, which precipitated a rapid decline in global coffee prices after 1897 and unsettled the economic and political foundations of Guatemala.[14] The economic crisis was also deepened by Guatemala's mounting dependency on coffee exports.[15] Silver money shortages rapidly appeared as Guatemala's new president Manuel Estrada Cabrera sought to address trade imbalances with a devaluation of Guatemalan currency. Inflation and monetary shortages were made worse by planter debt. During the period of high coffee prices and land speculation of the 1880s and 1890s, many coffee planters purchased plantations on credit and at high prices. When the market collapsed, highly indebted planters faced economic ruin. One German coffee planter wrote, "I will have to strain everything to pay the horrible loans and mortgages on my capital."[16]

In Alta Verapaz, a few German coffee planters with strong familial ties to banks in London, Bremen, and Hamburg were better situated to weather the storm of monetary instability and reaped the rewards of debtors who could not pay.[17] As a result, German ownership of land in Alta Verapaz expanded from 600 square miles in 1901 to 2,100 square miles by the beginning of World War I.[18] This land ownership, however, was concentrated in the hands of a very small number of German

---

[12] AGCA B Leg. 15858 Exp. 1320 and Exp. 348.

[13] The cost of passage per *quintal* (one quintal equals 100 Spanish pounds, or 46 kilograms) from Panacheje to Livingston was $1.60, from Livingston to New Orleans $0.40, and from Livingston to Europe $0.85. AGCA B 129 Leg. 22188.

[14] Record harvests in Brazil set the stage for the rapid fall in coffee prices in the world market, which had reached a high in 1895 at $37 per quintal. In 1896, those prices fell to $32 and then, in 1897, to $14 and then to $8. Wagner, *Los alemanes en Guatemala*, 280–2.

[15] Exports in coffee expanded from 40 percent of the nation's total exports in 1880 to 50 percent in 1889 to 64 percent in 1896. Wagner, *Historia del café*, 280–2.

[16] Oskar Weber, *Briefe eines Kaffee-Pflanzers, Zwei Jahrzehnte Deutscher Arbeit in Zentral-Amerika*, Schaffsteins Grüne Bändchen 50 (Cöln am Rhein: Schffstein, 1913), 70.

[17] See also González-Izás, *Modernización capitalista*, 335.

[18] Wagner, *Los alemanes en Guatemala*, 280–1.

Guatemalans. While German immigrants to Alta Verapaz had come from diverse class, religious, and regional backgrounds, two German settlers – Erwin Paul Dieseldorff and Richard Sapper – were particularly well situated to benefit from the economic crisis.[19] Through their privileged access to capital and markets, Sapper and Dieseldorff established vertically integrated enterprises that combined coffee production with processing and export, and they controlled virtually all the credit in the region. Far more than any other German residents, Dieseldorff and Sapper symbolized the idealized figure of a German settler and the measure by which the successes and failures of others were judged. Capital accumulation and wealth, evident in their expanding and prosperous plantations, supplied material proof of the virtue, diligence, and intelligence that Germans were presumed to embody.

Dieseldorff and Sapper had several advantages over other coffee planters due to their access to foreign currency and capital. The 1897 crisis generated a balance of payments problem and monetary instability that resulted in inflation. German Guatemalans benefited from this inflation by paying salaries in devalued national currencies and selling exports in strong foreign ones.[20] German Guatemalan planters also had advantages in capital acquisition.[21] As large merchants, Sapper and Dieseldorff accessed credit on better terms from foreign and national banks and in turn made these funds available to other Altaverapacence planters at higher interest rates.[22] Dieseldorff generally received loans at 6 percent annual interest, while he financed the operations of other planters at a rate of 12–16 percent. Annual interest rates reached as high as 20 percent.[23] Coffee planters who took out loans to pay for wage advances faced the

---

[19] According to records of the Deutsche Verein (German Club) in Cobán, of the pre–World War I immigrants, the majority were from the professional classes and had capital. Of the 291 Germans who registered at the Deutsche Verein, 241 classified themselves as "professionals" engaged in either commerce (174) or coffee planting (42). Of the 50 artisans, the majority self-identified as gardeners (24), followed by machinists and locksmiths (5 and 7, respectively). See King, *Coban and the Verapaz*, 338, see tables 126 and 127.

[20] On Guatemala's economic crisis, see Aníbal Martínez Muñoz and Bruno Busto Brol, "Agricultura," in *Historia general de Guatemala, vol. 5: Época contemporánea: 1898–1944*, eds. Jorge Luján Muñoz and J. Daniel Contreras R. (Guatemala: Asociación de Amigos del País, 1996). The Guatemala peso, equivalent to the US gold dollar in 1871, depreciated to 8.50 pesos in 1899, to 15 pesos in 1902, 18.50 pesos in 1909, and 45 pesos in 1914.

[21] AGCA PO, Córdoba, November 1, 1890.

[22] Wagner, *Los alemanes en Guatemala*, 184–96; Náñez Falcón, "Erwin Paul Dieseldorff."

[23] AGCA PO Jacinto Cordova 1899, No. 7, folios 10–17; No. 8, folios 17–22; No. 9, folios 22–5; No. 37, folios 90–6; No. 57, folios 146–7; No. 62, folios 162–5; No. 64, folios

highest risk, since they had to repay their loans regardless of whether they received the contracted labor.[24] The high cost and risks of credit often doomed a small grower to ruinous loans or to a permanent position as a dependent supplier of raw or semifinished coffee products to larger planters like Dieseldorff or Sapper.

When the 1897 coffee crisis hit, Dieseldorff and Sapper were particularly well situated to expand their land holdings by purchasing the properties of small planters who were unable to repay their loans. In 1901, for example, Manuel Vásequez Meza sold Dieseldorff three lots of approximately 6,000 acres for 6,000 pesos. These properties had been mortgaged to Vital Prado for 10,000 pesos.[25] In the midst of the coffee crisis, Dieseldorff purchased eight properties that totaled 24,278 hectares from indebted Guatemalan coffee planters. By 1929 Dieseldorff owned an astounding 865.4 caballerías of land.[26] Dieseldorff and Sapper channeled the capital they had accumulated from loans and exports into coffee-processing plants.[27] By the turn of the century, German Guatemalans exported over 80 percent of Alta Verapaz's coffee.[28]

In Alta Verapaz, Karl Sapper drew the first scientific maps of Alta Verapaz and published them in the *Mittheilungen der Geographischen Gesellschaft* in Hamburg in 1901.[29] Reflecting the changing nature of land ownership and use in Alta Verapaz, Sapper's maps illustrated the region's geology and vegetation, its political boundaries, and the linguistic distribution of Spanish, Q'eqchi', and Poqomchi speakers. The maps also illustrated plantation ownership. Like the maps of British and French colonial possessions, Sapper set apart German from non-German properties with dark coloring. Through this color-coded scheme, Sapper staged Alta Verapaz as a place of German occupation and projected a teleological future where uncolored plots awaited German ownership. On this map, the territorial boundaries of plantations also appeared in perfect linear fashion, with no jagged or irregular edges. The map's imagery

---

168–74; No. 65, folios 174–6; No. 70, folios 208–10; No. 88, folios 250–2; No. 104, folios 297–300.

[24] McCreery, *Rural Guatemala*, 229.

[25] AGCA Asunto Alemanes (hereafter AA) Exp. 1551. See also Náñez Falcón, "Erwin Paul Dieseldorff," 82–3.

[26] See Wade Kit, "Costumbre, Conflict and Consensus: Kekchí-Finquero Discourse in the Alta Verapaz, Guatemala 1880–1930" (PhD diss., Tulane University, 1998), 80–1.

[27] See Náñez Falcón, "Erwin Paul Dieseldorff."

[28] Wagner, *Los alemanes en Guatemala*, 211.

[29] Karl Sapper, "Die Alta Verapaz (Guatemala)," *Mitteilungen der Geographischen Gesellshcaft in Hamburg* 17 (1901): 78–223.

recalled a shattered piece of glass that had been carefully pieced back together. When viewed alongside Sapper's topographical map, which illustrated the region's many mountains and rivers, the careful viewer might have recognized that the territorial boundaries of these plantations were more fictive than real. Like other cartographic representations, Sapper's map created an illusion of spatial fixity and authority to German territorial possessions, while it actively erased the histories of those possessions. Sapper's map of Alta Verapaz was a model for, rather than a representation of, reality.[30] Like other efforts to render socially dense landscapes into the abstract principles of the map, cartographic illusions of fixity were, in practice, consistently interrupted by counterclaims to land ownership, movable boundary makers, multiple place names, and shifting and fragmented land tenure arrangements.

Like Sapper's cartographic representations of Alta Verapaz, el Q'eq also expressed German desires for territorial sovereignty. Unlike Sapper's maps, however, el Q'eq illustrated German plantation sovereignty not in the form of abstract and commodified space, but through the allegories of densely woven affective politics. As plantation workers such as Miguel Yat explained, German coffee planters owned el Q'eq and he was indebted to them. El Q'eq's sole purpose was to protect the plantation from thieves and capture runaway workers. Because of his debt to the plantation owner, el Q'eq also did much more. Imbued with extraordinary strength and ravenous hunger, el Q'eq wandered the plantation at night in search of food and material items to satiate his boundless hunger. During his nightly escapades, el Q'eq took what was not his without Tzuultqa'as' sanction or permission, and because he was owned by the German landowner these possessions enriched the planter. Stealing from the poor and carrying their loot to the rich, el Q'eq was an inversion of Robin Hood.[31] El Q'eq himself embodies the ravenous hunger of capitalism: the insatiable German appetite for wealth that dispossessed rural Mayas and upset Maya ethics of solidarity and reciprocity. Yet, as Q'eqchi' stories suggest, el Q'eq was necessary, in part, because German sovereignty was incomplete and the boundaries of plantations were never fully recognized.

Even as German coffee planters swallowed up productive land in Alta Verapaz, Mayas continued to grow coffee on stamp-sized plots, washing the beans in buckets late into the night and spreading them out to dry on

---

[30] Winichakul, *Siam Mapped*, especially chapter 2; Craib, *Cartographic Mexico*, chapter 1.
[31] Cabarrús, *La cosmovisión K'ekchi'*.

women's skirts and shawls by the roadside or in household patios. Q'eq-chi's also likely continued to plant coffee in the midst of their milpas and other crops. Due to a lack of available statistics, it is difficult to ascertain the extent of small-scale coffee production in nineteenth- and early twentieth-century Guatemala. At the turn of the century, many Q'eqchi's likely turned increasingly to food crops, due to low coffee prices and high cost of food staples.[32] Nonetheless, the documentary record leaves evidence of the ongoing struggle among Maya patriarchs and commoners to plant coffee and, at times, to become veritable coffee plantation owners. Unlike the Maya patriarchs of Quetzaltenango, who were largely urban artisans and traders, Q'eqchi' patriarchs often possessed land suitable to coffee production and continued to pursue these ends. In 1907 Francisco Coc Icó of San Pedro Carchá claimed to have 5,000 coffee plants and four mozos working for him.[33] The names of three Q'eqchi' coffee planters also appear in a 1912 list of mandamiento laborers requested from the state.[34] As this list also suggests, small-scale Maya growers likely continued to be subject to mandamientos, disrupting communal labor when it was most needed. In 1915 Maya coffee planters in San Cristobal Verapaz, for example, complained that large estate owners persecuted them relentlessly, trying to force them into mozo status. Coffee plantation agents harvested or burned their milpas and destroyed their coffee trees.[35]

In their efforts to earn public recognition as agents of progress, sometimes Q'eqchi' patriarchs posed for photographs to distinguish themselves from non-Mayas, and to assert their role as coffee planters or, increasingly, as military officers. By the late nineteenth century, Q'eqchi' patriarchs had risen through the ranks of the military and claimed a place in national progress by defending the nation from external enemies.[36] In a studio portrait (Figure 4.1), two young Q'eqchi' men appear side by side, representing the future horizon of civilized Q'eqchi' as coffee planters and military officers or soldiers. Unlike cartes de visites and ethnographic

---

[32] David Carey Jr., "'The Heart of the Country': The Primacy of Peasants and Maize in Modern Guatemala," *Journal of Latin American Studies* vol 51, no. 2 (May 2019) 273–306.

[33] AGCA JP-AV 1907 Paq. 1, "Fracisco Coc Icó al JP," May 2, 1907; "Antonio Tiul al JP," May 5, 1907; "Pedro Che al JP," May 3, 1907; "Tiburcio Caal al JP," May 2, 1907.

[34] The list included three Q'eqchi's out of a list of seventeen requests; CM Est. 4 Paq. 13 1912, "Nómina de mozos de orden superior solicita por un finquero," n.d.

[35] AGCA JP-AV 1915 Paq. 4, "Vecinos de San Cristobal Verapaz al JP," August 26, 1915; AGCA JP-AV 1906 Paq. 2, "G. Villatoro al JP," September 7, 1906.

[36] For lists of military battalions in Alta Verapaz, see AGCA B-127-58-2 Leg. 1854; AGCA B-127-59-2 Leg. 14280.

FIGURE 4.1 Two young Q'echi' men posing for the photographer.
Photograph courtesy of Colección Familia Hempstead, CIRMA

images of cultural others, these portraits were intended to be viewed only by the sort of people seen in them, rather than by an unknown and or foreign observer. Not simply a passive representation, the portrait reflected the subject's conscious will to be seen, reconstituted, and remembered as such by future generations.[37] This portrait is also saturated with Q'eqchi' patriarchs' control over the technologies of violence – the pistol is foregrounded and is as visible as the military uniform. These two men symbolize the Q'eqchi' patriarch's access to state and nonstate forms of coercive power: they can be imagined as battling insurgent political factions or attacks on the national territory and ensuring order on the plantation. Through their class positions, these two Q'eqchi' patriarchs suggest their control over the bodies of other lower-class men. As liberal patriots and civilized coffee planters, they united masculinity and

[37] Greg Grandin, "Can the Subaltern Be Seen? Photography and the Affects of Nationalism," *Hispanic American Historical Review* 84, no. 1 (2004): 83–111.

historical agency. As youthful men, they represented a future already in the process of actualization that defied the politics of postponement. This portraits also stands in stark contrast to studio photographs of urban K'iche patriarchs in Quetzaltenango, where K'iche families, including men, women, and children, poised for the camera with little reference to their occupations.[38]

Q'eqchi' coffee planters, however, have largely been written out of scholarly interpretations of coffee planting in Guatemala, and nineteenth-century German and ladino planters largely disavowed their activities. German and ladino planters attributed Q'eqchi's purported inability to become capitalists to an inherent racial defect. In 1901 Karl Sapper noted, "As successful as the Indians might be as merchants . . . it is very rare that an Indian becomes considerably wealthy, since he is missing entrepreneurial spirit [*Unternehmungsgeist*]."[39] Racializing Mayas as incapable of entrepreneurial will or, in the memorable words of Max Weber, the "spirit of capitalism," Sapper contended that Mayas were simply incapable of transcending their racial and class status to become agents of capitalist modernization. These views were often replicated in the writings of ladinos and state officials, who could hardly imagine Mayas who possessed economic reason sufficient to work for wages.

If Mayas lacked entrepreneurial spirit, then Germans were precisely the opposite, and German material wealth and social standing were allegedly due to their hardworking character and capitalist ingenuity, rather than their privileged position in global markets. According to Dieseldorff, coffee planters needed certain rational qualities, energies, and capacities to succeed. These characteristics included "knowing how to calculate costs and engage in rational planning, the ability to foresee adversities or favorable circumstances, the capacity to make decisions, [and] the possession of organizational talent, energy and certain practical and technical knowledge of the production and commercialization of the product."[40] A 1902 editorial entitled "Germany's Prosperity," published in the *Diario de Centro-América*, attributed superior German characteristics to the poverty of German soils compared with Guatemalan ones. "Will is a talent acquired by the [German] race, through the ages, in a

---

[38] Ibid.
[39] Karl Sapper, "Die Alta Verapaz (Guatemala): Eine Landeskundliche Skizze Mit Fünf Originalkarten," *Mittheilungen Der Geographischen Gesellschaft in Hamburg* 61 (1901): 208.
[40] Wagner, *Historia del café*, 117.

double fight against men and against nature," the editorialist explained, "The prodigious efforts to make the hard and infertile lands of the northern plains productive, has given the Germans qualities of energy that today bear fruit and which have come to include the very entrenched feeling of self-confidence."[41] If Mayas were indolent due to the fecund Guatemalan landscape, Germans clearly were born in poor soils that required hard work, making them into industrious men and agents of progress.[42] Thus, while German coffee planters possessed structural advantages in coffee production, popular narratives attributed their social class to innate racial characteristics, further solidifying the racial character of emergent capitalism in Guatemala. On the infamous fincas de mozos, these racial explanations for class distinctions were further entrenched through the structured hierarchies that undergirded daily life. If we listen carefully to Q'eqchi' interpretations, however, they reveal that German prosperity was the product of theft and violence, sexual conquest, and labor discipline. In short, planter wealth was an artifact of plantation sovereignty.

FINCAS DE MOZOS I: HISTORICAL FORMATIONS

At the turn of the century, Altaverapacence coffee planters were squeezed between low coffee prices and high debt ratios and thus looked to wring money out of a short supply of laborers when they could. This dire situation was expressed in a petition from eighty-seven Altaverapacence coffee planters ranging from medium-sized producers to the wealthiest German coffee planters. "An ominous epoch and true decadence in agriculture is crossing over this Department," the letter began, highlighting the decline in all agricultural activity, from coffee to subsistence crops. The planters implored the minister "to study and expose the determining causes of our extreme situation," for they feared that the department was headed toward "quick and sure ruin." According to the planters, the reason was simple: "the indigenous race and work." As evidence that Mayan indolence was to blame for the economic situation, Altaverapacence coffee planters noted that a decline in coffee exports from 64,800 *quintales* (one quintal is equal to 100 Spanish pounds or 46 kilograms) of coffee in 1902 to 47,600 in 1903 coincided with a scarcity of food,

[41] "La prosperidad de Alemania," *Diario de Centro América*, October 7, 1902.
[42] Jorge Ramón González Ponciano, "'No somos iguales': La 'cultura finquera' y el lugar de cada quien en sociedad en Guatemala," *ISTOR* 6, no. 24 (2006): 43–66.

including corn. Mayas, the coffee planters declared, would rather "face starvation" than engage in labor. As such, Mayas were a "stationary force that must be impelled to move." The planters suggested a combination of direct and indirect methods to compel Mayas to labor for wages. First, they requested exemptions from military and public service for workers who had fulfilled their labor obligations. Second, they asked that laborers who had defrauded their contracts or fled be required to work on public roads projects or on plantations far from where they had fled service. Finally, they wanted a register of all delinquent laborers in order to ensure strict punishment. The Altaverapacence coffee planters concluded: "With coerced labor the department would be saved and the Indian too would be saved, since honorable work is the most efficient civilizing method."[43] Wealthy planters, however, recognized that relying on state-enforced coercion alone was unsustainable. As el Q'eq suggests, coffee planters also needed a privatized discipline tied to the plantation territory, and they sought to create fincas de mozos to do so. By the turn of the century, fincas de mozos became more than simply planters' coffee groves and workers' homes and plots; they were also spaces of affection and intimacy, as well as rape and violence. Fincas de mozos became tenuous political formations, where laborers were made into racialized subjects and planters generated a partial and gradated sovereignty. Nonetheless, rural Mayas who resided on plantations mobilized their ingenuity and agency to assert their own power in highly asymmetrical relations.

Altaverapacence coffee planters turned to fincas de mozos, where rural Mayas signed contracts that granted them access to a limited amount of subsistence acreage and, in exchange, agreed to work for a wage for a period of one or two weeks per month as needed on the coffee plantation.[44] In contrast to mandamientos, which required coffee planters to work through the state and intermediaries, fincas de mozos privatized the acquisition of coffee plantation labor and fostered more direct relationships between coffee planters and laborers. In addition, augmenting coffee planters' control over laborers, fincas de mozos were, like the colonial hacienda, relatively flexible institutions that facilitated enduring the coffee market's ups and downs. During economic booms, planters could expand their coffee production and hire additional seasonal laborers either by advancing habilitación wages or, if labor was particularly

---

[43] AGCA MF B 129 Leg. 223304 Exp. 907.
[44] Tulane Latin American Library (hereafter TULAL) Erwin Paul Dieseldorff Collection (hereafter EDC) Vol. 63, Folio 168. For accounting in company stores, see Vols. 249–53.

scarce, by calling on the state to provide additional mandamiento workers. During a recession, coffee planters could allow residents to plant more subsistence crops and cut back on coffee production and labor.[45] Even more, fincas de mozos were a reservoir of labor that could be relied on in moments of rebellion against mandamiento labor. Most coffee planters thus deployed a shifting combination of resident labor (mozos colonos), indebted contract laborers (*jornaleros* or *enganchados*), and mandamiento laborers depending on the market.[46]

The turn of the century was also an opportune moment to establish fincas de mozos in Alta Verapaz. The region faced not only a fall in coffee exports but a decline in subsistence production, which made rural life precarious. Demographic growth made this insecurity notably worse.[47] By the early twentieth century, domestic food shortages and a growing population required Guatemala to import corn and other basic foodstuffs.[48] Commentators noted inflationary pressures that made basic necessities more expensive and deepened the gap between the rich and the poor.[49] In response, state officials reversed their emphasis on using town ejidos to plant coffee and sugar, and instead mandated that municipalities plant wheat, corn, beans, rice, potatoes, and yuca.[50] As the cost of basic food necessities climbed cyclically and annually, life for the poor grew precarious. As a result, rural Mayas frequently turned to the security offered by residence in a finca de mozos. At other times, Q'eqchi's had no choice; they were outbid at auctions (see Chapter 3) or they lost their property to debt, like other small- and medium-sized coffee planters.

[45] For an in-depth and insightful analysis of the shifting circumstances of peasants living on plantations, see Vincent C. Peloso, *Peasants on Plantations: Subaltern Strategies of Labor and Resistance in the Pisco Valley, Peru* (Durham, NC: Duke University Press, 1999).

[46] This was the norm for much of Latin American colonial economy, as well as certain areas where export production expanded in the nineteenth century. For an insightful summary of much of the early literature, see Steve J. Stern, "Feudalism, Capitalism, and the World-System in the Perspective of Latin America and the Caribbean," *The American Historical Review* 93, no. 4 (1988): 829–72.

[47] Unreliable census records, however, make it difficult to determine the precise nature of these shifts. For example, according to census records, the population of Alta Verapaz increased by 56 percent in twenty years – from 86,943 in 1880 to 136,024 in 1902. *Censo de la República de Guatemala: Levantado el 28 de agosto de 1921* (Guatemala: Tipografía Nacional, 1924), 16.

[48] Martínez Muñoz and Busto Brol, "Agricultura."

[49] "La cortesía," *La Voz del Norte*, April 15, 1904.

[50] See Sandra del Carmen Mérida, "Agricultura para el consumo interno," in *Historia general de Guatemala, vol. 5: Época contemporánea: 1898–1944*, ed. Jorge Luján Muñoz and Daniel Contreras R. (Guatemala: Asociación de Amigos del País, 1996), 358.

Either way, el Q'eq's voracious appetite for eggs can be read as a metaphor for the uncertainty of Maya life under coffee capitalism.

Coffee planters deployed several mechanisms to create fincas de mozos. First, some purchased Maya-inhabited lands outright as tierras baldías. In some instances, the documentary record suggests that the purchase of tierras baldías generated a relatively smooth transition from living as villagers on communally owned property to living as plantation laborers on a finca de mozos owned by a ladino, German, or Q'eqchi' coffee planter. Second, coffee planters purchased the individual titles of previously communal properties and then eventually stitched these individual titles back together in a newly reconstituted finca de mozos. This second method often required coercion or significant amounts of time. Shortly after the residents of Cojaj divided their communal property into individual titles, Richard Sapper threatened the residents with violence, forcing them to turn over four out of their twelve caballerías of land. Seeking to expand the emerging finca de mozos, Sapper then petitioned to title other parts of Cojaj as part of his adjacent property. The violent threats then escalated. Persecuted by soldiers commissioned by Sapper, the residents of Cojaj were rounded up and forced to work on Sapper's plantation. "These acts," wrote the patriarch Andrés Maquin, "could not be more abusive given that we are neither Sapper's [mozos] colonos nor renters, and we live in our own lands where we cultivate our small coffee plantations."[51] Asking for protection from the president, Andrés Maquin sought, ineffectively, to ward off the illegal appropriation of Cojaj. Three years later, the residents of Cojaj petitioned the local courts once again. Rather than fighting Sapper, they demanded payment for the lots that the Q'eqchi' patriarch Maquin had sold off to Richard Sapper.[52] Perhaps seeing no other possibility, Maquin illegally sold the remaining parts of Cojaj to Sapper and abandoned his role as a patriarch.

While the purchase of tierras baldías resulted in rapid change for some rural Mayas, the creation of fincas de mozos often took years, if not decades. Coffee planters sometimes cobbled together the individually titled plots of ethnic clan lands in a long-term process of reconstituting a finca de mozos. Grain shortages, inflationary pressures, and low coffee prices forced many smallholders to sell their individual plots. Erwin Paul Dieseldorff, for example, purchased the private titles of the ethnic clan land Tanchi-Raxaha over a period of nearly twenty years. In 1932

---

[51] AGCA B Leg. 28827 Exp. 2772 1892. See also AGCA J-AV 103 Leg. 26 E Exp. 23.
[52] See AGCA AA Exp. 1379, AGCA PO Jacinto Córdova 1895, folios 79–83.

Dieseldorff legally reconstituted these individual plots into a single finca de mozos.[53] Yet despite the coffee planter's best efforts to create a perfectly defined finca de mozos, with clear territorial boundaries as imagined in Sapper's map, many Maya smallholders tenaciously held on to their plots and defied efforts to re-create a complete ethnic clan territory. As a result of their resilience, the countryside, particularly around San Pedro Carchá, resembled an unfinished jigsaw puzzle. In 1922, for example, when Jorge Jähnig sought to determine the legitimate boundaries between his "German" and "indigenous" plots in the area known as Chimo, surveyors found it nearly impossible to go from one section of Jähnig's property to another without crossing the scattered properties of his Q'eqchi' neighbors.[54] These fragmented tenure arrangements were a far cry from Sapper's perfectly plotted map of landownership.

Whether plantations were purchased all at once or gradually pieced back together, coffee planters wanted Maya families to remain on the plantation and wanted to treat their property as a quantifiable asset that could be measured, bought, and sold. Such efforts required accurate maps and definite boundaries. German planters like Dieseldorff studied colonial-era Maya land titles as well as structures of governance to better understand Maya norms around land use and property, particularly ethnic clan lands.[55] These studies helped them model fincas de mozos on ethnic clan lands, and recognize that territorial boundaries were also about reaffirming community membership. As such, Q'eqchi' residents played an active role in land surveying not simply because of their intimate knowledge of the land but because such participation ensured that Q'eqchi' residents' memories of land use and community were embedded in the redefinition of territorial boundaries. In 1901, when Dieseldorff purchased the plantation Paijá, he assembled the Q'eqchi' residents and alcaldes auxiliares of the plantation, as well as those of Cucanjá, the neighboring *aldea* (small village), to participate in the survey

---

[53] The legal history of the purchase and sale of all the plots can be found in the German expropriation and agrarian reform records. See AGCA AA Exp. 1551, "Guillermo Erwin Dieseldorff Gressler," and AGCA DAN-AV Paq. 6 Exp. 6, "Raxaha, Carchá, W. E. Dieseldorff."

[54] AGCA ST-AV Paq. 99 Exp. 9.

[55] TULAL EDC "Old Titles of the Quecchí Indians" (September 15, 1903), 3. Dieseldorff discusses the meaning and implication of the land title in "Religión y arte de los mayas (continuación)," *Anales de la Sociedad de Geografía e Historia* 5, no. 2 (December 1928): 187. Karl Sapper similarly studied ancient Indian land titles; see *Título del Barrio de Santa Ana* (1900).

of the property. The field hands were instructed to bring their machetes and hatchets to clear trees and underbrush. The worker-residents assisted in the placement of the *mojones* (boundary markers).[56] The plantation territory was thus contingent on the knowledge and consent of the villagers, whom the planters purportedly governed.[57] Like the surveying of Q'eqchi' communal properties described in Chapter 2, coffee planters' efforts to spatially fix migratory Mayas and fluid landscapes was always partial, contested, and unfinished. Q'eqchi' laborers and neighboring villages constantly negotiated and moved the territorial boundaries of plantations, making absolute spatial fixity an illusion. Just as the Q'eqchi' patriarchs had reproduced the spiritual markers dividing communities by translating them into legal property boundaries, the Q'eqchi' laborers may have marked the locations of the Tzuultaq'as. They placed stones on hilltops, at trail crossings, and next to trees. By the early twentieth century, however, the descriptions of Maya markers and place names gradually disappeared in favor of supposedly universal and uniform scientific measurements.[58]

By involving all the residents in surveying, planters may have sought less to embed cultural meaning to territory than to stabilize boundaries as mutually agreed-on reality that made the plantation governable. Frequently, resident laborers reported trespassers on plantation property.[59] Conflicts nonetheless proliferated. Plantation borders, particularly those that divided communal lands, were often violently contested.[60] Like efforts to inscribe the abstract maps' fixed lines on agricultural lands and municipalities, coffee planters' efforts to stabilize the space of plantations did not erase earlier memories of land use. Rather, Q'eqchi' resident laborers continually sought to re-create their ethics of solidarity and reciprocity through Tzuultaq'as on a coffee plantation, and they fought over fixed boundaries that had once been fluid and subject to negotiation. Maya efforts to reproduce ontologies of reciprocity could never be

---

[56] AGCA ST-AV Paq. 42 Exp. 7. See also any of Erwin Paul Dieseldorff's land purchases in the Sección de Tierras as well as those of many other planters.

[57] See also Craib, *Cartographic Mexico*, 88.

[58] Julio César Méndez Montenegro, *444 años de legislación agraria, 1513–1957* (Guatemala: Revista de la Facultad de Ciencias Jurídicas y Sociales de Guatemala, 1960), 144–9.

[59] See AGCA J-AV 104 Leg. 2 A Exp. 2 and AGCA J-AV 104 Leg. 2 F Exp. 42.

[60] For those specifically relating to Erwin Paul Dieseldorff's properties, see AGCA J-AV 104 Leg. 9 A Exp. 10; AGCA MG B Leg. 29164 Exp. 10; AGCA J-AV 104 Leg. 9 C Exp. 38; AGCA J-AV 103 Leg. 29 A Exp. 10; AGCA J-AV 103 Leg. 36 A Exp.16; AGCA J-AV 103 Leg. 25 A Exp. 18.

entirely successful, and the voracious appetite of el Q'eq highlights the
perversion of Maya ethics under coffee capitalism. While the archival
record suggests that the colonos reported trespassers, according to oral
testimonies, el Q'eq policed the boundaries of the plantation. Those
caught trespassing or stealing were taken to the coffee planter. This
symbolized the kind of partial sovereignty that German coffee planters
sought to create – one based not on reason and the law but on sexual
transgression and moral perversion.

Like other forms of mapping, the creation of fincas de mozos involved
marking distinctions between "inside" and "outside" the plantation.
These boundary markers, however, also marked variations in state and
planter sovereignty. Like the worker camps and various penal, military,
settler, or agricultural colonies that formed a historical genealogy with
formal European colonies, the plantation was a designated space, a
holding pen that constricted sociality and confined people. It enclosed
and contained laborers and coffee plants as distinct from the uncivilized
lands outside the plantation itself.[61] German coffee planters frequently
evoked the civilization–barbarism binary to describe the dualism between
the ordered social and natural worlds of the coffee plantation and the
fecund tropics that dangerously lurked at its edges.[62] For coffee planters,
the plantation was a promise and anticipation of a future defined by
prosperity and civilization. For coffee plantation laborers, the plantation
was the suspension of time altogether. The plantations, as Ann Stoler
argued for the colony and camp, "are both containments, enclosures, and
unsettled encampments that are more closely allied than we may have
imagined."[63] Like colonies, the plantation was "a tenuous, illegitimate,
and provisional political formation" that rested on the racialization of
certain peoples and their political subordination. The plantation distinguished civilized order from barbarous chaos, and defined racialized
plantation residents as mozos in relationship to a hierarchy within the
plantation and beyond. The process of mapping did not simply reflect, but
also produced new agricultural practices and social relations and gave
structured meaning to the politics of postponement. The spaces of the

---

[61] Stoler, *Duress*.

[62] These are common tropes that appear in German writing on the tropics; see Christiane
Berth, "Between 'Wild Tropics' and 'Civilization': Guatemalan Coffee Plantations as Seen
by German Immigrants," in *Comparing Apples, Oranges, and Cotton: Environmental
Histories of the Global Plantation*, ed. Frank Uekötter (Frankfurt: Campus Verlag,
2014).

[63] Stoler, *Duress*.

plantation were further carved up into discrete areas for coffee and subsistence production, workers' and administrators' houses, as well as the coffee processing machinery. Like the plantations themselves, el Q'eq was produced and owned by German coffee planters. As the product of a sexual union between a German coffee planter and a cow, el Q'eq was said to have been born a slave to Germans. In his anthropological writings, David Sapper contrasted the Q'eq with the Tzuultaq'as, noting that this "maligned spirit . . . causes all types of evil and damage, bewitching people and crops and persecuting everyone and everything in his reach."[64] El Q'eq, like life on the plantation, was an inversion, rather than a realization, of Q'eqchi' ethics.

FINCAS DE MOZOS II: COERCION, DEBT, AND DEPENDENCY

Above all else, el Q'eq symbolized new regimes of discipline on coffee plantations. Roaming the plantation, el Q'eq's job was to maintain order and police the plantation's frontiers. Through its nightly escapades, el Q'eq induced fear and promoted good behavior among workers. Like Michel Foucault's panopticon, el Q'eq functioned not only through direct corporal punishment, but by creating self-regulatory norms – the ever-present sensation of being watched – so that workers would govern themselves. As Foucault suggested, capitalism created the need for new regimes of discipline, which were realized through workers' asylums and madhouses, where unfit laborers were removed from society and reeducated. Rather than the time-discipline and panopticon of the prison and factory, plantation punishment worked through the malignant figure of el Q'eq. In Alta Verapaz, labor training was not a state-directed project that relied on the scientific expertise of medical doctors and psychiatrists, or even judges and police officers. Instead, coffee planters took private control over labor education and punishment on the plantation, creating whipping posts and jails. Like the prison or the madhouse, fincas de mozos constituted a colony, where coffee planters deployed a combination of violent coercion, debt, and discipline to create good workers. Coffee producers in Alta Verapaz did not aim to create a fully formed proletariat entirely dependent on wage labor, but a hybrid that at once engaged in subsistence production to subsidize coffee production, while

---

[64] David E. Sapper, "Costumbres y creencias religiosas de los indios Queckchi," *Academia Sociedad de Geografía e Historia de Guatemala* 2, no. 2 (1926): 191.

remaining dependent on seasonal wage labor. As such, Q'eqchi' resident laborers also frequently thwarted coffee planters' efforts to make them dependent and drew on small spaces of power to assert their agency and autonomy.

Coffee planters like Erwin Paul Dieseldorff sought to fix Maya residents, who had long engaged in migratory forms of production, to the plantation by creating new dependencies and by deploying coercion. Coffee planters could threaten Mayas with the loss of access to subsistence lands and forced removal from their community of origin; sometimes they burned the milpas of those who failed to fulfill their labor obligations.[65] Shortly after purchasing the property Secac from Eduardo Felice, Dieseldorff removed "troublesome" mozos, including the alcalde auxiliar Joaquin Chub, from the property because these laborers refused "to obey the property rights" that Dieseldorff had acquired. Chub, along with the residents of Secac, however, claimed to be owners of the land, rather than resident laborers. In retaliation, Dieseldorff burned their milpas and ranchos, and confiscated all their objects of value.[66] In addition, coffee planters deployed coercive violence, including whippings and incarceration. This equipped coffee planters with the ability to punish defiant laborers and usurp the state's role in policing the population. Littered throughout the judicial archives and governmental records are reports of illegal detention, threats, and the use of force that speak to the centrality of violence in the plantation social worlds. Concepción Choc appeared in the local courts, for example, noting that Dieseldorff had illegally detained her daughter, Patrocina, who worked in his plantation store. Unable to account for a quintal of salt, Dieseldorff's administrator imprisoned Patrocina on an accusation of theft. The administrator whipped and beat Patrocina and then locked her in a dank plantation jail for three days without food. The administrator returned only to torment Patrocina, until he finally threatened to take her life if she did not confess.[67] Violence against resident laborers, while often unpredictable and irrational, was the essence of patriarchal plantation politics rather than an exception. While violent coercion weighed heavily on resident laborers, this violence – at once illegitimate and legitimating – also meant that the space of the plantation was a space of contention, particularly when it involved women.

[65] AGCA J-AV 104 Leg. 26 B Exp. 22 1925.
[66] AGCA J-AV 103 Leg. 29 A Exp. 10. See also AGCA J-AV 104 Leg. 26 B Exp. 22 1925.
[67] AGCA J-AV 105 Leg. 29 B Exp. 5. See also AGCA J-AV 104 Leg. 20 A Exp. 27.

As coffee planters expanded their properties, they assigned administrators to oversee the running of individual plantations and solidified structured racialized and gendered hierarchies. Administrators were frequently newly arrived German settlers and ladinos, but they were also occasionally Q'eqchi' patriarchs. They were charged with overseeing the day-to-day affairs of plantation life. These administrators then appointed representatives of the Guatemalan state, Maya alcaldes auxiliares and caporales, to directly oversee laborers. They worked for the coffee planters and were responsible to them. These plantation state officials were tasked with a wide range of responsibilities, from administering justice to rounding up workers, and facilitated the process of establishing planter sovereignty. Dieseldorff required these plantation alcaldes and caporales to inspect each mozo's plots and report Mayas who transgressed the new rules regarding the distribution of subsistence lands.[68] As Karl Sapper reminded us, coffee planters maintained a partial territorial sovereignty through their management of Guatemalan state officials on plantations. At the bottom of the hierarchical scheme were the resident laborers, which included entire families and villages of rural Mayas, themselves modeled on a patriarchal hierarchy. Across this hierarchical organization, each position was defined by gender, race, and class so that resident laborers were frequently demasculinized and, as the word "mozo" suggests, were referred to as mere boys. Despite this hierarchical organization, some women used the new plantation economy to advance their own interests, finding new roles as cooks and corn grinders (*molenderas*), who could often earn a degree of economic autonomy.[69]

As plantation hierarchy suggests, coffee planters played on patriarchal hierarchies and "gender pacts" in which men were responsible for protecting and providing for women. Coffee planters, thus, often described themselves as "good fathers" to their workers, and the various men occupying lower roles as alcaldes and administrators were folded into relative positions in this gendered hierarchy of paternal care. This plantation patriarchy was often reinforced through violent discipline and by Q'eqchi' appeals to higher men for protection. Coffee planters often jailed, beat, or punished the wife or mother of a delinquent laborer. The public wife-beating demasculinized laborers who failed to

---

[68] See, for example, TULAL EDC, Vol. 78, folios 443 and 880.
[69] See also David Carey Jr., *Engendering Mayan History: Kaqchikel Women as Agents and Conduits of the Past, 1875–1970* (New York: Routledge, 2006), 31–60.

fulfill their obligations. This demasculinization reproduced the plantation's racial–gender hierarchy, where coffee planters were at the top
with female laborers at the bottom. Within patriarchal politics women
appealed to higher authorities, such as other plantation owners, judges,
or the departmental governor, for protection on behalf of their husbands, sons, and brothers, and thus turned the racial–gender hierarchy
against coffee plantation administrators and owners.[70] Women's frequent calls to higher-status men to protect lower-class Q'eqchi' women
and men against the excesses of other men expanded rather than diminished patriarchal privilege.

While bolstering patriarchal privilege, women's efforts also forced
coffee planters to occasionally relinquish some of their plantation sovereignty.[71] As such, many coffee planters discouraged their laborers from
appealing to higher authorities and called on them to treat the coffee
planters as *the* superior authority. When Domingo Chub and Domingo
Caal from Yalpmech lodged a complaint, Dieseldorff asked the unhappy
laborers to settle their dispute with the administrator. If disputes could
not be easily settled, Dieseldorff explained that he would intervene directly on their behalf. Most importantly, however, he asked his workers to
refrain from appealing to other authorities or outsiders:

These people do not act in your best interests nor mine, but they only look to take
advantage of whatever they can for their personal interests.... Remember how
they treated you ten or more years ago. None of you asked to go to Chisec or to be
forced to work a number of days in someone else's plantation or for the municipality. They took you by force from your ranchos and they took you to Cubilguitz
where you had to work for three or four months in a row, leaving all your women
and children alone in your ranchos. In Cublguitz you had to work hard, to put up
with many illnesses. Today everything is completely different.[72]

Dieseldorff signed off as "les saluda su patron" (greetings from your
patron). Better than facing the hardships of mandamientos, Dieseldorff
reminded the laborers of the benefits of patriarchal plantation life, and
thus sought to reinstate both his authority and plantation sovereignty.

[70] AGCA J-AV 103 Leg. 15 Exp. 12. "Patriarchal pacts" build on Steve J. Stern, *The Secret
History of Gender: Women, Men, and Power in Late Colonial Mexico* (Chapel Hill:
University of North Carolina Press, 1995); see also David Carey Jr., *I Ask for Justice:
Maya Women, Dictators, and Crime in Guatemala, 1898–1944* (Austin: University of
Texas Press, 2013).
[71] Stern, *The Secret History of Gender.*
[72] TULAL EDC Fincas, Bound Vol. 63, Fol. 686, "Erwin Paul Dieseldorff a Domingo Chub
y Domingo Caal," January 10, 1912.

In addition to deploying violent coercion and patriarchal pacts, coffee planters also used the principle of dependency, which enabled coffee planters to promote voluntary consent in which laborers depended on coffee planters for their basic needs, including access to subsistence lands and the payment of their mandamiento and military exemptions, duties that had long been the domain of Q'eqchi' patriarchs. In exchange for these protections, every four years an administrator and the resident laborers agreed to the terms of a new contract that stipulated salaries and labor expectations. Through this subtler dependency, coffee planters aimed to limit subsistence production so as to prevent marketable surpluses that would grant resident laborers more autonomy. Coffee planters like Dieseldorff sought to restrict the size of the Q'eqchi's' milpa plots (generally twenty cuerdas) in order to limit their subsistence production to the confines of the plantation, and to require that laborers purchase their goods from the plantation itself.[73] Planters also paid wages in *fichas*, a kind of plantation currency, to limit autonomy and inhibit movement off the plantation. They argued that plantation coins were necessary because of the national scarcity of currency due to inflation.[74] Fichas, however, had limited circulation value and forced many plantation laborers to spend their earnings at the local plantation store.[75] Resident laborers, however, constantly violated their contracts. Although they were almost always forbidden to engage in commercial production for themselves on plantation land, many nevertheless sold the corn from their milpas on local markets; some sold even the food rations given them by their employer, confident that he needed their labor and would not let them starve. Bolder resident laborers sometimes brought in relatives or hired labor to cultivate corn on a commercial scale on plantation land. Others even attempted to title the land as their own.[76] Such acts, however, came with risks, including violent retribution or removal. By eroding the

---

[73] TULAL DC Fincas Bound Vol. 77, Fol. 909; Vol. 64, n.p.

[74] Carlos E. Nájera M., *Fichas de fincas: Acuñaciones particulares de moneda en Guatemala, que se utilizaron como instrumento de explotación* (Guatemala: Editorial de Cultura, Ministerio de Cultura y Deporte, 1998).

[75] Ricardo Terga, *Almas gemelas: Un estudio de la inserción alemana en las Verapaces y la consecuente relación entre los alemanes y los K'ekchies* (Cobán: Imprenta y Tipografía "El Norte," 1991), 263; Benjamin Caal interview with the author June 5, 2008. The municipality of Carchá often fought against Sapper's currency. SPCM 1907 Actas Municipales 1907; SPCM 1924, "Circular del Jefé Político of Alta Verapaz a las municipalidades de Alta Verapaz," September 19, 1924.

[76] McCreery, *Rural Guatemala*, 224, and AGCA JP-AV 1915 Paq. 1, "Indigenas de la Finca Primavera al JP," November 12, 1915.

material self-sufficiency of Mayas, coffee planters added another subtle instrument of discipline to their repertoire of weapons for ensuring a stable and compliant labor force.

Most potently, coffee planters tied laborers to the plantation through debt. Plantation laborers earned a wage that theoretically enabled them to pay off their wage advances. In practice, however, once rural Mayas were lured into debt, they found it practically impossible to regain their freedom. The cycle of debt was made worse by the decline in real wages, especially since the advent of coffee required the importation of most foodstuffs and drove up prices for goods. Wage levels thus not only failed to keep pace in good times, but were even worse in moments of ongoing inflation as occurred throughout Manuel Estrada Cabrera's rule. Ultimately, however, the real debt of the worker mattered little to the coffee planter. As David Gaeber has argued, what counted was that debts were quantifiable and backed by state and nonstate violence.[77] Coffee planters sometimes falsified records, passed a laborer's debts onto kin, or declared the laborer's indebtedness under oath. As a result, few plantation laborers were ever likely to escape the debt they owed. Drawing on his studies of Q'eqchi' cosmology, Karl Sapper, for example, concluded that "debts follow them [Q'eqchi's] into the afterlife."[78] In 1906 Dorotea Pop protested to the departmental governor, following the death of her husband, Santiago Yat, that her husband's outstanding debt with Fidel Ponce was transferred to her. "No human or divine law," Dorotea argued with the help of a tinterrillo, "requires a poor widow with minor children to be responsible for the labor debts contracted by her husband."[79] Indeed, these practices were used more generally in relations of debt peonage where women were required to pay the debts of their husbands, fathers, and brothers. Sons were sometimes also made responsible for the debts of their fathers.

Through debt, dependencies, and coercion, coffee planters sought to possess the time of laborers – both the time they were required to provide harvesting coffee and the time that future generations would be required to provide – and began to include this labor time as part of the capital value of a plantation. Debts owed for labor constituted assets that could

---

[77] David Graeber, *Debt: The First 5,000 Years* (New York: Melville House, 2014).

[78] Karl Sapper, "Religious Customs and Beliefs of the Q'eqchi' Indians," in *Early Scholars' Visits to Central America: Reports by Karl Sapper, Walter Lehmann, and Franz Termer*, ed. Marilyn Beaudry-Corbett and Ellen T. Hardy (Berkeley: Costen Institute of Archaeology, University of California, 2000), 37.

[79] AGCA JP-AV 1906 Paq. 2 "D.D. al JP," October 4, 1906.

be included with the sale of a coffee plantation or separated out and disposed of independently.[80] Erwin Paul Dieseldorff and Max Leippard complained about planters such as Kensett Champney, who stole their mozos by offering them higher wages or a plot of land.[81] Coffee planters regularly traded, transferred, and sold the rights of laborers among themselves.[82] Coffee planters also sold the debts of laborers they no longer wanted or needed, often not at the actual value of the debt but for whatever the market would bear.[83] Newspapers were littered with ads for the sale of fincas de mozos that included the number of workers in the sale. Fincas de mozos also commanded high prices. In 1908, for example, one plantation purchased thirty-one workers for the price of their debts plus 150 percent, and in 1913 another paid a premium of 250 percent for 209 workers.[84] According to coffee planters' accounting procedures, laborers and their time constituted an essential part of the territory and value of the plantation itself, much as slaves on plantations constituted a particularly important part of the overall capital value deployed in production. In Guatemala, ownership of space was associated with ownership of time and money.[85] Dieseldorff laid out three options for his resident laborers who decided to work for another coffee planter: leave, pay rent, or work for him one week per month.[86]

Just as el Q'eq was owned by German coffee planters, and thus his nightly raids served to enrich the coffee planter, Alta Verapaz's fincas de mozos, and the laborers who resided in those plantations, were owned by planters and existed for the sole purpose of enriching the highly capitalized coffee plantations of the ninety or so entrepreneurial planters who formed the heart of Alta Verapaz's bourgeoisie.[87] Some lambasted the purchase and sale of fincas de mozos as "slave trading." In 1906 Manuel Estrada Cabrera issued Decree 657 to put a stop to the "exchange or sale of workers."[88] Less than a year later, with the support of a sympathetic departmental governor, Jorge Ubico, the new law was challenged in the

---

[80] See *El Progreso Nacional*, May 3 and 4, 1898.

[81] AGCA JP-AV 1906 Paq. 1, "EPD, Max Leippard al JP," November 12, 1906.

[82] AGCA JP-AV 1905 Paq. 4, "N.M al JP," October 12, 1905; AGCA B 119.21.0.0 Leg.4773 Exp. 43.

[83] AGCA JP-AV 1896 Paq. 3, "6 mozos al JP," April 7, 1896.

[84] McCreery, *Rural Guatemala*, 232.

[85] J. T. Way, *The Mayan in the Mall: Globalization, Development, and the Making of Modern Guatemala* (Durham, NC: Duke University Press, 2012), 37.

[86] AGCA JP-AV 1907 Paq. 4, "Erwin Paul Dieseldorff al JP," January 22, 1907.

[87] Numbers drawn from King, *Cobán and the Verapaz*, 298.

[88] Skinner-Kleé, *Legislación indigenista de Guatemala*, 86.

regional courts by Alta Verapaz's largest coffee planters, Dieseldorff and Sapper. Earlier that year, Sapper purchased a finca de mozos from Dieseldorff, expecting that the resident laborers would remain on the plantation. He was furious when he discovered that the mozos colonos were no longer on the plantation and filed a lawsuit against Dieseldorff for theft. In his defense, Dieseldorff contended that Decree 657 prohibited the sale of mozos. Such sales, he claimed, constituted "the traffic of slaves." Sapper, however, retaliated by suggesting that if Decree 657 was applied in Alta Verapaz, it would be "a death attack on agriculture" that "would ruin the country by killing the only source of wealth." This wealth was not coffee, but rather the workers themselves. "Who would buy a plantation," Sapper asked, "without the most important factor, which is workers. What trust should a foreigner have in setting up a plantation in this country [*fincarse en este país*], if they can never sell or trade their properties because it is a plantation of mozos? What is a wellspring without water?" Awarding in Sapper's favor, the judge effectively turned resident laborers into capital. In Alta Verapaz, labor and territory were so indelibly linked that stealing labor equaled stealing land. When José Vidaurre allegedly signed Richard Sapper's laborers to new contracts, Sapper accused Vidaurre of the theft of his property.[89]

As the figure of el Q'eq suggests, fincas de mozos were constituted by debt; the debt of el Q'eq to the plantation owner mirrored the debt that laborers also owed. This debt was more than simply a perverse capitalism in which wages were insufficient to cover subsistence. Rather, like el Q'eq, it defined the limits of freedom, citizenship, and equality.[90] Within liberal thought, debt signified an inability to chart one's own path free of constraints; in short, it marked the politics of postponement as debt broadly restricted one's capacity to act as a fully constituted citizen and historical agent. Such relations of obligation and dependency established Q'eqchi' laborers as racialized others who were dependent. By representing laborers as wards, plantation owners and administrators also fashioned themselves as truly autonomous and self-mastered individuals, who possessed the right to govern not just themselves but others as well. Since racial hierarchy derived from assessments of morals, views, and affective

---

[89] AGCA JP-AV 1907 Paq. 4, "Don R. Sapper con don José L. Vidaurre por infracción de la ley de trabajadores," October 2, 1907.

[90] See Saidiya Hartman, *Scenes of Subjection: Terror, Slavery, and Self-Making in Nineteenth-Century America* (New York: Oxford University Press, 1997), especially chapter 5.

loyalties, coffee planters recognized that the management of sentiments was central to plantation life itself. Daily plantation life helped affirm racialized differences as laborers, administrators, and plantation owners performed tasks that seemed to confirm racialized ascriptions. When coffee planters punished mozos, it was for violating the coffee planters' vision of their own self-mastery and autonomy as good plantation patriarchs, which was constructed both literally and figuratively by the resident laborers themselves.

Coffee planters cemented the perception that their laborers lacked freedom and autonomous self-governance by running contracts collectively. In 1898, for example, more than 2,500 Q'eqchi' men gathered in front of the plantation house at the plantation Chijolóm in Carchá and listened as an interpreter read the terms of the contract, after which they issued a joint verbal agreement, formalized by a thumbprint.[91] While collective contracts violated liberal norms of individual will, coffee planters worked hard to maintain the myth of unanimity. Coffee planters strategically incarcerated troublesome workers during contract renewals. Erwin Paul Dieseldorff, for example, employed an administrator and a soldier to capture bothersome workers so as to facilitate the signing of new contracts. For ten days, Dieseldorff held his unruly workers in a damp prison, where Don José Barahona threatened to turn them over to the departmental governor, whose punishment, Barahona claimed, would be far greater. According to Dieseldorff, this was necessary so that "they begin to feel some respect and fear." With the troublemakers locked away, Dieseldorff requested that the administrator warn the other plantation laborers of the consequences of their failure to renew their contracts: military service and forced labor on railways. "You must persuade them that the contract is necessary for them," explained Dieseldorff to his administrator, "and if they are stubborn or unwilling tell them that without a contract they would be forced to pay rent for their subsistence plots."[92] Even while collective contracts made a farce of liberal notions of free will, they illustrated, like el Q'eq himself, that the space of the plantation defined the limits of liberalism and the sovereignty of the state.

For Q'eqchi' laborers, however, such practices, especially the accumulation of debts, did not merely signify the loss of autonomy and rights to self-governance within liberal ideas of the autonomous self. From within a

[91] Cited in Grandin, *The Last Colonial Massacre*, 26.
[92] TULAL EDC Vol. 61, Fol. 454.

Q'eqchi' political ontology, debt also signaled the mutual obligation between coffee planters and resident laborers, which mirrored Maya reciprocity. For Mayas, the accumulation of debts implied not simply an obligation to labor for a planter; it also conferred on Mayas certain protections and power in highly asymmetrical relations. By accruing debt, laborers increased the amount of capital a coffee planter invested in them and thus garnered greater bargaining power with the coffee planter. The more the plantation owner invested in a laborer in the form of monetary advances, the more power that laborer could wield in the relationship. While workers who violated norms could be made to leave, coffee planters had to face the problem of the laborers' debts and how to make them repay.[93] Likewise, Q'eqchi's could use growing competition among plantation owners to their advantage. While some rural Q'eqchi's might not have wanted to leave their ancestral lands located in a finca de mozo, others appeared willing to hop from finca de mozo to finca de mozo, searching for more favorable working conditions. In this way, workers were able to bid up advances and improve conditions and, to a certain extent, maintain some mobility.[94] In coffee planters' persistent claims of fugitive laborers, we can also then read that Q'eqchi' laborers were frequently challenging the terms of their debt agreements with a degree of success.

On fincas de mozos, coffee planters forged new disciplinary relations that combined patriarchal politics and coercion with debt and dependency. Unlike the state-directed efforts found in prisons and madhouses described by Foucault, coffee planters exercised a privatized discipline on the plantation, whether in the violent coercion of physical punishment or through the subtler mechanisms of dependency. Coffee planters sought to demarcate the plantation as a state of exception, where they set the limits of the liberal ideals of freedom, equality, and autonomy. While relations of dependency and debt signaled a lack of freedom within liberalism, they also signified mutual obligation from within Q'eqchi' culture. To fully understand how Q'eqchi's interpreted life on the plantation, it is thus necessary to also consider how coffee planters and workers built plantation life out of cultural translations across difference, and between liberal ideals and Q'eqchi' political ontologies. If we read el Q'eq as a window into Q'eqchi' commentary on plantation life, however, we can see that these cultural translations were not neutral. El Q'eq – who stole from the

---

[93] TULAL EDC Vol. 91, Fol. 95.   [94] See Reeves, *Ladinos with Ladinos*.

poor to enrich coffee planters – represented not only the enactment of reciprocity, but also its violation. As a solitary figure, el Q'eq also opposed Q'eqchi' ideas of community and spoke to atomization and individualism. Consuming symbols of reproduction, acting individually, and propelled by foreign interests, el Q'eq represented the epitome of disrespect and nonproductivity. While for German coffee planters, the plantation spoke of wealth and prosperity, for Mayas it expressed moral decay and the loss of social and economic reproduction.

FINCAS DE MOZOS III: GOOD PATRIARCHS, LOYAL WORKERS, AND THE MYTH OF TWIN SOULS

As the product of sexual violation and deviance, el Q'eq was also an expression of the emergence of new and rigidly policed racial and sexual politics. The fincas de mozos' racialized and gendered hierarchies were also labor-management strategies. Coffee planters based their labor management on a conscious adaptation of Q'eqchi' patriarchal norms and hierarchies. They assumed the helm of the plantation hierarchy and appropriated many of the tasks long attributed to Q'eqchi' patriarchs. These new patriarchal duties included distributing subsistence land, administering justice, overseeing religious festivities and celebrations, organizing communal labor obligations, and, finally, representing Maya interests to the state. While there were some apparent similarities between the patriarchal obligations of communal properties and those of fincas de mozos, patriarchal obligations on fincas de mozos were always shaped by the racial and class hierarchies of coffee capitalism.

Just as coffee planters used cartographic inscriptions of land tenure to incorporate and redefine Q'eqchi' ontologies, they also incorporated and reworked Q'eqchi' forms of patriarchal community.[95] German coffee planters understood themselves as new patriarchs in Q'eqchi' community life. From their studies of Q'eqchi' culture and history, German coffee planters recognized the strategic value in translating and adapting Maya patriarchal ethics into a new plantation patriarchy. From his studies of the "peaceful" conquest, Karl Sapper, for example, concluded that "while, for example, in southern Guatemala almost everywhere a tolerably strict [labor] regime can be maintained, in the Alta Verapaz, the planter must adapt himself, as much as possible, to the more or less

---

[95] For a different example of how new land tenure regimes modified indigenous ethnic lineages, see Mallon, *Courage Tastes of Blood*.

patriarchal discipline; the Indians of the latter locality say of their master, that 'he lives as a father among them,' and expect a corresponding treatment from him; and here especially it is important to learn the native language of the Indians, since through translation of the interpreters many misunderstandings arise, which may engender ill feeling."[96] Sapper's call for patriarchal relations with Q'eqchi's was based not just on interpretations of Q'eqchi' culture. For German settlers in the colonies, images of patriarchal affection between planter and laborer, as well as the promise of founding respectable families abroad, were central organizing metaphors and models.[97] These metaphors were powerful discourses that elicited notions of obligation, duty, rights, and loyalty that merged with new relations of violence, affection, and dependency on plantation life.

Yet concerns with the familial sentiments that bound coffee planter and resident laborer were not just metaphors. Attention to affective bonds was also a strategy of governance, a calculated effort to shape proper conduct, to foster good work habits, and to cultivate fidelity and obedience. These efforts also reproduced and stabilized racialized difference.[98] But they were not entirely new. Patriarchal authority blended German aspirations for familial governance with Q'eqchi' patriarchal norms.[99] Everyday life on coffee plantations was marked by the strategic and hybrid blending of Q'eqchi' patriarchal norms of reciprocal obligations with the purportedly civilized coffee planters who oversaw the uncivilized and backward laborers.

Acting as good patriarchs involved a number of different facets ranging from learning Q'eqchi' to participating in the ritual life of Maya communities to enacting local justice, and even becoming new intermediaries between rural Mayas and the state.[100] Through these efforts, German coffee planters supported the translation of the Q'eqchi' ethics of reciprocity, solidarity, and mutual obligation into a new plantation

---

[96] Sapper, *Das Nördliche Mittel-Amerika*, 223.

[97] Woodruff D. Smith, "Colonialism and the Culture of Respectability," in *Germany's Colonial Pasts*, ed. Eric Ames, Marcia Klotz, and Lora Wildenthal (Lincoln: University of Nebraska Press, 2005), 3–20. See also Lora Wildenthal, *German Women for Empire, 1884–1945* (Durham, NC: Duke University Press, 2001).

[98] Ann Stoler examines colonial rule as attempts to manage affective relations. See *Carnal Knowledge and Imperial Power: Race and the Intimate in Colonial Rule* (Berkeley: University of California Press, 2002).

[99] See Lynn Hunt, *The Family Romance of the French Revolution* (Berkeley: University of California Press, 1992).

[100] Erwin P. Dieseldorff, *Der Kaffeebaum: Praktische Erfahrungen über seine Behandlung im nördlichen Guatemala* (Berlin: Verlag Hermann Paetel, 1908), 35–6.

patriarchy centered on German planters. As coffee planters reassembled ethnic clan lands as fincas de mozos, Q'eqchi' ethics and ontologies blended with a new overlapping set of rules, authorities, and meanings that governed life on the plantation.

German coffee planters claimed a special propensity to be not only good plantation patriarchs but also good civilizers. Richard Sapper's cousin David explained that "while the Indians were still not accustomed to formal work as well as punctuality, they generally accepted with goodwill the teachings and they demonstrated to be a good-hearted people that could be educated through peacefulness and perseverance."[101] Shortly after his arrival in Alta Verapaz, Erwin Paul Dieseldorff noted that "all of the Indians, for example, are very dirty. But when they enter into more intimate contact with Europeans, to serve them, etc., then they generally become very clean, sometimes even scrupulously clean."[102] In contrast, ladinos, according to Dieseldorff, were infamous for avarice, violence, and falsehood. Through romanticized representations of Maya–German relations, Maya resistance to coerced labor on coffee plantations was carefully recast as the laborers' need for more contact with civilized European patriarchs.

The patriarchal politics of plantation life also rested on sex and rape.[103] Foreign immigrants, especially Germans, often relied on concubinage to facilitate permanent settlement. In Alta Verapaz, Q'eqchi' women of wealthy landowning families afforded German immigrants the means to quickly acclimatize to the region by providing local medical and cultural knowledge, access to land, and a quicker way to learn the language. In many cases, concubinage entailed demands on women's labor and legal rights, and was simply portrayed as companionship or cohabitation outside marriage or as domestic service.[104] The common

---

[101] David Sapper, "Memorias," unpublished translation from German, trans. Regina Wagner (March 1952). See also Julie Gibbings, "'Their Debts Follow Them into the Afterlife': German Settlers, Ethnographic Knowledge, and the Forging of Coffee Capitalism in Nineteenth-Century Guatemala," *Journal of Comparative Studies in Society and History* 62, no. 2 (April 2020): 389–420.

[102] Erwin Paul Dieseldorff, "Letters to His Mother" (1879–90), 172.

[103] For a discussion of Q'eqchi'–German sexual and familial relations, see Adrian Roesch, *A Medley from the Alta Verapaz: Images of German Life in Guatemala, 1868–1930*, trans. Petra Fischer (Stuttgart: At Home and Abroad Publishing, 1934), 101–4; Karl Sapper, *Die Tropen: Natur und Mensch Zwischen Den Wendekreisen* (Stuttgart: Strecker und Schröder, 1923), 117; King, *Coáan and the Verapaz*, 64, 70, 86–9, 224–68; Terga Cintrón, *Almas gemelas*.

[104] Roesch, *A Medley from the Alta Verapaz*; and Terga Cintrón, *Almas gemelas*, 7–21.

discourse of "living maritally" (*viven maridablemente*) in fact suggested more social privileges than most women who were involved in such relations would have actually enjoyed. They could be dismissed without reason, severance, or even pay.[105] Women who worked as domestic and sexual servants provided the daily needs of coffee plantation administrators, without imposing either the emotional or financial obligations of a European family. In other cases, Q'eqchi' and ladina women became abiding and faithful companions who shared the same quarters as the German man. These interracial relationships transgressed and solidified racial hierarchies and patriarchal politics. Eventually, German coffee planters sought to marry proper German wives as symbols of their status as successful entrepreneurs.

The relatively harmonious and stable Q'echi' cook–German planter relationships were not the only forms of interracial sex on plantations. Frequently, coffee planters took advantage of their patriarchal status to engage in interracial sex that was little more than rape. The Bostonian cousins Kensett and Walter Champney, who arrived at the end of the nineteenth century, each fathered more than a dozen children. "They fucked anything that moved," recalled a neighboring planter.[106] David Sapper, who fathered a son named Ernesto with Candelaria Ac, was said to have maintained relationships with at least three other indigenous women, and fathered twenty-six children. Yet he claimed in his memoirs: "Instead of imitating my friends, much older than I, who looked to make the monotonous life on the plantation more bearable through distractions called 'fun' such as orgies and other pleasures, I lived very much within myself being that my only rest were my stays of two or three days every half year in Chimax."[107] Intimate relations between German men and Q'eqchi' women evinced German power over Q'eqchi' men.

On rare occasions, protests to a German man's perceived rights to Q'eqchi' women entered the historical record. José de Laza, for example, complained that the German administrator Eduardo von Möeller demanded to have twelve-year-old María Bol, the daughter of one of Laza's resident laborers. According to Laza, Bol's parents had hidden their daughter in a distant village. Even more, Laza complained that this

[105] AGCA JP-AV 1936 Paq. 2, "Carta de Angela Xoy al JP," October 29, 1936.
[106] Cited in Grandin, *The Last Colonial Massacre*, 32.
[107] Sapper recognized Ernesto Ac during World War II; see CM Libros de Reconocimiento, folio 245. For his other children, see Terga Cintrón, *Almas gemelas*, 277.

was the third time von Möeller had "taken" a laborer's daughter.[108] In 1908 Mercedes Yat accused Samuel Hoenes, a German plantation administrator, of demanding that she "turn over" her fourteen-year-old daughter, Josefa, so that he could "make use of her as is Señor Hoenes' custom." According to court testimonies, Hoenes threatened to revoke Mercedes's right to occupy and plant milpa on a small plot of plantation land. When the court questioned Hoenes, the administrator claimed that he had only requested that Josefa work for him as a domestic servant.[109] At other times, Q'eqchi' women sought the restoration of their honor via the courts. Juana Pacay, for example, accused Maximo Krings of "forcing himself" on her one night and offering her "great things." When Juana became pregnant, she requested that the departmental governor intervene so that Krings would comply with his promises.[110] Like the plantation itself, el Q'eq was a hypersexualized being. The origin of el Q'eq in a sexual union between a German planter and a cow spoke to the sexual subjugation of Q'eqchi's on the plantation, as well as to the ravenous sexual appetites of German landowners and administrators who took whomever they wanted whenever they wanted.

The patriarchal politics of affection and sexual violence on the plantation, however, also bled into highly romanticized mythologies of inter-racial love between German plantation administrators and Q'eqchi' laborers. One priest, for example, argued that Germans and Q'eqchi's were "twin souls," bound together by similar cultural characteristics such as the desire for hard work, moral sensibilities, and a love of nature.[111] Arne Sapper, grandson of Richard, proclaimed in an interview that "both groups [Q'eqchi's and Germans] had to struggle against nature and both pulled their weight equally, they depended on each other. The *indios* were aided by their customs and the Germans brought scientific knowledge, and other things that aided them in their struggle against nature."[112] These romantic representations of Q'eqchi's form part of a broader movement in nineteenth-century Germany. In novels, travel writing, and ethnographic displays of indigenous peoples, nineteenth-century Germans grew fascinated with exotic peoples and proclaimed a special affinity

---

[108] AGCA JP-AV 1907 Paq. 3, "José Laza al JP," July 3, 1907.
[109] AGCA JP-AV 1908 Paq. 2, "Criminal contra Samuel Hoenes."
[110] AGCA JP-AV 1907 Paq. 1, "Juana Pacay al JP," August 20, 1907.
[111] Terga Cintron, *Almas gemelas*.
[112] Arne Sapper, film transcripts from Uli Stelzner and Thomas Walther, *Los Civilizadores: Alemanes en Guatemala*, Colección DVD Guatemala (Alemania: Producción ISKA, 1998).

between Native American and German cultures. Both Germans and
Native Americans were representatives of a pure *Kultur* that was based
on an opposition to material and technological improvement, struggles
against conquest by outsiders, and that was free from peoples despoiled
by racial intermixing.[113] This special affinity can be found in Karl
Sapper's descriptions of Q'eqchi' life as a "whole picture of patriarchal
primitiveness and innocence, the likes of which will probably never again
be found in Europe," or in his claim that German women could learn
much from Q'eqchi' women's preparation of cacao.[114]

The Germans' desire to govern the countryside as good patriarchs
and thus elicit the loyalty of laboring classes, however, was neither new
nor unique to Germans. Q'eqchi' patriarchs, too, had fashioned themselves as good patriarchs whose special ability to govern the countryside
came from their fatherly connection to the rural classes and their desire
for national progress. Individuals such as Tiburcio Caal, Mateo Chub,
Pedro Coc, and Fabian Tiul had, in very distinct ways, engendered
patriarchal forms of community that combined both communal solidarity and reciprocity with liberal individualism, the hierarchy of inherited
status with the ability to rise through the ranks through service to the
community as good patriarchs. The mid-1880s crisis of legitimacy
within the indigenous patriarchy, however, generated the emergence of
new intermediaries from outside the ranks of indigenous society. Outsiders like Juan de la Cruz posed new threats and offered new promises
and forms of protection for disillusioned rural Q'eqchi's. If Juan de la
Cruz filled a vacancy in indigenous society, Germans, too, exploited the
same cracks and fissures. The plantation, however, was also distinct.
Fincas de mozos were produced through an uneasy combination of
loving guidance and violence, affection and intimidation, as planters

---

[113] For examples and development of this broader movement, see Harry Liebersohn,
Aristocratic Encounters: European Travelers and North American Indians (Cambridge:
Cambridge University Press, 1998); Susanne Zantop, *Colonial Fantasies: Conquest,
Family, and Nation in Precolonial Germany, 1770–1870* (Durham, NC: Duke Univer-
sity Press, 1997); Colin G. Calloway, Gerd Gemünden, and Susanne Zantop, eds.,
Germans and Indians: Fantasies, Encounters, Projections (Lincoln: University of Neb-
raska Press, 2002); H. Glenn Penny, *Kindred by Choice: Germans and American Indians
since 1800* (Chapel Hill: University of North Carolina Press, 2013). Sapper establishes
affinities between Germans and Mesoamerican Indians, especially the Q'eqchi' in *Das
Nördliche Mittel-Amerika*.

[114] Sapper, *Das Nördliche Mittel-Amerika*, 20; Karl Sapper, "Food and Drink of the
Q'eqchi' Indians," in *Early Scholars' Visits to Central America* (Los Angeles: Cotsen
Institute of Archaeology, 2000), 17–28.

sought to establish relations of dependency, coercion, and consent in the governance of their plantations. Through such affective politics and disciplinary practices as limiting the size of plots and paying wages in plantation fichas, coffee planters sought to fix laborers in place and solve the problem of migration. The management of sentiments, of what counted as a good, docile laborer, however, was never completely within the reach of coffee planters. Nor were such disciplinary efforts fully in the realm of the modern rational self.

For laborers, residence on the plantation involved the suspension of time even as their bodies were linked to territory that signaled planter sovereignty, a delimited territory that marked the limits of liberalism's promise of freedom, equality, and self-governance. For coffee planters, the plantation was both a promise and anticipation of future prosperity. On plantations, then, coffee planters imagined their civilized selves and luxuries violently squeezed from the bodies of Maya laborers. The plantation existed by virtue of its dependent status on the nation-state, but those who inhabited it stood in a skewed relationship to national biopolitical and legal norms: their time was not their own, and the meaning of freedom was circumscribed by debt and dependency, even as these relations repeated and sustained some of the aspects of patriarchal politics that guided Maya villagers. Coffee plantations were a space of affection and intimacy, but also of rape and violence, if not threats of violence. Fincas de mozos, then, were a tenuous political formation that sustained themselves by turning laborers into other kinds of people and their political position into a partial and gradated sovereignty.

CONCLUSION

By the first decade of the twentieth century, Alta Verapaz had undergone a dramatic metamorphosis. The short leafy rows of coffee plants replaced milpas, forests, and pasturage. Machine houses, processing plants, and cramped workers' quarters rose up on fincas de mozos, and roads and railways were etched into the region's mountains and valleys. The coffee plantation economy consolidated in Alta Verapaz then was significantly different from other parts of Guatemala, where highland Mayas traveled to the Pacific coast for the coffee harvest, propelled by mandamientos and eventually debt servitude. In these regions, the relatively large distances between workers' residences in the highlands and plantations in the lowland coasts created

administrative difficulties that facilitated worker resistance.[115] In Alta
Verapaz, because land suitable for coffee production overlapped with
preexisting Maya communities, and because there was an abundance of
land primarily in the hands of Maya communities, acquiring both sufficient land and labor were paramount. By the turn of the century,
mandamientos and the liberal state had undermined Q'eqchi' patriarchs'
role as native intermediaries, resulting in the need for new systems of
governance. The preferred mechanism was fincas de mozos, which
sought to reestablish patriarchs' relations that drew on Q'eqchi' norms
of mutual obligation, even as el Q'eq illustrated how coffee plantations
and the capitalist imperative reformulated Q'eqchi' ontologies. Unlike
the violence of Marx's metonymic chain of exchangeable commodities,
el Q'eq revealed Q'eqchi' interpretations of capitalism through allegories and metaphors that highlight the perversion of Q'eqchi' ethics and
the violence of sexual and political subjugation.

Even while some Q'eqchi's continued to plant coffee and shelter Maya
commoners, a large portion of the rural population by the second decade
of the twentieth century resided on coffee plantations owned by non-
Maya planters. In San Pedro Carchá, for example, the state recorded
3,114 mozos colonos and 437 indebted laborers working on 37 plantations. Since only male heads of households were counted in the records of
mozos colonos and indebted laborers, the actual number of people residing on the plantation was much higher. According to the official 1921
census, the rural population residing on fincas de mozos in San Pedro
Carchá totaled 20,717 individuals, or 39 percent of the rural population.
Other municipalities had much higher numbers – including Cobán where
54 percent of the rural population resided on fincas de mozos, or even
more dramatically Tucurú with 70 percent and Senahú with 60 percent
residing on fincas de mozos.[116] These numbers, like all state-collected
statistics from the time, probably undercounted the numbers of actual
laborers as coffee planters refused to permit state officials on their plantations, and thus self-reported the numbers. Coffee planters also may have
had an incentive to underrepresent the number of laborers who worked
for them to avoid paying taxes and being required to set up schools or out
of fear that they might be subject to another form of state intervention.

For Q'eqchi' commoners, the consolidation of the coffee plantation
economy by 1914 had important implications that were expressed

---

[115] Reeves, *Ladinos with Ladinos*, 87.
[116] *Censo de la República de Guatemala 1921*, 472–3.

through el Q'eq. Village members had less time or energy to maintain and reproduce social and ideological structures of cofradías or to meet their basic subsistence needs. This precarity was expressed in the notion of el Q'eq as a thief who stole from the poor to enrich the wealthy. The position of Q'eqchi's was further undercut by declining access to land, evidence of soil erosion, and climatic changes. Likewise, general population growth exacerbated these problems, and food shortages had become chronic by the early twentieth century. These same dynamics drove some Mayas to accept the relative comfort of fincas de mozos, which offered guaranteed subsistence production and exemption from military service and mandamientos. Fincas de mozos moved the system of labor from a largely coercive system to one that sought to make Maya laborers dependent on coffee planters. This new system combined patriarchal protections with coercive violence, displays of affection with discipline.

For coffee planters, fincas de mozos also ensured a new self-reliance and allowed them to construct spaces of partial sovereignty within the nation. They were no longer reliant on the state to provide labor through mandamientos, nor were they reliant on the state to discipline and punish laborers. Fincas de mozos enabled coffee planters to create their own kind of judiciary and jails, as well as more subtle mechanisms of discipline such as threats of loss of access to land. For planters, fincas de mozos were separated spaces that resembled camps and colonies in that their real and imagined boundaries distinguished between different kinds of people with different kinds of access to freedom and equality. Fincas de mozos, thus, were spaces of exception that allowed the metanarrative of liberal democracy overcoming enslavement to endure, since these others were relegated to a different place in space and time. Fincas de mozos enabled German planters to represent themselves as civilized men and agents of progress, and to imagine their future prosperity forged from Maya labor. In some cases, Germans imagined themselves as good patriarchs who protected Mayas and brought them into civilization. In this sense, German planters' sense of self rested on the performances of labor and good discipline on the part of mozos colonos.

For Q'eqchi's and German coffee planters alike, the social and political forms that emerged in the fincas de mozos transcended both space and time. When I asked different Altaverapacences why el Q'eq still roams the countryside, even though German-owned properties have all but disappeared, they explained that el Q'eq does not die. "The only thing that can kill a Q'eq," explained Miguel Yat, "is getting struck by a bolt of lightning." As the notion of el Q'eq suggests, the social formations

produced on the plantation have endured to haunt, steal, and scare
subsequent generations of Altaverapacences. To kill a Q'eq, he suggested,
required a natural force or perhaps, as in Xucaneb, a mountain spirit to
set the world straight. It is telling that el Q'eq still roams at night,
voraciously consuming eggs, stealing from the poor, and terrorizing those
whom he encounters.

For the small- and medium-sized planters squeezed out of coffee
planting in the late nineteenth and early twentieth centuries, desires for
modernity and progress had yet to be fulfilled. Planters pushed out of
coffee felt betrayal and postponement, what Michael Kirkpatrick has
called a "culture of waiting."[117] The feeling among aspiring ladinos and
Q'eqchi' patriarchs that modernity had been postponed was clearly symbolized in the Verapaz railway. While it had promised to catapult the
region into the orbit of the modern world, instead the railway was
truncated, inefficient, and unreliable, marked by constant disrepair and
delays that frequently left passengers stranded in the fetid lowlands. The
delays they endured cast a shadow over bourgeois notions of progress.
For many ladinos and Q'eqchi' patriarchs, their growing frustrations and
anxieties about becoming full participants in progress and the civilized
world made them susceptible to Manuel Estrada Cabrera's promises of
educational uplift and social mobility and his celebration of hardworking
ladino artisans against lazy aristocratic Europeans. Rural Mayas forced
to toil on coffee plantations, however, did not acquiesce to their fate, but
continued to seek alternative political futures grounded in Maya ontologies. By the turn of the century, the contradictions wrought by the politics
of postponement inherent in Guatemalan liberalism and racial capitalism
demanded resolution, and frustrations boiled up, generating cycles of
populism, dictatorship, and revolution that defined Latin America's twentieth century. By the 1920s, the mixed-race children born of unions
between German coffee planters and Q'eqchi' women also came to act
as strategic new intermediaries who disrupted and reworked traditional
forms of Q'eqchi' mediation.

---

[117] Michael Kirkpatrick, "Optics and the Culture of Modernity in Guatemala City since the
Liberal Reforms" (PhD diss., University of Saskatchewan, 2013).

PART II

ASPIRATIONS AND ANXIETIES OF UNFULFILLED MODERNITIES

5

On the Throne of Minerva

The Making of Urban Modernities, 1908–1920

And the indigenous race is listening, to the softness of your melodious accent, and driven by Good, there is forming, another race more worthy of the present.

—José D. Prado, "A Minerva," *El Norte* (October 1917)

As the nation plunged into economic calamity after the 1897 coffee market crash, Manuel Estrada Cabrera envisioned an extravagant annual festival to display Guatemala as a civilized nation on par with Europe and North America. As in the case of Alta Verapaz's railroad, Estrada Cabrera hoped the festivals would represent Guatemala's entrance onto the world stage, as a nation worthy of international recognition and, most importantly, foreign investment. In honor of Western civilization, the obligatory festivals were celebrations of Minerva, the Roman virgin goddess of music, poetry, medicine, wisdom, commerce, weaving, and the crafts. For three days every November, Guatemalans of all social classes gathered in Greco-Roman temples first in Guatemala City and then in the replicas that speckled the nation's countryside. Surrounded by tropical landscapes, the Minerva temples' heroic white columns offered a startling contrast. Foreign observers remarked that the Minerva temples dotting the countryside transported them across time and space from a remote and uncivilized countryside to the highest classical Western civilization.[1] "And it will be a festival worthy of a new time," noted one

[1] See Harry O. Sandberg, "Central America of Today – Guatemala," *Bulletin of Pan American Union* 218 (1916): 218–28; Catherine Rendón, *Minerva y la palma: el enigma de Don Manuel Estrada Cabrera* (Guatemala: Artemis Edinter, 2000).

observer in 1899. "The festival will raise spirits to previously unknown heights, and will proudly close the bright sky of Guatemala history during this century and foreigners will regard us as a cultured nation, lover of peace and progress."[2] While ostensibly the festivals were to display Guatemala on the world stage, the Minerva feasts, or Minervalias as they came to be known, were also profoundly important to national life and quickly became the nation's most important annual celebration, far exceeding in pomp and prestige the annual independence commemorations.[3] Estrada Cabrera commissioned illustrious poets and novelists to contribute to the festivals. Central America's renowned intellectuals, including the Guatemalan Maximo Soto Hall and the Nicaraguan Rubén Darío, delivered lavish speeches and recited poetry to the masses. In Guatemala City, German, French, Italian, Lebanese, and Chinese diplomats also exhibited their national traditions in pavilions, allowing for spectators to imagine Guatemala situated as a nation among nations on the world stage.[4]

While the Minerva festivals began in Guatemala City, during the first decade of the twentieth century Greco-Roman temples came to speckle the countryside as villages across the nation erected their own monuments to civilization, progress, and education. In 1908 Cobaneros constructed a Minerva temple on the city's western edges, and by 1915 smaller towns, such as San Pedro Carchá, San Cristobal Verapaz, Santa Cruz, and Tactic, all erected temples. In each town's Minerva temple, state officials honored teachers and students; the martial band and orchestra played; and the town's prominent citizens delivered flowery speeches exalting Manuel Estrada Cabrera and Western civilization. Everyone from the resident laborers of German coffee plantations to the departmental governor attended. For the participants, the festivals generated extraordinary feelings of being present at the center of Western civilization, with romantic floral arcs, scenic landscapes, and elaborate Greco-Roman temples and symbols. For the three days of Minervalias, all Guatemalans gained full access to modernity's promise of civilization, momentarily relieving the persistent feeling of being relegated to history's waiting room.

[2] "Panateneas," *Diario de Centro América*, October 21, 1899, p 1.

[3] See Clemente Marroquín Rojas, *Memorias de Jalapa o recuerdos de un remichero* (Guatemala: Editorial del Ejército, 1977), 96.

[4] See *Organización del desfile escolar en la marcha del veintiséis de los corrientes, con motivo de las festividades escolares del año de mil novecientos trece* (Guatemala: Tipografía Nacional, 1913).

Manuel Estrada Cabrera's dictatorship has been memorialized in Miguel Ángel Asturias's Nobel Prize–winning novel *El Señor Presidente* (1946) as a reign of political terror and arbitrary brutality. Secret police and *orejas* (spies) generated fear, obedience, and political exile. His dictatorship also offered marginalized urban social classes the promise of modernity and the illusion of social mobility through staged and choreographed spectacles such as the Minerva festivals.[5] This ambivalence between terror and the popular spectacle of social uplift was central to Estrada Cabrera's regime. At the very moment that German settlers consolidated their economic predominance, Estrada Cabrera sought to reconcile the feeling among the urban social classes of being left behind in the march toward progress. To do so, he promoted a new ladino nationalism that combined celebrations of the honorability and social mobility of ladino artisans with diatribes against corrupted aristocrats and European immigrants. With his praise of upwardly mobile ladinos and affronts to aristocracy, Estrada Cabrera's ladino nationalism strategically fashioned liberal–democratic and civilizing metanarratives into a novel nationalism. It also made race an invisible, but potent, discourse. In Alta Verapaz, ladinos as well as Q'eqchi' patriarchs took advantage of Estrada Cabrera's nationalism as well as liberal associations and clubs, and social welfare and artisan societies promoted by him, to face down racism, cement alliances, and remake the city and themselves in images of a distinctive urban modernity. As they built hospitals and new urban plazas, and cleaned and electrified the streets, ladinos and Q'eqchi' patriarchs staged and stabilized the meaning of modernity based on technology, aesthetics, and culture that symbolized their social mobility and progress, rather than liberal democracy and an end to slavery of the masses.[6] While these associations were vehicles for political patronage, Q'eqchi's and ladinos also utilized them to promote a new modern social order. The very festivals that Manuel Estrada Cabrera created to generate popular support, however, eventually became symbols of his reign of terror. Through his protopopulism, Estrada Cabrera embodied the beginning of twentieth-century efforts to reconcile the politics of postponement and the liberal promises of freedom and equality. For Guatemalan

---

[5] Miguel Ángel Asturias, *El señor presidente* (San José: Editorial Universidad de Costa Rica, 2000 [1946]).

[6] See Mark Overmyer-Velázquez, *Visions of the Emerald City: Modernity, Tradition, and the Formation of Porfirian Oaxaca, Mexico* (Durham, NC: Duke University Press, 2006), especially chapter 2.

Liberals, however, these efforts to modernize the city and reconcile modernity were frequently troubled by the growing number of lower-class, working women, who crowded Cobán's streets and marketplaces. Gaining access to wages gave women in the city more sexual and economic autonomy, which challenged patriarchal orders, while the urban public spaces working women occupied were sites of potential corruption, disease, and racial degeneration, which challenged visions of orderly progress and racial whitening.

EL SEÑOR PRESIDENTE AND LADINO NATIONALISM

For many Guatemalans, Manuel Estrada Cabrera himself embodied the promise of ladino nationalism and social uplift. Born to a domestic servant and a wealthy ladino, he was an illegitimate child of less-than-pure lineage. He nonetheless rose through the social hierarchies via education; Estrada Cabrera studied at the Instituto Normal de Varones, and then completed a law degree at the Universidad de Occidente in Quetzaltenango.[7] As a Liberal ladino from the western highlands city of Quetzaltenango, he was a proponent of the 1871 Liberal revolution and the belief that ladinos – regardless of their mixed-race origins – also harbored the historical agency to lead the nation to greatness. More than his Liberal predecessors, however, Estrada Cabrera obsessively sought to produce a unified ladino nation from a racially diverse body of lower-class ladinos, who had recently migrated to the nation's growing cities.

Emphasizing honorability and social class over lineage and physiognomy as social status determinants, Estrada Cabrera promised to create a ladino society without caste hierarchies. Whiteness, in this scheme, was defined not by skin color but by honor and social standing and was thus available to all. He celebrated the honorable working classes and called for the aristocratic elites' moral reform. By applauding ladino artisans, teachers, and other semi-skilled workers, he argued that the future of the country resided not with European immigrants and other white aristocrats but with ladinos who had risen up from humble origins.[8] In a society

---

[7] Rendón, *Minerva y la palma*, 1–6. See also Rafael Arévalo Martínez, *¡Ecce Pericles!: Historia de la tiranía de Manuel Estrada Cabrera* (San José: Editorial Universitaria Centroamericana, 1971).

[8] See Ramón Salazar, *Conflictos* (Guatemala: La Tipografía Nacional, 1898). For a discussion, see Julie A. Gibbings, "Another Race More Worthy of the Present: Race, History, and Nation in Alta Verapaz, Guatemala, c. 1860–1940s" (PhD diss., University of Wisconsin–Madison, 2012), 296–300.

where most lower-class ladinos possessed some indigenous blood, Estrada Cabrera's silence about familial origins and devaluation of skin color was empowering. His ladino nationalism erased histories of mestizaje but also granted little, if any, place for Mayas in the nation. Their dangerous promixity to Indianness made both poor ladinos and Q'eqchi' elites more susceptible to a political language that cast them as capable of civilization. Such racial silencing enabled some Q'eqchi' patriarchs – as members of Liberal clubs and artisan and welfare societies – to participate in displays of ladino nationalism without ever ceasing to be Q'eqchi'.[9] Alliances with ladinos thus helped Q'eqchi' patriarchs to distinguish themselves from Q'eqchi' commoners who increasingly toiled on German plantations.

When Estrada Cabrera promoted popular associations and celebrated artisans against aristocrats as the true embodiments of the Guatemalan nation, he also became a protopopulist. He skillfully applied many political techniques that later came to define mid-twentieth-century populist dictatorships including Rafael Trujillo (1930–61) in the Dominican Republic and Anastasio Somoza (1937–47, 1950–6) in Nicaragua.[10] Like Estrada Cabrera, these populist dictatorships combined terror with the extension of the state into everyday life through patronage networks and extravagant state theater that drew on popular idioms of masculinity and fantasies of social mobility. Estrada Cabrera declared himself "Protector of the Studious Youth" and thus the guardian of the national future. He rapidly expanded public education. He also actively supported the working classes by mandating mutual aid societies, labor unions, and artisan societies, which he sought to control as vehicles for political patronage. Minerva festivals were extravagant state theater designed to instill in ladinos their destined role as historical agents of progress. While Estrada Cabrera promoted these orchestrated scenes in the name of the betterment of the ladino national subject, he also installed an omnipresent reign of terror through a diffuse police-state apparatus and low tolerance for political dissidence.[11]

Historians, however, have often glossed over Estrada Cabrera's dictatorship, placing it alongside a number of other late nineteenth-century Central American regimes, including those of Justo Rufino Barrios,

---

[9] Thus, Q'eqchi' elites could be something akin to what Marisol de la Cadena has described as "indigenous mestizos." See *Indigenous Mestizos: The Politics of Race and Culture in Cuzco, Peru, 1919–1991* (Durham, NC: Duke University Press, 2000).

[10] See, especially, Lauren Derby, *The Dictator's Seduction: Politics and the Popular Imagination in the Era of Trujillo* (Durham, NC: Duke University Press, 2009).

[11] Rendón, *Minerva y la palma*; Arévalo Martínez, *¡Ecce Pericles!*.

Marco Aurelio Soto, and José Santos Zelaya, who emphasized the values of progress and order over democracy and liberty. Estrada Cabrera, in fact, owed much to caudillismo. As John Charles Chasteen has argued, caudillismo fashioned strongmen as cultural heroes who created loyalty among their followers by means of clientelism, patronage, and political prestige. Through their heroism, caudillos became collective symbols of masculine values such as bravery and skilled oratory. Like Estrada Cabrera, their appeal to the masses was based on their humble origins, and their leadership was ostensibly a product of skill and providence.[12] Historians, however, have also elided what made Estrada Cabrera different from nineteenth-century caudillos and dictators: his use of state theater and the appropriation of popular culture to address the politics of postponement and his efforts to incorporate the masses more directly into the state through mutual aid societies and elaborate festivals.[13]

Late nineteenth-century economic changes (described in Chapter 4) also set the stage for Estrada Cabrera's brand of urban protopopulism. The consolidation of foreign and, particularly, German control over coffee exporting and finance, as well as the growing concentration of landownership in German hands, stimulated a potent desire for national integrity and agency among Guatemalan Altaverapacences. Guatemalans wished to control their destiny, propel the nation toward the future, and participate on the world stage – they desired access to modernity, rather than unfulfilled promises of a modernity yet to come. If German coffee planters carved out plantation sovereignty where they enacted their own ideologies of personal progress, then ladinos and Q'eqchi' patriarchs looked to the city and Manuel Estrada Cabrera for self-actualization. Q'eqchi' patriarchs' and ladinos' modernity was not the liberal-democratic modernity promoted by those who lambasted the slavery of mandamientos, but a modernity derived from dreams of Western culture, social betterment, and technological progress. When Estrada Cabrera promoted the nation abroad through extravagant Minerva festivals celebrating the studious youth, he connected these individual desires to the state. When he bestowed great public praise on the building of hospitals

---

[12] See John Charles Chasteen, *Heroes on Horseback: A Life and Times of the Last Gaucho Caudillos* (Albuquerque: University of New Mexico Press, 1995).

[13] While emphasizing reform among the urban poor, Manuel Estrada Cabrera's regime did not contain any of the elements of mass consumption associated with more classical cases of populism, such as Peronism. See, for example, Eduardo Elena, *Dignifying Argentina: Peronism, Citizenship, and Mass Consumption* (Pittsburgh, PA: University of Pittsburgh Press, 2011).

and schools, ladinos and Q'eqchi's took up the opportunity to create a new prosperous era. When Estrada Cabrera silenced racial discourses by emphasizing morality and social mobility over lineage and physiognomy, he helped ladinos and Q'eqchi's face down racism.

For middle- and upper-class ladinos, the dramatic socioeconomic changes with the rise of coffee production generated anxieties about disease and urban space in the 1880s and 1890s. Urban population growth and dislocation, particularly after the 1886 frost, swelled the ranks of Cobán's urban poor.[14] In 1903 Cobán's town councilmen wrote to Estrada Cabrera asking for increased funds for a police force, because the city had become "a fertile ground for thefts and stealing" since "a disequilibrium in resources between the proletariat class, naturally leads to an increase in crimes against property."[15] Perhaps most disturbing for Liberals, however, was the growing number of lower-class, working women, who crowded the streets working as laundresses, market women, and seamstresses. Gaining access to wages gave women in the city more sexual and economic autonomy. Unhygienic marketplaces, schools, and hospitals were sites of potential corruption and racial degeneration. According to miasmic theories of the time, disease and, thus, racial degeneration emanated from public spaces and floated in microbes. "The predominant diseases are those that come from the use of well water as well as the infection of the air as a result of the lack of drains for the toilets," explained one 1894 report to Cobán's alcalde.[16] Many claimed prostitution was on the rise, and the marketplace was described as the city's "nucleus of corruption" for its unsanitary conditions and the growing number of street vendors who ventured to the city from the countryside.[17] When ladinos expressed their fears about infectious disease and prostitutes, they were also voicing anxieties about disruptions in the social order that arose from migration to Cobán.[18]

---

[14] According to existing statistics, Cobán's urban population grew by 23 percent between 1880 and 1894 (from 4,871 to 5,996). These statistics, however, are widely regarded as unreliable and should be taken only as rough approximations. See *Censo General de la República de Guatemala* (Guatemala: Tipografía Nacional, 1880), 140; and *Censo General de la República de Guatemala* (Guatemala: Tipografía Nacional, 1894), 149.

[15] CM Est. 1 Paq. 16, "Correspondencia 1903, Municipalidad de Cobán al Presidente de la República," July 3, 1903.

[16] CM Est. 3 Paq. 4, "Policía e higiene," 1894.

[17] "Policía," *El Demócrata*, May 1, 1887; "El mercado es un foco de corrupción," *El Demócrata*, November 21, 1886.

[18] On the relationship between fears about disease and social-boundary crossing, see Sandra Lauderdale Graham, *House and Street: The Domestic World of Servants and Masters in*

Ladinos channeled these fears of social disorder into demands for increased state surveillance, social welfare, and the reordering of public space. For Q'eqchi's, the disruptions in the moral and social order as evident in the 1886 frost could also lead to illness.[19] Cleaning up the city also offered an opportunity for lower-class men to shape public debates about sanitation and morality and provided opportunities for Liberal elites to consolidate power. Many believed that social upheaval could be rectified by delineating the boundaries of social class to incorporate honorable workers, while moral attacks on the poor solidified a new social identity for the bourgeoisie and social climbers aspiring to join the bourgeoisie.

While uncontrollable laboring women of diverse racial backgrounds challenged elite ladino men in Cobán, Estrada Cabrera had also recognized the power of organizing the urban working classes, and urban ladinos and Q'eqchi' patriarchs alike took up the opportunity. In Alta Verapaz, an extensive network of political clubs, social-welfare organizations, artisan societies, workers' unions and cooperatives, and Liberal Party newspapers dedicated to the regime flourished, establishing political patronage mechanisms. Liberal societies administered schools and mobilized members and townspeople to celebrate national holidays, such as Estrada Cabrera's birthday and the Minerva festivals. They also campaigned for political candidates and published newspapers that ran articles promoting work discipline, improved technology, and the image of Guatemala as a democratic republic of liberal artisans.[20] Newspapers also disseminated Estrada Cabrera's image through the streets, bringing the once-distant president close to the people. Local liberals crafted an image of Estrada Cabrera as a great benefactor of the nation and fostered the feeling that he was in complete control. By 1904 Cobán had three Liberal clubs, and San Pedro Carchá had at least one. Quickly, Liberal clubs sprouted up in far-flung places such as Cahabón.[21] As the regime's repression mounted, every literate

---

Nineteenth-Century Rio de Janeiro (Cambridge: Cambridge University Press, 1988), 108–36.

[19] Wilson, *Maya Resurgence in Guatemala*, 123–57.

[20] Liberal clubs and artisan societies founded the following newspapers during Estrada Cabrera's regime: *Propagandista Liberal, La Voz del Norte, El Anuncio, Eco del Norte, General barrios, Minerva, Alta Verapaz, El Pueblo, 15 de Marzo, La Verapaz,* and *El Paladín.*

[21] The clubs were Pro-Patria, Alta Verapaz, and Tezulutlán. For their merger, see "Nuestros trabajos," *La Voz del Norte,* January 15, 1904.

citizen was required to be a member of a Liberal club; and to demonstrate their goodwill and allegiance to the regime, many gave donations beyond their means. By 1915 more than 500 Liberal clubs had sprouted across the country and at least 200 publications dedicated to the regime circulated.[22]

Members of Liberal clubs and other associations were mostly ladino elite men, other socially mobile ladinos, and Q'eqchi' patriarchs. Listed among the members of Cobán's "Club Liberal Estrada Cabrera" were the Q'eqchi' patriarchs Gualberto Cu and Tiburcio Caal, who had served as *alcalde tercero* in the town council. Members also included higher-ranking officials in the army, notaries, and artisans.[23] Of the fifty-six members of Cobán's Artisan Society, thirteen were Q'eqchi' and forty-three were ladinos.[24] By 1915 the region's artisan society, renamed "Minerva" in honor of the dictator, had become one of Estrada Cabrera's workers' cooperatives.[25] The association's multiclass and multiracial character brought together Q'eqchi' patriarchs and ladinos in a common cause of racial and national progress.

The associations also generated multiracial spaces of sociability that effectively allowed Q'eqchi's to distinguish themselves from the negative traits associated with lower-class, uneducated Q'eqchi's, without necessarily losing their indigeneity. The Society of Sport in Cobán, for example, made its primary mission the physical and moral improvement of its members. The Welfare Society sought to instill the morally uplifting practice of charity, and the Artisan Society aimed to guide workers toward their racial perfection.[26] These ideals of social welfare, education, and philanthropy privileged inward sentiments and morality derived from the soul rather than the exterior manifestations of race on the body. A reprinted poem in Cobán's newspaper *El Norte* captured this sentiment well: "True nobility, is the nobility of the soul.... It is better to be the founder of a family or a race that begins humbly but with dignity, than a gravedigger of one filled with titles that ends unhappily," the author declared.[27] As Edgar Esquit has described for Comalapa, social mobility allowed Maya patriarchs to *superarse*, which means literally to

---

[22] Rendón, *Minerva y la palma*, 218.
[23] CM Est. 1 Paq. 2, "Nómina de los miembros del Club Liberal 'Estrada Cabrera,'" April 3, 1908.
[24] AGCA JP-AV 1892 P4, "Nómina de los socios la sociedad de artesanos de Cobán."
[25] Rendón, *Minerva y la palma*, 220.
[26] See, for example, "Minerva," *Ecos de Cobán*, September 14, 1918.
[27] "Nobleza," *El Norte*, Cobán, December 19, 1915.

"overcome oneself" and connotes the ability to improve oneself by transcending circumstances.[28] In Peru, social mobility allowed educated indigenous mestizos to maintain their indigeneity while transcending the negative connotations of Indianness.[29] Since at least the 1871 Liberal revolution, Q'eqchi' patriarchs had promoted education and were among the first to establish mandated schools on their coffee plantations.[30] Through education and social class, Q'eqchi' patriarchs possessed civilization and historical agency without necessarily ceasing to be Q'eqchi.' As both civilized and Q'eqchi's, they unpinned efforts to render them as mere anachronisms in the nation and demonstrated that citizenship need not be racially white.

The Liberal associations' activities and self-promotions allowed ladino and Q'eqchi' members to assert civilized sentiments and customs and to reaffirm the racial and class boundaries between themselves and lower-class "darker" ladinos and Q'eqchi's who required their special tutelage and charity. As one editorialist noted, "It is not possible to see a poor man suffering in the bed of pain, without us feeling the need to alleviate him and his aches. It is impossible to contemplate the spectacle of hunger and nudity and not try to satisfy the first and remedy the other in those unfortunate beings, victims of such misfortune. Mutual aid was a duty born of the highest sentiments of human nature and makes necessary the constitution of these societies."[31] Mutual aid and social welfare united individual self-actualization with the common good. The practice of charity was a liberal and secular remaking of the colonial practice of giving alms and pious bequests to earn salvation. As such, charity fostered personal character and morality, and increased social prestige. By 1919, for example, Cobán boasted seven such associations dedicated to social and racial improvement – the Welfare Society, the Artisan Society, the Club Liberal "2 de Abril," the Scientific and Literary Society, the Academy of Teachers, the Society of Sport, and the "Minerva" Mutual Aid Society and Workers Cooperative – as well as

---

[28] Edgar Esquit, *La superación del indígena: la política de la modernización entre las élites indígenas de Comalapa, siglo XX* (Guatemala: Universidad de San Carlos, 2010).

[29] De la Cadena, *Indigenous Mestizos.*

[30] See, for example, JP-AV 1884 Paq. 5, "Vicente Yat se pone escuela en su finca Tantun," February 8, 1884; JP-AV 1884 Paq. 5, "Juan Coc se establece una escuela en su finca Chimote," August 27, 1884. See also the list of coffee planters who had established local schools in JP-AV 1885 Paq. 2. On indigenous support of education as early as 1866, see CM Est. 3 Paq. 14 1866, "Disposiciones dictadas por este despacho."

[31] "La beneficencia," *El Polochic*, October 7, 1894.

two additional cultural centers, the Artisan Library and the Technical School for Men.[32]

Liberal societies, in short, solidified the mechanics of Estrada Cabrera's protopopulism. They operated as vehicles for political patronage, produced locally the benevolent theatrics of Estrada Cabrera's rule, shored up the ideal of social and racial mobility, contained and controlled the lower classes, and solidified a common "other" – the aristocracy and foreigners. Estrada Cabrera's regime witnessed a marked turn toward celebrating hardworking citizens against the degenerate aristocracy. In an editorial entitled "Los Parásitos," the author condemned the unnoticed "parasite" of immorality among the higher classes. The editorialist maintained that "a pathetic invalid of the disinherited class who for hunger commits a crime" perpetrated less damage to society than "a man of illustrious blood who having given over to gambling, drunkenness and immorality, lives by spreading his seed of corruption through all parts." Cobán thus did not need a "panopticon for the town criminals," but a correctional facility for "industrial gentlemen, to teach the inept to work, and to make useful citizens of professional corruptors, frock-coated vagrants, and lepers of the soul."[33] Another editorialist declared that "the time has now passed in which work was considered unseemly and improper for well-to-do families; today to work is to make oneself worthy of social esteem," and advised wealthy families to educate their children in a useful craft. Such an education would encourage the morality of children, since "humble, but honorable, vocations are much more valuable than the higher ones which only serve to create vanity."[34] During moments of economic crisis in coffee capitalism, state officials and coffee planters often blamed the nation's poverty on Maya indolence. However, as German economic predominance solidified in the first decades of the twentieth century, many decried the indolence of the wealthy. "Work must be for all," declared one editorialist. "It must not only be the *indio*, who fulfills this duty; we are all obliged to sustain the strength of the nation. The labor of a few who serve the royalty should not sustain others who live by exploiting the work of everyone else."[35] In their diatribes

---

[32] J. M. Eduardo Portocarrero, *Alma y vida de Cobán* (Cobán: Tipografía Escuela Práctica, 1919), 25. For the official statutes of Cobán's Welfare Society, see AGCA B Leg. 29092 1905, and AGCA B Leg. 29261 Exp. 13 1913.

[33] "Los parásitos," *El Norte*, December 25, 1915.

[34] "El porvenir de los niños," *El Norte*, September 26, 1915. See also "El trabajo," *El Norte*, February 9, 1918.

[35] "¿Por qué hay pueblos pobres?," *El Norte*, December 5, 1915.

against the wealthy, newspaper editorialists appealed to the liberal–democratic metanarrative's anti-aristocratic and egalitarian impulses, even while downplaying the republican aspects of that narrative.

Through their celebrations of humble origins, Liberal editorialists also helped shift racial discourses and promoted wider participation in ladino nationalism. Whereas racial whiteness had once evoked European origins, in the hands of Liberals racial whiteness conjured the colonial past's moral corruption, caste hierarchy, and stalled development. Under Estrada Cabrera, the hardworking artisan assured national progress. Honorable artisans were not, however, Mayas, who remained associated with coffee plantation labor, ignorance, and indolence. Nor did Liberals' praise for ladino artisans produce nationalist rejoicing in mestizaje. Rather, the humble and honorable artisans were ambiguously neither Maya nor white; rather, they were an empty racial category. The ladino artisans' racial ambiguity enabled Q'eqchi' patriarchs, who had separated themselves from the ignorance and poverty of lower-class Q'eqchi's, to partake in ladino nationalism, rather than being fully excluded from it.

Mutual aid societies united Q'eqchi' and ladino men in social welfare and racial improvement, and they also allowed for the controlled participation of respectable women. While men governed mutual aid and welfare societies, ladinas participated in fundraising events and later in advocacy for child welfare. Through mutual aid and welfare societies, middle- and upper-class women channeled their early feminist interests into respectable domains. As Donna Guy and Ann S. Blum have demonstrated for Argentina and Mexico, women converted these social welfare societies over time into spaces of sociability and acceptable forums for women's participation in politics. Eventually, they were able to shape the development of the twentieth-century welfare state.[36] Whereas men could grow morally through social service in municipal politics, as well as political clubs, Masonic lodges, sports societies, and social clubs, women found a similar venue in the fundraising and advocacy work of welfare societies. Through social welfare societies, women shaped public opinion and partook in state patronage, and later became sources of political radicalization for women during a

---

[36] Donna J. Guy, *Women Build the Welfare State: Performing Charity and Creating Rights in Argentina, 1880–1955* (Durham, NC: Duke University Press, 2009); and Ann S. Blum, *Domestic Economies: Family, Work, and Welfare in Mexico City, 1884–1943* (Lincoln: University of Nebraska Press, 2009).

democratic efflorescence in the 1920s and during Guatemala's "revolutionary spring" of 1944–54.[37]

Liberal club members also played a crucial role in legitimizing the nation's elections. Every six years, Liberal clubs across the nation promoted the president and gathered the masses to cast their collective vote for the only choice on the ballot. In 1903 Estrada Cabrera modified the 1879 constitution, which had prohibited reelection. Thereafter, on election day, local officials from Liberal clubs gave each citizen trinkets after they cast their ballot. These tokens were prominently displayed by voters. Tokens were not just symbols of the president's gratitude, but also confirmed popular support for the regime. Many voted more than once to demonstrate their pronounced dedication to the president.[38] Coffee planters brought their laborers to vote in the elections. As the historian D. G. Munro, who was in Cobán at election time, explained, "To make the *indios* realize how fortunate they were that they resided in a democratic country, each group was received with a band or at least a delegation of schoolchildren carrying the national flag."[39] According to Munro, an official passed along the line of Maya laborers with each one stating that they had voted for Estrada Cabrera. Afterward, state officials rewarded them with sugar cane liquor. When the votes were counted and the National Assembly declared Manuel Estrada Cabrera elected, more ballots were cast in his favor than eligible voters in the entire nation. Some 200,000 fictitious votes were cast.[40] Rituals and propaganda, staged performances, and symbols were repeated with ever-greater force during elections in 1915.

Participation in Liberal clubs was crucial to separating oneself from the stain of indigeneity and establishing lines of patronage and political support among the urban ladinos and Q'eqchi's. These associations, however, were rarely only state-funded, and they did not often achieve their stated goals. The Artisan and Welfare Societies of Cobán relied on a combination of private initiative and state support. The Welfare Society

---

[37] Indeed, San Pedro Carchá's welfare society El Centenario, created in 1920, was primarily governed by women (including Belen Guay and Julia Chavarria, who became vocal anticommunist activists in Carchá in the 1940s and 1950s). AGCA B Leg. 29482 1920. Despite the later politics of many its members, the Welfare Society declared itself "free of political and religious interests."

[38] See Rendón, *Minerva y la palma*, 218–20.

[39] D. G. Munro, *A Student in Central America, 1914–1916* (New Orleans: Middle American Research Institute, Tulane University, 1983), 43.

[40] Rendón, *Minerva y la palma*, 172.

of Cobán, however, fought with only limited success to ensure that taxes destined for social welfare reached Cobán, rather than ending up in Guatemala City's Welfare Society. While Liberal societies and public works projects, including the Hospital del Norte, were meant to support the urban lower classes, they may not have actually achieved that goal. As Silvia Arrom has demonstrated for Mexico City's Poor House, social welfare institutions did not always function as officially intended, and over time Mexico City's Poor House ceased to become a refuge for the urban poor, but rather followed the timeworn patterns of philanthropy in the Hispanic world, where institutional relief often helped an advantaged sector struggling to maintain its status.[41] Thus, through social welfare, ladinos and Q'eqchi's could both espouse the rhetoric of containment, discipline, and social uplift of the "darker" lower classes, as well as protect middling Q'eqchi's and ladinos who struggled in times of crisis. The role of mutual aid societies in maintaining social hierarchies was also evident in modernizing Cobán's urban landscape.[42]

FORGING NEW CITIES, CULTIVATING NEW SELVES

In the late nineteenth century, Cobán underwent dramatic demographic and socioeconomic changes that elevated social tensions and escalated elites' fears. Not only did desirable German settlers populate the city, but a burgeoning class of new plebeians also crowded the city's streets and central plaza. Ladino, Q'eqchi', and German elites sought mechanisms to regulate, control, and clean the city in ways that often stigmatized this new urban poor and subjected them to state intrusion. In part, anxieties about urban space grew out of Cobán's unique landscape. Except for a section near the central plaza, an agrarian aesthetic defined by trees and gardens dominated the town. Urban properties likewise were ordered in a distinctly Q'eqchi' fashion. Like the rural landscape – dotted by single households surrounded by or near to milpa plots – urban houses were set back from the road, surrounded by a garden, trees, and bushes, and separated from the road by a thick hedge. The church, government offices, and local market were framed by quaint homes, cultivated plots of coffee and corn, and scattered trees that troubled the boundaries

---

[41] Silvia Marina Arrom, *Containing the Poor: The Mexico City Poor House, 1774–1871* (Durham, NC: Duke University Press, 2000).

[42] See Teresita Martínez-Vergne, *Shaping the Discourse on Space: Charity and Its Wards in Nineteenth-Century San Juan, Puerto Rico* (Austin: University of Texas Press, 1999).

FIGURE 5.1 Alta Verapaz, 1928.
Colección de la Familia Hempsted, Fototeca CIRMA

between the agrarian countryside and the modern city (see Figure 5.1). For modernizing Altaverapacences, the rural aesthetic of Cobán's urban landscape was a distressing symbol of the region's incomplete modernity.[43]

The social dislocations caused by the rise of coffee production and the events of Xucaneb had also propelled migration of undesirable Q'eqchi's to the city. Cobaneros complained about "suspicious Indians hanging around the corners day and night," and the "Indians and ladinos who were completely taken over by drunkenness and other vices." Crime and prostitution, according to many, were on the rise. Indians were dirty and, besides selling themselves in the street, did not seek a medical doctor when they got sick.[44] The hospital had become "a mansion of vices and

[43] As Raymond Williams has argued, the countryside was the necessary counterpoint for the modernizing city; see *The Country and the City* (New York: Random House, 2013).

[44] See "El mercado," *El Demócrata*, Cobán, July 4, 1886; "El mercado es un foco de corrupción," *El Demócrata*, November 21, 1886; "A la policía," *El Demócrata*, March 27, 1887; "Policía," *El Demócrata*, January 30, 1887; "Policía," *El Demócrata*, May 1, 1887; "Sociedad de caridad i beneficencia," *El Demócrata*, September 26, 1886; "A la policía," *El Demócrata*, March 27, 1887. On the marketplace, see also CM Est. 4 Paq. 13, "Actos de la Municipalidad 1887"; "A grandes males, grandes remedios," *El Porvenir*, December 8, 1889; "Mejoras necesarias," *El Porvenir*, November 2 and December 14, 1890. For the creation of the hospital, see AGCA MG B Leg. 28734

disorder" and the scene of "scandalous orgies."[45] Also worrisome for many Cobaneros was the swelling number of working-class women among the Q'eqchi's crowding the streets. Working-class women did not generally conform to dominant notions of female respectability and made visible the tenuous racial boundaries between ladinos and Q'eqchi's.[46] Urban plebeian women also often settled their conflicts through shouting matches and fisticuffs in the streets, their yards, and the market.[47] In town, poor women's behavior was present for everyone to see. They not only filled the marketplace and ambled along the streets, selling foodstuffs, sweets, clothing, and other goods during the day, but they also socialized at night, often drinking in local taverns.

As commerce and population expanded, itinerant men and women moved from town to town, staying for days or weeks to trade. They especially raised the specter of criminality and indecency, while their foreignness confounded racial hierarchies. Late one night, thieves broke into Dolores Paredes de Aguilar's store and stole some merchandise. Dolores's neighbor Julian Ponce reported to the departmental governor: "At ten o'clock at night, looking from my house to the street, I saw six men huddled together in the corner, talking in low voices. Upon examining them they must have been Indians dressing up as Ladinos, with diverse clothing, but shoeless and in the company of Manuel Saquil, a cart man ... who was up to an illegal act, since the mentioned Saquil has

Exp. 2573 1886; AGCA MG B Leg. 28741 Exp. 249 1887; AGCA MG B Leg. 8754 Exp. 2725 1887; AGCA MG B Leg. 28777 1889; AGCA MG B Leg. 28766 Exp. 1906 1888; AGCA MG B Leg. 28769 Exp. 134 1889; "El hospital," *El Porvenir*, February 3, 1889. For the police force, see AGCA MG B Leg. 28789 Exp. 1125 1890; CM Est. 3 Paq. 1 1891, "Partes del Director de la Policía." For the school police, see "República de la policía escolar en Cobán," *El Guatemalteco*, September 7, 1893. In 1895 the Municipality of Cobán also began the practice of nominating alcaldes auxiliares for each barrio and canton in the city. See AGCA MG B Leg. 28896 Exp. 1083.

45 In a hospital with only twenty beds, 4,023 people had come: 274 people were quarantined, including 194 men and 80 women in 1892. AGCA MG B Leg. 28829 Exp. 3206 1892. In 1894 the Municipality of Cobán began to seek donations to build a new hospital. See CM Paq. 1894, "Carta del Municipalidad de Cobán a Cirujano Militar," May 16, 1894; CM Paq. 1894, "Carta al Alcalde Municipal del Sociedad Dramática," August 15, 1894; "Hospital del Norte," *El Polochic*, May 17, 1895.

46 The work on plebeian women's honor codes is now extensive. See Stern, *The Secret History of Gender*; Eileen Findlay, *Imposing Decency: The Politics of Sexuality and Race in Puerto Rico, 1870–1920* (Durham, NC: Duke University Press, 1999).

47 See judicial records, especially slander and assault cases. For example, AGCA J-AV 103 Leg. 17 Exp. 15 1887; AGCA J-AV 103 Leg. 17 Exp. 18; AGCA J-AV 103 Leg. 17 Exp. 19; AGCA J-AV 103 Leg. 17 B Exp. 10; AGCA J-AV 104 Leg. 17 A Exp. 12; AGCA J-AV 103 Leg. 18 A Exp. 27; AGCA J-AV 104 Leg. 20 Exp. 20.

had bad conduct before as a thief."[48] Later that day, the police apprehended two men and three women, along with a seven-year-old child, in possession of Dolores's stolen merchandise. In the court hearing, the police officers racially darkened the accused through explicit descriptions of hair, skin, and eye color as well as stature. From Julian Ponce's rumors about unsavory Mayas masquerading as ladinos, and hanging out in the street corners, to the arrests of darkened outsiders, the court case expressed ladino anxieties about public space, itinerant workers, vendors, and the boundaries of race demarcating ladinos and Mayas.[49]

When permanent vendors, state officials, and bourgeois Cobaneros expressed their concerns about the marketplace and itinerant vendors, they also voiced unease about rural peoples in urban spaces. Rural people, coded as Mayas, were understood to have a polluting presence that generated not only foul smells, but also dangerous microbes that threatened to bring epidemics.[50] As Alain Corbin has argued, there is often a striking congruence between perceptions of social hierarchy and fears of disease.[51] The itinerant people who passed through the streets and markets symbolically linked the dangers of mobility and the failure to fix Mayas to plantations with the discourse of disgust, and ladino elites railed against the perils of microbes, foul smells, poor drainage, prostitutes, and peddlers. For urban ladinos and Mayas, the street was like a virus that threatened to engulf the respectable townspeople. The city itself was thus understood as a body that required proper circulation and movement by healthy and respectable residents, rather than unknown migrants. These mobile and unsavory characters manifested social degeneracy and crime that weakened the city's overall health.

Due to ladino fears of prostitution, vagabonds, crime, and immorality in the streets of Cobán, town officials cracked down on urban crime through the 1880s and 1890s.[52] Finding themselves persecuted by the local police force, Cobán's lower classes fought back with insults. Reclaiming honor through insults was crucial for urban working classes, since an individual's reputation influenced their livelihood, particularly their ability to secure work and sell goods. When the police arrested

---

[48] AGCA JP-AV 1885 Paq. 1, "Sr. Juez de Paz desde el JP," June 26, 1885.   [49] Ibid.
[50] CM Est. 3 Paq. 18 Leg. 8 1894; "Policía e higiene" and "Mejoras necesarias," *El Porvenir*, November 2, 1890.
[51] Alain Corbin, *The Foul and the Fragrant: Odor and the French Social Imagination* (Cambridge, MA: Harvard University Press, 1986), 226.
[52] CM Est. 2 Paq. 22, "Sr. Alcalde 1° de Cobán del JP," July 2, 1892; CM Est. 2 Paq. 22, "Sr. Alcalde 1° Municipal del JP," July 5, 1892.

Adolfo Leal for public drunkenness, he called the officers "shameless cowards" for attacking the poor.[53] Other urban plebeians recuperated their honor by charging police officers with violating the law. Manuel Fernandez Barrios accused a policeman of slander for calling his wife an "old *india*."[54] Still others denounced the illegitimacy of charges: Pedro Juarez claimed he was persecuted by the police for personal vendettas.[55] As socioeconomic inequality rose in the early twentieth century, the municipal council requested a larger police force: "Today, that scarcity [of currency] is causing in the Republic a disequilibrium in the resources of the proletariat classes, it is natural that there is an increase in the crimes against property."[56] As this suggests, the expansion of the police during Estrada Cabrera's regime was not only the product of a dictators' desire to quell popular dissent and monitor the population, but also the expression of social anxieties among respectable urban classes. In addition to official policing efforts, Cobaneros actively regulated their neighbors' social conduct and cleanliness. They publicly complained in newspapers about the unclean habits of their neighbors, the lack of moral virtues among schoolteachers, or the spread of immorality through the town.[57] By publicly deriding the habits and morality of their lesser neighbors, these concerned citizens also performed their own honorability and enacted civilized customs.

By the turn of the century, Cobán's body of frustrated urban plebeians, who were eager to defend their honor after years of stigmatization, latched on to new social discourses honoring the poor and keenly participated in urban social reforms and Liberal clubs as means to elevate their social status. Liberal associations were an important forum for individuals whose precarious racial and class status was threatened by changes in the city and who could easily become the targets of charges of uncleanliness and immorality. These social sectors were made up of "marginal dons" – artisans, shopkeepers, teachers, and social-climbing lower classes – who struggled for honorability and recognition. They had a

---

[53] AGCA JP-AV 103 Leg. 22 Exp. 9 1893.   [54] AGCA J-AV 103 Leg. 27 D Exp. 20.

[55] AGCA J-AV 103 Leg. 36 B Exp. 3. See also AGCA J-AV 103 Leg. 36 B Exp. 5.

[56] CM Est. 8 Paq. 16, "Carta al Sr. presidente de la Municipalidad de Cobán," January 8, 1903.

[57] The number of these letters appears to have taken off after 1915. See, for example, "Higiene," *El Norte*, May 9, 1915; "¡Esto es chusco!" and "Calles," *El Norte*, June 6, 1915; "El beneficio de ganados," *El Norte*, January 20, 1917; "El aseo de la población," *El Norte*, February 17, 1917; "Baños en chío," *El Norte*, May 12, 1917; "Las fiestas agostinas," *El Norte*, August 18, 1917; "Nuestros calles," *El Norte*, February 16, 1918.

penchant for bringing up slander cases to defend their honor against accusations of theft or charges of inadequate teaching abilities and lack of hygiene.[58] Brought together into associations promoted by Estrada Cabrera, the honorable lower and middle classes worked in alliance with elite Germans, Q'eqchi' patriarchs, and ladinos in remaking the city, and in the process distinguished themselves from dishonorable and darker others and thereby secured not only their reputation but also their livelihood.

Urban associations and labor unions were a medium for artisans and elites alike to become active participants in the city's modernization. In the process, these diverse citizens also forged collective memories and a shared sense of time and space.[59] It is difficult to overestimate the importance of urban modernization to the regional experience of Estrada Cabrera's regime. To commemorate and celebrate their accomplishments, the municipal council elaborated short histories, called *memorias*, of the public works projects completed.[60] Memorias evinced the importance of urban projects to the forging of a common Altaverapacene regional identity as modern and urban. In contrast to Alta Verapaz's characterization as rural, backward, and indigenous, the memorias privileged Cobán as civilized, urbane, and progressive. The memorias also spoke to the reorganization of knowledge and the disavowal of Maya political ontologies. Through the writing of memorias, municipal officials devised new ways of knowing that emphasized certain events and decreed how they should be framed.[61] In the process of narrating modernization, municipal officials also rejected Q'eqchi' political ontologies including the agency of Tzuultaq'as, disciplinary functions of el Q'eq, and Maya practices of reciprocity and solidarity.

Among the new modernizing projects promoted by urban associations and the municipality was a modern central plaza. In 1915 iterant vendors – cast as rural, dirty, and degenerate – were expelled to the margins of the city, and replaced by a stylized, Europeanized central plaza

---

[58] Findlay, *Imposing Decency*.

[59] See Anthony King, *Spaces of Global Cultures: Architecture, Urbanism, Identity* (London: Routledge, 2004); Abidin Kusno, *The Appearances of Memory: Mnemonic Practices of Architecture and Urban Form in Indonesia* (Durham, NC: Duke University Press, 2010).

[60] CM 1911, "Sr. Alcalde 1° del Manuel Ponce," January 20, 1911; AGCA JP-AV 1919 Paq. 5, "Nómina de obras públicas llevadas durante la administración de E. Cabrera."

[61] For more on memorias as history-making, see Paul K. Eiss, *In the Name of El Pueblo: Place, Community, and the Politics of History in Yucatán* (Durham, NC: Duke University Press, 2010), 45–8.

that defined the heart of the city. This shift can be seen in the contrast between two photographs: the first around 1890 (Figure 5.2) and the second in the early 1920s (Figure 5.3). The municipality of Cobán transformed its central plaza from a marketplace into a central park, with a

FIGURE 5.2 Photograph of Cobán's central plaza, c. 1890.
Courtesy of Hugo Rodríguez

FIGURE 5.3 Photograph of Cobán's central plaza, c. 1920s.
Courtesy of Hugo Rodríguez

gazebo, a monument to Minerva, and a unique garden design.[62] As a highly visible demonstration for visitors and residents alike, the central plaza was an ideal stage from which to project a new modern identity. As an interpretation of nineteenth-century English gardens, the new central square turned Cobán's unruly green aesthetic into a carefully tended garden. Modernizing Cobaneros transformed the central square from a disorderly and racially darkened marketplace into a theater for bourgeois sociability. With the installation of elegant statues and ornamental street-lights, paths for evening strolls, and rows of French wrought-iron benches, the central plaza became a stage for promenades and splendid concerts, where honorable townspeople could come to see and be seen. In the highly gender-segregated worlds of respectable townspeople, the central square was one of the few spaces where youth could mingle without chaperones. It was also a space for choreographed ceremony and spectacle where Liberals would deliver elaborate speeches praising President Estrada Cabrera.[63] The square was completed with two monuments: one to the great Liberal general don Miguel García Granados, and the other to Minerva.[64]

The project to build a central plaza, like the remaking of other aspects of the urban-built environment, was an instrument of both remembering and forgetting, shedding the indigenous past embedded in the urban landscape and ushering in a modern ladino future. By redesigning aesthetics and erecting new structures, Cobaneros from diverse social classes envisioned themselves not as passive observers or colonial holdovers, but rather as active participants in the making of a new era that brought Guatemala into the fold of civilized nations. By reordering space, Cobaneros could thus also remake their location in the forward march of time. As Abidin Kusno has illustrated for modern Indonesia, in the process of reinventing the urban environment, urban planners and citizens alike

---

[62] CM Est. 1 Paq. 2, "Al Sr. presidente Constitucional de El Comité de Minerva de la Municipalidad de Cobán," April 23, 1908; CM Est. 4 Paq. 13, "Al Alcalde Municipal de Comité de las Fiestas de Minerva," September 24, 1912.

[63] On central parks as spaces of sociability, see, for example, David Scobey, "Anatomy of the Promenade: The Politics of Bourgeois Sociability in Nineteenth-Century New York," *Social History* 17, no. 2 (1992): 204–27; Silvia Marina Arrom, "Introduction: Rethinking Urban Politics in Latin America before the Populist Era," in *Riots in the Cities: Popular Politics and the Urban Poor in Latin America, 1765–1910*, ed. Silvia M. Arrom and Servando Ortoll (Wilmington, DE: Scholarly Resources, 1996); and Derby, *The Dictator's Seduction*, 84–8.

[64] For a description, see Portocarrero, *Alma y Vida de Cobán*, 72–6.

attained a sense of being subjects of history.[65] The ordering of urban space was thus disciplining and empowering.

Estrada Cabrera encouraged social welfare societies and municipal councils to promote urban improvement and technical schools. Alta Verapaz's urban associations built new schools and a hospital, which projected a new modern aesthetic and were a visible testament to society's role in the unfolding drama of national progress. By incorporating artisans, teachers, and other honorable working classes in modernizing projects, once-stigmatized groups participated in their own personal social uplift as well as that of family members, neighbors, or friends. In 1906 the Artisan Society built a technical school. Estrada Cabrera promoted technical schools as a means to prepare young men and women for meaningful and moral lives as tradesmen, artisans, and housewives. Technical schools promised to transform dishonorable women and men into productive ladino citizens. Schoolteachers taught women domestic trades useful for their future roles as wives and mothers. Men were instructed in manual trades such as carpentry, cabinetmaking, shoemaking, saddlery, typography, book binding, the making of candles and soaps, and others.[66] The schools sought to form good citizens through classes in mathematics, language, civics, and ethics.[67] Widely celebrated by Estrada Cabrera, the students and teachers of the technical schools were lavished with the dictator's praise as model citizens. In addition to training a new generation of honorable citizens educated in the trades, schools were intended to keep unruly children off the streets. When these efforts failed, state officials turned to discipline. Cobán created a special police unit dedicated solely to rounding up vagrant children and punishing parents whose children did not attend school.[68] Likewise, the municipality required teachers to submit weekly registers of attendance,

---

[65] Kusno, *The Appearances of Memory.*

[66] For practical schools, see Felipe Estrada Paniagua, *Algo sobre educación* (Guatemala: Tipografía Nacional, 1907).

[67] See, for example, CM Est. 3 Paq. 18, "Correspondencia del año 1903: Informe relativo al ramo de instrucción pública," October 27, 1903; AGCA JP-AV 1906 Paq. 1, "Al Tesorería Municipal del presidente del Comité de Construcción de la Escuela Práctica," March 1, 1906; CM Actas Municipales de 1907; CM Est. 3 Paq. 15, "Al alcalde municipal del Director de la Escuela Práctica," August 10, 1910.

[68] See CM 1894, "Poner en vigor el reglamento de policía escolar," and, for example, CM 1894, "Lista de niños que han citado seis veces por la policía i no se ha logrado de asistir al colegio"; and CM 1894, "Orden militar, citar los padres de familia ... adentro de cinco días presentan en este despacho a sus hijos."

recording absences so that parents and children could be held accountable for absences.[69]

Across the nation, Estrada Cabrera promoted the construction of hospitals in the name of social welfare and the well-being of the poor. In Alta Verapaz, notable businessmen, coffee planters, engineers, ladino artisans, and Q'eqchi' patriarchs formed a Hospital Construction Committee in 1903 with the aim of building a new hospital on the outskirts of the city. With its location in an idyllic rural space and an interior layout separating men and women, the hospital represented a future vision of Cobanero society.[70] According to the miasmic theories in vogue at the time, the environment itself influenced moral character as well as physical health, particularly in the tropics, so the location of the hospital needed to foster health and stimulate within each patient the desires associated with a moral life.[71] In contrast to representations of rural space as dirty, poor, and immoral, the hospital committee painted a picture of an idyllic rural society, where the "small houses of indigenous people" who dedicated themselves entirely to the cultivation of cereals provided a model of a simple, rural, and healthy life that contrasted with the foul and morbid life of the urban poor. To the south, uncultivated land gave way to a river that drained out of the city, ensuring that disease and dangerous microbes would be washed away from, rather than toward, the rest of the population. The dominant northern and western winds, too, would carry away the bad air of illness and immorality. The plot of land was well above the riverbank and on firm ground, which would provide for a year-round source of fresh water.

Before the project could be completed, however, grain shortages and a coffee crisis dried up the financial support, and the project was officially suspended in 1905.[72] When a makeshift hospital was opened three years later, the president of the Welfare Society, Rafael Ordoñez Solís, narrated the history of the hospital as a tale of corruption. Noting the poor

[69] These records can be found in the municipal archives of Cobán and San Pedro Carchá. A sustained statistical examination of the ethnic dynamics of attendance warrants future analysis.

[70] *Comité de Construcción del Hospital del Norte: Informe emitido á la Jefatura Política del Departamento de Alta Verapaz* (Guatemala: Tipografía Sánchez & Guise, 1904); Portocarrero, *Alma y vida de Cobán*, 113–14.

[71] See Nancy Leys Stepan, *"The Hour of Eugenics": Race, Gender, and Nation in Latin America* (Ithaca, NY: Cornell University Press, 1991).

[72] See AGCA JP-AV 1906 Paq. 1, "El director del Hospital de Cobán propone arbitrios para sostener el Establecimiento."

conditions of the previous hospital and the "hurricane of disgrace" that
swept over the "badly directed, ill-serviced and poorly assisted" hospital,
he declared: "Such is the general outline of the history of sham that has
been the hospital." However, it was saved by the livestock tax that the
president created for poor households, and the honorable efforts of the
departmental governor Jorge Ubico. Implicitly linking the failure of
the hospital project with immigrants' exploitation of poor Mayas, Ordoñez blamed foreigners, "who discredit and incapacitate [efforts to
improve the welfare of society], those who have come to this land worthy
of a better fate, who become accomplices with the ruffians, exploit the
poverty of the town, sell justice, and put themselves on the side of the
tycoons and the powerful and fill their insatiable pockets with gold, a
product of their disgrace."[73] Far from a celebratory narrative, Ordoñez
presented the history of the hospital as a moral tale for Cobanero society,
and articulated Estrada Cabrera's protopopulist discourses that emphasized the honorability of the poor against the rich. The capital invested in
the hospital, however, was not lost. Rather, in 1909, the military began to
use the hospital, and renewed efforts to complete the hospital became
indispensable.[74] That year, in honor of the president, the hospital was
renamed after Estrada Cabrera's mother, Joaquina. By the end of 1910,
the hospital was completed, and by participating in its construction,
ladinos, Q'eqchi's, and Germans alike joined together in defining themselves against those who might occupy its corridors. The hospital, however, continued to function more as a prison for the destitute than a
sanctuary for the ill. Patients such as Patrocina Acala or Margarito Jor
fled the horrible conditions they faced.[75] Q'eqchi' patients may have also
rejected the hospital since the notion of seclusion stood in contraposition
with Q'eqchi' conceptions of illness as the result of spirit loss that was
worsened by separation from one's place of origin.[76]

---

[73] "Discurso pronunciado por el Licenciado don Rafael Ordoñez Solís, al inaugurase el
    edificio del Hospital del Norte, el 29 del mes próximo pasado primer aniversario del
    atentado contra la vida del Presidente de la República," *El Anuncio*, May 10, 1908.
[74] See AGCA MG B Leg. 29164 Exp. 11 1909; AGCA MG B Leg. 29189 Exp. 16 1910;
    AGCA MG B Leg. 29181 Exp. 3 1910; "Se autoriza un contrato con el Ing. don José
    D. Moran para el ensanche del Hospital del Norte," in *Recopilación de leyes*, vol. 28
    (Guatemala: Tipografía Arturo Siguiere, 1910), 145.
[75] CM Est. 8 Paq. 16, "Carta al Alcalde Municipal de Cobán de Control del Hospital del
    Norte," March 26, 1895; and AGCA J-AV 104 1915 Leg. 16 B Exp. 34.
[76] On spirit loss and separation from community, see Wilson, *Maya Resurgence in
    Guatemala*, 145.

The discourses of hygiene and social welfare, and the importance of the city in representing civilization to the outside world, were also mobilized by the poor. Urban market vendors, for example, utilized cleanliness and hygiene, as well as existing municipal regulations, to shape the ordering and use of urban market space. For example, Felisa Tziboy, Rosa Chocoj, Candelaria Pacay, Tomasa and Petrona Pacay, and Manuela Quix petitioned to the departmental government to have their location inside the municipal market reinstated after they had been forcefully relocated next to the public sanitary facilities. Complaining of unhygienic conditions, the market women argued that if they sold their wares next to public bathrooms, travelers "would speak poorly of the town." The market women also appealed to the departmental governor as "poor women" who "make our living from this [sale of coffee and food]" and requested that they be allowed to operate inside the market "as long as we continue to pay our rent punctually."[77] The departmental governor granted their request, and on numerous similar occasions – in small but significant ways – market vendors and the urban poor shaped the city. Indeed, while the remaking of urban space could solidify social and racial divisions, proliferating regulations around hygiene and order allowed lower-class residents to petition the local authorities and thus participate in making the urban landscape.

The allocation of urban space, too, became a mechanism for patronage politics. Between 1911 and 1913, Estrada Cabrera expropriated agricultural land surrounding Cobán and created a new barrio in which he distributed 126 lots to militiamen for their faithful service to the nation.[78] When the new marketplace was created in 1905, the women who had rented market stalls from the municipality feared losing them to individuals who could pay higher rent. When the municipal government placed the stalls in public auction, Estrada Cabrera personally intervened to protect poor Cobaneras' interests.[79] Estrada Cabrera likewise provided personal donations and raised new taxes to support hospitals, erect schools, and support labor unions and artisan societies that garnered support from the urban working classes. These new spaces of sociability brought Q'eqchi's and ladinos together in a project to improve themselves by transcending their humble origins and recuperating their honor. Yet

---

[77] CM Box 1, "Carta al Señor JP de Felisa Tziboy," July 14, 1926.
[78] AGCA MG B Leg. 29261 Exp. 10. See also Portocarrero, *Alma y vida de Cobán*, 124.
[79] CM Est. 8 Paq. 16 "Actas sobre las nueva obras de construcción del mercado," November 4, 1905. See also AGCA Leg. 29109 Exp. 13.

the remaking of urban space also divided and reorganized, policed and demarcated, the boundaries between healthy urban laborers and elites, on the one hand, and racially degenerate and rural others (especially women), on the other.

MINERVALIAS

Even though the Minerva festivals fell during the rainy season in Alta Verapaz, making travel treacherous and outdoor festivities uncomfortable, coffee plantation owners brought laborers in from the countryside and townspeople gathered with great enthusiasm.[80] Estrada Cabrera envisioned the Minerva festivals as truly national celebrations and mandated that the entire nation – young and old, rich and poor, landowners and laborers – gather in unison to celebrate education and the youth.[81] Thus, across the nation for at least three days at the end of the school year in October, schoolchildren, teachers, state officials, local elites, and masses of workers from the countryside simultaneously celebrated Greco-Roman culture, education, and progress and paid tribute to their great benefactor, Manuel Estrada Cabrera. The synchrony of public rituals fostered a sense of common purpose and destiny that linked each village and town to the nation's capital. Joined across time and space, each village performing Minervalias was a serial repetition of another; each school child marching in line represented all other schoolchildren so that everyone at once embodied the totality of the nation. From organized marches of students all dressed in white to recitations of poetry, singing the national anthem, military exercises, and demonstrations of physical prowess through sport, Minervalias brought the nation together in a public spectacle of civilization and order.[82] Estrada Cabera distributed to diplomats and other presidents ornate albums of these annual affairs filled with memorabilia from the festival, including photographs and copies of the speeches of respected intellectuals and statesmen, as well as reports from foreign newspapers.

[80] SPCM 1918, "A los propietarios de las fincas, del Alcalde Municipal de Carchá," October 11, 1918; SPCM 1918, "Al JP del Comité de las Fiestas de Minerva," October 20, 1918; "Correspondencia desde Alta Verapaz," *Diario de Centro-América*, November 6, 1903; and "Minerva en Cobán," *El Norte*, November 14, 1915.

[81] Decreto 604, October 29, 1899, in *Recopilación de leyes*, vol. 18 (Guatemala: Tipografía Arturo Siguiere, 1909).

[82] *Crónica de las fiestas de Minerva* (Guatemala: Tipografía Nacional, 1904), 3.

The Minervalias were also designed to support Estrada Cabrera's strategic blend of the liberal–democratic and civilizing metanarratives and sought to create a new calendrical time. While celebrating Western civilization and education, the festivals effaced spatial reminders of Catholicism and the colonial past through itineraries that carefully avoided past religious processional routes and showed new symbolic representations of pagan, classical Greece that overshadowed Catholic traditions. Instead of ecclesiastical processions marching toward the church on saint's days, cofradías were organized and brought together in processions, leading to a pagan, classical Greco-Roman temple. Just as the Church had preached the cultivation of the self for a future divine salvation, the Minerva festivals preached the cultivation of the self for an earthy future material progress. The symbols of modernity – science, reason, democracy – were to triumph over the conservatism, clericalism, and hierarchy of the Church. "In all ages and all times," declared José Montealegre, in his Minerva speech in 1903, "the clergy have hidden books of science, they prohibited them and shot anathemas against them, the men who believe them are unfortunately large in number and remain blind, and crimes follow crimes, just like error follows ignorance."[83] Reciting an anti-Catholic history, Montealegre called on Guatemalans to follow the men who "build schools, creating communication routes towards progress." Indeed, he proclaimed, "the Guatemalan Nation has understood all of this [history] and is inspired by a profound desire to be counted among the most civilized nations of the Globe. The citizen who faithfully interprets his aspirations is placed in front of destiny.... To worship the cult of Minerva is to worship the cult of science; science is the truth itself; it is God."[84] Similar to the words of José Montealegre, the Minervalia speeches were replete with allegories between schools and temples, science and the ultimate truth, worshiping Minerva and worshiping progress and reason, in which teachers were apostles of progress. The Minerva festivals marked the beginning and the end of the school year as a chief calendrical event that eclipsed religious holidays. Even more, the Minervalias elicited the feeling that a new history – modern, secular, democratic, and rational – was on the horizon. Society was recast with a new secular religion based on the celebration of education and progress. A new space-time would also demand that the population take up historical agency and become citizens working alongside the state

[83] José Montealegre P. "Minerva," *Minerva*, October 25, 1903.   [84] Ibid.

FIGURE 5.4 Minerva temple, Cobán.
Photograph by Felipe Sierra Cú, photograph courtsey of Felipe Sierra Cú's family

toward progress. Estrada Cabrera and other state officials thus attempted to institutionalize liberalism by making the world of liberalism fully real and instilling it into the meaning of the epoch.[85]

For ladino and Q'eqchi' organizers, the Minerva festivals fulfilled a civilizing pedagogical impulse to cultivate particular senses of self and nation among the lower classes, as well as to represent and produce the truth of themselves as participants in the highest forms of modernity. The line between participant and spectator was purposefully blurred.[86] This civilizing desire is captured in the photograph of Cobán's Minerva temple (Figure 5.4). In the image of an indigenous woman walking toward the temple, the photographer produces the visual narrative of a march toward civilization. The role of the festivals was to direct society toward new heights. Festival organizers and participants drawn into the Minerva festivals were also invited to take up the reformative power of education

---

[85] In this sense, the Minerva festivals have something in common with the festivals celebrating the French Revolution; see Mona Ozouf, *Festivals and the French Revolution*, trans. Alan Sheridan (Cambridge, MA: Harvard University Press, 1988).

[86] "Las fiestas de Minerva," *La Juventud Liberal*, November 7, 1909; and "Discurso presentado por Felipe Estrada Panigua," in *Álbum de Minerva*, 1907, 6.

and science that promised to break down barriers of social inequality and to silence racial discourses. As one Minerva participant declared, science "is the mysterious scale that without exception of classes, lineage or color, elevates and dignifies man, bringing him closer to God. Youth follow in his beautiful footsteps, climb the stairs of his altar, one by one, and occupy in society an honorable post that Minerva grants to those who pay tribute to the sciences and the arts."[87] Just as Estrada Cabrera promoted artisan societies, cooperatives, and youth clubs to uplift the working class, the Minerva festivals represented an effort to civilize the urban poor. The Minerva festivals themselves thus were akin to the metaphysical theater described by Clifford Geertz in nineteenth-century Bali. The festivals were designed to express a truth about Guatemalan social reality and the degree of civilization that it inhabited, while at the same time inculcating and educating, stimulating and disciplining the nation's population to live up to that truth.[88] After an evening of dancing, one observer noted, "all the social classes were given a place to enjoy the sweet and rhythmical notes of the guitars, mandolins, and violins that transported impassioned souls to the nation of their dreams."[89]

For organizers, the spectacles also represented the democratization of this civilized culture, once available only to a select few. The organizers' ownership of that culture allowed them to end the politics of postponement. The Minerva festivals, as Elías Barrientos of San Pedro Carchá noted, "could only be actualized in an era of high civilization, that in gigantic steps had advanced in the search for intellectual, moral, and material perfection."[90] Statesmen, intellectuals, and teachers sought to stimulate these ideals and utopian visions of Guatemalan society through their carefully crafted speeches, which were obsessively reprinted in special newspapers dedicated to Minerva. Like the building of the Hospital del Norte, the ladino and Q'eqchi' participants and organizers of Minerva festivals recast space and time and fashioned new modern selves.

The Minerva festivals were also highly choreographed affairs that bear the marks of an increasingly repressive dictatorship. From marches and games to speeches and poetry, the events bore a remarkable similarity across the nation. Participants were obligated to pay tribute to great past civilizations, strategically position Guatemala within the scheme of

[87] M. V. M. "Pensamiento," *Minerva*, October 25, 1903.
[88] Clifford Geertz, *Negara: The Theater State in Nineteenth-Century Bali* (Princeton: Princeton University Press, 1981), 104.
[89] "Minerva en Cobán," *El Norte*, November 14, 1915.   [90] Ibid.

universal history, and glorify Estrada Cabrera as a benevolent dictator. As Lauren Derby has explored, scripted forms of political oratory helped forge an official identity crucial to explaining the enduring power of dictatorship and the normalization of everyday forms of domination and terror.[91] Official speech protocols drew participants into the regime even if they were required to perform according to a set of scripts not of their own making. As Catherine Rendón has noted, the Minervalias were an important vehicle for Estrada Cabrera's popular control.[92] The Minerva festivals had a psychological lure that could be understood as a cover for and distraction from the brutality of the regime – its prisons filled with political dissidents, its victims of repression, and its growing body of exiles. Awe and spectacle, rather than merely distracting from the realities of political repression, might guarantee safety from his wrath. For Guatemalans and immigrants alike, the Minerva festivals were opportune moments to demonstrate a Liberal political affiliation and support for Estrada Cabrera. The Liberal club's members played an active role in the organization of the festivities. Indeed, around the time of Estrada Cabrera's reelection, the eloquent speeches about science, education, and the youth of the nation were framed to an increasing degree as praises of and tributes to the achievements of his presidency. As fear increased, so did the extravagance of the celebrations.

Sometimes, however, choreographed speeches erupted with uncensored details that functioned as criticisms of Estrada Cabrera's regime. In 1900 Sofia Chavarria, a schoolteacher in Carchá, delivered the closing speech for the ceremony by congratulating the schoolchildren and parents, and remarking with some disdain on the decadence of the festivals themselves. Indeed, she asked, "What brilliance would this work [the adornments of the festival] have if it lacked expensive objects that win our love, our affection and our friendship? ... If in this manner school work was celebrated, then there is no doubt that next year, the children will dedicate themselves with greater energy to their studies, and it will awaken enthusiasm in them." In order to salvage the celebration, the Minerva festival committee immediately called on another schoolteacher and town official to follow Chavaria's closing speech with a different conclusion to the ceremonies. Making vivid reference to the gods of Roman mythology, the town councilmen noted that the time of regeneration and progress

---

[91] Derby, *The Dictator's Seduction*, 136.
[92] Rendón, *Minerva y la Palma*; and Rendón, "Temples of Tribute and Illusion," *Americas* 54, no. 4 (July–August 2002): 17–23.

had arrived, and placed Guatemala's efforts to achieve civilization through education in the universal history of civilized nations, from Rome to the United States.[93] Chavarria's seemingly unscripted and critical remarks highlight, however, that some ladinos viewed the Minerva festivals not as symbols of wealth, or the civilization and grandeur of their nation, but as state theater that detracted from the much-needed work of education and the reality of poverty in their midst. The Minerva festivals, rather than granting a reprieve from the politics of postponement, might have been further evidence of the nation's stagnation.

Since the extravagance of the Minervalias grew in direct proportion to the brutality of Estrada Cabrera's regime, the Minerva festivals' symbols of grandeur easily transformed into representations of banality and vulgarity. As political opposition mounted in 1918 and 1919, editorialists criticized the festivals for the pompous displays of civilization and the free flow of liquor and moral disorder. In 1918, in an article sarcastically titled "Pro-Minerva," one editorialist noted that Minervalias were actually celebrations of Bacchus, the Roman god of wine and debauchery. The festivals, he decried, had been "converted from more or less respectable displays of merriment into scandalous saturnalias, where the cult of the beautiful Bacchus is worshipped, insulting the legendary poverty of the teachers with the popping of vulgarized champagnes and displaying before the eyes of children the triumph of vice, the ostentation of riches as if this festival was not itself eminently democratic."[94] The festivals were merely a "pretext for speculators" and "the festivals of knowledge were made into the apple of discord, and the rock of scandal." Mineravalias, according to the editorialist, fomented political corruption as money collected for the events rarely reached the children and teachers it was meant to honor.[95] A year later, the same newspaper reported that "still the municipality expends liquors in the Minerva camp, producing scandals that still make many blush, because they were truly *orgies* that happened under the infamous influence of liquor."[96] As these accounts suggest, Altaverapacences, frustrated with Estrada Cabrera's tyranny, expressed disgust with the Minerva festivals themselves. The festivals thus were a metaphor for Estrada Cabrera's moral and political corruption, as well as the vulgarity and viciousness of his politics.

---

[93] Biblioteca Nacional, "Programa de las Minerva Festivales, San Pedro Carchá," 1900.
[94] "Pro-Minerva," *El Norte*, October 26, 1918.
[95] Untitled editorial in *El Norte*, October 26, 1918.
[96] "Festejos," *El Norte*, November 29, 1919.

Shifting global and regional contexts may have also played an important role in the growing disgust with the Minerva festivals. The devastation and destruction wrought by World War I gave rise to profound global uncertainty about European civilization's own descent into barbarism. Most famously, these doubts were articulated in Oswald Spengler's *Der Untergang des Abendlandes* (The Decline of the West), published in Spanish in 1923 as *La decadencia del Occidente*.[97] As Europe lost its claim to civilization and culture, Latin Americans also articulated a new regional vision that granted Latin America a privileged place in the metanarrative of democracy and, more than ever, peace.[98] For Altaverapacences, celebrations of Western civilization likely seemed out of step with global events and an emergent anti-European and anticolonial regionalism.

DETHRONING MINERVA

Between 1917 and 1919, a series of political and economic crises as well as natural disasters revealed the fault lines of society and unraveled Manuel Estrada Cabrera's base of support among the urban working and middle classes, and eventually coffee planters, Germans settlers, and other elite sectors. The outbreak of World War I disrupted trade and credit with Germany, causing difficulties in the coffee economy.[99] Two massive earthquakes struck, in December 1917 and January 1918, leaving Guatemala City in shambles. In the words of Miguel Ángel Asturias, the earthquakes "not only shook the earth but also jolted our consciences."[100] When rumors reached Guatemala eight months later that

[97] Oswald Spengler, *La decadencia de Occidente: Bosquejo de una morfología de la historia universal* (Madrid: Calpe, 1923).

[98] See Ricardo Melgar Bao and Mariana Ortega Breña, "The Anti-Imperlialist League of the Americas between the East and Latin America," *Latin American Perspectives* 35, no. 2 (March 2008): 9–24. See also Sanders, *The Vanguard of the Atlantic World*, 225–6.

[99] Coffee exports to Germany fell from 458,037 quintals in 1912 to 99,998 quintals in 1916 to zero in 1918; those to England fell from 75,013 quintals in 1912 to 9,452 quintals in 1916 to 4,216 quintals in 1918. Likewise, in 1913, 27 percent of exports went to the United States, while 53 percent went to Germany and 11 percent went to Great Britain. By 1915, however, this situation had reversed: 60 percent of exports were destined for the United States, 0 percent went to Germany, and 11 percent to Great Britain. Dana G. Munro, *The Five Republics of Central America: Their Political and Economic Development and Their Relations with the United States* (New York: Oxford University Press, 1918), 274.

[100] Miguel Ángel Asturias, cited in Joseph A. Pitti, "Jorge Ubico and Guatemalan Politics in the 1920s" (PhD diss., University of New Mexico, 1975), 197–8.

the global influenza pandemic was knocking on its door, the capital city still lay in rubble. Makeshift refugee camps peppered the outskirts of the city as displaced people scrambled for inadequate housing. Resources had already been spread thin, and corruption in Estrada Cabrera's regime appeared to be reaching new heights. The nation was unprepared. When the epidemic swept the Pacific Coast and western highlands in August, Altaverapacences braced themselves for the horrors on the horizon. By September 1918, only a month before the coffee harvest got under way, planters in Alta Verapaz had reported cases of influenza, although the departmental governor did not officially report any instances of the epidemic for another two months. At the same time, the Mexican and Russian Revolutions offered new language that helped turn Estrada Cabrera's anti-aristocratic discourses into more radicalized calls for equality and social justice for the poor in Alta Verapaz. World War I not only stoked the flames of anti-German sentiment, but also angered German, ladino, and Q'eqchi' coffee planters, who faced difficulties in exporting coffee at the very moment prices were set to skyrocket.

The influenza epidemic was more devastating than any other recent natural disaster in Guatemala. The earthquakes of 1917 and 1918 had primarily affected the urban centers. The 1918 influenza pandemic attacked ladinos and Mayas, rural and urban folks, and rich and poor alike, although not all in the same way. Additionally, Estrada Cabrera failed to respond appropriately to the epidemic, and the country lacked an official branch to deal with public health. In Alta Verapaz, local sanitation committees were hastily organized to clean drains and streets, disinfect the interior and exterior walls of homes, pick up garbage and debris "that could feed microbes of contagious diseases," and cut down trees surrounding homes in order to ensure that "the movement of pure air not be interrupted."[101] The municipal council obliged townspeople to be vaccinated, and schools closed their doors. Local newspapers promised "to reprimand those who disobey and do not attend to the orders that are dictated for the welfare of everyone" by printing publicly the names of people who shirked their sanitation responsibilities.[102] All in all, however, most people believed the nation was entirely unprepared.

Like other natural disasters, the influenza epidemic also threw into sharp relief social inequalities that unveiled the mythical quality of

---

[101] SPCM 1918, "Correspondencias, Circular del JP a Carlos Torres Q Alcalde de 1° Municipal," September 13, 1918.
[102] "Ecos y rumores," *El Norte*, January 11, 1919.

Estrada Cabrera's promise of social uplift. Editorialists began to blame the rising death toll on the moral corruption of state authorities and the coffee-planting elite.[103] Even before the outbreak, anti–coffee planter critiques had been brewing alongside the Mexican Revolution. Beginning in 1917, newspaper articles about socialism, the 1910 Mexican Revolution, and the plight of Maya laborers speckled Cobán's newspaper *El Norte*.[104] If planters had long been guilty of exploiting the masses, coffee planters' notable lack of concern for their workers in the midst of a deadly epidemic was the final proof of their moral depravity. According to one editorialist, coffee planters demonstrated greater concern for the welfare of their horses, dogs, and cattle than of their laborers.[105] Another editorialist appealed to the coffee planters' patriotism and humanity: "We do not doubt that the planters of this beautiful region will hear our voice in favor of the primitive race, owner of these lands, and they will do all that is possible to rescue them from the fatal blow, of the terrible calamity decimating humanity."[106] One editorialist, writing in the *Diario de Centro-América*, contended that Alta Verapaz's wealthy German immigrants had a special obligation to save the nation's indigenous population.[107] If German settlers had grown wealthy from Guatemala's fertile soils and Mayas' arduous labor, then, the editorialist suggested, Germans had a special duty to give back to their host country. Perhaps, he intimated,

---

[103] See David McCreery, "Guatemala City," in *The 1918–1919 Pandemic of Influenza: The Urban Impact in the Western World*, ed. Fred R. van Hartesveldt (Lewiston, NY: Edwin Mellen Press, 1992), 161–84; David Carey, *Our Elders Teach Us: Maya-Kaqchikel Historical Perspectives: Xkib'ij Kan Qate' Qatata'* (Tuscaloosa: University of Alabama Press, 2001), 119–27. The available data from Alta Verapaz suggest that the epidemic began in September 1918 and reached its height in the first months of 1919. For the daily reports from municipalities as well as comandantes locales, see the AGCA Jefatura Política-Alta Verapaz records for 1918–19. The first report of the epidemic I found was from September 13, 1918, two months before it appeared in official reports. See SPCM 1918, "Carlos Torres Q. al Alcalde 1° Municipal, 13 septiembre 1918"; AGCA B Leg. 29404 Exp. 20.

[104] "Lucha de clases," *El Norte*, January 27, 1917; Virgilio Rodríguez Beteta, "Situación del indígena en Guatemala," *El Norte*, March 9, 1918; "Habilitaciones ytrabajadores," *El Norte*, March 9, 1918; Virgilio Rodríguez Beteta, "Por los indios," *El Norte*, March 23, 1918.

[105] JEMP, "La influenza nos ha invadido," *El Norte*, January 18, 1919.

[106] JEMP, "Continuamos hablando al corazón de los hijos de la Alta Verapaz," *El Norte*, February 1, 1919.

[107] "A los finqueros de Alta Verapaz," *Diario de Centro América*, February 15, 1919; M.A.R.G, "La salubridad en las fincas," *El Norte*, January 25, 1919; "Ejemplo digno de imitarse," *El Norte*, February 15, 1919; and Portocarrero, *Alma y vida de Cobán*, 152–3.

German immigrants should demonstrate where their true national loyalties resided.

In response to US pressure and mounting domestic concerns, Estrada Cabrera passed anti-German wartime measures. In 1917 he prohibited commerce with German firms and plantations that figured on the *listas negras*, or Enemy Trading lists, compiled by the Allied forces. Three months after the ceasefire on November 11, 1918, he confiscated German properties and assets owned by Germans who had remained in Germany during the war.[108] Erwin Paul Dieseldorff was among those affected.[109] Frustrated Guatemalan coffee planters found themselves unable to acquire credit for cash advances to laborers, heightening anti-German sentiment and enflaming Guatemala's own brand of anti-Semitism that often conflated Jewish ancestry with German nationality. Decrying the lack of credit available for Guatemalan coffee planters, one editorialist noted: "There is no one that can lend them even a cent." Even worse, "the Jews who live there give them some advances for their harvests, but the conditions are so sad and so degrading that they are not useful."[110] Anti-Semitic arguments bled into conflicts between German and ladino coffee planters. In 1919 Víctor Ramírez cited the local newspaper in his conflict over laborers with the German settler Víctor Wellman: "With just reason the local press has said that 'how many have also arrived to this land and after amassing a fortune with the bitter sweat of the poor *indio*, who has been enslaved like a beast of burden, from night to day they take flight and do not leave any more trail than the black memory of the sad history of dishonorable, Jewish exploitation.'"[111] Ladino editorialists were influenced not only by World War I but also by German economic predominance, the epidemic's devastation, and the unfulfilled expectations of social mobility and progress. Some coffee planters even went so far as to call for the nationalization and redistribution of German-owned properties, an ominous warning for German settlers.[112]

The influenza epidemic, alongside World War I, accelerated open resistance to Estrada Cabrera's regime. Before 1918 newspaper editorialists had rarely criticized the government. Even after the earthquakes

[108] The properties intervened by the government reached an astounding total of 527,792 Guatemalan pesos. Regina Wagner, *Los alemanes en Guatemala*, 260.
[109] Náñez Falcón, "Erwin Paul Dieseldorff," 61–3.
[110] "Por la Vera-Paz, notas de interés público," *Diario de Centro América*, June 7, 1919.
[111] AGCA JP-AV Paq. 16 1919, "Víctor Wellman para mozos fraudulentas," April 21, 1919.
[112] AGCA JP-AV 1919 Paq. 5, "Al JP de Agricultores de Alta Verapaz," July 18, 1919.

jolted Guatemalan political consciousness, the newspaper pages were filled not with news about the local dictators but with reports from war-ravaged Europe. Domestic concerns were relegated to the back pages, when they were given any attention at all. When influenza reached Central America via El Salvador in August, however, the *Diario de Centro-América* turned its focus from events in Europe to the immediate internal threat. As the death toll surged precisely during the height of the coffee harvest, this danger grew in strength, and some in Alta Verapaz feared the "loss of hands [*brazos*]" would result in food shortages and a stalled coffee harvest.[113] As had occurred with earlier natural disasters, Estrada Cabrera and regional authorities underreported the devastation caused by the epidemic, which fueled rather than assuaged grievances.[114] Alta Verapaz was no different. When the epidemic reached its peak in January 1919, the departmental governor remarked that there had been "a few cases," even while the Municipality of Cobán alone had reported more than 150 confirmed cases of influenza and several deaths by mid-January.[115] That May, the departmental governor reported that the region was "completely free from the epidemic," even though municipalities reported influenza cases daily. Reports from the departmental governor also tended to downplay the impact of the epidemic, emphasizing the region's healthy climate and robust indigenous population.[116] While the census data are incomplete, extant data suggest a negative population growth rate.[117] The pandemic also had a profound economic impact on the coffee economy. Coffee exports dropped by 13.9 percent in 1918, even as coffee prices skyrocketed the following year.[118] Not only was the

[113] "Previendo el hambre," *El Norte*, January 18, 1919.
[114] McCreery, "Guatemala City," 161–84; and Richard N. Adams, "La epidemia de influenza de 1918–1919," in *Historia general de Guatemala, vol. 5: Época contemporánea, 1898–1944*, ed. Jorge Luján Muñoz and J. Daniel Contreras R. (Guatemala: Asociación de Amigos del País, 1996), 313–38.
[115] AGCA Leg. 29404 Exp. 20.
[116] Richard N. Adams, "Estado e indígenas durante la epidemia de influenza de 1918–1919 en Guatemala," *Mesoamérica* 34 (December 1997): 554.
[117] Thirteen out of twenty departments experienced negative population growth. The highest negative population growth was in the Department of Guatemala, as a result of both the earthquakes and the influenza epidemic, at 15.53 percent. The highest population growth was in the Department of Jutiapa at 4.41 percent. *Censo de la República de Guatemala: Levantado el 28 de agosto de 1921* (Guatemala: Tipografía Nacional, 1924), 67.
[118] McCreery, *Rural Guatemala*, 301. For prices for Guatemalan coffee for the years 1914–40, see *World's Coffee: Studies of the Principal Agricultural Products of the World Market*, no. 9 (Rome, 1947), 432.

devastation, which predominantly affected rural, highland Mayas, profoundly underreported, but the epidemic's social, political, and economic impact was also widely underestimated.[119] Along with the coffee crisis, however, the pandemic helped unite coffee planters and workers, urban middle classes and intellectuals, army officers and even his own hand-picked state officials, against the aging dictator. The tides of social and political change in Guatemala were reaching a crescendo that could not be stopped.

CONCLUSION

Encouraged by Estrada Cabrera's protopopulist politics, urban bourgeois and honorable working-class ladinos and Q'eqchi's worked together to forge a new social identity by modernizing urban space and participating in public festivals that redefined hierarchy and distinguished them from the poor, the rural, the sick, and the uneducated. Together they forged a modern identity against the stereotypes of Indianness. This social identity was not based on mestizaje – it did not signify a transition between the rural Indianness and European whiteness. Ladino was in itself an end point that could contain a spectrum of racial differences, ranging from Q'eqchi' patriarchs to Creoles. It was an open and ambiguous social identity whose power derived from fluid and uncertain social and racial hierarchies. Ladino nationalism made people on the margins of urban social worlds liable to charges of being an indio, just as it could incorporate people like the Q'eqchi' patriarchs, who were ethnically indigenous but socially and politically prominent. Ladino nationalism worked because race, particularly in the context of such unstable social classifications, was based on performances that would become manifest in the context of particular interactions. Every interaction was a ritualized performance in which status claims were processed and made based on shared criteria of racial markers, ranging from name and face to occupation and language and to dress and residence. As Eileen Findlay has argued, those who occupied a lower rung in class terms were at a disadvantage, and so had to work harder to demonstrate their honorability, while at other times they defied elite norms altogether.[120] One way of achieving this honorability was to emphasize one's association with "Western civilization, modernity,

[119] Carey, *Our Elders Teach Us*, 123–6.   [120] Findlay, *Imposing Decency*.

upward mobility ... the cash market," which ladinos did through urban modernization projects, Liberal clubs, and social welfare.[121] Manuel Estrada Cabrera's Liberal clubs, welfare associations, and the like provided opportunities for the lower classes to shore up their status and worth, and to legitimately claim to be ladino.

Through participation in festivals and events, education and social welfare programs, and the building of a hospital, social groups as diverse as workers, emerging middle-class ladinos, and Q'eqchi' elites had also come to understand themselves through narratives of progress and providence and defined their social status in historical terms. Through the period of Estrada Cabrera's dictatorship especially, diverse social sectors had begun to see progress narratives in a new light, as historical agency and civilization was made available to all. In addition to the memorias celebrating public works, Altaverapacence ladinos also sought to write their own history chronicling the achievements of the region. In December 1919, as anti-Estrada Cabrera political mobilization erupted in Guatemala City, J. M. Eduardo Portocarrero, a teacher at Cobán's Practical School for Boys, printed *Alma y vida de Cobán*. The 158-page book sought to dispel Alta Verapaz's obscurity within the national imagination. Portocarrero opened his book declaring that "it seems strange that this beautiful and rich region of our beloved nation is much better known in Europe, than by ourselves."[122] Undertaking to rectify the region's oblivion, the teacher chronicled Alta Verapaz's history, its morals and customs, and most of all, the great material progress Alta Verapaz had achieved. Portocarrero extolled the virtues of the region's "humble" and "peaceful" Mayas, celebrated the region's beauty, and admired the many great ladinos who had forged the region into a beacon of modernity with roads, a modern central square, and a railway. He assembled his narrative from municipal and departmental archives, newspapers, and popular memory. Portocarrero chronicled Alta Verapaz's modernity and helped articulate an emergent regional identity.

Portocarrero's *Alma y vida de Cobán* also spoke of the coming legacy of Estrada Cabrera's protopopulism: a flexible and shifting ladino identity forged through expectations of modernity on the horizon, frustrations with German economic predominance and the structural

---

[121] Mary Weismantel, *Cholas and Pishtacos: Stories of Race and Sex in the Andes* (Chicago: University of Chicago Press, 2001), 90.

[122] Portocarrero, *Alma y vida de Cobán*, 5.

barriers to social mobility, and efforts by ladinos to distinguish themselves racially from darker others. Portocarrero lamented German domination of the coffee economy, which was due not to a ladino racial defect but rather to the "lack of lending firms that supply money at reasonable and equitable rates ... and make us independent of the exorbitant Jewishness of certain firms that give money at conditions much too ONEROUS for the nation's planters, industrialists, or artisans."[123] Potocarrero's observations gave voice to ladino sentiments about social and economic barriers to their advancement and transposed their fears into a global anti-Semitism. In crafting his history of modernization, Potocarrero also recounted the events of Xucaneb some thirty years earlier. Based on rumor and popular memory, he described Juan de la Cruz as "very dark colored" and attributed the apparition of a deity to the Black Christ of Esquipulas, long associated with African heritage.[124] The pilgrimage to Tzuultaq'a Xucaneb is notably absent from his recounting. Instead, the reader is left to surmise that Juan de la Cruz is of African descent. Portocarrero's erasure restored Q'eqchi' patriarchs' and ladino artisans' honor by relegating Juan de la Cruz to another category altogether: Afro-Guatemalan. Blurring fact and fiction, Portocarrero's narrative was pregnant with alternative stories that served as an index of social hierarchies and power on the eve of political change.

As Portocarrero's narrative also suggests, racial identifications were contingent and shifting.[125] The fluidity of social relations and hierarchies, the multiple contexts and interactions, meant that racial differences were neither stable, nor based on a simple either/or formula. As I have sought to demonstrate, ladino nationalism proved much more inclusionary than a racial binary between ladinos and Mayas would suggest. Who constituted a ladino was subject to multiple interpretations. "Ladino artisans" did not have any single, unitary connotation – they could be racially darkened and represented as the cause of stalled national development, or they could be the symbol of an honorable people, capable of participating in progress. The meaning of ladino thus continually shifted, not just in everyday interactions, but also over time. As opposition mounted to Estrada Cabrera, ladino artisans formed some of the principal opponents of his regime. Estrada Cabrera's failure to fully resolve the politics of postponement generated escalating demands for meaningful reform, including democratic expansion. In the aftermath of his overthrow, a

---

[123] Ibid., 23–4.   [124] Ibid., 44.   [125] See Taracena Arriola, *Etnicidad, estado y nación.*

general reflection on the meaning of the Liberal revolution of 1871 led many Guatemalan intellectuals, however, to blame ladinos, and their racial defects, for Estrada Cabrera's dictatorship. With each successive turn, the concept of ladino as well as the meaning of modernity developed historical genealogies of ruptures and reencasements that were neither progressive nor linear.

6

Freedom of the Indian

Maya Rights and Citizenship in a Democratic Experiment, 1920–1931

The Indian is unaware that Guatemala is a republic and is unaware of his rights and obligations as a citizen.
—Miguel Ángel Asturias, *El problema social del indio*

As the influenza epidemic stole rural lives, imperiled coffee harvests, and unleashed critiques of coffee planters, Cobán's town councilmen celebrated the nation's independence in September 1919 by laying the first stone of a future monument to the heroic Q'eqchi', Manuel de la Cruz Tot.[1] A Cobanero patriarch, Manuel Tot was famed for his participation in early independence agitation and his untimely death at the hands of Spanish royalist forces. According to J. M. Estrada Paniagua, a local historian and schoolteacher, Tot exemplified "Indians who love national progress and liberty" and provided an objective lesson of "what is and could be a civilized Indian." The local indigenista Celso V. Reyes contended that Manuel Tot offered irrefutable historical evidence of Q'eqchi's' ability to become modern, civilized citizens. "Because today this poor race is arrested under the oppression that sustains their ignorance,"

[1] See "Noble idea," *El Norte*, November 25, 1917; "La gratitud de la Verapaz," *El Norte*, July 26, 1919; Celso V. Reyes, "El gran indio," *El Norte*, November 1, 1919; "Para el centenario" and "El alma de la raza," *El Norte*, September 15, 1921; Mario Selis Lope, "Orientamos a la juventud," *El Norte*, September 24, 1921; AGCA JP-AV 1919, Paq. 1, "Informe de la municipalidad de Cobán al JP," December 30, 1919; and Portocarrero, *Alma y vida de Cobán*, 108–10. For references to Manuel Tot, Alejandro Marure, *Bosquejo histórico de las revoluciones de Centro-América desde 1811 hasta 1834* (Guatemala: Tipografía de "El Progreso," 1877), 19; and Felipe Estrada Paniagua, *Pasatiempo* (Guatemala: Tipografía Nacional, 1902), 22.

Reyes wrote in *El Norte*, "there are those who cannot conceive that yesterday they could have been nothing less than a heroic race, that knew how to spill, as much as others, their blood for the integrity of the land in which they were born."[2] The Tot monument, however, did not grace Cobán's central plaza for nearly another sixty years. In December 1919, construction was temporarily delayed due to a financial shortfall. After the abrupt end to Manuel Estrada Cabrera's regime the following April, the project was stalled, and the florid discourses about Manuel Tot's heroic virtues disappeared from the newspapers and other public forums. By September 1921, when the centenary was celebrated, speeches praising the Q'eqchi' leader were virtually absent from public commemorations.[3]

During the twenty-nine months between Estrada Cabrera's overthrow and the centenarian celebrations, José Ángel Icó, a dynamic and relentless Q'eqchi' patriarch, led Q'eqchi's in efforts to reshape local power relations through electoral politics and political organizing. Together, they unsettled Alta Verapaz's social and political order and challenged coffee planters' sovereignty. In striking contrast to celebrations of Guatemalan independence, Altaverapacence Q'eqchi's avowed that colonialism had never come to an end and took up the promises of liberalism by demanding full rights as citizens, the end of debt contracts, and control over municipal councils. Q'eqchi' mobilizations, however, struck fear in the hearts of planters, fostered rounds of escalating political violence, and silenced treatises about noble Q'eqchi' patriarchs heroically defending the nation. By the mid-1920s, state officials and coffee planters violently cracked down on labor mobilizations, reinstated mandamiento labor, and drafted constitutional reforms that limited Maya citizenship. In Guatemala, no national popular coalition solidified to incorporate Maya demands into a redefined nation-state as happened in neighboring Mexico.[4] Rather, the 1920s witnessed the vigorous re-entrenchment of the civilizing metanarrative and racially ordered social and political worlds. As Q'eqchi's formed an insurrectionary politics, state officials

---

[2] Celso V. Reyes, "El gran indio," El Norte, November 1, 1919.

[3] J. Fernando Juárez Muñoz would also later argue that Tot represented the need to incorporate Mayas into national history alongside other independence leaders. See J. F. Juárez Muñoz, "Apología del prócer Manuel Tot," *Anales de la Sociedad de Geografía e Historia* 17, no. 5 (March 1942): 327–32.

[4] See Florencia E. Mallon, "Indian Communities, Political Cultures, and the State in Latin America, 1780–1990," *Journal of Latin American Studies* 24, Quincentenary Supplement: The Colonial and Post-Colonial Experience (1992): 35–53.

and others denounced Mayas as anachronisms in the nation. Guatemalan intellectuals also began to view Alta Verapaz's fincas de mozos, German immigrants, and racial mixing between Germans and Mayas as a laboratory for national progress.

This chapter examines Guatemala's experiment with electoral democracy in the early 1920s to the beginning of the Great Depression, the Communist Red Scare, and the election of Jorge Ubico as president of Guatemala in 1931. It first charts how Q'eqchi's, led by José Ángel Icó, sought to use the democratic opening following Estrada Cabrera's forced resignation to challenge racial hierarchies and the politics of postponement, and to demand rights and freedoms. Maya political organizing, however, sparked escalating rounds of violence and retribution. As Q'eqchi's pursued electoral politics and then land invasions and labor strikes, they also redefined Q'eqchi's mediation. Just as the early nineteenth-century constitutional experiments challenged Maya caste hierarchy, the early twentieth-century democratic opening promoted new forms of native-state mediation that empowered lower-class Mayas. Ladino and German coffee planters, however, faced a common enemy and reunited in a new alliance against Mayas. This chapter then explores how elite ladino-European immigrant alliances were expressed in a new mestizaje project that celebrated the union of European men, principally Germans, with Maya women as the racial solution to Guatemala's stalled development. Finally, it details how, by the mid-1920s, soaring coffee prices led coffee planters first to reinstate mandamiento labor, and then with the help of the Association of Agriculturalists, lay the foundations for a new vagrancy law. The Great Depression, along with the Central American Communist red scare, concluded Guatemala's democratic experiment.

UNIONISTS AND THE INDIAN QUESTION IN GUATEMALA

In the first months of 1919, opposition to Manuel Estrada Cabrera formed among the celebrated ladino artisans. Making use of Estrada Cabrera's cooperatives and Liberal clubs, artisans and railroad workers turned Estrada Cabrera's instruments of state patronage into weapons of political resistance. As political opposition spread to the countryside, Mayas like José Ángel Icó challenged planter abuses and mandamiento labor through the local courts. In early 1919, the ladino coffee planter Jorge Méndez charged that Icó was "an enemy of all the authorities."[5]

---

[5] AGCA JP-AV 1919 Paq. 4, "JP de Jorge Mendez B.," March 17, 1919.

Q'eqchi's also once again adopted the languages of slavery to confront their status as resident laborers. With a tinterillo's support, Juan Chub and Mateo Bol demanded the right to leave the plantation they resided in, "because we are not slaves and, although ignorant, we understand that no man, no citizen, has the obligation of serving another person without pay."[6] By the end of 1919, the departmental governor reported to the president that the region's exceptionally high crime rate was a result of "a lack of deference."[7]

The 1920 National Assembly elections provided another flash point for the urban middle class, intellectuals, and even coffee planters to join the anti-Estrada Cabrera movement. In December 1919, a broad coalition of dissidents revived the defunct Unionist Party to unite political opposition and support candidates.[8] The Unionist Party members hastily penned a political program that expressed its diverse base. The platform ranged from establishing vagrancy laws to abolishing mandamientos, the building of roads to redistributing rural properties, as well as regenerating the Indian via education and sanitation. The proposal also included an expansive definition of citizenship that granted citizenship to all Guatemalan men, without literacy and property requirements. From this diverse and contradictory platform, small branches, known as Unionist clubs, popped up across the countryside as a forum for Guatemalans to participate in shaping the new political era on the horizon. Mayas from across the nation were active in the anti-Cabrera movement, as both actors and intellectuals, but their participation was often met with surprise, disdain, or hesitant collaboration. As one contributor recorded, "Even *los indios* are arriving to support our campaign."[9] Mayas subscribed to Unionist and regional newspapers, to the expressed surprise of newspaper editorial boards.[10] Some Maya patriarchs fostered relationships with Guatemalan intellectuals affiliated with the Unionist Party.[11] As a bottom-up alternative to state-controlled Liberal clubs, the Unionista clubs prompted El Señor Presidente's wrath.[12] In March alone, the secret police arrested

---

[6] AGCA JP-AV 1919 Paq. 6, "Sr JP de Juan Bol y Mateo Chub," July 8, 1919.

[7] AGCA JP-AV 1919 Paq. 1, "Informe del JP de Alta Verapaz," December 2, 1919.

[8] See "Partido Unionista: Acta de organización," cited in Arévalo Martínez, *¡Ecce Pericles!*, 475–8.

[9] "Segunda carta de Manuel Cobos Batres a su hermana, Adela, del 23 de marzo de 1920," in Arévalo Martínez, *¡Ecce Pericles!*, 467–70.

[10] Ibid.   [11] Esquit, *La superación indígena*, 73.

[12] Wade Kit, "The Unionist Experiment in Guatemala, 1920–1921: Conciliation, Disintegration, and the Liberal Junta," *The Americas* 50, no. 1 (June 1993): 61. See Arévalo

more than 400 members of the Unionist Party. But the pace of arrests could not keep up with the tide of resistance sweeping the nation. In Guatemala City, an estimated 60,000 people came together in a series of events, meetings, and increasingly violent confrontations.

Nowhere was the radical democratic potential of the Unionist clubs more dramatically realized than with the Altaverapacence Club Unionista "Freedom of the Indian." On April 3, 1920, only days before Manuel Estrada Cabrera's forced resignation, 123 Q'eqchi's from the Club Unionista "Freedom of the Indian" presented a petition to the National Assembly. "We are knocking on the door of our political emancipation," they proclaimed. Their letter went on to call for the recognition of the individual rights of *all* Guatemalans, including Mayas:

Newspapers all over the nation constantly complain of the abuses that are committed daily by the authorities against us, but nothing has been done. It is therefore necessary that we ourselves demand before the National Assembly the rights that belong to us. Just as we have been regarded as citizens for the purposes of service and defense of the Nation, in the same way we want to be guaranteed our constitutional rights as Citizens, so that we can enjoy liberty. And we believe that if Guatemala wants to take its place among the civilized nations of the world so as to celebrate with dignity the centenary of its independence, before anything else it needs to give the Indian complete liberty.

During its ninety-nine years of independence, the AUTHORITIES have not recognized the citizenship and liberty of the Indian. It would therefore be just, very just, to today concede the rights that belong to him. . . .

IN VIRTUE OF THIS:

TO THE HONORABLE NATIONAL REPRESENTATIVES, we come to use the rights that our foundational laws grant us, in Article 23, asking:

1. That the Authorities of the entire Republic recognize the citizenship rights that we are entitled . . .
5. Decree the immediate suspension across the entire Republic of the contracts between PATRON AND WORKER, because this practice is one of the foremost causes of suffering for the Indian, leaving instead FREEDOM OF LABOR.

. . .

Martínez, *¡Ecce Pericles!*; Wade Kit, "The Fall of Guatemalan Dictator, Manuel Estrada Cabrera, U.S. Pressure or National Opposition," *Canadian Journal of Caribbean and Latin American Studies* 10 (winter 1990): 105–27; R. Witzel de Ciudad, *Mas de 100 años del movimiento obrero urbano en Guatemala* (Guatemala: Asociación de Investigación y Estudios Sociales de Guatemala, 1991); Carlos Figueroa Ibarra, "Contenido de clase y participación obrera en el movimiento antidictatorial de 1920," *Política y Sociedad* 4 (July–December 1977): 5–51; and Carlos Figueroa Ibarra, "La insurrección armada de 1920 en Guatemala," *Política y Sociedad* 8 (July–December 1979): 91–146.

So we say, Gentlemen Representatives, please honor our humble petition and take into account regarding our decisions, that an entire PUEBLO is looking upon Us, as the only ones called upon to resolve their situation of LIBERTY OR SLAVERY. Even more, this same pueblo that today works to bring together the United Great Nation of Central America, to concede them what they so justly request, and remember with sincere gratitude that History will collect in its pages our names, writing them with gold letters.[13]

Q'eqchi' Unionistas drew on the liberal–democratic metanarrative to demand an immediate end to the purgatory of history's waiting room. They also wrote themselves into narratives of national progress as heroic agents of a long-anticipated change: the final realization of Guatemala's entrance into modernity as a fully independent nation-state. Like other anticolonial and antiracist movements, in the words of Achille Mbembe, Q'eqchi's "demanded the status of full subjects in the world of the living."[14] Calling for the abolition of labor contracts and the end of plantation abuses, Q'eqchi' Unionistas sought to challenge racist exclusions and coffee-planter sovereignty. Q'eqchi's understood themselves to be on the brink of a new and undefined era, where Mayas inaugurated a new dawn as the "civilized nations of the world" watched.

Q'eqchi' Unionistas were not alone in their feeling that history had suddenly become tangible. Rural workers refused to honor outstanding labor contracts, declaring that democracy had brought an end to slavery, injustice, and exploitation.[15] The president's office and the ministry of government were flooded with land claims, accusations of planter abuses, and demands for the removal of unpopular departmental and municipal officials.[16] In Guatemala, the first months of 1920 were a historic moment in which peasants and indigenous peoples experienced and helped produce a revolutionary time that not only rejected the deferment of the liberal promises of citizenship, but also allowed them to imagine they were historical actors producing a new society.[17]

A mere five days after the petition by the Club Unionista "Freedom of the Indian," Manuel Estrada Cabrera's handpicked National Assembly

---

[13] AGCA B Leg. 29466, Cobán, April 3, 1920.
[14] Achille Mbembe, *Critique of Black Reason* (Durham, NC: Duke University Press, 2017), 3.
[15] See Wade Kit, "Precursor of Change: Failed Reform and the Guatemalan Coffee Elite, 1918–1926" (MA thesis, University of Saskatchewan, 1989).
[16] For examples from other regions, see ibid.
[17] Walter Benjamin, "On the Concept of History," in *Selected Writings*, ed. H. Eiland and M. W. Jennings (Boston: Harvard University Press, 2003), 389–400.

declared him mentally incompetent to govern and removed him from office. The next day Guatemalans awoke to the shattering roar of gunfire and bombs, and for the following week people in the capital lived in chaotic terror. At week's end, Manuel Estrada Cabrera acquiesced, the gunfire stopped, and the National Assembly appointed the Unionist candidate, Carlos Herrera, as interim president. The end of Manuel Estrada Cabrera's twenty-two-year dictatorship shook not only the capital, but also the very multiethnic, multiclass alliances that had brought his dictatorship to an end.

Maya participation, as actors and intellectuals, opened up a vociferous debate across national forums about Maya nature, the limits of freedom, and the weight of the past. The Club Unionista "Freedom of the Indian" petition generated a debate that spilled across the pages of Guatemala's premier newspaper, *El Diario de Centro-América*. Jorge García Salas began his editorial, "Worthy of applause is the initiative taken by the Club Unionista de Cobán 'Freedom of the Indian.' Today, however, we must be practical and logical." With this conservative pragmatism, García Salas responded to the Q'eqchi's liberal demands by rehearsing old arguments about Mayas' incapacity for citizenship: "If consulting *el indio* about their ideals and desires, surely, they would not request rights and duties equal to ours but would rather be left independently in their jungles [*selva*] and their lands, free to live according to the customs of their ancestors. We are not co-citizens for them: instinctively they continue to consider us the enemy who overthrew their idols and shattered their civilization, as the conquerors who seized their riches." Postponing Maya demands, García Salas argued that Mayas were not yet ready for citizenship and that "they must be obliged to work, because lacking needs, lacking the spirit of saving, without notions of the improvement of the family, and left to their own devices, they would live the better part of the year in complete idleness. *El indio* constitutes 70 percent of the nation's population, and if these masses remain inert, our economic development, our progress, will be severely compromised."[18] At the very moment when Q'eqchi's sought to build a more inclusionary and democratic Guatemalan nation, García Salas rendered them dangerous anachronisms who imperiled national progress and prosperity. As often was the case, García Salas used the civilizing metanarrative that privileged capitalist

---

[18] Jorge García Salas, "Comentarios a la iniciativa del Club 'La Libertad del Indio,'" *Diario de Centro-América*, May 1, 1920.

expansion and the cultural attributes of Western civilization to deny cultural and racialized others access to modernity.

García Salas's ideas were also dangerous for coffee planters. He articulated the view – spreading across the hemisphere in the wake of the Mexican Revolution – that the state should play a definitive role in ensuring justice, including intervening on behalf of poor and exploited workers and guaranteeing certain protections. For coffee planters, this new role for the state was nothing short of a direct attack on their carefully negotiated territorial plantation sovereignty. A month later, a coffee planter penned an anonymous editorial which argued that coffee planters, not state bureaucrats, were best situated to civilize Mayas. The anonymous planter maintained that Mayas were best judged by planters who worked closely with Mayas and knew their true nature and desires.[19] Of course, he too reasoned that Mayas were not yet ready for freedom and self-governance and, like children, needed a strong guiding hand to discipline them and educate them in proper conduct.

Months later, the Unionist Party also responded to the Club Unionista "Freedom of the Indian's" petition, printing a three-part editorial, "Redemption of the Indian," written by Alicio Montt and published in Unionista newspapers across the country. While the Unionist Party had declared in December 1919 that they planned to expand citizenship, abolish mandamientos, and redistribute rural property, they now argued that Mayas were distrustful and prone to alcoholism and idolatry. Despite Maya participation in the Guatemala City anti–Estrada Cabrera demonstrations, Alicio Montt declared that Mayas "confuse politics for religion." Suggesting that Mayas blindly followed Estrada Cabrera, the editorialist noted that "statesmen for them are like gods, their pictures are carried and adored like idols." Like García Salas, the editorialist contended that Mayas were *not yet* fit for citizenship. To resolve Mayas' cultural stagnation and prepare them for national participation, Montt proposed education. In addition, Montt maintained that the nation should look to Alta Verapaz's fincas de mozos as a laboratory for the nation's modernity. The system of fincas de mozos in Alta Verapaz, Montt reasoned, "pleases the Indian by giving them lands to plant themselves in exchange for services" and "[has] given excellent results." Ignoring the regional origins of the Club Unionista "Freedom of the Indian," the editorialist made Alta Verapaz into a model for the nation itself: a

---

[19] "El indio su educación y progreso. Reflexiones de un finquero," *Diario de Centro-América*, June 17, 1920.

national future built on an idyllic and paternalistic rural space characterized by fixed residence, indigenous subsistence production, and nonindigenous-owned coffee plantations, where Mayas would be instructed and made into healthy citizens by good-father planters. The Unionist editorial was also reprinted in Cobán's Unionist paper, *El Federal*, in the weeks leading up to the 1920 elections, and it is likely that literate Q'eqchi' Unionists read the editorialist's suggestions with some interest.[20] The editorialist's dismissal of Q'eqchi' demands, however, did not stop Q'eqchi's from organizing in support of the Unionist candidate, Carlos Hererra, for the elections scheduled that August. Instead, Q'eqchi's such as José Ángel Icó believed that electoral politics offered a possibility for Mayas to shape the national political landscape.

ELECTORAL POLITICS, DEMOCRACY, AND CITIZENSHIP

In weekly meetings held in a small hermitage on the outskirts of San Pedro Carchá, José Ángel Icó rallied Q'eqchi's around the Unionist candidate and interim president, Carlos Herrera. Although we may never know the content of Icó's meetings, the Unionistas likely discussed not only the upcoming elections but also the national debate over Maya rights as citizens. If local officials are to be believed, however, Icó and his followers were also mounting a local revolution that echoed Jorge Yat's attempt to overthrow the town council on San Pedro Carchá's saint's day forty-five years earlier. Local authorities filed a charge of sedition against Icó for purportedly scheming to remove them from office.[21] The local police commander, Ciriacano Delgado, who also happened to be Icó's uncle, reported that he had heard news that Icó was fomenting plans "to rob him [*dar a palos*] of his personal authority, as well as that of the Alcalde 1° and the Sanpedranos Francisco Paredes and Elías Barrientos."[22] Witnesses called to give their account of Icó's meetings remarked that "the alcalde 1° must be an *indio* in order for them to be free." Icó, for his own account, denied all the charges and simply stated he was collecting funds "to hold a mass to give thanks for the new government and to pay for children orphaned in Guatemala" (as a result of the bombing in

---

[20] See "La redención del indio," *El Federal*, no. 10, July 14, 1920; no. 12, July 30, 1920; no. 13, August 10, 1920.

[21] On the meeting, see AGCA J-AV 104 Leg. 21 A Exp. 40 1920, and on the sedition charges, see AGCA J-AV 104 Leg. 21 A Exp. 41.

[22] AGCA J-AV 104 Leg. 21 A Exp. 41.

April). Charges against Icó had to be taken seriously. While Jorge Yat was an elderly, illiterate patriarch from a small village distant from the center of power in Carchá, Icó had roots in an elite Q'eqchi' family from San Pedro Carchá. Before his political involvement, he had received loans from Erwin Paul Dieseldorff, and was said to have been invited to dine with the Germans.[23] On his maternal side, Icó had ladino family members such as Cirilaco and NIcólas Delgado, who occupied crucial posts within the municipal council reserved for ladinos.

Organizing Mayas to participate in electoral politics, Icó represented a new type of native intermediary. With changes in meaning and form, Q'eqchi' patriarchs had acted as intermediaries between indigenous communities and the state since the conquest. By 1920, however, decades of political marginalization in local town councils, the hardships of mandamiento labor, and the privatization of property, as well as the growth of planter sovereignty and fincas de mozos, had eroded the civil–religious hierarchy that enabled Q'eqchi' mediation. While Greg Grandin has argued that Maya elites' power increased in tandem with the Liberal state, state expansion in Alta Verapaz was spatially uneven, especially in the coffee-planting countryside where planters exercised their own sovereignty.[24] Within town councils, Liberals also eroded Mayas' authority and systematically relegated Maya patriarchs to lesser positions. The 1920s, however, offered some Q'eqchi' patriarchs an opportunity to reimagine their roles as native intermediaries. Just as early nineteenth-century electoral politics allowed Maya commoners to challenge caste hierarchy, the democratic elections of the early 1920s served to channel their frustrated expectations into a vigorous struggle for meaningful access to political power in which Maya patriarchs like Icó could play a central role as party organizers.

From the socially embedded networks of Q'eqchi' patriarchal lineages, José Ángel Icó should have been like his father, Tomas Icó, and his uncle José Coc Delgado, who had both sought to negotiate the new era of liberalism and coffee production by translating communal properties into coffee plantations and thus securing mandamiento exemptions for their ethnic clans and other Maya commoners. In 1875, the year Icó was born, his father titled Chitaña's clan lands to represent of all the inhabitants and, as did so many other Q'eqchi' patriarchs, fashioned himself as a

---

[23] TULAL Dieseldorff Collection, Box 10, Fol. 1, "Señor Erwin Paul Dieseldorff de José Ángel Icó," Cobán, October 26, 1906.
[24] Grandin, *The Blood of Guatemala*.

Maya coffee planter on an expanding coffee plantation.[25] In 1878 Icó's uncle obtained the title to the lands of Cobanero residents of Setoc, and acting as the "sole and legitimate owner of the entire property," protected his resident laborers from oppressive mandamientos.[26] As representatives of their communities, José Ángel Icó, like José Coc Delgado, often aided Q'eqchi's in their petitions, drawing on his legal and bureaucratic knowledge, as well as familial and political connections with ladinos and Germans. Like his father and brothers, Icó was a coffee planter who presided over eighty Q'eqchi's who lived and worked on the parcel of land he had inherited, and Icó procured military and other exemptions for the laborers.[27] Yet Icó's plantation was not officially recognized by the state. In a 1921 official list of plantations with mozos, colonos, and enganchado laborers in the municipality, state officials did not record his plantation. Instead, they likely treated the residents of Chitaña as Icó's extended family members.[28] Nor did Icó's plantation appear on the 1921 census of coffee plantations.[29] Of course, unlike his uncle and his father, Icó may have preferred that his plantation not be recognized by state officials.

José Ángel Icó was also very different from his uncle and grandfather and from most Q'eqchi' patriarchs who had preceded him. Icó defied Q'eqchi' patriarchal norms. He never married, nor is he known to have fathered any children; as a result, he could not or did not participate in cofradías or the civil–religious hierarchy. His marginalization from Q'eqchi' patriarchal institutions' prestige may have permitted Icó to find new ways to be a patriarch who represented the interests of the Maya pueblo. In the 1920s, Icó discovered electoral and party politics, as well as more radical measures such as labor strikes and land invasions, as tools for expressing Maya norms of reciprocity and solidarity. "We spoke for our race," explained José Ángel Icó's great-nephew Alfredo Cucul in an interview.[30] Cucul, who was born in 1926, would first meet his uncle as he was being dragged off to jail in 1932. Operating outside Q'eqchi'

---

[25] AGCA ST-AV Paq. 3 Exp. 13 1879.   [26] AGCA ST-AV Paq. 4 Exp. 4 1879.

[27] AGCA JP-AV 1925 Paq. 2, "Carta al JP de José Ángel Icó," April 5 and June 30, 1925; AGCA J-AV 104 Leg. 9 A Exp. 27; AGCA J-AV 104 Leg. 8 A Exp. 24; AGCA J-AV 104 Leg. 8 A Exp. 26; AGCA J-AV 104 Leg. 15 A Exp. 14. See also Grandin, *The Last Colonial Massacre*, 19.

[28] AGCA JP-AV 1921 Paq. 2, "Nómina General de los mozos colonos y enganchados de las fincas existentes en el Departamento de Alta Verapaz."

[29] *Censo de la República de Guatemala: Segunda parte* (Guatemala, 1924), 472–3.

[30] Cited in Grandin, *The Last Colonial Massacre*, 33.

patriarchal institutions, but within Q'eqchi' patriarchal norms, Icó represented Maya peasants and workers and became the target of state officials' and coffee planters' anger.

Breaking with Q'eqchi' patriarchal institutions, José Ángel Icó was
rumored to be homosexual. His great-grandnephews and nieces tended
to agree: "It was somewhat rare, strange," said his great-nephew Alfredo
Cucul, "but that's how he lived, he never had a compañera."[31] Yet, as
Greg Grandin has noted, Icó's family and friends dismissed the reports
that Icó was a homosexual as hateful and jealous gossip. The rumors and
hearsay about his homosexuality articulated an excessive masculinity
derived from his domination and power over other men. As Roger
Lancaster has illustrated, male homosexuality in Nicaragua does not hold
the same rigid stigmas that define North American representations of it. In
Central America, male homosexuality is often more ambiguous and
defined by encounters that are divided into active and passive roles. The
man who is penetrated is feminized and shamed, while the man playing
the active/penetrating role achieves greater masculinity. He is an
"hombre-hombre" (a manly man). Like sexual encounters with women,
masculine status is attained by conquering many male partners.[32] Because
Icó was perceived as an active rather than a passive partner, hearsay
about his homosexuality granted him an excessive masculinity derived
from dominating other men. Icó's hypermasculinity also helps explain the
equally prolific accounts of the great number of children Icó sired. Tales
of homosexuality, whether founded or not, also operated as metaphors
for Icó's extraordinary ability to summon Mayas into radical political
action and generate dread among planters and state officials. By providing an alternative plot, stories of Icó's homosexuality and prowess speak
to the hypermasculine, revolutionary agency required to overturn the
modernity of the coffee plantation.

While Icó rallied rural Mayas around the Unionist Party, ladinos and
some Q'eqchi' patriarchs also sought to mobilize themselves politically
around the newly formed Republican Party and its presidential candidate, José León Castillo, in the lead-up to the elections scheduled for
August 23, 1920.[33] Deepening politicization erupted in violence in the

---

[31] Ibid.

[32] Roger N. Lancaster, *Life Is Hard: Machismo, Danger, and the Intimacy of Power in
Nicaragua* (Berkeley: University of California Press, 1992), 238–75. For an example in
Alta Verapaz, see AGCA J-AV 104 Leg. 15 A Exp. 34.

[33] AGCA B Leg. 29468, "Al Señor Presidente de la República de Guatemala, Don Carlos
Herrera de José Ángel Icó," Carchá, August 15, 1920.

streets.[34] Icó, addressing President Herrera himself, reported that, on July 28, the "Castillistas" attacked him and "his one hundred indios," leaving dozens injured. Many others, including Icó himself, were arrested and abandoned in Cobán's dank prison cells.[35] Despite violent outbreaks, the coalition candidate of the Unionist Party and Democratic Party, Carlos Herrera, swept the elections with 94.6 percent of the vote. José León Castillo, the Republican Party candidate, received only 3.04 percent of the vote.[36]

Following Herrera's sweep of the national vote, infuriated ladinos unleashed a new round of political violence in Alta Verapaz. José Ángel Icó's relatives and members of the Freedom of the Indian faced illegal arrests on fabricated charges.[37] Dozens of Q'eqchi' Sanpedranos wrote to President Herrera, in the name of "more than 10,000 compañeros," declaring that they were victims of the Republican Party's "oppressive force." Following the elections, the Sanpedrano Q'eqchi's claimed to be "victims of outrage" who were subject to incessant threats and insults.[38] In addition to ladinos' political backlash, the August 1920 elections ruptured Alta Verapaz's racial order based on the postponement of Maya citizenship, and exposed ladinos' deepest fears. Ladinos' anxieties about racial order and Maya political agency found expression in renewed apprehensions about prostitution and venereal disease, vagrants and dirty streets, deviant Mayas and crimes of blood, that mandated social reform, sanitation officers, and ladino police forces.[39] In response, Carchá's town council founded a ladino police force, since the Q'eqchi' municipal officers, whose duty it was to police the streets, were not reliable. "Being Indians," explained the alcalde primero, "they have no respect," and as a result, "continuous scandals erupted in the streets at night."[40] Newspaper editorialists denounced the "overgrown, narrowed, and garbage-filled" streets, which offered proof that "we are surrounded by gossip, politics, and partialities."[41] Ladinos

---

[34] Ibid.   [35] Ibid.

[36] TULAL Dieseldorff Collection, Personal papers, Box 10, Folder 7, "Sr. Don Erwin Paul Dieseldorff de JM Isaac Sierra," July 25, 1920.

[37] AGCA J-AV 104 Leg. 21 Exp. 20 1920.

[38] AGCA B Leg. 29456 Exp. 9 1920. For an example of such violence, see AGCA J-AV 104 Leg. 21 Exp. 20 1920 and AGCA J-AV Leg. 22 B Exp. 14 1921.

[39] See AGCA B Leg. 29452 Exp. 15 1920; AGCA JP-AV 1920 Paq. 1, "Informe del JP de Alta Verapaz al Ministro de Gobernación," May 20, 1920; AGCA B Leg. 29456 Exp. 15; AGCA JP-AV 1926 Paq. 1, "Carta del Consejo Superior de Salubridad al Ministerio de Gobernación," May 28, 1920.

[40] SPCM 1926 "Libro de Actas, Sesión Pública Ordinaria," February 4, 1926, No. 9.

[41] "De sábado a sábado," *El Norte*, March 4, 1922.

expressed their fears of disruptions in racial order by decrying deviance and disorder. For anxious ladinos, social reform, sanitation, and discipline provided the language to rearticulate racial and class boundaries as well as a state apparatus through which surveillance could be enacted.

For Q'eqchi's, the election of Herrera was an affirming victory that symbolized Maya political potency and rallied them to push for local and regional political representation. Across Alta Verapaz, Q'eqchi's reclaimed ladino-held positions within municipal councils. Pedro Caal ran for alcalde primero in Cobán, a seat that no Maya had occupied for nearly fifty years.[42] While no Q'eqchi's referenced nineteenth-century debates, many seemed intent on turning back the clock on Liberal policies that had taken away Conservative-era indigenous-only municipalities. Q'eqchi's sought the return of indigenous municipalities, however, not because Mayas were wards of the state, as Conservatives contended, but because Q'eqchi's demanded a democracy responsive to the people. In San Pedro Carchá, Icó vigorously campaigned for a return to an indigenous-only municipal council. The council, he argued, was an institution that should be run by representatives of the masses, not a few ladinos.[43] His efforts intensified ladinos' fears that Mayas would take over all municipal posts. In a preemptive attack, Sanpedrano ladinos prevented Q'eqchi' patriarchs from voting in the 1921 municipal council elections.[44] For Q'eqchi's, the ladino backlash made clear that what was at issue was the racist politics of postponement that rendered them as servile laborers, rather than citizens. In a petition to the president, the Q'eqchi' patriarchs of San Pedro Carchá declared: "We understand that they [the ladinos] would like to exile and exterminate us from the land in which we were born and of which we are owners through our ancestors; and they would like to take away our citizenship rights, because according to them we are only good for carrying heavy loads, serving as mules for the municipality in order to satisfy the whims and interests of magnates who see us as nothing more than miserable slaves."[45] The departmental governor, Camilo Bianchi, too, became an object of attack

---

[42] AGCA JP-AV Paq. 3 1920, "Elecciones municipales de Cobán," December 12, 1920.
[43] AGCA B Leg. 29468, "Al Señor Presidente de la República de Guatemala, Don Carlos Herrera de José Ángel Icó," Carchá, August 15, 1920.
[44] See AGCA B Leg. 29456 Exp. 9 1920; AGCA B Leg. 29536 1921; AGCA J-AV 104 Leg. 21 B Exp. 35 1920; AGCA J-AV 104 Leg. 21 Exp. 20 1920; AGCA B Leg. 29515 1921, "Telegrama Oficial al Presidente de Carchá, 29 de enero, 1921"; J. V. Arévalo, "Defensa," *El Republicano*, January 30, 1921.
[45] AGCA B Leg. 29456 Exp. 9 1920.

when he supported new elections in San Pedro Carchá.[46] Within a month, Bianchi was replaced by a Republican Party member.[47] Many Altaverapacence ladinos were willing to do whatever it took to halt the erosion of their local political power. While the Unionist Party might have swept the national elections, entrenched interests halted Q'eqchi' efforts to take over local political power.

In addition to pressing for change in municipal councils, Icó also sought to exercise a new intermediary role between coffee planters and laborers. Mere weeks after Herrera's victory, Icó wrote to Erwin Paul Dieseldorff asking the coffee magnate to work alongside the Unionist Club to resolve the many complaints that Dieseldorff's mozos had brought to Icó.[48] Ignoring Icó's request for dialogue, Dieseldorff penned an angry letter to the Ministry of the Interior demanding that the state remove Icó from the department. Icó, he claimed, had gained many followers by making "Bolshevik offers: that he was going to distribute the plantation among *los indios*, that the salary would raise to $2 daily, that foreigners must leave, followed by the ladinos." According to Dieseldorff, Icó "maintained the Indians in constant revolt, the majority of mozos in the plantations are not fulfilling their contracts, even as far as the district of Senahú, the majority of mozos are on strike." Dieseldorff complained that "it was a mistake from the start to give *an indio* so much power, as has been given to Icó," and concluded, "now that the problem exists, it is up to the government to fix it."[49] As Dieseldorff's animated comments suggest, coffee planters' unwillingness to improve working conditions signaled to rural Q'eqchi's the need for new methods: labor strikes and land invasions. For rural Mayas, the day had come to repossess labor time and plantation territory.

INSURRECTIONARY GEOGRAPHIES

By January 1921, the frustration of rural Q'eqchi's in Alta Verapaz was growing palpable, while coffee planters anxiously commenced harvesting. While José Ángel Icó pursued mass mobilization as the mechanism

---

[46] Arévalo, "Defensa," *El Republicano*, January 30, 1921.

[47] "Nuevo JP," *El Republicano*, February 20, 1921.

[48] TULAL Dieseldorff Collection, Box 10, Folder 8, "A Erwin Paul Dieseldorff de José Ángel Icó," September 5, 1920.

[49] AGCA B Leg. 29462, "Al Ministerio de Gobernación y Justicia de Erwin Paul Dieseldorff," September 9, 1920.

toward a democratic road to social and political change, this tactic had by 1921 demonstrated its limitations to challenge either local or national political and economic structures. Emboldened by their expectations of a new just political order, Q'eqchi' laborers turned to labor strikes and land invasions to bring about the more just world they imagined on the horizon. As Q'eqchi' laborers took control over their time, and sometimes even the space of the plantation itself, coffee planters and then state officials responded with escalating rounds of violence and deepening political polarization. By focusing on Q'eqchi' actions, we can read against the archival grain to see what freedom and rights might have meant to rural Q'eqchi's. Blaming the Unionists for the radicalization of the region and Icó's "celebrity," one editorialist noted, "It is not the parrot's fault, but he who teaches him to speak."[50]

Acting individually but in concert, rural Q'eqchi's fled plantations and went on strike, sparking the ire of coffee planters.[51] They struck strategically to hurt planters the most, during the height of the harvest in January and February. More than a hundred coffee planters desperately pleaded to the minister of agriculture: "The Indians, on whom we have counted for the support of our coffee plantations and subsistence production, today have decided not to work, which has resulted in the loss of a good part of the harvest.... Even the colonos of our properties have declared themselves on strike and do not obey the orders of the owners, adopting an insolent attitude toward the planters and even the authorities."[52] To further ensure order, the planters argued for the implementation of vagrancy provisions and asked state officials to punish strikers by sending them to build a new road to the capital city. If the words of caporales on Dieseldorff's plantation are to believed, Q'eqchi's were intent on more than just reclaiming their labor time. They also sought to challenge the patriarchal politics of plantations that reduced them to mere boys. According to the caporales, the laborers on strike avowed that "no one told them what to do because they are not children." Such words suggest that Q'eqchi' plantation laborers knew precisely the value of their work and disagreed with the plantation hierarchy that planters had so carefully constructed. In June 1921, resident laborers from Richard Sapper's plantation Campur complained that the administrator "treats us exactly like

---

[50] "No tiene culpa," *El Republicano*, February 20, 1921.
[51] AGCA JP-AV 1921 Paq. 1, "José Ma. Mollino al JP," March 9, 1921.
[52] AGCA JP-AV Paq. 4, "Al Ministro de Agricultura de los infrascritos agricultores de la Departamento de Alta Verapaz," February 21, 1921.

slaves for the only crime of being Guatemalans." The workers explained how they were paid in fichas (the currency of the plantation), and that the planter measured their subsistence allotments arbitrarily, and prevented them from tending their milpas.[53] After the coffee harvest, rural Q'eqchi's turned to a new tactic: land invasion. Encroaching on German properties, rural Mayas burned coffee bushes and planted milpa in the ashes.[54] Their actions were symbolic and material: in place of export coffee, a symbol of foreigners and exploitation, they planted milpa, a symbol of local culture and reproduction. In addition, they refused to obey the plantations' gendered and racialized hierarchy of command.

Labor strikes and land invasions also united Altaverapacence coffee planters and ladinos in their common anxieties about racial disorder and their desire to return to the liberalism of the past. Those anxieties and desires were channeled politically into the newly formed Liberal Party.[55] Planters also directed their anger into revenge. In a special municipal council meeting held in Carchá to discuss the labor issue, some planters called on the state to punish laborers with obligatory service on public works projects.[56] Other planters took matters into their own hands and refused to grant permission to plant milpas to resident laborers who had gone on strike during the coffee harvest. Erwin Paul Dieseldorff kicked off the resident laborers of one particularly troublesome plantation and replaced the laborers' milpas with cattle.[57] When one laborer complained about the loss of his subsistence production, Dieseldorff counseled the administrators: "This is the venom of the Bolshevik, the venom that comes once every century to ruin nations guided by weak leadership."[58] As much as Q'eqchi's imagined themselves inaugurating a new era and acting on the world-historical stage, German coffee planters like Dieseldorff continually referenced Bolsheviks and century-long cycles of revolution in Europe. By placing Maya actions within a Eurocentric historical frame, they laid bare the historic stakes of the conflict. Soon rumors spread of a planned Maya insurrection. Some coffee planters requested

---

[53] AGCA JP-AV Paq. 1, "De Marcos Caal, Pedro Choc, et al al JP," June 21, 1921.

[54] AGCA J-AV 104 1921 Leg. 22 A Exp.24

[55] "Confirmarnos lo dicho," *El Norte*, April 9, 1921.

[56] AGCA JP-AV Paq. 1 1920, "El infrascrito secretario municipal de San Pedro Carchá certifica: Haber tenido a la vista el acta de la sesión celebrada el día de hoy," May 20, 1921.

[57] TULAL Dieseldorff Colllection, Fincas Bound Volumes, Vol. 73, Fol. 975, 977, 978.

[58] TULAL Dieseldorff Collection, Fincas Bound Volumes, Vol. 73, Fol. 491.

arms to defend themselves, and others called for military intervention to punish rebellious Mayas.[59]

As coffee planters feared a revolution on a grand historical scale, they quickly blamed the labor strikes and land invasions on José Ángel Icó. The departmental governor launched an inquiry into the "habits and customs" of the deviant Q'eqchi' troublemaker. To justify the inquiry, the minister of the interior proclaimed that Icó "incites the mozos to disobey their patrones, maliciously inculcating them with the idea of unlimited freedom."[60] Coffee planters from across the region testified how Icó had driven laborers to strike, to press charges against administrators, and to claim freedom and access to land. Drawing on the trope of the outside agitator, coffee planters made the actions of Q'eqchi's across the region appear not as popular mobilizations or logical responses to injustice, but rather as the result of the malicious and manipulative character of one individual. Icó's actions were labeled dangerous and threatening to the natural social order, and his ability to enthrall the Mayas conjured up images of supernatural powers. For coffee planters like Dieseldorff, the rapid succession of events made their world seem out of order, and the resulting anxiety demanded some kind of equally disturbing explanation: supernatural powers, Bolshevik agitation, as well as racial degeneration and sexual deviance.

Q'eqchi's and sympathetic state officials, however, contested the coffee planters' efforts to resignify Q'eqchi' political mobilization as the mere workings of one social deviant-cum–Bolshevik agitator. In response to the Ministry of the Interior's inquiry, the departmental governor wrote to the minister to clarify the events. Instead of blaming the strikes on one man's subversive acts, the departmental governor legitimated the complaints raised by Q'eqchi' laborers. "In this department, Señor Minister," he began, "the question of mozos always presents great difficulties for the Authorities, as a result of the custom that planters have of making *el indio* . . . into a slave . . . paying them a wage (4 reales or some 2 or 3 pesos a day) that, as the Señor Minister can see, cannot satisfy their most basic needs."[61] In the inquiry, Q'eqchi' commoners also contested charges laid against them by coffee planters, stating that the planters' upset had more to do with politics than with any unlawful actions on their part. Q'eqchi' laborers also contested the outside agitator trope that vacated their

---

[59] AGCA JP-AV Paq. 3 1921, "Los vecinos de Cahabón al JP," August 9, 1921; AGCA J-AV 104 Leg. 22 E Exp. 4 1921.
[60] AGCA J-AV 105 Leg. 28 B Exp. 21.   [61] AGCA J-AV 104 Leg. 22 B Exp. 33 1921.

political agency, explaining that Icó informed them of the political situation but had not incited them to rebellion.[62]

The crescendo of political violence in Alta Verapaz continued to grow. In September, the minister of war sent a telegram to all the municipalities saying, "All subversive movements that threaten public order and peace and those in charge or who are promoters will be punished according to military law."[63] A month later, when workers on the plantation Transval gathered peacefully to demand higher wages, local authorities sent to the plantation opened fire, leaving an unknown number wounded and dead. State officials arrested José Ángel Icó.[64] Despite the growing violence, rural Mayas continued to protest, invade plantations, and prepare for a new round of labor strikes.[65] On October 3, Marcos Caal, along with a small group of Mayas, invaded one of Richard Sapper's properties, declaring that they had received word that the lands now belonged to the nation and would be redistributed, even though confiscated German plantations had been returned to their owners three months earlier.[66] Other Mayas rebelled against plantation modernity by returning wage advances and declaring themselves free.[67]

Q'eqchi' labor strikes and land invasions speak to the creation of insurrectionary Maya geographies of time and space that unsettled plantation modernity. The colonial power inherent in state archival records makes accessing the motivations and political ideals of illiterate and subaltern actors difficult. If, instead, we focus on the actions taken by rural Mayas, we can imagine what freedom meant to them. In violation of the fixed boundaries of the plantation, Q'eqchi's planted milpa on the charred remains of the coffee trees, which demonstrates the importance of subsistence production to their social and cultural worlds. Against the plantations' regimented labor time, surveillance, and debt obligations, laborers refused to show up, went on strike, and declared themselves free. In the face of planters' claims to patriarchal order and affection, laborers declared their manhood and refused to obey. When they

[62] AGCA JP-AV Paq. 1, "De Marcos Caal, Pedro Choc, et al al JP," June 21, 1921.
[63] AGCA JP-AV 1921 Paq. 3, "Telegrama del Ministerio de Guerra al Comandante de Armas de Panzós," September 14, 1921.
[64] AGCA J-AV Leg. 23 A. Exp. 41 1921; see also SPCM 1927, "Libro de Actas Municipales," August 25, 1927.
[65] AGCA JP-AV 1921 Paq. 3, "Al JP de M. Cheves y Romero," December 3, 1921.
[66] AGCA J-AV 104 Leg. 22 Exp. 22 1921.
[67] AGCA JP-AV 1921 Paq. 2 "Jesús de Prado al JP," October 10, 1921.

demanded higher wages and violated their contracts, they gave voice to the injustice of the exchange value of their labor and the need for reciprocity. And when they worked together to go on strike and press for changes, they articulated communal solidarity. In the process, they also upset society's racial ordering, unleashing a fury that covered up ladino and German planters' silent fear that their wealth and prosperity was not the product of entrepreneurial coffee planters but the work of the hands and bodies that toiled daily in the fields. Indeed, by taking action in the midst of coffee harvests, Q'eqchi' laborers may very well have been making this point: they were the essential engines of prosperity.

By December 1921, as political violence exploded across the country-side, President Carlos Herrera's government was clearly coming to an end. A decline in coffee prices to nearly half of their 1919 level further unsettled the precarious coalition surrounding the Unionist Party.[68] Despite the government's crackdown on worker strikes and land invasions, Herrera's inability to control the countryside also hastened his demise. On December 5, 1921, dissident army officers forced the president's resignation. Shortly thereafter, General José María Orellana (1922–6) assumed the presidency backed by the Liberal Party and the military.[69] While not returning to the levels of repression that marked Estrada Cabrera's dictatorship, Orellana swiftly clamped down on political opposition across the country. In January, Cobán's police arrested Unionist Party supporters for causing commotion in public spaces.[70] Celso V. Reyes, a young indigenista, was forced to halt the publication of his newspaper *Juventud Verapacence* after it printed editorials denouncing

---

[68] Kit, "The Unionist Experiment in Guatemala, 1920–1921"; and Victor Bulmer-Thomas, *The Political Economy of Central America since 1920* (Cambridge: Cambridge University Press, 1987). In the fall of 1920, Dieseldorff was beset by foreign creditors who demanded he extinguish outstanding debts, and he was forced to liquidate portions of his vast holdings. See TULAL Dieseldorff Colllection, Box 10, Fol. 10, "Dieseldorff to W. R. Grace & Co., 18 de septiembre de 1920"; Box 10, Fol. 10, "Dieseldorff to H. P. Operfamann, agent of W. R. Grace, 20 de octubre 1920"; Box 10, Fol. 12, "Paso que los gobiernos de los países cafeteros podrían dar para contrarrestar la baja del café," E. P. Dieseldorff, December 16, 1920; Box 10, Fol. 12, "E. P. Dieseldorff 16 de diciembre 1920"; Box 10, Fol. 13, "Dieseldorff to Chalmers, Guthrie & Co, Ltd., 26 de enero 1921"; Box 10, Fol. 14, "Dieseldorff to W. R. Grace & Co, 22 Febrero 1921."

[69] SPCM Libro de Actas Municipales "No. 23 sesión pública ordinaria, 25 de agosto de 1927." In October 1921, Dieseldorff similarly used military forces to resolve a dispute over one of his properties. See SPCM, "Al Alcalde 1° de Erwin Paul Dieseldorff, 22 de octubre de 1921" and "Al Alcalde 1° del Juzgado de 1ª Instancia de Alta Verapaz, 24 de octubre de 1921."

[70] AGCA JP-AV 1922 Paq. 1, "Del alcalde de San Pedro Carchá al JP," January 23, 1922.

censorship and the military's "hunting of men, healthy and sick citizens alike," in the streets of Cobán.[71]

While the military overthrow of Herrera may have dampened the spirits of some, political oppression radicalized others and prompted the birth of new organizing. In the wake of the military coup, Altaverapacence coffee planters were ready to respond violently to worker resistance. On February 7, in the midst of the coffee harvest, Richard Sapper reported that resident laborers on plantation Sasis had "risen up in an alarming manner, refusing to go to work without just cause." The departmental governor responded by sending the military to propel the laborers back to work.[72] Military repression did not, however, put an end to Maya resistance in Alta Verapaz. In Guatemala City, ladino artisans were also radicalized by the changing political climate, where they formed the Communist Party of Guatemala.[73] As both the Unionista and Communist parties demonstrate, the left in Guatemala was not born among intellectuals, as was the case for much of Latin America. Guatemalan intellectuals of the famed "Generation of 20" were more interested in the theories of Auguste Comte and Herbert Spencer than Karl Marx and Vladimir Lenin and in celebrating European immigrants rather than the working or indigenous classes.[74]

Maya resistance in Alta Verapaz also helped cement new alliances between the German diaspora, Guatemalan coffee planters, intellectuals, and other elites. Throughout the period of 1920–2, Erwin Paul Dieseldorff called on coffee planters to put aside their differences and unite in resolving the labor problem.[75] They also sought more symbolic forms of

---

[71] AGCA Leg. 29601 Exp. 4 1922. On the articles, see "Liberalismo cimarrón," *La Juventud Verapacense*, May 20, 1922; and "El reclutamiento militar con mengua de los derechos ciudadanos," *La Juventud Verapacense*, May 20, 1922.

[72] AGCA JP-AV 1922 Paq. 1, "Richard Sapper al JP de Alta Verapaz," February 7, 1922.

[73] Carlos Figueroa Ibarra, "Marxismo, sociedad, y movimiento sindical en Guatemala," *Anuario de Estudios Centroamericanos* 16, no. 1 (1990): 59. See also Asociación de Investigación y Estudios Sociales (ASIES), "Movimiento obrero urbano," in *Historia general de Guatemala: Época moderna*, ed. Jorge Luján Muñoz (Guatemala: Asociación de Amigos del País, Fundación para la Cultura y el Desarrollo, 1996), 293–306.

[74] Figueroa Ibarra, "Marxismo, sociedad, y movimiento sindical en Guatemala," 67. See also Marta Elena Casaús Arzú, "La generación del 20 en Guatemala y sus imaginarios de nación (1920–1940)," in *Las redes intelectuales centroamericanas: Un siglo de imaginarios nacionales (1820–1920)*, ed. Marta Elena Casaús Arzú and Teresa García Giráldez (Guatemala: F&G Editores, 2005), 253–90.

[75] See personal and business communication in the TULAL Dieseldorff Collection for these years and, for example, TULAL Dieseldorff Collection, Box 10, Folder 11, "Al General don José Ma. Orellan de Erwin Paul Dieseldoff," November 21, 1920.

union. Instead of the celebrations of Manuel Tot for the September 1921 centennial of Guatemalan independence, the German community hosted an elaborate and solemn affair, opening the doors of the German Club to state officials and ladinos.[76] Shortly after the commemoration, Altaverapacence ladinos called out for reconciliation with the Germans. "The national ladino element and the German element have lived in this city with enormous distance due to prejudices and motives that we all know," began an editorial in *El Norte*. The time had come, however, for the beginning of a new era: "The German residents among us ... can today have complete assurances that new friendships have been established and can be put to use in the name of heralding progress and proclaiming social union."[77] While the editorialist might have simply been referencing the generous centennial celebrations hosted by the German community, he may also have been referring to how Germans and elite ladinos were uniting, not only for social union or progress, but also against a common enemy.

IMAGINING A NEW NATION: EUROPEAN IMMIGRATION AND MESTIZAJE

While ladino artisans flocked to labor unions and the Communist Party and Q'eqchi's boldly envisioned a new future beyond the exploitation of coffee plantations, Guatemala's Generation of 20 intellectuals expressed their great despair regarding the national future. Disheartened by Liberal dictatorships and Guatemala's failed democratic experiment, these urban Creole and ladino elites sought a broader rethinking of Guatemala's ladino nationalism, exemplified by the prominent intellectual Miguel Ángel Asturias. In 1923 Asturias completed a thesis entitled "Sociologia guatemalteca: el problema social del indio" (Guatemalan Sociology: The Social Problem of the Indian), which set the stage for a national rethinking. In the early 1920s, Asturias was deeply influenced by his experience in Mexico as a delegate to the First International Student Congress. In Mexico, Asturias studied under José Vasconcelos, who was then developing his renowned philosophy of mestizaje. Vasconcelos sought to challenge Spencerian racial theories that condemned miscegenation. Instead, Vasconcelos celebrated mestizaje between Indians and Spaniards as the

---

[76] AGCA JP-AV 1921 Paq. 3, "Invitación de la Club Alemán," August 30, 1921.
[77] "Apuntes de crónica," *El Norte*, September 24, 1921.

basis for a new cosmic race that would withstand imperialism.[78] Returning to Guatemala after studying under Vasconcelos, Asturias toured the countryside to see how Mayas lived, and then returned to Guatemala City to write his thesis. Like Vasconcelos, Asturias refuted Spencerian theories, which asserted that racially hybrid societies were unstable and disorganized. In contrast, Asturias regarded racial mixing as a viable way to create a homogeneous society out of a heterogeneous one. Yet, unlike Vasconcelos, Asturias found little to celebrate in Guatemala's past or present. He claimed that Guatemala's failure to become a modern unified nation could be traced to colonial legal prohibitions on interracial mixing, large civilizational differences between Mayas and Spaniards, and Spaniards' ill-treatment of Mayas.[79] More importantly, the majority of ladinos, Asturias contended, were not civilized enough to undertake the mission of "racially whitening" through interracial mixing and cultural influence. The ladino population, he noted, was too small – they made up only one-third of the total national population. Moreover, only the best of this ladino group, he argued, could be considered even "semi-civilized."[80] Ladinos, in other words, did not have sufficient European blood. The only way of saving the nation, declared Asturias, was new blood. "Let us transform the indigenous environment by means of immigration, honoring the confidence the future has deposited in our hands in the form of a second life, nothing more," he concluded.[81]

By the mid-1920s, Asturia's thesis about the national indigenous problem gained further force. As Estrada Cabrera's celebrated ladino artisans expanded their unionization efforts and engaged in labor strikes, many of Guatemala's aristocratic elites from a Creole background blamed Estrada Cabrera's dictatorship on marginalized ladinos of mixed race and lower-class standing. Jorge García Granados maintained that the political turmoil Guatemala was currently facing and, even more importantly, the dictatorships that had preceded it, were blatant evidence of ladinos' – or more precisely mestizos' – racial defect.[82] Cesar Brañas likewise believed that a "better racial mixture" was needed and could be fostered through selective immigration. "Redemption for our race should occur through the fertilization of our Indian women with Saxon semen!" declared

[78] José Vasconcelos, *La raza cósmica* (México: Espasa-Calpe Mexicana, 1966).
[79] Miguel Ángel Asturias, *Guatemalan Sociology: The Social Problem of the Indian*, trans. Maureen Ahern (Tempe: Arizona State University, 1977), 99–100.
[80] See ibid., 63, 65–6, 86–7.   [81] Ibid., 105–6.
[82] Jorge García Grandos, *Ensayo sobre sociología guatemalteca* (Guatemala: Tipografía "Sánchez & Guise," 1927), 41.

another intellectual.[83] Following ideologies of mestizaje across Latin America, they postulated that the "mixing of blood" would result in racial improvement because "superior" European racial characteristics would dominate both the inferior indigenous and Afro–Latin American ones.

The Generation of 20 intellectuals, however, were not simply theorizing about abstract possibilities, but specifically referencing the emergence of a class of mixed-race Maya–Germans. When Asturias traveled the countryside in the midst of the 1921 labor strikes and land invasions, he found proof that immigration could give rise to a new race in Alta Verapaz and parts of the western highlands. In Alta Verapaz, especially, miscegenation between Germans and Mayas had resulted in Q'eqchi'–German children who were "robust and well-endowed; physically one could not ask for more from an aesthetic point of view."[84] If the German–Q'eqchi' experiment was conducted on a much larger scale, Asturias believed it would be a "radical remedy" that would attack the "roots of [the nation's] illness," opening the door for Guatemala to join the world of civilized nations. While in Mexico Vasconcelos's project of racial mixing heralded a future race born of Spanish and indigenous blood, some Guatemalan intellectuals firmly believed this mestizaje could be achieved only through further European immigration.

In practice, the Q'eqchi–Germans Asturias celebrated comprised an unstable social class and could just as easily be excellent intermediaries between coffee planters and their laborers as unruly troublemakers who, like Icó, rallied the masses. Q'eqchi'–Germans were potent intermediaries precisely because social-class mobility and interracial status did not necessarily lead to de-Indianization. Francisca Wellman Coc worked for her father, Víctor Wellman, as a plantation overseer. Francisca traveled to the jail to retrieve laborers who had fled their obligations, to negotiate to lessen sentences, and to advance wages.[85] When addressing coffee plantation laborers, she went by the name Francisca Coc, but when she addressed state officials she went by the name Francisca Wellman. Such fluid identifications, however, generated anxieties among Germans about ethnic loyalty and political affiliation. After Carlos Chub Sarg's German father lost his job as a plantation administrator and abandoned his

---

[83] Cited in Joseph A. Pitti, "Jorge Ubico and Guatemalan Politics in the 1920s" (PhD diss., University of New Mexico, 1975), 217.

[84] Asturias, *Guatemalan Sociology*, 101–3.

[85] See AGCA J-AV 103 Leg. 33 B Exp. 18 1932.

Q'eqchi–German family in Cobán, Carlos joined forces with the Club Unionista "Freedom of the Indian " and José Ángel Icó.

The Germans' anxiety about their Guatemalan children's ethnic loyalty was also entrenched by the experience of anti-German nationalism and internment of German assets during World War I. Some Germans, such as Erwin Paul Dieseldorff, promoted deeper alliances by schooling their children in German culture and language.[86] Shortly after the end of World War I, Dieseldorff sent his Q'echi–German daughter, Matilde Cu, to Germany. Under the careful guidance of her stepmother, Albertina Johanna Gressler, Matilde attended school in Germany where she learned the German language, habits, and customs. After her return to Guatemala, Matilde married Max Quirin, Dieseldorff's most trusted administrator. Responsible for the organization of servants and the operation of Dieseldorff's household, Matilde became the perfect intermediary between Q'eqchi' workers and German visitors and clients. She also reinforced, rather than threatened, German cultural reproduction. Alongside her husband, Matilde socialized with the German women of Cobán. Matilde also owned and administered coffee plantations with him.[87] The question of the relative Germanness of Q'eqchi'–German children was crucial to defining both ethnic loyalty and political affiliation. Such racial identifications were largely contingent on effective performances and highly subjective judgments about cultural competency.[88]

By the mid-1920s, newspaper editorialists in Alta Verapaz had abandoned their World War I–era nationalism and begun to celebrate German immigration and call for racial mixing. One Altaverapacence editorialist noted that "we need a true social and spiritual evolution to cure us. It is a work of time and of racial amalgamation."[89] Another editorialist advocated for more immigration: "It is certain that Latin American nations cannot nor will not prosper without intermixing with European races that have to forcefully infiltrate our customs, our laws, our life with the civilization that has been achieved by nations of the old world." Proof

---

[86] See Guillermo Náñez Falcón, "Erwin Paul Dieseldorff, German Entrepreneur in the Alta Verapaz of Guatemala, 1889–1937" (PhD diss., Tulane University, 1970), 45–6.

[87] See Matilde Quirin Dieseldorff, interview with Uli Stelzner for the documentary by Uli Stelzner and Thomas Walther, *Los Civilizadores*.

[88] On racial difference defined by sentiment and cultural attributes and competencies, see, for example, Ann Laura Stoler, *Carnal Knowledge and Imperial Power: Race and the Intimate in Colonial Rule* (Berkeley: University of California Press, 2002), and de la Cadena, *Indigenous Mestizos*.

[89] "El mal está en la sangre," *El Norte*, February 25, 1926.

could be found in Alta Verapaz: "The foreign colonies resident in Alta Verapaz ... have become publicly renowned for their temperate customs, for their habit of working, for their friendliness and good treatment of the children of the nation and for their unity with the members of their own nationality." Above all the foreign communities, the most successful and distinguished was the German community. And from this experience, the author exhorted that "it is agreeable that all of the children of the nation and all of the foreigners know that Alta Verapaz is eager to welcome the immigration of people with capital and with industry, who come to work with us in the project of progress and that here we have so much wealth to nourish a population twenty times larger than that which we have."[90]

Celebrations of German immigrants paralleled a surge of post–World War I German immigration and the reestablishment of diplomatic and commercial ties with Germany in 1922. With the coffee boom of 1924–8, Germany also regained its share of Guatemalan coffee exports, which had been lost to the United States due to the war.[91] As German plantations prospered, coffee planters contracted German immigrants as plantation administrators, mechanics, and accountants. Escaping post–World War I Germany, new German settlers were more often receptive to new political ideas emanating from their homeland. They were also less likely to be able to afford the expense of a German wife and thus established intimate relationships with Q'eqchi' women, fulfilling the promise of a new nation on the horizon. Even as Asturias's dream of German–Maya miscegenation seemed viable, the coffee boom also set the stage for the revival of mandamiento labor.

FROM INTERWAR COFFEE BOOM TO GREAT DEPRESSION

The mid-1920s witnessed skyrocketing global coffee prices as prohibition in the United States generated a spike in demand for coffee, and Brazil undertook measures to regulate its domestic production, resulting in a steadier flow of coffee onto the international market.[92] Coffee prices

---

[90] "Colonias extranjeras," *El Norte*, February 28, 1926.

[91] In 1924, of the total exports of coffee (888,005 quintales of coffee), 384,638 (43.3 percent) went to the United States and 361,582 (40.7 percent) to Germany. Wagner, *Historia del café de Guatemala*, 156.

[92] William Gervase Clarence-Smith and Steven Topik, eds., *The Global Coffee Economy in Africa, Asia, and Latin America, 1500–1989* (Cambridge: Cambridge University Press, 2003); Steven Topik and William Gervase Clarence-Smith, "Introduction: Coffee and Global Development," in ibid., 1–20.

increased from 13.70 pesos per quintal in 1922–3 to 24.50 in 1924–5 and 22.80 in 1926–7.[93] To expand production, coffee planters had to over-come a series of barriers: ongoing monetary instability that generated inflation and scarce credit; expensive, treacherous, and irregular transpor-tation by railway from highlands coffee plantations to the lowland port; and, crucially, the lack of a reliable labor force.[94] After Herrera's over-throw, President José María Orellana enacted much-needed monetary reform, adopting parity with the US dollar and establishing the quetzal as the official currency in 1924.[95] In June 1926, the government also created a centralized banking system, which helped reduce the inflation-ary pressures of the previous decades and made capital loans more accessible. In 1928 President Lázaro Chacón (1926–30) created the Cen-tral Coffee Bureau (La Oficina Central del Café) to promote Guatemalan coffee abroad and support Guatemalan producers in the export of their coffee.[96] The more pressing issues of labor unrest and local political power proved much more difficult to overcome and required promoting political alliances across different elite sectors and reasserting the racial hierarchies needed for Maya labor recruitment. Struggles between differ-ent sectors of the Guatemalan elite culminated in the 1927 constitutional reforms, which was an affirming victory for coffee planters. The new constitution outlawed labor strikes, restricted citizenship according to literacy requirements, and laid the foundations for vagrancy laws. Guate-malan coffee producers responded to these favorable circumstances with increases in production, and Guatemala became the third largest producer of coffee in the world.[97] On the eve of the 1929 stock market crash, Alta Verapaz coffee production soared to new heights, reaching 188,807 quintales in the 1927–8 harvest, seven and a half times the peak produc-tion of the 1880s, according to extant statistics.[98]

As coffee producers faced difficulties with their resident laborers, the departmental governor responded in the mid-1920s with the renewal of

[93] Wagner, *Historia del café de Guatemala*, 155.
[94] For a particularly vivid description, see "Desde Panzós," *El Norte*, July 5, 1924.
[95] Paul Jaime Dosal, *Power in Transition: The Rise of Guatemala's Industrial Oligarchy, 1871–1994* (New York: Greenwood Publishing, 1995), 54; Guillermo Díaz Romeu, "Del régimen de Carlos Herrera a la elección de Jorge Ubico," *Historia general de Guatemala* 5 (1996): 39.
[96] Wagner, *Historia del café de Guatemala*, 152.   [97] Ibid., 152.
[98] *Informe de la Dirección General de Estadística 1888* (Guatemala: Tipografía la Unión, 1889), 60; *Memoria de las labores del Ejecutivo en el Ramo de Agricultura durante el año administrativo de 1928 presentada a la Asamblea Legislativa en sus sesiones ordinarias de 1931* (Guatemala: Tipografía Nacional, 1929), 48.

coerced labor and violent repression. He viciously repressed labor strikes, jailed political troublemakers like Icó, and limited freedom of the press. The departmental governor also authorized the use of mandamientos.[99] In 1926 Q'eqchi's from San Pedro Carchá protested that coffee planters and public authorities seized them violently and forced them to carry heavy loads to unhealthy areas of the department, while army press gangs invaded their houses and assaulted their women.[100] Q'eqchi' patriarchs and some sympathetic ladinos, however, loudly contested the reintroduction of mandamientos.

Despite political repression, Mayas regularly elected sympathetic ladinos to positions on the municipal council. Local coffee planters and the departmental governor frequently decried the local ladino authorities, who had come into office on "absurd promises" they made to the indigenous masses.[101] In February 1926, the departmental governor and some of Carchá's ladinos called on the municipality to reinstate mandamiento labor drafts to ensure sufficient labor for the region's bountiful harvest. The alcalde primero, Manuel Chavarría, was vehemently opposed to mandamiento drafts: "The municipality believes that no one has the right to remove someone from their house so that they go to work for another person, perhaps for a meager wage that they decide to pay or is fixed by the authorities." Such methods, the alcalde primero declared, "would not achieve the regeneration" that the government desires. "The Indian of Alta Verapaz who resides in the countryside is a human beast of burden." Instead of this, Chavarria claimed, Mayas "should enjoy the rights of citizens just as all of the Indians of foreign nations enjoy." A few months later, the departmental governor forced the troublemaker Chavarría to resign.[102] Others, including José Ángel Icó's nephew Benjamin Caal, were similarly forced out of office for voicing their opposition to mandamientos.[103] In Cobán's town council, two years later, Domingo Caal Caal, the son of Tiburcio Caal, suggested to the council that it was

---

[99] Witzel de Ciudad, *Mas de 100 años*; Paul J. Dosal, *Doing Business with the Dictators: A Political History of United Fruit in Guatemala, 1899–1944* (Wilmington, DE: SR Books, 1993).

[100] McCreery, *Rural Guatemala*, 205.

[101] AGCA JP-AV 1925 Paq. 1, "JP al Ministerio de Gobernación," July 25, 1925.

[102] SPCM 1926, "Libro de Actas Municipales," sesión pública ordinaria, February 18, 1926, No. 2.

[103] See SPCM 1927, Libro de Actas Municipales 1927, "No. 7 Sesión pública ordinaria celebrada el día jueves 21 de abril, 1927," and "No. 17 Sesión pública ordinaria celebrada jueves 7 de julio, 1927."

time "to trade in the mecapal for mules."[104] In addition to political opposition within the municipal council, coffee planters also faced renewed modes of resistance that had long dominated labor regimes in the region. Some Q'eqchi' patriarchs-cum–coffee planters in Carchá paid their colonos higher wages, sparking the ire of many ladinos.[105]

As coffee planters and state officials backed the reintroduction of mandamientos, they also reasserted racial ascriptions of Mayas as laborers and narrated the past to justify coercion. If the future beckoned Mayas as they sought to create an inclusive and just world beyond racial hierarchies and exploitation, then the past consumed coffee planters who were invested in reinstating social order. No past events were more central to coffee planters' imagination than the 1886 revenge of Xucaneb. Writing in Guatemala's premier intellectual journal *Academia Sociedad de Geografía e Historia de Guatemala* in 1926, German banker and coffee planter-cum-anthropologist David Sapper described the incident in Xucaneb:

> Sometime ago, the press reported that in the mountains of Cucanep [*sic*], close to [San Juan] Chamelco, an alleged *Indian prophet* appeared preaching all the fortune and misfortune and the coming end of the world for all sinful humanity, since he told them that god was tired of his law becoming so scandalous and he wanted to severely punish its offenders. He declared that the only way to offset divine ire was to return to a state of primitive life, to absolute poverty and complete nudity. He ordered the destruction of all kinds of crops and seedbeds that were not indispensable for sustaining the indigenous race and brazenly affirmed that all coffee plantations must be destroyed or devastated, because they only served for the profit of coffee planters, who trampled the laws of God, obligating the poor *indios* to work. Naturally, with such ideas and doctrines, this group of charlatans was able to conquer many followers and live like nawabs, without thinking about work.[106]

While Juan de la Cruz had been racialized as ladino and then as Afro–Guatemalan, Sapper suggested that he was, in fact, Maya. While Juan de la Cruz's representation as Afro–Guatemalan reflected Estrada Cabrera's silencing of ladino artisans' racial origins, Sapper's narration reflected the fear that half a decade of Maya political action had generated. This fear was also about the dangerous potential of Maya spirituality – the

---

[104] CM Libro de Actas Municipales Sesiones ordinarias, Sesión número 39 celebrada el 8 de noviembre de 1928, no. 6, "El Señor Alcalde 3° presentó el memorial," 257–61.
[105] SPCM "Actas Municipales, Sesión Pública Ordinaria," February 18, 1926, no. 10.
[106] Sapper, "Costumbres y creencias religiosas de los indios Queckchi," 194–5 (emphasis mine).

complete return to primitive life that would happen when the disruptive and regressive force of Maya culture was unleashed. Popular memory and rumor impregnated stories of Juan de la Cruz and reflected more about the storyteller and the stories' historical context than the past. The events of Xucaneb, thus, could not simply be relegated to Alta Verapaz's bygone past; these events were alive and shaping the present.

In order to record and control the past, San Pedro Carchá's municipal council also penned memorias of the events of 1920–2. Compiled in the form of witness testimonies, these memorias confirmed interpretations of José Ángel Icó as a social deviant who corrupted other Q'eqchi's, much as Juan de la Cruz had in David Sapper's narrative. According to one coffee planter, Icó "implanted the idea that now they [laborers] did not have to work for their patrones, that they were free, and that soon the government would award them their land titles." Mirroring the language and fears of ladinos' reaction to Jorge Yat in 1865, Icó had even gone so far as "to convince the Indians of Lanquín that it was necessary to get rid of all the Ladinos in town by setting fire to their houses at night." According to the report, Icó was constantly drunk and fomenting rebellion; he also lacked respect for state authorities and coffee planters. "With his faulty Spanish he insults anyone who passes by, without distinction of sex nor class," they claimed.[107] Icó embodied the barbaric and primitive, the threatening and deviant. These memorias were strategic performances of racial difference: they not only described events in the past, but inscribed the sentiments, actions, and cultural traits that defined Mayas. Narratives of Maya anachronism were also spectacular and menacing, showing how the Maya, as a racialized group, threatened progress and required state vigilance and repression, if necessary.

The ongoing struggles over racial hierarchies and labor coalesced during the 1927 constitutional reforms. Following the death of President Orellana in 1926, Lázaro Chacón (1926–30) came to power on the promise of constitutional change. The 1927 amendments reflected the desire to secure a new era of democratic politics that limited the powers of the presidential office, separated judicial and legislative bodies, prohibited reelection, and secured individual rights such as habeas corpus and rights to private property. The modifications also reflected the desire to secure a new era of coerced labor that was not simply a relic of the colonial past, to lay the basis, in other words, for a vagrancy law. The

---

[107] SPCM 1927 "Libro de Actas Municipales," August 25, 1927, No. 23.

constitutional convention defined "productive work" as a necessary transitional step in the transformation of the nation from an agricultural society into an industrial one, and required the incorporation of Indians as "the nation's progressive and laboring peoples."[108] As such, the constitutionalists defined work as a social obligation for all Guatemalans in the name of national progress, and those unwilling to fulfill their duties were defined as vagrants and were subject to punishment.[109] The constitutional changes also deemed labor strikes illegal; a proposal to establish a labor tribunal was deferred; and the 1921 literacy-based definition of citizenship was sustained despite vociferous opposition.[110] Even Cobán's municipal council recognized that a literacy-based definition of citizenship would discriminate against Mayas and turn them into secondary citizens. The majority of the council voted in opposition to the reforms, since "the Indian like all of the children of Guatemala should enjoy such rights."[111] These voices, however, were ignored, and Guatemala's 1927 social constitution bore little resemblance to Mexico's 1917 constitution, with its protection of labor, land, and social rights.[112]

As the 1927 constitutional reforms concluded, the left in Guatemala also began to shift focus from ladino workers in the cities to Maya laborers in the countryside.[113] José Ángel Icó continued to provide refuge for victims of abusive patrones, to denounce local corruption, and to represent indigenous claimants from Panzós to the Petén.[114] Along with his brother-in-law, Santiago Cucul, Icó also participated actively in land invasions, leading forty-five other Q'eqchi's to plant corn on land claimed by Dieseldorff, about ten kilometers north of Icó's home village. "Hypnotized by Icó's promises," Dieseldorff complained, "these mozos refuse

---

[108] *Génesis de la reforma constitucional de la República de Guatemala en el año de 1927* (Guatemala: Tipografía Nacional, 1931), 75–6.

[109] Ibid., 25–31.   [110] Ibid, vii. For the debates on labor, see 40–2, 71–2, 74–8, 80, 94–5.

[111] CM Libro de Actas Ordinarias 1925–1929, Sesión No. 12 extraordinaria celebrada 24 de mayo de 1927, No. 2, "Por encardo del Señor Presidente, el Sindico 2° Lic. Prado B. hizo saber el objeto de la sesión," 170–1; see also Numero 5 realizada el 27 de enero de 1927, No. 5, "Se dio lectura a la moción presentada por el Sr Alcalde 2° Don Alberto D. Durán," 157–8. See also CM Est. 1 Paq. 16, "Lic. Francisco Contreras B. y Ing. Miguel Nuila al Diputados," May 24, 1927.

[112] For Mexico, see Charles A. Hale, "Political and Social Ideas," in *Latin America: Economy and Society, 1870–1930,* ed. Leslie Bethell (New York: Cambridge University Press, 1989), 225–300.

[113] See Arturo Taracena Arriola, "Presencia anarquista en Guatemala entre 1920 y 1932," *Mesoamérica* 9, no. 1 (June 1988): 18.

[114] AGCA J-AV 104 Leg. 28 A Exp. 28 1927; see, especially, AGCA J-AV 105 Leg. 29 C Exp. 8 1928, which contains three cases against Icó.

to return [to work], nor will they pay me what they owe; they have said to my representative that I should not send a commission to arrest them, because they will shoot him with their rifles."[115] Altaverapacence Q'eqchi's thus often sought to live the discontinuous, disrupted, and undeferred fulfillment of revolutionary time as they engaged in insurrectionary Maya geographies of time and space.

The first chill winds of the Great Depression, however, descended on Guatemala in 1929 as overflowing Brazilian coffee warehouses signaled the coffee bonanza's untimely conclusion. Only weeks before the stock market crash, the Brazilian Coffee Institute collapsed, heralding the end of relatively stable and high coffee prices.[116] The Guatemalan government responded to the crisis by creating a National Bank of Mortgage and Credit to provide small loans for agriculturalists and small industrialists, which helped to mitigate the impending disaster.[117] As Regina Wagner has argued, the real crisis, however, did not set in until 1931, when major banks began to recall loans, creating a solvency crisis and a virtual panic.[118] Planters responded by aggressively increasing production, cutting wages, and halting advances. Erwin Paul Dieseldorff addressed the Ministry of Agriculture in 1930, calling for government action to reduce wages even further: "It would be helpful if the government would begin by cutting wages and salaries.... Of course, there will be opposition among the agricultural workers to lowering their wages, and the landowners need the help of the government to put such cuts into effect."[119] As some plantation owners stopped advancing new wages or only credited a workers' debt in the midst of the economic crisis, coffee laborers declared themselves free, despite their remaining debts.[120] These reactions ignited coffee planters' fears of a new wave of political radicalization.

The first years of the Great Depression sent shock waves across the region, and many coffee planters feared the expansion of communist organizing in the countryside. In 1931 the organized labor movement

---

[115] Kit, "Costumbre, Conflict and Consensus," 210; and AGCA JP-AV 104 Leg. 26 B Exp. 29.
[116] Clarence-Smith and Topik, "Introduction: Coffee and Global Development."
[117] Wagner, *Historia del café de Guatemala*, 165; McCreery, *Rural Guatemala*, 315.
[118] Wagner, *Historia del café de Guatemala*, 166.
[119] Cited in McCreery, *Rural Guatemala*, 313.
[120] When Erwin Paul Dieseldorff sent some mozos to work in road construction, they complained they were not mozos because they did not have contracts. SPCM 1932, "Al alcalde 1° del Erwin Paul Diesledorff," April 2, 1932.

and the Communist Party attempted to organize coffee workers in San Marcos. That same year, J. Fernando Muñoz Juárez, a Guatemalan intellectual and indigenista, penned a strong warning against the dangers of political unrest among the indigenous population in the countryside and the possible emergence of "indigenous communism" that would, like a disease, attack the social body. "We are before a forced solution of the great problems that agitate the consciousness of the masses," he wrote. "The disease spreads through the towns and decides destinies by way of tumultuous crowds . . . and [as] the contagion comes nearer, it is necessary for those who direct national destinies, that they are aware it is more sensible to prevent than to later resolve. The day could arrive in which the remedy is entirely futile."[121] As Mayas sought to build alternative political futures, Muñoz Juárez reduced Mayas to dangerous anachronisms, easily infected by the disease of communism.

With heightening anxieties spreading among Guatemalan elites and the middle class, the military and political elite turned to a rabid anticommunist, law-and-order populist Jorge Ubico, for solutions. As departmental governor in Alta Verapaz (1907–9), Ubico had a considerable reputation as an able administrator, and headed a strong and well-organized political party, the Progressive Liberal Party (Partido Liberal Progresista), with a growing base of support among intellectuals, the middle class, and planters. When Ubico campaigned against Lazaro Chacón in the 1926 elections, he promised social reform inspired by labor movements and the discourses of the Mexican presidents Álvaro Obregón (1920–4) and Plutarco Elías Calles (1924–8).[122] By 1930 Ubico's growing reputation for cruelty and efficiency, energy and decisive action also attracted the support of a broader spectrum of society that believed he would put an end to Communist advances. Opportunity struck when President Chacón suddenly succumbed to a cerebral hemorrhage in December 1930. A military revolt gave way to hasty elections in February 1931, and Ubico managed to secure his position as the only candidate on the ballot.

Only a few days after Ubico took office, José Ángel Icó wrote to Guatemala's newly elected president with a tone of remarkable

---

[121] J. Fernando Muñoz Juárez, *El indio guatemalteco, ensayo de sociología nacionalista* (Guatemala: Tipografía Nacional, 1931), 117–18.

[122] See Joseph A. Pitti, "Jorge Ubico and Guatemalan Politics in the 1920s" (PhD diss., University of New Mexico, 1975), 191–260; and Arturo Taracena Arriola, "El APRA, Haya de la Torre y la crisis del liberalismo," *Cuadernos Americanos* 37, no. 1 (January–February 1993): 190.

familiarity. In the spirit of Club Unionista "Freedom of the Indian," Icó requested that Ubico create a free labor market by legislating a guaranteed minimum wage as well as canceling all debts and existing labor contracts. "Señor don José Ángel Icó," Ubico began his measured response, "I believe that it is an opportune moment to express to you, that it is more advisable for you to dedicate yourself, as you have always, to work. Do not foster grievances among the Indians for any reason, because soon I will establish new, analogous or similar regulations to those that you propose. This legislation will try to rectify the difficulties that the population of your region currently experiences."[123] Ubico's inaugural address, published a few days later in the newspaper *El Imparcial*, made clear what Ubico had meant in his letter to Icó. As if announcing the repression and terror on the horizon, he declared to the nation: "One of the hypocritical forms of vagrancy, that has been among us, is the habit of occupying oneself with politics."[124] Ubico's speech equated political troublemakers like Icó with criminal vagrants, and the crime of vagrancy with political troublemaking. His response foreshadowed both his law-and-order approach to Guatemala's labor question as well as his brutal crackdown on the political movements that had blossomed over the prior decade.

The ink had barely dried on President Ubico's response to Icó when Icó faced criminal charges of fraud, assault, and land invasions.[125] According to local lore, Ubico personally ordered Icó's arrest and made him walk the seven miles from Cobán to Carchá tied to the tail of a horse. According to one sympathetic local historian, this humiliating act "mock[ed]" Icó's arrogant pretensions of "riding around on a horse" and served to "remind him that he was an Indian."[126] Only a few months later, repression escalated into a massive assault on both the rural and urban labor movements. Ubico violently confronted the labor movement in cement, beer, and sugar plants. In December 1931, he ordered the arrest of key labor leaders. The Guatemalan press also reported Ubico's dismantling of

---

[123] AGCA J-AV 105 Leg. 29 C Exp. 8.
[124] Cited in Figueroa Ibarra, "Marxismo, sociedad, y movimiento sindical en Guatemala," 76.
[125] AGCA B Leg. 30267 Exp. 7; AGCA J-AV 105 Leg. 31 B Exp. 16; AGCA B Leg. 30507 Exp. 27; AGCA B Leg. 30507 Exp. 1; AGCA B Leg. 30506 Exp. 40; AGCA J-AV 104 Leg. 26 B Exp. 29; AGCA B Leg. 30455, "Al Sr. Presidente de la República de José Ángel Icó," July 27, 1932; AGCA J-AV 105 Leg. 33 B Exp. 13; AGCA J-AV 105 Leg. 33 B Exp. 18.
[126] Grandin, *The Last Colonial Massacre*, 32.

a Communist plot in January 1932.[127] A massive Communist uprising in El Salvador that ended in a brutal massacre later that month escalated the perceived Communist threat and corresponding repression. Two months later, Ubico dissolved unions. By June 1934 the Department of Labor was placed under the management of the National Police.[128] The message could not have been more clear – Ubico equated communism with criminality and political opposition, concluding that anyone who disrupted the political order or opposed his regime was automatically espousing communism. When Icó attempted to seek justice for other inmates from his own dank prison cell, where he spent much of the 1930s, he found his political connections vanquished, leaving his efforts frustrated and his reputation in question among the Q'eqchi's he had sought to protect.[129] José Ángel Icó's abandonment in prison represented the closing-down of a democratic opening and signaled new efforts on the horizon to dismantle emergent alliances between Mayas and the Guatemalan left.

CONCLUSION

The 1920s offered Guatemalans a brief democratic opening. Spearheaded by José Ángel Icó, Q'eqchi's took advantage of the moment to organize the Club Unionista "Freedom of the Indian" and to demand Maya rights as citizens, an end to coerced labor and debts as well as other abuses perpetuated by coffee planters and state officials alike. Disrupting the politics of postponement, some Mayas lived in an undeferred, revolutionary time and imagined themselves on the world stage inaugurating a new and yet undefined era. State officials, intellectuals, and coffee planters responded to Maya demands by pointing out Mayas' uncivilized cultural traits and sentiments, their insolence and indolence, and their need for a guiding hand. Even though Q'eqchi's claimed citizenship and equal rights, they could not measure up because, behind the set of capacities ascribed to all human beings, there lies a dense collection of social credentials and characteristics that constitute the real bases of political inclusion. Far from abstract and universal, citizenship was defined by shifting cultural competencies. According to some coffee planters and state officials,

---

[127] Taracena Arriola, "Presencia anarquista en Guatemala," 19–23.
[128] Kenneth J. Grieb, *Guatemalan Caudillo, the Regime of Jorge Ubico: Guatemala, 1931–1944* (Athens: Ohio University Press, 1979), 16; Piero Gliejeses, "La aldea de Ubico," *Mesoamerica* 17 (1989): 25–60.
[129] See AGCA J-AV 105 Leg. 33 B Exp. 18 1932; AGCA B Leg. 30507 Exp. 27 1932; AGCA B Leg. 32234 Exp. 34 1943.

Mayas were not yet modern enough. As Bliss Cua Lim has argued, "the rhetoric of anachronism is consistently employed by proponents of homogenous time whenever a stubborn heterogeneity is encountered. One comes to expect that whenever anachronism is shouted conflicting, coexisting times are being hastily denounced."[130]

In the 1920s Q'eqchi' political actions, however, were met with escalating cycles of violence, revenge, and persecution. But within these cycles of labor strikes and incarcerations, land invasions and violent reprisals, we can catch furtive glimpses into Maya notions of freedom, justice, and equality. When they demanded higher wages or violated contracts, they spoke to a desire for greater reciprocity. When they planted maize on coffee plantations, they gave voice to a desire for land and subsistence production and perhaps greater autonomy. When they united against coffee planters and state officials, they embodied Maya practices of communal solidarity. And when they stood up to administrators, planters, and state officials, they made real the desire to be recognized as citizen-agents and not subjects.

Nonetheless, the escalating rounds of political violence that dominated the 1920s also generated deepening racial divisions and renewed celebrations of German immigrants and German–Maya mestizaje that illustrated the resurrection and reinvention of the civilizing metanarrative, deployed strategically to counter the radical liberal–democratic one articulated by Icó and others. Land invasions and labor strikes also expressed desires to promote new kinds of mediation between indigenous communities, the state, and coffee planters. In 1929, when the state required coffee planters to comply with national legislation requiring them to educate the children of resident workers, coffee planters could only imagine that education would further agitate Mayas to political action. Erwin Paul Dieseldorff complained: "Of what value is it to a mozo to be able to read and write, or to know about history and geography?" Indeed, Dieseldorff seemed to be suggesting that such education might only help Mayas place their experience in the broader, global contexts of slavery. "Is it not true," Dieseldorff continued, "that giving the Indian classes a higher education than their social position merits only serves to disrupt their work? We have learned from experience that Indians who have learned to read and write are no longer useful as agricultural workers.... We need workers who are content with their social status, not an abundance of learned

[130] Lim, *Translating Time*, 84.

persons who look upon manual labor with arrogant disdain."[131] Rather than hiring trained schoolteachers and building schools, Dieseldorff ordered that old plantation outbuildings function as schools and commanded an illiterate resident laborer to instruct the students for the required hours.[132] Whereas at the turn of the century Mayas and ladinos united in opposition to aristocratic elites (including German settlers) and celebrated social mobility via education, by the mid-1920s, Germans and ladinos despised social mobility and education and united against a common enemy: Mayas. The Great Depression, alongside a Communist Red Scare, set the stage for the close of Guatemala's democratic experiment and a return to a populist dictatorship.

---

[131] In Náñez Falcón, "Erwin Paul Dieseldorff," 344; see also Grandin, *The Last Colonial Massacre*, 36.
[132] TULAL DC Bound Volumes, Vol. 73, Fols. 217, 227, 233.

7

Possessing Tezulutlán

Splitting National Time in Dictatorship, 1931–1939

> Political ideas can be inherited, ... they're carried in the blood and there's
> no more dangerous kind of inheritance. That's how one revolutionary is
> born from another, how one policeman is born from another.
> —Miguel Ángel Asturias, *The Green Pope*

> The Alta Vera Paz has been conquered by white men a couple of times.
> First, in the sixteenth century by Bartolomé de las Casas as a demonstration
> of what could be done peacefully; and in the nineteenth century by Germans
> leaving a fatherland which offered more goose-stepping than opportunities
> for advancement.
> —Erna Fergusson, *Guatemala* (1937)

As the nation plunged into the Great Depression and elite Guatemalans
trembled at the Communist threat looming over Central America, President Jorge Ubico envisioned a massive program of rural modernization
that expanded the state into the countryside; brought racial improvement
through eugenics, health, and sanitation; built roads and bridges; and
ended discontent among rural laborers by abolishing debt peonage and
halting planter abuses. Like Manuel Estrada Cabrera's protopopulism,
Ubico envisioned Guatemala's entrance onto the world stage, as a nation
worthy of international recognition, via a vigorous campaign to improve
the health, wealth, and morality of Guatemalans. In honor of rural
modernization and economic progress, Ubico created annual state and
national fairs where each department displayed their market wares, rural

produce, and crafts for sale.[1] In Alta Verapaz, state officials held competitions for the best coffee, the healthiest baby, and the oldest indio, and each region was celebrated with a specific regional bird and flower that defined their unique landscape. In addition, Ubico promoted beauty pageants for "coffee queens" and "indias bonitas," who highlighted the feminine qualities of coffee planters and plantation laborers. In promoting Maya beauty contests during state fairs, Ubico safely relegated Maya culture to the past as an authentic tradition. Under Ubico, the postcolonial predicament and historical time were resolved through the promotion of a sanctioned *indigenismo* that fixed Mayas in the past in folkloric traditions and rendered other aspects of Maya culture threatening in the present. At the same time, Ubico rapidly persecuted Mayas for their cultural practices, including subsistence and boj production, and shamanism. Ubico thus not only engaged the politics of postponement to counter other heterogeneous times and political imaginings; he also criminalized Maya practices that reproduced Q'eqchi' ontologies.

In Alta Verapaz, the first departmental state fair coincided with the region's 400th anniversary of the peaceful conquest in 1936. Preparations for the festivities began a year in advance as upwardly mobile ladinos and Q'eqchi' patriarchs sought to demonstrate their modern and patriotic sentiments for the public. Alta Verapaz's state fair quickly gained national predominance as a fierce national debate emerged over the meaning of the peaceful conquest, filling the newspapers with hundreds of editorials. In Alta Verapaz, the state fair was further complicated by brewing nationalisms. Only three years earlier, officials from the Party of German National Socialist Workers (Nationalsozialistische Deutsche Arbeiterpartei, NSDAP) marched into the board of directors' meeting of Cobán's German club to demand control, proclaiming themselves to be the Führer's true representatives.[2] Ladinos responded to German nationalism with their own anti-German nationalism. These competing nationalisms were expressed in debates and efforts to control the meaning and history of the region's peaceful conquest. Many ladinos and Q'eqchi' patriarchs referred to the region as Tezulutlán (Land of War), the name given to the region by Nahua allies of Pedro de Alvarado.

---

[1] Walter E. Little, "A Visual Political Economy of Maya Representations in Guatemala, 1931–1944," *Ethnohistory* 55, no. 4 (2008): 633–63.

[2] Martin Frey, *Deutschtum in der Alta Verapaz: Erinnerungen Herausgegeben Anläßlich des 50 Jährigen Bestehens des Deutschen Vereins zu Coban, Guatemala, 1888–1938* (Stuttgart: Deutsche Verl. Anst., 1938), 46.

Through the symbolic renaming of Alta Verapaz as Tezulutlán, Altaver-apacence ladinos celebrated undefeated Maya warriors' fierce defense of the territory from foreign invaders as a kind of metaphor for their own anti-German, anti-foreign nationalism. German nationalists in Alta Ver-apaz, too, adopted the peaceful conquest to imagine Alta Verapaz as a land free from the stains of racial mixing and colonialism, and the ideal place for a German diasporic nation. For Q'eqchi' patriarchs, the state fairs generated spaces for them to reinforce their identities as both indigenous and modern. Q'eqchi', German, and ladino uses of Maya culture were shaped by and helped bolster Ubico's own brand of sanctioned indigenismo.[3] Unlike indigenismo in Mexico, which assumed the incorporation of Indians into Mexican society and their ultimate Europeanization, Ubico's indigenismo classified Mayas as contemporary relics of past civilizations and noncitizens.[4]

Some Guatemalans still whisper admiration for Jorge Ubico's strong-arm dictatorship, remembering the safety and security offered by his law-and-order approach. Many others shudder with fear recollecting his regime. Under Ubico, the state expanded directly and indirectly through the National Police and a series of low-level state officials who occupied positions as sanitation officers, rural policemen, postal workers, and census takers. Through state positions, Ubico enabled social climbers to position themselves as apostles of progress. His dictatorship also offered marginalized rural and urban classes the promise of modernity through the building of roads and choreographed spectacles like the fairs. At the very moment when some German settlers espoused a virulent racist nationalism, Jorge Ubico sought to reconcile the feeling of being left behind in the march toward progress among the racially mixed and socially marginal. To do so, he reined in planter sovereignty and enlarged state presence in rural areas as well as the intimate spheres of life. He promoted a new nationalism that combined celebrations of Maya culture and tradition with diatribes against threats to modernization, particularly elements of Maya culture like subsistence and boj production and shamanism. The time of the nation was strategically split between the

---

[3] In some respects, his sanctioned indigenismo mirrored the scientific and apolitical indigenismo that was established later in the Insituto Indigenista Interamericano (III). See, for example, Laura Giraudo, "Neither 'Scientific' nor 'Colonialist': The Ambiguous Course of Inter-American Indigenismo in the 1940s," *Latin American Perspectives* 39, no. 5 (2012): 12–32.

[4] Charles A. Hale, *The Transformation of Liberalism in Late Nineteenth-Century Mexico* (Princeton, NJ: Princeton University Press, 1989), 260.

archaic, dangerous past and the modern and progressive present. With his praise of economic modernization, Ubico strategically fashioned the liberal–democratic and civilizing metanarratives into a new state-directed program that combined material progress through infrastructure, and social and moral progress through eugenics policies such as a focus on child-rearing and sanitation that sought to improve the innate qualities of a race.[5] In Alta Verapaz, ladinos, Germans, and Q'eqchi's took advantage of Ubico's nationalism to face down racisms, recuperate their honor, and rearticulate the boundaries of the nation. What Ubico did not count on, however, was the strength of evolving anti-German sentiments. Shortly after the populist was inaugurated, Cobán's municipal council wrote a memorandum to the president entitled "The Most Important Public Works Projects That Must Be Undertaken in the Department to Achieve Progress." Alongside calls for potable water, modern drains, and roads, Cobaneros proposed a legislative accord that would "require foreigners who owned property anywhere in the Republic, to be obliged to take Guatemalan nationality and that they could not acquire more than fifteen caballerías of land, which they would be required to cultivate."[6] Erwin Paul Dieseldorff himself owned nearly 900 caballerías.[7] Few, however, anticipated what this combination of economic and anti-immigrant nationalism and state-directed modernization would mean by the time that Guatemala entered World War II on the side of the Allied forces in December 1941.

THE CHIEF OF SANITATION: LABOR LAWS AND THE EXPANSION OF STATE POWER UNDER UBICO

From the modest comfort of his Guatemala City home, the great-nephew of José Angel Icó, Alfredo Cucul, recalled Jorge Ubico's dictatorship with a mixture of horror and awe. Under Ubico, Cucul explained, the state's disciplinary power extended its tentacles into the countryside. The state even reached underneath the dirty fingernails and into the lice-ridden hair follicles of schoolchildren who, on orders from Ubico – the self-proclaimed chief of sanitation – were reprimanded by their teachers. Alfredo's voice quivered as he also recalled the first time he saw a public

---

[5] Francis Galton, *Essays in Eugenics* (London: Eugenics Education Society, 1909).

[6] CM Est. 1 Paq. 16, "Memorándum: de las obras más importantes que hay que llevar a cabo en el Depto. para el progreso efectivo," May 23, 1931.

[7] Guillermo Náñez Falcón, "Erwin Paul Dieseldorff, German Entrepreneur in the Alta Verapaz of Guatemala, 1889–1937" (PhD diss., Tulane University, 1970), 169.

execution in San Pedro Carchá's town square. Alfredo remembers most
vividly the grisly sound of the execution. The condemned Q'eqchi' man
was only accused of adultery.[8] In 1934 Ubico had decreed the death
penalty for "unsavory individuals or those with communist tendencies."[9]
He frequently sentenced to public execution or jail union organizers and
opposition leaders, and during his annual inspection trips he singled out
Maya patriarchs, such as José Angel Icó, as community leaders for the
simple fact of being literate.[10] Even military officers were afraid. One
coronel noted: "We were always scared; the military code was draconian,
prescribing the death penalty for virtually every offense. Spies were everywhere."[11] Others recall the political repression wrought by the National
Police, known as the "Gestapo." Jails were overflowing with political
prisoners. The state expanded through an elaborate system of *orejas*
(spies) and sanitation officers not only into bedrooms and brothels, but
also onto plantations challenging the coffee planters' sovereignty. Ubico
also radically reconfigured state power through vagrancy laws and new
municipal *intendentes* that eroded Maya patriarchs' political power.[12]
Despite Ubico's efforts, these institutional and legal reforms were imperfectly applied as Mayas, local state officials, and coffee planters alike
confounded efforts to direct modernization from above.

Historians have often portrayed Ubico's dictatorship as thirteen years of
brutal terror.[13] Ubico himself is often represented as irrational, if not
deluded, for his self-styled likeness to Napoleon Bonaparte and his palace
filled with busts of his great hero. Ubico, however, ruled not by terror

---

[8] Interview with the author, May 17, 2008; see also Grandin, *The Last Colonial Mas-
     sacre*, 47.
[9] Beatriz Paloma de Lewin, "La universidad de 1920–30 y durante el régimen de Ubico,"
     Estudios, anuario de la Universidad de San Carlos 6 (1975): 207.
[10] Federico Hernández de León, *Viajes presidenciales: Breves relatos de algunas expedi-
     ciones administrativas del General D. Jorge Ubico, presidente de la República* (Guate-
     mala: Publicaciones del Partido Liberal Progresista, 1940 and 1943).
[11] Cited in Piero Gleijeses, *Shattered Hope: The Guatemalan Revolution and the United
     States, 1944–1954* (Princeton, NJ: Princeton University Press, 1992), 16.
[12] Michel Foucault, *"Society Must Be Defended": Lectures at the Collège de France,
     1975–1976* (New York: St Martin's Press, 2003); Giorgio Agamben, *Homo Sacer:
     Sovereign Power and Bare Life* (Stanford, CA: Stanford University Press, 1998).
[13] Richard Newbold Adams, Brian Murphy, and Bryan Roberts, *Crucifixion by Power:
     Essays on Guatemalan National Social Structure, 1944–1966* (Austin: University of
     Texas Press, 1970); Richard H. Immerman, *The CIA in Guatemala: The Foreign Policy
     of Intervention* (Austin: University of Texas Press, 2010); Kenneth J. Grieb, *Guatemalan
     Caudillo, the Regime of Jorge Ubico: Guatemala, 1931–1944* (Athens: Ohio University
     Press, 1979).

alone; he was also a populist. In typical populist fashion, Ubico rode his Harley Davidson motorcycle around the countryside on annual inspection trips, known as *viajes presidenciales*.[14] Walking through villages, Ubico listened to the residents and visited schools, public offices, and prisons. He invited complaints about the conduct of local authorities, often overruling their decisions, and removing or arresting them on the spot. On occasion, he demanded improvements in working conditions and pay on plantations. On his first such annual inspection trip in 1932, Ubico scolded Altaverapacence coffee planters. According to newspaper accounts, he chided the planters: "The general welfare of a region is not possible when the salaries paid to workers are too low." Ubico required the planters to come to an agreement to raise wages.[15] Ubico also inquired into the needs of the villagers, and often responded favorably to requests for the extension of public services. Ubico's regular visits and public displays of violence and goodwill elicited a powerful combination of fear and awe, terror and justice. Thus, even while the state enacted violent repression, Ubico cultivated enthusiastic support in the countryside. Like the Dominican dictator Rafael Trujillo, Jorge Ubico strategically adopted a popular masculinity that included defending women and the poor, riding on a motorcycle, and dressing in military uniform.[16]

In his inaugural speech, Ubico outlined his government's three guiding principles:

JUSTICE, because without this the maintenance of harmony and social stability is inconceivable; MORALITY, within the governmental sphere, in order to increase the efficiency of the state, and outside of it, to aid society in the fight against some damaging habits, falsely attributed to inheritance and the environment; PROGRESS, in moral and material spheres, with the purpose of neither halting nor regressing us in the great march of humanity, toward the perfection of the lives and souls that we call civilization.[17]

To promote material progress, Ubico passed legislation that required every Guatemalan to pay an annual road tax or provide two weeks'

---

[14] Hernández de León, *Viajes presidenciales*; and Grieb, *Guatemalan Caudillo*, 35–8.

[15] "Ubico visita Petén y Alta Verapaz," *Diario de Centro América*, February 14, 1932.

[16] See, for example, Lauren Derby, *The Dictator's Seduction: Politics and the Popular Imagination in the Era of Trujillo* (Durham, NC: Duke University Press, 2009); Richard Lee Turits, *Foundations of Despotism: Peasants, the Trujillo Regime, and Modernity in Dominican History* (Stanford, CA: Stanford University Press, 2004); Jeffrey L. Gould, *To Lead as Equals: Rural Protest and Political Consciousness in Chinandega, Nicaragua, 1912–1979* (Chapel Hill: University of North Carolina Press, 2014).

[17] Jorge Ubico, *Hacia un futuro mejor: Importantes documentos para la historia patria* (Guatemala: Tipografía Nacional, 1932), 7–8.

unpaid labor in constructing roads.[18] More than promoting material progress, he also sought justice, progress, and social order in Guatemalan social life through his personal interventions and a broad program of eugenics and sanitation. Ubico was concerned with domestic affairs, where popular justice was most intimate and where, many eugenicists contended, the future of the nation resided. In January 1934, for example, Candelaria Cuc wrote to Ubico about her husband's murder, pleading, "Help me Señor President, you are just and will bring out the truth. Here the poor die underneath the foot of the rich."[19] Ubico personally ordered the capture of the accused murderer. Through direct interventions in personal affairs, Ubico shifted the focus of popular demands from better working conditions and access to land to personal disputes in intimate affairs. Abusive husbands, thieving neighbors, and cheating bosses were all subject to Ubico's wrath. As Francisco Panizza has argued, populism "blurs the public–private dividing line and brings into the political realm both individual and collective desires that had previously no place in public life."[20] This was especially true in the context of an age of state intervention and eugenics. While intervening directly in local and domestic affairs, Jorge Ubico rapidly implemented a new law-and-order regime and reconfigured state power.

In order to extend the territorial reach of the state, Ubico implemented state reforms that centralized state power in the figure of the president, created new local intermediaries, and dealt a decisive blow to Q'eqchi' patriarchs. Ubico took control over the nomination and removal of judges, limited the exercise of rights such as freedom of the press, and prohibited oppositional parties. Most significantly for Q'eqchi's, Ubico suspended municipal autonomy and elections and created new state-appointed *intendentes municipales*.[21] Instead of ladino and Maya alcaldes, Ubico appointed intendentes municipales as mayors.[22] Intent on ending political corruption and ensuring political loyalty, Ubico

---

[18] Rosendo Méndez, *Leyes vigentes de agricultura* (Guatemala: Tipografía Nacional, 1937), 214–15, 244–7.

[19] AGCA B Leg. 30792 Exp. 3.

[20] Francisco Panizza, *Populism and the Mirror of Democracy* (New York: Verso, 2005), 24.

[21] See *Reforma constitucional de 1935: Antecedentes texto taquigráfico de los debates sostenidos en la comisión de la constituyente* (Guatemala: Tipografía Nacional, 1936).

[22] Antonio Goubaud discusses the new relationship between the intendentes and the Q'eqchi' elites in regard to the provision of local justice; see Antonio Goubaud Carrera, "*Notes on San Juan Chamelco, Alta Verapaz*," Microfilm Collection of Manuscripts on Middle American Cultural Anthropology. University of Chicago Library (Chicago, 1949), 5.

personally selected intendentes and required that they serve in regions where they had few connections. Occasionally, however, Ubico appointed Altaverapacence ladinos and Q'eqchi'–Germans who had demonstrated great personal loyalty to serve in their home departments.[23] Juan Turkheim, the son of a Q'eqchi' mother and German father, was named intendente of San Juan Chamelco for nearly the entire duration of Ubico's rule.[24] Possessing absolute authority in local affairs, intendentes further undermined the Q'eqchi' patriarchs' role as mediators in local conflicts and representatives of the Maya lower class.[25] Alta Verapaz's local press celebrated the intendente system as the final blow to "the Chinese-wall politics that was inherited from Colonialism."[26] These editorials presented the intendentes not as part of a top-down system of administrative government that eroded local democracy but as progress toward a homogeneous and liberal nation-state.

Ubico also extended state authority into the countryside, and even into plantations, through new vagrancy, labor, census, and sanitation laws. Over the preceding decades, coffee planters had forged a provisional territorial sovereignty on their plantations by preventing the entrance of state agents and appointing state representatives. In 1932 Alta Verapaz's sanitation officer complained that "leaving coffee planters to request assistance from the physician has demonstrated results that are absolutely insufficient," and recommended new state legislation that would grant the state medical access to plantations.[27] Many coffee planters found themselves increasingly within the purview of an expanded state bureaucracy charged with keeping up-to-date lists of men who were due to report for road service. Municipal and departmental archives are replete with road censuses (*censos de vialidad*), indicating that, for the first time, the state sought to keep accurate records of the numbers of people living on plantations. Under Ubico's direction, local officials were instructed to collect statistics down to the very last cuerda of coffee cultivated by small-scale Q'eqchi's producers.[28] Ubico's largest affront to planter sovereignty, however, was from two labor laws passed in 1934: Decree 1995, which abolished debt peonage and mandamientos; and Decree

---

[23] Juan von Turkheim Pacay was named intendente in San Juan Chamelco, for example. See "Intendentes," *El Norte*, October 12, 1935.
[24] Cobán Municipal Archive, Libros de Actos Municipales 1932–9.
[25] Goubaud Carrera, "Notes on San Juan Chamelco," 187.
[26] "Intendentes municipales," *El Norte*, June 29, 1935.   [27] AGCA Leg. 30507 Exp. 26.
[28] SPCM 1938, "JP a los alcaldes municipales," August 20, 1938; SPCM 1938, "Circular, Dirección General de Estadística," June 8, 1938.

1996, which made vagrancy illegal.[29] Through provisions in these two laws, coffee planters were required to provide state officials access to their plantations for sanitation and school inspections, as well as for the collection of local statistics.[30] Likewise, the state once again took control over the management and provision of labor on coffee plantations. As Kenneth Grieb argued, "The government became the patron, and the seat of power was transferred from the local *hacienda* to the Presidential Palace."[31]

While the new labor laws hindered coffee planters' sovereignty, they also benefited coffee planters by providing two years of free labor at a crucial juncture during the Great Depression and promised to create a steady stream of laborers much as mandamientos had in the past. In April 1934, Ubico passed Decree 1995, which forbade coffee planters and habilitadores to give new advances to their workers and allowed coffee planters two years to compel their indebted laborers to work off what they already owed. After the two-year period, all remaining debts were to be canceled. Worker debt, however, was largely an accounting fiction: no worker could ever pay off what they owed to a planter in their lifetime.[32] In effect, Ubico's legislation granted planters free labor for two years.

While Decree 1995 abolished debt peonage, Guatemala's new vagrancy law, Decree 1996, ensured a steady labor supply for coffee plantations. The legal code labeled any man (women were not subject to the vagrancy law), regardless of race, a vagrant under the following conditions: anyone who did not practice a recognized profession or have a business or adequate income, had contracted for work on a plantation but failed to comply with the agreement, or did not have a contract for agricultural labor. Men were required to cultivate at least three *manzanas* (one manzana equals 1.727 acres) of coffee, sugar, or tobacco; four manzanas of corn, wheat, potatoes, vegetables, or other subsistence products; or three manzanas of corn that gave two harvests a year. Most Mayas did not have access to sufficient land to be exempt from vagrancy laws.[33] As a result, many Mayas were required by law to provide between 100 and 150 days

---

[29] Méndez, Leyes vigentes de agricultura, 214–15, 244–7.
[30] Grieb, *Guatemalan Caudillo*, 34.   [31] Ibid., 39.
[32] McCreery, Rural Guatemala, 318–19.
[33] See ibid., 317. See also Douglas E. Brintnall, *Revolt against the Dead: The Modernization of a Mayan Community in the Highlands of Guatemala* (New York: Taylor & Francis, 1979), 107; Charles Wagley, *Economics of a Guatemalan Village* (Washington, DC: American Anthropological Association, 1941), 26; Sol Tax, *Penny Capitalism: A Guatemalan Indian Economy* (Washington, DC: US Government Printing Office, 1953), 107.

per year of labor for wages to be paid at the going rate. The new laws applied to a wide swath of people, ranging from agricultural laborers who had not completed their obligations as outlined in their contracts to beggars on the street and students who did not attend class regularly. Agricultural laborers were also required to carry a *libreta*, in which employers noted the number of days each individual worked for wages. Police agents were empowered to detain men to review their libretas. If the person had not worked the required quota of days, a judge sentenced him to jail for thirty days. Departmental governors and intendentes, however, often assigned vagrants to work for coffee planters.[34] In practice, the vagrancy law replicated rather than replaced mandamientos. It also created incentives for poor Mayas and ladinos to seek contracts with agricultural plantations rather than be subject to vagrancy charges. Indirectly and directly, the vagrancy law transferred control over labor acquisition from coffee planters to the state.

Newspapers heralded Ubico's abolition of debt peonage as the end of slavery in Guatemala and the nation's emergence from the dark ages, even while it represented vagrants as a new class of social deviants. Ubico himself claimed that he had "rescued [the Indians] from slavery."[35] Regional newspapers declared that the new law would lead to the "emancipation of workers" as the state had finally brought an end to "the hateful inheritance of the past that is the slavery in which people labored for the good of all."[36] Likewise, the vagrancy law appeared to be proof that the state was taking a more active role in civilizing the population by instilling in them the custom of hard work. The vagrancy laws, local editorialists declared, would usher in a new class of laborers who would "be freed from the jail of their customs, forgetting the habit of fraud and the marked indolence that has characterized the majority of Indian workers."[37] As ladinos and state officials narrated the vagrancy law within the liberal–democratic metanarrative, they often overlooked the fact that all Guatemalans still had a duty to promote national progress via their labor, capital, or other investments. Labor in Guatemala was not free – at least not in the sense demanded by José Angel Icó and other Q'eqchi's and ladino allies. Indeed, Ubico's vagrancy law relegated many

---

[34] SPCM 1938, "Ignacio Valiente al JP de Alta Verapaz," March 29, 1937.

[35] Victor Bulmer-Thomas, "La crisis de la economía de agroexportación (1930–1945)," in *Historia general de Centroamérica, vol. 4: Las repúblicas agroexportadoras*, ed. Víctor Hugo Acuña Ortega (Madrid: FLASCO, 1993), 367.

[36] "La redención de trabajador," *El Norte*, May 12, 1934.

[37] "La redención de trabajador," *El Norte*, May 12, 1934.

Guatemalans to the criminalized category of nonproductive subjects and social deviants. They were cast as a racialized disease in the body politic. "We know all too well that the vagrant is a harmful parasite," declared one newspaper editorialist.[38] Vagrancy was the opposite of modern citizenship. The law quantified and measured this social deviance according to the principles of abstract labor time plotted in the number of days worked or not worked, and subject to state intervention. The vagrancy law thus brought together the emancipatory promise of the liberal–democratic metanarrative (heralding the end of slavery) and the disciplinary force of the civilizing metanarrative (denouncing vagrants as noncitizens).

While Guatemala's vagrancy law applied to all Guatemalans regardless of race, court cases show that the overwhelming majority of people charged with vagrancy were Mayas, and the records themselves demonstrate how the law's application produced racialized distinctions. Between 1936 and 1940, only eleven vagrancy cases out of 190 were filed against individuals with recognizably non-Maya names.[39] A sampling of vagrancy cases also illustrates how police officers racialized lower-class Mayas as vagrants. On February 2, 1938, as Esteban Caliz Coc was returning home after working a plot of land, he passed through the city where a police officer grabbed him and forcibly took Caliz's machete and his mecapal, which he was using to carry wood. The arresting officer, a ladino originally from Antigua by the name of Antonio Castillo, put him in jail to await a hearing with the local judge.[40] The exceptions also seem to prove the rule. In 1938 Jorge Schambach Schabel, a seventy-one-year-old German immigrant, was charged with vagrancy for not caring a libreto even though he a well-known accountant for German firms in San Pedro Carchá. The judge handling his case noted that "taking into account his age, as well as his honorability, he cannot be defined as a vagrant."[41] Ladino and Q'eqchi'–German police officers' decisions to stop some individuals and not others established a set of shifting visual codes of conduct and appearance by which race and class was evaluated.

If the vagrancy law extended the authority of the state and created agreed-on norms to evaluate racial ascriptions of laziness, the courts also generated a space for those persecuted as vagrants to fight back. Like the marginalized urban poor under Manuel Estrada Cabrera, individuals charged with vagrancy frequently used the courts to reclaim their

[38] "Persiguiendo la vagancia," *El Norte*, June 12, 1937.   [39] AGCA J-AV Índice 105
[40] AGCA J-AV 105 Leg. 39 Exp. 40.   [41] AGCA J-AV 105 Leg. 39 "G" Exp. 9 1938.

honorability and masculinity. When questioned by the judge, Esteban Caliz Coc claimed that he had just left work on a plantation in Panzós, where he had caught malaria, and was returning to Carchá to work as a servant, the job he normally occupied. Caliz was released and freed of charges, having successfully defended himself – and thus his honorability and status – against the charge of vagrancy.[42] At times, the men contested the association between Mayas and unproductive labor, and could have their sentences reduced or waived altogether.[43] The public performances involved in the persecution of vagrancy thus both produced racial and class criteria and enabled some to contest charges of vagrancy and their status as criminals.

Despite Ubico's efforts to centralize power, extend the state's tentacles, and stamp out corruption, the new vagrancy law was imperfectly applied as local state officials resisted central orders and coffee planters adapted the law to the laborers' demands. William Dieseldorff complained that "the persecution of vagrancy among workers is without a doubt one of the most assured methods of supporting agriculture, but it is clear that there exist anomalies and tendencies to circumvent the law." Dieseldorff pointed out that laborers "filled [their libretas] with imaginary work through whatever form of remuneration."[44] Despite oversight by an intendente, local officials granted libretas to small-scale vendors and Maya peasants who did not legally qualify.[45] Given such practices, we might surmise that these local officials did not believe that small-scale vendors and subsistence producers were social deviants requiring state coercion. In their actions, municipal officials instead demonstrated a tenacious desire to protect rural Mayas from the disruptions that forced labor brought to rural communities, much as their nineteenth-century counterparts had done. Despite decades of the gradual erosion of Q'eqchi' patriarchal reciprocity, municipal officials still sought to reproduce those norms even if their actions violated the law.

Coffee planters and state officials also discovered that Q'eqchi's still frequently required wage advances to pay for any number of expenses ranging from family emergencies to contributions to the annual saint's day festivities. Courts, however, refused to uphold long-term debts, in effect

---

[42] AGCA J-AV 105 Leg. 39 Exp. 40.

[43] See, for example, AGCA J-AV 105 Leg. 39 Exp. 40.

[44] CM Est. 2 Paq. 19 Exp. 11, "W. E. Dieseldorff al Intendente," Cobán, June 3, 1943.

[45] SPCM 1938, telegrama oficial, 18 de febrero de 1938; see also "Los jornaleros," *El Norte*, June 5, 1937.

limiting wage advances to what could be worked off in a single season.[46] If smaller wage advances were insufficient, coffee planters changed the name of the advance from *habilitación* (wage advance) to *prestamo* (loan) in their ledgers.[47] In reality, however, most rural laborers would have no other means to pay off their loans than through their labor, thus creating a new cycle of debt peonage. This created an additional risk for coffee planters, since the state rarely recognized debts if the worker fled. As a result, sometimes worker requests for wage advances were denied. In 1938, for example, William Dieseldorff responded to a request for a wage advance with: "We no longer provide habilitaciones."[48]

The territorial expansion of the state apparatus under Ubico meant fundamentally different things to different social classes. While coffee planters experienced an erosion of their sovereignty, and Q'eqchi' patriarchs were further marginalized from municipal councils, workers and mothers may have gained new access to a paternalistic populist who was willing to intervene on their behalf.[49] Ubico's legislation also helped generate a labor market, and workers regularly pressed coffee planters for increased wages and won. For some aspirational ladinos and Q'eqchi'–Germans, the expanding state offered new forms of employment that allowed them to face down racisms and claim a place in the march of progress. To overcome their troubled racial heritage, social-climbing ladinos, Q'eqchi' patriarchs, and Q'eqchi'–Germans also celebrated symbols of modernity, including new roads, electricity and public lighting, and the arrival of the telegraph. New positions available within the state helped these social climbers participate in state-directed modernization, thus representing themselves as agents of history. Just as urban modernization under Manuel Estrada Cabrera had been both disciplining and empowering, so too were state-directed rural modernization efforts in the 1930s. Ladino newspaper editorialists also helped produce, for the reading public, a new time for the nation defined by progressive advancement as they catalogued, narrated, and celebrated the region's progress.

---

[46] McCreery, *Rural Guatemala*, 316.

[47] SPCM 1938, "Telegrama oficial 18 de febrero 1938"; SPCM 1938, "Al JP de Ignacio Valiente," March 29, 1937; SPCM 1938, "Circular a los propietarios, administradores, o representantes de las fincas del municipio."

[48] TULAL Dieseldorff Collection Unbound Finca records, Folder 27, "Sr. don Jacobo Viadex, Raxaha de WED," June 2, 1938.

[49] Julie Gibbings, "Progressive Mothers, Populist Politics: Eugenics, Race, and Progress during Jorge Ubico's Guatemala," paper presented at Latin American Studies Association annual conference, Boston, May 2019.

Sometimes state modernization efforts resulted in meaningful change for a wide swath of Altaverapacences, even though those symbols of national development likely meant very different things to different social sectors. In 1938 a major highway linked Cobán to Guatemala City via Salamá for the first time, resulting in a significant reduction in travel time to the capital. A number of smaller roads were also built. By 1943 Guatemalans had quintupled the reach of their road system and constructed 10,200 kilometers of roads, bridges, and tunnels.[50] These roads helped facilitate the expansion of trade among a variety of classes. For itinerant vendors, coffee planters, and middle-class professionals, the experience of traveling on new roads may very well have confirmed their belief that Guatemala was marching toward a destined future. We can surmise that others might have privately lamented how roads also facilitated the extension of the state into the countryside. For the poor Q'eqchi' and ladino laborers, who undertook the arduous and unpaid labor of road construction, the new roads might have also symbolized a different kind of modernity that was defined not by mobility and commerce but by ongoing coerced labor. For others, Ubico's reforms failed to address the root of poverty and exploitation. In 1934 Adrian Zelaya, a teacher at Cobán's premier private school Pedro Nufio, penned a strongly worded essay entitled "Renewal." Zelaya condemned German commercial dominance and declared that the time had come to end "the slaughter of commercial slavery that every year closes in more on the children of the nation." Repurposing the anti-slavery liberal–democratic metanarrative for anticolonial ends, Zelaya proposed that Guatemala reclaim its national riches.[51] Zelaya's essay reveals the growing tensions among Altaverapacences over perceived German imperialism and the hardening of racialized and national boundaries between Guatemalans and Germans.

POLICING MODERNITY: DRINKING, PROSTITUTION, SHAMANISM, AND OTHER CRIMES

Municipal archives themselves are a testament to Guatemala's incredible state expansion across the 1930s. In addition to booklets full of telegraphs, daily reports fill Cobán's municipal archive detailing everything from the names of guests at local establishments and private homes, the

---

[50] Grieb, *Guatemalan Caudillo*, 35.
[51] CM Est. 1 Paq. 6, "Renovación por Adrian Zelaya," Cobán, June 29, 1934.

vehicle registration numbers of automobiles entering and leaving the town, the number and causes of arrests made, the quantity of *aguardiente* (sugarcane liquor) produced in the state-run distilleries, the state of municipal finances, and even, on occasion, the number of stray dogs destroyed.[52] As these records suggest, state expansion materialized, directly and indirectly, through the National Police.[53] Local police officers were deployed to enforce the program of public works, and the Department of Labor was transferred to the general management of the police. While the National Police, particularly its criminal investigation police, violently repressed political opposition to the regime, most police operations occurred through a network of collaborators that included telegraph and post office workers, taxi and bus drivers, office workers, sanitation officials, and prominent citizens. Local sanitation officers, for example, provided reports to the National Police on the social relations, habits, and customs of individuals on request.[54] Some have estimated that by the end of Ubico's regime in 1944, one in every ten citizens had acted as spies for the government.[55] Rather than simply repressing the population, the state's police apparatus incorporated nearly everyone into a system of discipline and surveillance of social deviants, including vagrants, prostitutes, shamans, and boj producers, all of whom were perceived as threats to modernity.

Since Ubico emphasized turning delinquents into disciplined workers, local state officials were charged with eradicating one particularly troublesome practice that imperiled worker health: the production and consumption of boj. The vagrancy law included articles prohibiting the production and sale of spirits, activities that had hitherto been largely beyond the control of the state. Under Ubico, then, the state persecuted clandestine alcohol production not only to increase state coffers but also

---

[52] These reports are found in the JP records; see, for example, AGCA JP-AV 1939 Paq. 2, "Señor JP Departmental, Oficio No. 12, del Comisionario de la Policía Nacional," Cobán, January 8, 1939.

[53] Stefan Karlen, "Orden y progreso en el gobierno de Ubico: Realidad o mito?," in *Historia general de Guatemala, vol. 5: Época contemporánea: 1898–1944*, ed. Jorge Luján Muñoz and J. Daniel Contreras R. (Guatemala: Asociación Amigos del País, 1996), 70; and Stefan Karlen, *Paz, Progreso, Justicia y Honradez: Das Ubico-Regime in Guatemala, 1931–1944* (Stuttgart: F. Steiner, 1991).

[54] See, for example, CM Exp1 Paq. 6, "Intendente Municipal del Comisaria de la Policía Nacional, referente a investigar acerca de las relaciones sociales, vida y costumbres de TOMASA TOC CHUB," oficio 260, Cobán, February 13, 1942; and Karlen, "Orden y progreso en el gobierno de Ubico," 68.

[55] Karlen, "Orden y progreso en el gobierno de Ubico," 62–70.

to combat the vice of alcohol consumption and the racial degeneration it supposedly produced. Boj, the traditional corn liquor of Mayas, was associated with all that was nonmodern and was said to have particularly deleterious effects. The National Police commissioner in Alta Verapaz noted, "Boj is the preferred beverage of the indigenous which makes them impulsive, leading them in all cases to madness or crime. Experience and statistical evidence in this Department have shown us that all the criminal acts which occur in the jurisdiction are committed by Indians under the influence of boj and not under the influence of state-produced aguardiente. From this we deduce that this primitive ferment produces enormous mental upheavals in those who imbibe it, and due to this we constantly have to remit a good number of indigenous addicts of this nefarious beverage to the asylum."[56] Alcoholism, Guatemalan scientists had long argued, resulted in a host of physical illnesses and social ills that imperiled one's racial makeup – genetic degeneration, insanity and mental defects, epilepsy, tuberculosis, criminality, and spreading venereal disease. "Alcoholism of *el indio*," explained one scientist, "is a national danger against which we must fight; ignorant and inebriated, the indigenous worker represents a social asset that is constantly declining, which constitutes a true threat to our agricultural riches and to our national progress."[57]

Unable to pay the fees and dependent on income from boj, marginalized Q'eqchi's routinely disregarded the law. If court registers are any indication, local judiciaries, jails, and municipal offices must have overflowed with Mayas arrested, sentenced, and jailed for illegal production of alcohol. In 1935 the police announced to the public a new crackdown on clandestine boj production, declaring that those arrested would be sent to the treacherous lowlands around Panzós, where the men would work on building a road and the women would work in the camp.[58] Despite harsh penalties, arrests continued to be reported as late as 1940. In addition to persecuting boj producers, the police also attacked public drunkenness. Police reports included an astounding array of drunkenness categories for which people were arrested, including "scandalously drunk," "habitually drunk," "helplessly drunk," and "falling-down drunk," all of which corresponded with different degrees of racial

---

[56] AGCA JP-AV 1938 Paq. 2, "Memoria de la Policía Nacional," December 8, 1938; see also "Contra los defraudadores," *El Norte*, September 7, 1935.

[57] Dr. Poitevin, "El alcoholismo y la higiene social," *Boletín Sanitaria* 2–4 (1929): 62.

[58] "Contra los defraudadores," *El Norte*, September 7, 1935.

degeneration and potential for criminality.[59] Like individuals charged with vagrancy, boj producers often recast their incrimination in terms of their poverty. Women appealed to gendered discourses about their crucial role as responsible mothers who cared for the needs of their children and thus the future of the nation.[60] When local judges listened to these appeals and reduced sentences, the system of courts and police officers incorporated the demands of even those it criminialized and thus helped to produce the feeling that justice had been served.[61] Even as the state criminalized the poor and all those it deemed to be insufficiently modern, the expansion of the police and courts served to bolster rather than diminish state legitimacy in the countryside. Thus while in 1865, changes to liquor regulation and labor laws helped to provoke Yat's rebellion, the 1930s witnessed the expansion of the state without a similar revolt in the countryside.

Local police officers also pursued prostitutes and indigenous shamans, whom the government deemed to be dangerous to the health and welfare of the nation.[62] Prostitution raised the specter of venereal disease, which threatened to imperil national progress and racial improvement. Jorge Ubico reminded local authorities, "I do not need to remind you of the importance of studying this legislation [on sexual prophylaxis and venereal disease] in order to be able to cooperate with the Supreme Government in the actualization of this important work of social evolution that proposes the persecution of venereal disease and the moral and economic elevation of the young women who have fallen into commercial sex."[63] This, he argued, was central to the great national project "in favor of the

---

[59] Rachel Sieder, "Paz, progreso, justicia, y honradez: Law and Citizenship in Alta Verapaz during the Regime of Jorge Ubico," *Bulletin of Latin American Research* (2000): 283–302.

[60] Gibbings, "Progressive Mothers, Populist Politics"; David Carey Jr., *I Ask for Justice: Maya Women, Dictators, and Crime in Guatemala, 1898–1944* (Austin: University of Texas Press, 2013), 58.

[61] Carey, *I Ask for Justice*, 61.

[62] "Medida profiláctica," *El Norte*, September 26, 1936; "La obra de profilaxis," *El Norte*, October 10, 1936; Nancy Leys Stepan, *"The Hour of Eugenics": Race, Gender, and Nation in Latin America* (Ithaca, NY: Cornell University Press, 1991). On campaigns to regulate prostitution, see Natalia Milanesio, "Redefining Men's Sexuality, Resignifying Male Bodies: The Argentine Law of Anti-Venereal Prophylaxis, 1936," *Gender and History* 17, no. 2 (2005): 463–91; and Katherine Bliss, "The Science of Redemption: Syphilis, Sexual Promiscuity and Reformism in Revolutionary Mexico," *Hispanic American Historical Review* 79, no. 1 (1999): 1–40.

[63] CM Est.1 Paq. 6, "Circular a los señores JPs, Comandantes de Puertos, médicos Departamentales, y Intendentes Municipales," July 30, 1938.

preservation of health and the improvement of the race of Guatemalans."[64] Arrests were often made on nothing more than rumors. Cristina
Sierra was captured in her parents' home in San Pedro Carchá, on November 9, 1936, and taken to the hospital for testing and isolation, because
sanitation officials had received "reports in respect to her conduct."[65] By
1936 venereal disease had become such a "grave social danger" that the
National Police took control of the hospital's newly constructed isolation
wing. The presence of the National Police, contended the departmental
governor, would have "practical benefits for the indigenous class."[66]
Editorials in *El Norte* applauded the efforts of the police to clean the
streets, noting that "while such methods seem drastic, they are completely
necessary and urgent in their application in order to save the pueblo from
the contamination that is a harmful and pernicious threat since it causes
the degeneration of people."[67] In addition to rounding up suspicious
women, police officers "cleaned" the streets of the mentally ill and dis-
abled. Juan Chun, Matilde Cu, Rosa Cuc, Vicenta Maquin, Eusebio Xol,
Julian Teyul, Miguel Gutierrez, and Valeriano Chavarría were captured
and sent to the insane asylum in Guatemala City.[68]

Emboldened by thinly veiled descriptions of Maya culture as unsanitary
and antisocial, and fearful of the deleterious effects of non-Western medicine, local police and sanitation officers also cracked down on Q'eqchi'
curanderos (shamans) and other so-called dangerous individuals who
threatened the health of the public with their superstitious practices. By
definition, the superstitious were not modern, and irrational practices were
associated with barbaric people and semicivilized places. In 1937 the
National Police director H. Ordoñez underscored the campaign against
Maya shamanism and witchcraft by asserting that "superstition ... principally occurs in the least civilized regions."[69] For police and sanitation
officers as well as medical doctors, shamanism constituted an anachronistic
threat to the nation. Such fears easily bled into fantastical representations

---

[64] Ibid. For earlier campagins, see also "Celo que aplaudimos," *El Norte*, December
22, 1934.
[65] AGCA JP-AV 1936 Paq. 3, "JP del Hospital del Norte," Cobán, November 9, 1936, and
"JP del Hospital del Norte," November 16, 1936.
[66] AGCA JP-AV 1936 Paq. 5, "Al Director General de Sanidad Pública Guatemala, del JP,"
October 6, 1936; and AGCA JP-AV 1936 Paq. 7, "Al Director General de Sanidad
Pública del JP, informe sobre la profilaxis sexual," October 2, 1936.
[67] "La obra de profilaxis," *El Norte*, October 10, 1936.
[68] AGCA JP-AV 1936, "Al Director General del Asilo de Alienados del Hospital del Norte,"
August 21, 1936.
[69] Carey, *I Ask for Justice*, 53.

of political and other threats to public safety. Teodoro Caal Tot, for example, was investigated under the pretext of "having established a pact with el Duende and other spirits" to threaten his "unsuspecting neighbors."[70]

In Alta Verapaz, however, coffee planters like Erwin Paul Dieseldorff had long relied on Maya shamans to provide medicine for plantation workers, and non-Maya Altaverapacences also visited Maya shamans. While Guatemalan medical doctors and scientists, including Dieseldorff, were interested in studying Maya herbal remedies as potential sources of knowledge for new medicines, most believed that without scientific backing and in the hands of Maya shamans such remedies were dangerous to public health.[71] While it is possible that Maya shaman also drew on scientific medicine and Mayas likely visited medical doctors, the two-way exchange of medical knowledge and practice is largely absent from the archival record.[72] Like individuals charged with vagrancy and boj production, shamans fought back. In 1933 a sanitation judge charged Domingo Chub Chun with practicing as a curandero in his treatment of the now-deceased ladina María Mencos Valizón.[73] Dionisio Chub confessed: "For many years, without being able to say precisely how many, I have been curandero and as such I go where I am called to cure with grasses and herbs as they are called. Sometimes my patients get better and at other times they die as a consequence of the severity of their pain." Chub stated that María Mencos Valizón had called on his services twice, and that he had given her water containing leaves of a plant known as "Perec-max," in addition to plastering her forehead with the same leaf. For Chub's services, María's mother had paid one quetzal. Proud of his locally esteemed profession, Chub declared that "many people in Carchá know him as [a curandero] and he is highly sought after."[74] Chub refused to submit that his profession as a shaman – an anathema to modern medicine and national progress – belonged to the past. Much like the

---

[70] "El duende" refers to a woodland spirit or elf, but its actual meaning also includes notions of possession or being overcome with emotion, the feeling of getting chills for example. AGCA JP-1939 Paq. 2, "Al JP y Comandante de Armas, del Comandante de la Policía Rural Montada, Se remita una escopeta," December 5, 1939.

[71] "Estudio y utilización de las plantas medicinales del istmo," *El Imparcial*, November 19, 1936; Erwin Paul Dieseldorff, "Aliviando a los enfermos: En sus propios lugares aún distantes," *El Imparcial*, May 2, 1936

[72] David Carey Jr., "The Politics and Culture of Medicine and Disease in Central America," in *Oxford Research Encyclopedia of Latin American History* (New York: Oxford University Press, 2019).

[73] AGCA B Leg. 30792 Exp. 11 1934.   [74] Ibid.

persecution of vagrancy, criminalizing shamans racialized Q'eqchi' cultural practices and excluded them from legitimate participation in the national progress, even while the court cases illustrate how marginalized people subject to state power redeployed popular notions of justice, progress, and the health and welfare of the nation to claim a place in the present.[75]

If marginalized actors targeted by state actions sought to reclaim their honor, the police and sanitation officers who persecuted them, too, used their positions to participate in a drive for progress. New, low-level positions in the state system were often occupied by an aspiring middle class. Q'eqchi'–Germans, privileged for their role in the national mestizaje project and ideal intermediaries who could move between social classes, often took these positions. Domingo Winter Tot was one of three rural mounted police, and Victoriano Yat Wellmann was the sergeant in charge of roads in Chahal.[76] Through their participation in the state, these aspiring ladinos and Q'eqchi'–Germans found elevated positions of respect and authority. Riding a horse and wearing a uniform – in contrast to alcaldes auxiliares, who wore traditional Q'eqchi' dress and traveled on foot – were a means of status-marking.[77] For Q'eqchi'–Germans and ladinos, participation in the police apparatus was a means of facing down racism and the stereotypes of laziness, moral corruption, and effeminacy associated with racial mixture.[78] Police and sanitation officers, like militiamen elsewhere, pronounced their status as orderly and manly, superior to Q'eqchi' plantation laborers or even alcaldes auxiliares who policed the plantations.

The magazine *La Gaceta: Revista de la Policía y Variedades* often published cases such as Dionisio Chub's and helped shape images of criminals as racialized others and a menace to modernity. The magazine not only had editorials preaching social morals and knowledge about infectious diseases and sanitation but also had a special section entitled

---

[75] Alejandra Bronfman, *Measures of Equality: Social Science, Citizenship and Race in Cuba, 1902–1940* (Chapel Hill: University of North Carolina Press, 2004), 95–106. For medical opinions against curanderos, see "Clame contra el curanderismo en el Congreso Sanitario," *Boletín Sanitaria* 46 (January–December 1938): 530–1.

[76] AGCA, JP-AV 1939 Paq. 2, "La policía rural montada," January 8, 1939; AGCA, JP-AV 939 Paq. 3, "Cuerpo militar de caminos," November 18, 1939.

[77] On police uniforms, see *Ordenanza de la Policía Nacional de la República de Guatemala* (Guatemala: Tipografía Nacional, 1925), 4–5.

[78] On identities as racially improved, see Julie Gibbings, "Mestizaje in the Age of Fascism: German and Q'eqchi' Maya Interracial Unions in Alta Verapaz, Guatemala," *German History* 34, no. 2 (2016): 214–36.

"Archives of Delinquency." These archives featured vagrants, shamans, prostitutes, witches, and other petty criminals captured by the National Police. The criminals' photographs staged them as true threats to health, morality, and social order: they wore worn-out clothing, their faces were scowling and dirty. The detailed accounts of their crimes reinforced this imagery. Criminal cases were frequently recounted in a tabloid-like fashion, in exaggerated, scandalous language.[79] These sensationalist accounts of criminals were followed by articles penned by doctors, police officers, and scientists regarding the evils of shamanism, sexual laxity, and improper hygiene.[80] If the act of reading national, regional, and international events in newspapers, as Benedict Anderson argued, delivers a fantasy of "simultaneous consumption" in a collective present, then the role of tabloids like La Gaceta was not to create the homogenous time of the modern nation. Rather, La Gaceta helped split national time into the time of archaic, dangerous customs practiced by darker races, and that of the modern readership. As such, this tabloid newspaper not only bound a collective readership together in thrilling and sensationalist accounts of supernatural menaces and social deviancy, but also exemplified perceived differences among distinct social classes in Guatemala. The reading public was purportedly kept apart by taste and cultivation, on the one hand, and dangerous gullibility and sensationalism, on the other. Tabloid newspapers thus encoded a new politics of postponement that relegated Mayas not simply to the past but to the dangerous past of the supernatural and socially deviant. Mayas, in this form of postponement, were alien to modernity.

LOS SECRETOS DE LA RAZA: GERMAN AND LADINO APPROPRIATIONS OF MAYA CULTURE

While for some state officials and medical doctors, Maya medicine represented a threat to national health and safety, for other ladinos and

---

[79] "Archivo de la delincuencia: Curanderismo, brujerías y otros timos, que bajo la capa de asistir enfermos, se venían registrando en un cubil de la 3ª Avenida de Chinautla," *La Gaceta: Revista de Policía y Variedades*, 17, Año XIX, No. 7, February 19, 1939, 325–7.

[80] "La Policía Nacional en su labor científica de profilaxis social," *La Gaceta de la Policía*, August 16, 1936, 2016–17; "El peligro de los curanderos," *La Gaceta de la Policía*, August 16, 1936, 2044; "El criminal instintivo," *La Gaceta de la Policía*, August 23, 1936, 2063; "Lecturas para la agente de la policía: Moralidad y disciplina," *La Gaceta de la Policía*, August 23, 1936, 2097; and "La vagancia es rémora para el progreso," *La Gaceta de la Policía*, March 12, 1939, 1.

Germans, Maya medicine was both a repository of secrets to be mined for commercialization and an enduring tradition to be possessed as evidence of one's own modernity. If the *Gaceta de Guatemala* represented the splitting of national time into the archaic and racially darkened time of Mayas, and that of the modern-citizen readership, then ladino and German appropriations of Maya culture reconciled time by reintegrating a sanitized version of Maya culture into an authentic and timeless landscape. Despite positive celebrations of Maya cultural artifacts, ladinos and Germans situated contemporary Maya culture within the civilizing metanarrative as a relic of the past – as a set of cultural practices doomed to vanish in modernity's forward march. The decontaminated account of Maya culture, then, became a battleground as Germans, ladinos, and Q'eqchi' patriarchs struggled over claims to authority and presence in Alta Verapaz.

While German settlers in Alta Verapaz had studied Maya language, culture, and history since the late nineteenth century, Altaverapacence ladinos also began studying regional Maya culture in the 1930s as part of broader efforts to define a regional, Altaverapacence identity. In 1931 Emilio Rosales Ponce, the longtime editor of *El Norte*, published *Secretos de la raza: creencias, costumbres, medicina y supersticiones de los indígenas de la Alta Verapaz* (The Secrets of the Race: Beliefs, Customs, Medicine, and Superstitions of the Indians). In his book, Ponce sought to "conserve" in written form a "contingent of curious legends for national folklore" and create an enduring record of a culture doomed to vanish with modernity. "If each region of the nation was able to recover these relics of the primitive race, which tend to disappear with the invasion of modern ideas," Ponce wrote, "it would be a labor equally patriotic and important for the annals of history, since customs vary greatly across regions and are worthy of being copied in living books so that future generations may know about them."[81] Filled with curious legends, folkloric tales, and medicinal cures, Ponce must have culled the material from conversations with Q'eqchi's, but nowhere does he reference where he gathered the evidence for his book. Instead, Maya knowledge and practices appear disembodied and timeless, as if they emerged from the landscape itself and thus were available for possession by ladinos. Ponce's appropriation mirrored the Guatemalan ladino tradition of dressing up in Maya clothing during the annual celebrations of the Virgin of

---

[81] Mario Selis Lope, *Secretos de la raza: creencias, costumbres, medicina y supersticiones de los indígenas de la Verapaz* (Cobán, A: Tipografía "El Norte," 1931), 1.

Guadalupe.[82] During these festivities, ladinos across the nation disguised themselves as Mayas, allowing ladinos a temporary ethnicization while also distinguishing them from the darkened masses. A similar dynamic can be found among other middle- and upper-class individuals across Latin America, who included within their cultural repertoires elements that they identified with the lower-class, darker-skinned masses. These cultural appropriations often involved resignifying elements, mystifying their origins, and repositioning them within racial hierarchies so that, for example, Argentine and Uruguayan tango, Brazilian samba, Colombian cumbia, and Cuban rumba were nationalized.[83] Possession of cultural others thus strengthened rather than weakened racial hierarchies. In Guatemala, dressing up as Maya helped some ladinos confirm their cultural, racial, and temporal distance from Mayas. In Alta Verapaz, these cultural appropriations legitimated ladino possession not only of Maya culture but of their place in Alta Verapaz as true bearers of progress.

As anti-German nationalism surged among Altaverapacence ladinos, German–Guatemalan coffee planters needed to transform their presence in the region from foreign usurpers to naturalized inhabitants. As they had in the past, Germans relied on ethnographic knowledge and practices to stage their affinity with Maya culture and history, and naturalize their possession of land and laborers.[84] While most of these studies focused on archaeology, language, and history, Erwin Paul Dieseldorff also studied Maya medicine with the Q'eqchi' shaman Félix Cucul, and applied Cucul's cures on his plantations.[85] In the 1930s, Dieseldorff engaged in

---

[82] Arturo Taracena Arriola, *Guadalupanismo en Guatemala: Culto mariano y subalternidad étnica* (Mérida: Universidad Nacional Autónoma de México, 2008).

[83] De la Cadena, *Indigenous Mestizos*. On the appropriation of popular culture, particularly of dance, the literature is large and expanding. See, for example, Peter Wade, *Music, Race, and Nation: Música Tropical in Colombia* (Chicago: University of Chicago Press, 2000); John Charles Chasteen, *National Rhythms, African Roots: The Deep History of Latin American Popular Dance* (Albuquerque: University of New Mexico Press, 2004); Marc A. Hertzman, *Making Samba: A New History of Race and Music in Brazil* (Durham, NC: Duke University Press, 2013).

[84] For a more detailed examination of German ethnographers, see Julie Gibbings, "'Their debts follow them into the afterlife': German Settlers, Ethnographic Knowledge, and the Forging of Coffee Capitalism in Nineteenth-Century Guatemala," *Comparative Studies in Society and History* 62, no. 2 (April 2020): 389–420.

[85] See Erwin Paul Dieseldorff, *Las plantas medicinales del Departamento de Alta Verapaz* (Guatemala, 1940); Erwin Paul Dieseldorff, "Sida rhombifolia," *La Juventud Médica*, no. 197 (October 15, 1919): 153–6; "Statement Made by Erwin P. Dieseldorff," March 22, 1935, DC Medicinal Plants Papers; Guillermo Nañez Falcón, "Erwin Paul Dieseldorff," 73–9.

FIGURE 7.1 Two indigenous men from Alta Verapaz.
Courtesy of Colección Hermann Heinemann, CIRMA

a more systematic study of Maya medical plants with the assistance of a German administrator-cum–Q'eqchi' linguist, Paul Wirsing. Shamans were also a great source of interest for German settlers, who used exotic representations of Mayas to naturalize their presence as foreigners in the region. The German coffee planter Herman Heinemann staged several ethnographic-style photographs of Maya shamans that allowed him and other viewers to possess Maya culture. For example, the photograph shown in Figure 7.1 had the following typed description: "2 medicine men in front of the hut. They belong to the esteemed caste of wizards, herbalists and fortune-tellers." These men were, of course, Q'eqchi' shamans, who were not only medical healers (herbalists and wizards) but also daykeepers (diviners) who tended to the Maya calendar. Q'eqchi' shamans, however, were rendered as mere fortune-tellers who belonged to a class of social deviants and charlatans, or simply curiosities. Resignifying these practices as mere superstitions, Heineman relegated the Q'eqchi' men of this "esteemed class" to an anachronistic past that was outside modern reason, science, and historical time directed by human agents. Like other ethnographic photographs, the Q'eqchi' men were subjected to an outside gaze, while being placed within their seemingly naturalized habitat. Through ethnographic staging, Mayas were rendered as a timeless culture ready for possession by foreign observers. In possessing this authenticity, German settlers naturalized their own presence in a foreign land. Ladino and German efforts to possess Maya culture, however, directly threatened Q'eqchi' patriarchs, who increasingly understood themselves to be guardians of Maya culture.

In the 1930s, Q'eqchi' patriarchs also wrote their own ethnographies and catalogues of Maya medicine and culture. Unlike the works of ladinos and Germans, Q'eqchi' writings are not preserved in national or even regional libraries, but in faint archival traces that can easily be overlooked. By reading along and against the grain of German and ladino ethnographies, Q'eqchi' ethnographic writings emerge as a largely unacknowledged body of knowledge that ladinos and Germans accessed to write their own accounts and stage their own expertise. Antonio Goubaud Carrera, a young Guatemalan anthropologist living in San Juan Chamelco in the late 1930s, briefly mentions Tiburcio Caal's ethnographic writings in his own field notes.[86] At times, the appropriation of Maya knowledge angered Q'eqchi' patriarchs, who understood the political stakes. In an angry letter, Domingo Caal, for example, charged Erwin Paul Dieseldorff with stealing Maya knowledge and customs. In his accusation, he noted how he, too, had written about medicinal plants, and indigenous language and customs. Even more, Caal had imagined a world in which Q'eqchi's would write Cobán's history.[87] Caal likely also knew that Maya medicine was more than just a highly fought-over cultural symbol of authenticity and belonging. It was also a new frontier in the commodification of indigenous knowledge. In 1939 Ubico's government published Dieseldorff's study, and the following year Ubico requested that all municipalities provide samples and seeds of local medicinal plants, since the government was interested in "growing them on a large scale for export."[88] While some Q'eqchi's may felt validated by state and German interest in Maya medicine, others, like Domingo Caal, were likely angered by these appropriations. Ladino, German, and Q'eqchi'

---

[86] Goubaud Carrera, "Notes on San Juan Chamelco, Alta Verapaz," 75.

[87] See, especially, TULAL DC Maya Papers Box 148, "Domingo Caal to Erwin Paul Dieseldorff," December 27, 1926.

[88] For Dieseldorff's field notes on medicinal plants, see TULAL DC Box 161. See also Náñez Falcón, "Erwin Paul Dieseldorff," 74, and *El Norte*, July 25, 1926. Dieseldorff also created a private institute to study *sida rhombifolia*, known as mesbé, in Berlin in 1913. While Maya shamans rarely used mesbé, Dieseldorff argued it relieved chronic bronchitis and tuberculosis. Partly because of World War I, the Mesbé Institute ceased operation in 1919 when Dieseldorff left Germany for Guatemala. CM Est. 3 Paq. 16 Exp. 2, "Plantas medicinales en el municipio," 1940; and Dieseldorff, *Las plantas medicinales*. For Dieseldorff's field notes on medicinal plants, see TULAL DC Box 161; for his correspondence, see Boxes 160 and 162.

struggles over the possession of Maya culture took place within a broader context of competing nationalisms vying for the region, and exploded with particular fervor around the 400th anniversary of Alta Verapaz's so-called peaceful conquest.

BETWEEN LITTLE GERMANY AND TEZULUTLÁN: GERMAN NATIONAL SOCIALISM AND ANTI-IMPERIALISM IN ALTA VERAPAZ

By the mid-1930s, Guatemala had made a startling recovery from the worst effects of the Great Depression: the nation's gross domestic product had not only well surpassed its Great Depression nadir in 1932, but had also well exceeded pre-1929 levels.[89] Ubico had invigorated the nation with dreams of modernization and popular justice, centralized power in the president, and enlarged the state; he had stabilized the government's finances, averted bankruptcy and economic collapse, and eliminated political agitators. But the conditions that had enabled Ubico's populism – the economic crisis of 1929 and the political crisis stemming from the Central American Red Scare – had also evaporated. As his popularity waned between 1936 and 1940, Ubico cracked down on dissent, removed departmental governors from posts, and tightened press censorship.[90] Even his annual inspection trips to the countryside became less tours to address popular grievances than choreographed celebrations of Ubico himself.[91] To bolster his waning popularity, Ubico staged elaborate departmental and national fairs in honor of economic modernization and the nation's great regional diversity.[92] Alta Verapaz, however, also bustled with heightened nationalisms. By the mid-1930s, Nazi Party membership was growing, particularly among a younger generation of Germans who settled in Guatemala after World War I.[93] In response, Altaverapacence ladinos also articulated an anti-imperialist regional identity and Q'eqchi' patriarchs laid claim to their positions as guardians of Maya culture. These rival nationalisms came into conflict during the celebration of the

---

[89] In thousands of dollars, Guatemala's GDP in 1929 was 431,065, reached a low in 1932 of 366,919 and then jumped by 1936 to 665,639. See Jurgen Buchenau, *Tools of Progress: A German Merchant Family in Mexico City, 1865–Present* (Albuquerque: University of New Mexico Press, 2004); Max Paul Friedman, *Nazis and Good Neighbors: The United States Campaign against the Germans of Latin America in World War II* (Cambridge: Cambridge University Press, 2003), 30.
[90] Grieb, *Guatemalan Caudillo*, 265–7.   [91] Ibid.   [92] Ibid., 268–9.
[93] See Frey, *Deutschtum in der Alta Verapaz*, 48.

400th anniversary of the region's peaceful conquest in 1936, and competing interpretations of history were at the heart of conflicts over national
boundaries and the place of the German diaspora. Ubico's own support
for fascists in Europe, and his self-styled likeness to Napoleon, however,
would eventually clash with the tide of anti-German, and increasingly
anti-fascist, sentiment. At the outbreak of war in 1939, students in Guatemala City denounced their German counterparts in the streets by chanting
"Long live Poland!" and "Let the Germans die!"[94]

After Hitler's rise to power in 1933, German national socialism spread
through established networks of associational life. The Auslandsorganisation (AO, Foreign Organization) supported demonstrations, festivities,
and holiday celebrations, and made efforts to provide financial support to
poor Germans in Alta Verapaz.[95] The German Club raised the German
national flag in honor of events ranging from Hitler's birthday to Guatemalan independence.[96] German propaganda films – *The Fifth Congress of
Germans Abroad in Stuttgart 1937*, *Far from the Land of Ancestors*, and
Trips to Beautiful Germany – produced specifically for the *Auslandsdeutsche*, were screened in Cobán's newly operating theater.[97] Many
Germans, like Oda Droege and Max Noak, recalled the incessant buzz
of the German radio breaking the silence and isolation of plantation life.[98]
As Oda Droege, the coffee planter Hugo Droege's wife, recalled, "The
German Club became National Socialist, as well as the Club in Guate-
mala City, then there were groups for women and men who were
members of the party. Some hid the party's insignia underneath the flap

---

[94] AGCA Ministerio de Educación (hereafter ME) B Legajo 34915, "Del Director del
Deutsche Schule al Secretario de Educación," September 18, 1939, and "Del Director
del Instituto Nacional Central de Varones al Secretario de Educación," September
20, 1939.

[95] See, for example, CM ET3 P19, "Deutsches Konsulat, Cobán, Guatemala al Sr Alcalde
1°," Cobán, November 15, 1933. See also Gerhard Enno Buß, "Zur Biologie des
Deutschtums in Guatemala" (Hamburg: Institut für Schiffs- und Tropenkrankheiten,
1942), 17; Regina Wagner, "Los alemanes en Guatemala" (PhD diss., Tulane University,
1992), 712.

[96] See AGCA JP-AV 1936 Paq. 3, "Carta al JP de F. Feske, Secretario del Club Alemán,"
January 3, 1936; "Carta al JP de H. Martin Luther, Secretario del Club Alemán," March
14, 1936; "Carta al JP de H. Martin Luther, Secretario del Club Alemán," April 19,
1936; "Carta al JP del Consulado de Alemania," April 30, 1936; AGCA JP-AV 1936
Paq. 5, "Al Martin Frey del JP," January 3, 1936, and "Carta al JP de Martin Frey,
Secretario," September 14, 1936.

[97] AGCA B Leg. 31402 Exp. 32 1938.

[98] Among the Germans reported as owning radios are the Dieseldorffs, Sappers, and
Droeges. See SPCM Libro, "Memorandum de 1940," folio 5.

of their bag, but others wore it with great joy. And there were also those armbands with the Swastika, all of it."[99]

Even though the Nazi promise of a unified ethnonational community (*Volksgemeinschaft*) drew on the deep ties fostered by German associational life, support for the Nazis was not uniform nor was the German community in Alta Verapaz unified. By the 1930s, Germans were divided along class and generational lines, as well as by political affiliation, religion, and region of origin. The first generation of settlers in Alta Verapaz in the late nineteenth century was well established and prosperous, and was generally less inclined to join the Nazi Party. The older members of Cobán's German Club, for example, resisted the efforts of a younger generation to remove iconography of the Kaiser, at least in part because, for many of them, German national politics was not relevant to their cultural affairs.[100] While some of the early German settlers' German and Q'eqchi'–German sons and daughters had lived or studied in Germany, many had never stood on German soil nor breathed German air. Younger generations of immigrant settlers, however, who had left Germany after World War I and who worked largely as administrators, mechanics, technicians, and gardeners, welcomed the advent of a strong leader promising economic renewal and national greatness in Germany. Nazism's violent hostility to communism also appealed to German coffee planters in Alta Verapaz, for whom labor strikes, land invasions, and Bolshevik agitators had been a vivid reality throughout the 1920s. Tailored for a Latin American audience, Nazi propaganda emphasized anti-communism.[101] Nazism also struck a chord with many Germans whose sense of racial superiority had been bolstered by the racial stratification of Guatemalan society. Some Germans were offended by the Nazi Party's anti-Semitism and others simply stopped spending time at the German Club. But by the end of the war, Guatemala – and especially Alta Verapaz – had become a Nazi stronghold. Yet only approximately 10 percent of Germans residing in Guatemala were members of the Nazi Party,[102] this figure does not represent the extent of Nazi support,

---

[99] All oral testimony from Oda Droege, unless otherwise stated, comes from the transcripts of an interview with Oda Droege by Uli Stelzner for the documentary *Los civilizadores*.
[100] Hugo Droege, transcribed interview with Uli Stelzner and Thomas Walter, *Los civilizadores*.
[101] Buchenau, *Tools of Progress*; Friedman, *Nazis and Good Neighbors*, 30.
[102] Guatemala was only surpassed by Honduras (20 percent) and Haiti (30 percent). Friedman, *Nazis and Good Neighbors*, 27. Compare 10 percent party membership with the less than 5 percent for Latin America as a whole; Jürgen Müller, *Nationalsozialismus in*

since party membership often also entailed activism: a willingness to organize and attend meetings, engage in fundraising, and submit to party discipline.

German National Socialism also produced tensions within German settlers' mixed-race families as some Germans sought to harden the fluid boundaries between German and Guatemalan national affiliations. Nazi obsessions with racial purity clashed with sexual and social practices in Alta Verapaz. Party standards explicitly rejected a large segment of the German population in Guatemala: those who married non-Aryans, who did not speak German in their daily life, who dedicated themselves to local political issues, or who adopted Guatemalan citizenship. The Nazi Party in Guatemala went so far as to expel members who "profane the race" by marrying Guatemalans.[103] For many Germans in Alta Verapaz, however, Nazi rules regarding racial hygiene were more flexible and the question of who counted as German and by what measure was far more fluid and now highly problematic. Federico Schleehauf, for example, married a Q'eqchi' woman, Teodora Pacay, and joined the Nazi Party on February 4, 1934.[104] Federico and Teodora's son Otto was sent to Germany for education where he learned German and participated in the Hitler Youth.[105] For many German settlers in Guatemala, there was no contradiction between loyalty to the German nation and to their children, like Otto Schleehauf Pacay, who spoke Q'eqchi' and wore Nazi garb.

Nazi Party concerns about German racial purity and reproduction in the tropics fostered new scientific investigations into the living conditions of Germans in Alta Verapaz. In 1938 Gerhard Enno Buß, a senior physician in the German military, traveled to Alta Verapaz to study German racial preservation abroad in the children in Cobán's newly operating German school. At the school, Buß explicitly set out to "certify the thesis of Aryan superiority. He examined the genealogical composition of the "pure Aryan German," "half-German," "non-Aryan Northern European," and "ladino" children. This was the basis for comparisons in mental acuity, weight, and other racial characteristics. The doctor's study confirmed the thesis of Guatemalan intellectuals such as Miguel Ángel

---

Lateinamerika. Die Auslandsorganisation der NSDAP in Argentinien, Brasilien, Chile und Mexico, 1931–1945 (Stuttgart: Verlag Hans-Dieter Heinz, 1997), 100.

[103] Friedman, *Nazis and Good Neighbors*, 13.

[104] NSDAP List provided by Christiane Berth.

[105] Helen Schleehauf, interview with the author, April 12, 2008. Helene also shared Otto's personal diaries from his time in the Hitler Youth.

Asturias, who celebrated German–Maya mestizaje. Half-Germans, he claimed, had a significantly higher level of psychological maturity than either their indigenous or ladino counterparts, since they had been born with many German physiological characteristics, which at that time were associated with psychological characteristics.[106] The American travel writer Erna Fergusson concurred. Referring to German–Maya unions, she noted: "This putting milk into the coffee seems to make a successful cross racially; the children are often fine-looking and intelligent."[107]

Q'eqchi'–German children, however, posed thorny questions about ethnic affiliation and loyalty to the German nation. According to Buß, German–Q'eqchi' interracial mixing was politically and socially danger-ous.[108] Being close, but not quite or fully German meant that many Q'eqchi'–Germans were imagined to have intimate, but possibly volatile relationships with Germans. Interracial mixing posed significant dangers to the Germany colony in Guatemala, he claimed. In an ominous warning, for example, Dr. Buß claimed that a Q'eqchi'–German had instigated a pro-Jewish demonstration in Guatemala City.[109] Yet, for Germans like Federico Schleehauf, who educated their mixed-race children in Germany or who ensured their children's well-being and upbringing within their means, there was no contradiction between German nationalism and sexual unions with Q'eqchi' Mayas. Many Germans in Guatemala, includ-ing Dr. Buß, advocated mediating the dangers posed by interracial unions and mixed-race children by encouraging men to seek German wives.

As German men returned to Germany in search of a "proper wife," Q'eqchi'–Germans experienced a profound betrayal at being reduced to "second families."[110] As Fergusson noted, Q'eqchi'–German children "may be very unhappy, especially if the father refuses them a good education or if they are left in the mother's class. The arrival of a wife from Germany hardly makes for harmony, though it all makes for drama. A thousand and one tales only await the teller."[111] The betrayals of Q'eqchi'–Germans illustrate how familial ideals and norms express national progress: in Western ideas of kinship, genealogical time is

---

[106] Buß, "Zur Biologie des Deutschtums in Guatemala."
[107] Erna Fergusson, *Guatemala* (New York: Alfred A. Knopf, 1937), 212.
[108] Buß, "Zur Biologie des Deutschtums in Guatemala," 27–8. See also Mary von Kreutzer, "'3; Der Auslandsdeutsche kann nichts anderes sein als Nationalsozialist!' Deutsch-österreichischer Faschismus in Guatemala," *Context* 21, nos. 3–4 (2002): 3–4.
[109] Buß, "Zur Biologie des Deutschtums in Guatemala," 27–9.
[110] For a detailed case study, see Gibbings, "Mestizaje in the Age of Fascism."
[111] Fergusson, *Guatemala*, 212.

progressive and linear.[112] Children are further along in time than their parents, and unions with advanced races like Germans hastened the speed of advancing toward a future of racial improvement. Q'eqchi–German betrayals by their German fathers thus often spoke in the temporal register of unfulfilled expectations about the acquisition of modernity.

For the abandoned Q'eqchi' concubines of German settlers, German nationalism revealed the tribulations inherent in a modernity founded on German settlement and Maya sexual labor at the heart of Guatemala's plantation economy. On April 1, 1936, Fidelia Bol wrote to the departmental governor requesting his support. "I am a single woman and I live in great poverty for the following reasons," she began. "Sixteen years ago, as a domestic servant in the plantation 'Sacoyou' and since don Oscar Flöhr had need for love [*amores*], I accepted his propositions, procreating with him four children.... After twelve years of marital living with the señor Flöhr, administrator of this plantation, in 1932 he abandoned me to go to Germany and get married. Since then he has not taken care of the needs of his children, who have remained in my care. These children need education, clothing and food and my scarce resources are not sufficient for them." She asked President Ubico to make Flöhr obey his duties as a father. "It is custom," she went on, "that the majority of the German men resident in our country take advantage not only of our personal labor but also satiating their appetites with us, leaving afterwards their children abandoned and increasing the bitterness of the needy citizens of the Republic. Fleeing very smugly and satisfied to enjoy in Europe the capital they have amassed with our sweat and lacking any humanitarian sentiments, they leave behind small beings in disgrace and without any education. In this one can see the scorn with which they view our poor nation and its inhabitants."[113] In her petition, penned with the help of a local lawyer, Fidelia Bol unveils the centrality of sexual labor to the plantation economy. As a result of this exploited labor, she illustrates how negligent German fathers were evidence that a desire for the accumulation of wealth, combined with an excessive individualism, led not to national progress, but to impoverished mothers and exploited children. The German abandonment narrative, and its critique of sexual labor, elicited images of children who were culturally on the loose, economically impoverished, morally neglected, and politically dangerous. The narrative also

[112] On kinship and linear time, see Peter Wade, "Hybridity Theory and Kinship Thinking," *Cultural Studies* 19, no. 5 (2006): 602–21.
[113] AGCA JP-AV 1936 Paq. 5, "Al JP de Fidelia Bol," April 1, 1936.

acted as a metaphor for the exploitation of an entire nation. In early 1937, in an ominous warning, the Local Committee on Uncultivated Lands began processing claims to German lands, including Erwin Paul Dieseldorff's properties, which qualified as latifundios for expropriation or forced rental.[114]

As Germans and Q'eqchi'–Germans struggled over national and political affiliations, Ubico relied increasingly on symbolic events such as state and national fairs to bolster his own popular appeal, celebrate progress, and construct a strategic and depoliticized space in the nation for Mayas. In light of growing German nationalism, Altaverapacences, however, quickly appropriated state fairs to pursue an anti-German nationalist agenda. In 1936 Ubico elevated Cobán's annual fair to a widely celebrated "departmental fair," which showcased the region's modern industry and agricultural production as well as indigenous culture and the exotic natural landscape. Special reports and magazines dedicated to the fair brimmed with evidence of modernization – roads, buildings, and coffee – of each municipality, supported by new infrastructure, images of regional flora and fauna, and picturesque landscapes. Magazines and newspapers staged modernization through visible evidence and demonstrated that the nation's excruciating wait for modernity was coming to an end.

The new status of Cobán's state fair bolstered already existing regionalism and nationalisms. In 1935, for example, *El Norte* ran an editorial calling on Altaverapacences "to love what is ours: our language, school, religion, and glorious transitions that extol the nation and its great men."[115] True nationalism, the editorialist concluded, was "to preferably consume the goods that our nation produces with the end of stimulating production."[116] Appeals to regional commerce and industry stood in stark contrast to a region overflowing with imported German products ranging from candies and beer to clothing and machinery. In part, this was due to Hitler's ASKI marks scheme, which required German importation firms to pay for Central American exports, such as coffee, in ASKI marks. The ASKI marks currency could only be used to purchase German goods.[117]

---

[114] CM Box 1, "La Junta Local de Eriales de Cobán, califica de latifundio los terrenos de Erwin Paul Dieseldorff," October 4, 1937; and SPCM 1938, "Al Alcalde 1° de Carchá de la Plantation Seamay," August 3, 1937.

[115] "El nacionalismo," *El Norte*, July 13, 1935.   [116] Ibid.

[117] Hitler's government issued ASKI marks in exchange for Central America's exports, which had profound consequences for trade in the region. ASKI marks encouraged the Guatemala to reduce its imports from other countries in favor of Germany, and as result between 1932 and the late 1930s, Germany tripled its market of imports in Guatemala.

In an era of import-substitution industrialization and economic nationalism, the German ASKI marks scheme likely appeared to be imperial to many Central Americans. If Ubico's state fairs were meant as symbolic proxies for state policies promoting homegrown industrialization, then the real experience of Alta Verapaz's economy made as much a farce out of Ubico's economic nationalism as Manuel Estrada Cabrera's Greco-Roman temples dotting the countryside. Nonetheless, Cobán's annual fair celebrations fostered a regional identity that combined an ethnic past and a modern future.[118]

Alta Verapaz's state fair celebrations reached dramatic heights in 1937, when Altaverapacences celebrated the 400th anniversary of the peaceful conquest and its new identity as Tezulutlán (Land of War). What the commemorations meant, however, varied widely across different social sectors, even as people united in a common celebration. The commemoration also generated a fierce national debate over the meaning of the conquest and restored the prestige of Hispanic heritage.[119] When President Ubico passed through Alta Verapaz's mountains on a presidential sojourn, his travel spokesperson Fernando Hernández de León passionately remarked how his travels reminded him of the "moral imperative" to revindicate the Spanish conquest, through a new and "honored interpretation of the facts."[120] From its very inception, the Spanish conquest of the Americas has been a deeply political world-historical event.[121] Across the hemisphere, indigenous peoples and their

Bulmer-Thomas, *The Political Economy of Central America since 1920* (Cambridge: Cambridge University Press, 1987), 78–9.

[118] See SPCM 1932, "Carta al Alcalde 1° Municipal del Comité de la Feria Nacional," May 20, 1932; AGCA JP-AV 1936 Paq. 1, "Solicitud que se eleve a la categoría de 'Feria Departamental,' la feria local de Santo Domingo," March 18, 1936; AGCA JP-AV 1936 Paq. 3, "Al JP del Presidente del Comité Pro-Feria de agosto," April 4, 1936; AGCA B Leg. 31079 Exp. 28 1936. The monja blanca orchid, which became the national flower, was widely found in Alta Verapaz and became, and continues to be, an important source of regional pride. A literary competition was held in 1937, and the results were published by the Secretary of Education. See *Monja Blanca (Lycaste skinneri alba): Flor nacional de Guatemala* (Guatemala: Tipografía Nacional, 1937). Ubico likewise encouraged scientific studies of Maya civilizations as part of his program to buttress nationalist sentiment and publicize Guatemalan contributions to Latin American intellectual endeavors. On folklore during Ubico, see also Way, The Mayan in the Mall.

[119] Marta Elena Casaús Arzú, "El gran debate historiográfico de 1937 en Guatemala: 'Los indios fuera de la historia y de la civilización'. Dos formas de hacer historia," *Revista Complutense de Historia de América* 34 (2008): 209–31.

[120] Hernández de León, *Viajes presidenciales*, 396–7.

[121] Steve J. Stern, "Paradigms of Conquest: History, Historiography, and Politics," *Journal of Latin American Studies* 24 (1992): 1–34.

allies denounced the conquest and the centuries of exploitation it created. These condemnations of Spanish colonialism could easily slide into the "black legend": an anti-Hispanic caricature and prejudice voiced by the Anglo heirs of a sordid racial history. For others, commemorations of peaceful conquest evoked a certain desire to redress the record, to move beyond a language of blame by defining more positive counterpoints in the "white legend": a celebration of Hispanic defenders of indigenous peoples, such as Bartolomé de las Casas.

In Guatemala, a deep suspicion of the socialist indigenismo emanating from Mexico helped foster Hispanism, which located the nation's heritage not in the indigenous past but rather in the conquest and its consummation through independence.[122] Alta Verapaz's peaceful conquest – with its romanticized mythologies of the goodwill and nonviolence of Dominican friars, and Mayas embracing the Christian faith – enabled Guatemalans to imagine the possibility of a fully reconciled society in this Hispanism. David Vela, a famous indigenista, narrated the region's history as a parable for the redemption of the Maya race. Emphasizing Mayas' connection with the region's natural riches and extreme beauty, he argued, "The spirit of Las Casas seems to illuminate the future rebirth of their [Maya] culture, which will be the redemption of the race." Vela suggested that national redemption and racial regeneration could take place only with the adoption of Las Casas's visionary aim of protecting Mayas. From the ashes of Alta Verapaz's heroic past, Vela envisioned a national future where all Guatemalans were citizens.[123] Newspaper articles likewise attributed the "spirit of Las Casas" to Ubico.[124]

Altaverapacence ladinos also adopted the peaceful conquest, but they often celebrated not Las Casas, but the fierce and noble native warriors who defended their freedom and autonomy from foreign invaders. Tezulutlán anti-imperialism began shortly after Nazis took over the German Club in 1933 and culminated in 1937 with the commemoration and state

[122] See, for example, Rebecca Earle, *The Return of the Native: Indians and Myth-Making in Spanish America, 1810–1930* (Durham, NC: Duke University Press, 2007). On Hispanism in Guatemala, see also Kirsten Weld, "The Other Door: Spain and the Guatemalan Counter-Revolution, 1944–54," *Journal of Latin American Studies* 51, no. 2 (2019): 307–31.

[123] Beyond the florid renditions that national intellectuals penned for Cobán's state fair, a much longer and heated debate took place in Guatemala's national newspapers. Between 1936 and 1937, more than eighty articles appeared in major newspapers on the history, meaning, and legacies of the conquest. See Casaús Arzú, "El gran debate historiográfico de 1937 en Guatemala."

[124] "Forjando una nueva Guatemala," *El Norte*, February 13, 1937.

fair. In 1934 ladino town councilmen renamed Cobán's central plaza Bartolomé de las Casas and officially renamed the city the "Imperial City of Carlos V." Local ladino editorialists took the pseudonym "Matalbatz," after the great cacique who had negotiated the peaceful conquest on behalf of Mayas. When foreign archaeologists discovered ancient Maya artifacts, San Juan Chamelco founded a museum in honor of "the great cacique Juan Matalbatz."[125] Newspapers regularly published articles celebrating Alta Verapaz's colonial history, particularly the valiant efforts to defend the region from foreign intruders. Editorialists now often referred to Alta Verapaz as Tezulutlán.[126]

As Cobán's state fair approached, ladinos subtly articulated Tezulutlán anti-imperialism that granted ladinos, rather than German settlers, an enduring and authentic claim to Alta Verapaz. Manuel Chavarría Flores contributed an excerpt from his book, *Tezulutlán*, to the annual state fair magazine published later that year. Entitled "Tierra Bravía (Untamed Land)," Chavarría described Alta Verapaz as a site of Spanish desire and defined the region through a dualism between an indomitable Maya spirit and surreal natural beauty. Chavarría then ascribed the Maya indomitable spirit to a set of ladino regional heroes – poets and writers, departmental governors, lawyers, and coffee planters. As the new modernizing agent, Alta Verapaz's authentic spirit – derived from Maya caciques and splendid natural beauty – was embodied in ladino men. Chavarría relegated Mayas to the timeless natural landscape and the German diaspora to foreign intruders. Rosendo Santa Cruz, a young Cobanero poet and novelist, similarly penned a series of articles celebrating the 400th anniversary of pacification by Dominican friars. As a result of the conquest, Santa Cruz declared that a "hardworking and peaceful" Verapaz was born a "child of love and faith."[127]

Neither Altaverapacence ladinos nor Guatemalan intellectuals controlled the meaning and political uses of the peaceful conquest. In the midst of celebrations of the anniversary, the German geographer Karl Sapper delivered a lecture to Cobán's German Club about the region's history of peaceful conquest.[128] During his first visit to the region in the

[125] "El museo Matalbatz," *El Norte*, Cobán, May 1, 1937; and "Museo Matalbatz en Chamelco," *Diario de Centro-América*, May 1, 1937.

[126] "De tiempos atrás," *El Norte*, June 13, 1936.

[127] Rosendo Santa Cruz, "El IV centenario de la conquista pacífica de la Verapaz," *El Norte*, May 15, 1937.

[128] Located in TULAL, DC, Maya Studies, and published as "Fray Bartolomé de las Casas und die Verapaz (Nordost-Guatemala)," *Baessler-Archiv* (1936): 102–7.

early 1890s, Sapper had, with the aid of a Q'eqchi' guide, traced the steps of the Spanish friars across the region, narrating the region's conquest and its effects on the cultural and physical landscape.[129] For the commemoration of the conquest, Sapper concluded before Cobán's Nazi-controlled German Club that "the strength of these people [Q'eqchi' Mayas of Alta Verapaz] has remained outstanding because of the actions and ideas of Fray Bartolomé de las Casas about the best manner of Christian mission work and about the maintenance of racial purity."[130] Virtually erasing the ladino presence, Sapper argued that Alta Verapaz's protection from Spanish settlement had left an untainted and noble race, and an ideal cultural landscape for a German diaspora. This vision of Alta Verapaz as a special place for a particularly national socialist German diaspora is also evident in rumors that Adolf Hitler harbored an abiding affection for Q'eqchi's. Admiring not only their industrious nature, Hitler, Altaverapacences maintain, believed the Q'eqchi' to be racially pure and superior, almost on the same plane as the Aryan race. In fact, some Altaverapacences claim that Hitler so loved the Q'eqchi's that he used the Q'eqchi' language as a code to transmit state secrets. The imagined relationship between Q'eqchi's, Germans, and Nazism sustains a mythical quality, laden with fables, rumors, and whisperings that unravel and invert racial hierarchies and legitimize the dispossession of Altaverapacence land. For Germans, ladinos, and perhaps even Q'eqchi's, the peaceful conquest was compelling perhaps precisely because of the impossibility of ever fully depoliticizing it; thus, the conquest would always be open to multiple interpretations, uses, and meanings.[131]

While ladinos and Germans wrestled over the meaning of Alta Verapaz's colonial history, Q'eqchi' patriarchs contributed to departmental and national fairs to locate themselves as the true representatives of Maya culture.[132] Q'eqchi' alcaldes were asked to select Mayas "to represent their town." The Q'eqchi' men, state officials counseled, should be accompanied by their wives adorned "in their traditional clothing." Participants

---

[129] For example, in region around Lake Izabal, he noted, "The future cruelty of the Spaniards weighs like a heavy curse on these fertile countries and hinders their agricultural development." Karl Sapper, *Das Nördliche Mittel-Amerika: Reisen und Studien aus den Jahren 1888–1895* (Braunschweig: Druck und Verlag, 1897), 39, 30–59.

[130] Sapper, "Fray Bartolomé de las Casas und die Verapaz (Nordost-Guatemala)," 107.

[131] On the politicization of the conquest, see Stern, "Paradigms of Conquest."

[132] SPCM 1937, "Carta al Sr. Intendente Municipal Carchá del Comité Central de la Feria Nacional," Cobán, October 2, 1937.

were also asked to demonstrate their "music and industrial artifacts."[133]
The Maya representatives attended the national fair in Guatemala City
and public spectacles. *India bonita* contests held annually during the state
fair provided opportunities for Maya patriarchs to represent indigenous
culture in a public setting. Q'eqchi' patriarchs, too, used folklorization to
distinguish themselves, as they had in the past, from uncivilized and lower-
class Q'eqchi's.[134] Q'eqchi' patriarchs' self-representations in the 1930s
were notably different from the early twentieth-century staged studio
photographs, where Q'eqchi' patriarchs envisioned themselves as coffee
planters and defenders of the nation (see Chapter 4). By the 1930s,
Q'eqchi' patriarchs represented themselves as simultaneously indigenous
and nonindigenous, ethnic and modern. As Q'eqchi' reciprocity and solidarity dissolved, Q'eqchi' patriarchs increasingly relied on indigenous
female dress to represent indigenous culture much as their K'iche counterparts in Quetzalentango had since the 1890s.[135]

Unlike heroic masculine images that Q'eqchi' patriarchs had used in
the past, the india bonita contests focused on the feminine domains of
Maya language and culture. While the contestants for india bonita need
only have indigenous parents, over the years, the candidates usually came
from the most prominent and wealthy Q'eqchi' families from Cobán. The
india bonita demonstrated not only the standard traits extolled by beauty
pageants – femininity, beauty, and innocence – but also a strategic balance between modernity and ethnic tradition, universality and particular-
ism, that both appealed to and represented rural Mayas and their urban
counterparts. Armenia Macz, the daughter of a prominent Q'eqchi' elite
family in Cobán, was the first india bonita elected in 1936 (and then
reelected in 1937). Drawing on a gendered ethnicity, Armenia represented
an authentic version of rural Maya culture. In a photograph from the

[133] CM Est. 8 Paq. 3, "Sr. Alcalde 3° Municipal," January 7, 1907.
[134] Two years earlier, the K'iche Sociedad El Adelanto Quetzaltenango had initiated an
annual contest for the "Reina Indígena." Unlike the event in Cobán, however, Quetzal-
tenago's indigenous beauty queen was selected by popular vote. In this regard, Cobán's
festival bore a greater resemblance to Mexico's 1921 India Bonita contest. In 1936, the
judges of the India Bonita contest were Erwin Paul Dieseldorff, Margarita S. de Ponce,
Abigail Figueroa, and Carlos Enrique Martinez. See CM Est. 1 Paq. 2, "Al Intendente
Municipal del Erwin Paul Dieseldroff," July 29, 1936. On the "ethnicization of Mexico"
through the 1921 India Bonita contest, see Rick A. López, "The India Bonita Contest of
1921 and the Ethnicization of Mexican National Culture," *The Hispanic American
Historical Review* 82, no. 2 (May 2002): 291–328. On Quetzaltenango, particularly
the much later 1955 contest, see Grandin, *The Blood of Guatemala* , 195–6.
[135] See Grandin, *The Blood of Guatemala*.

India Bonita de la Feria 1936 1937.

FIGURE 7.2 Indigenous beauty queen, Feria de Cobán (1936).
AGCA biblioteca.

1936 election (see Figure 7.2), a barefoot Armenia stands adorned in traditional Q'eqchi' clothing and surrounded by nature, portraying a scene of indigenous domesticity that associated indigenous culture with the countryside. Yet her silver necklace, a symbol of wealth, highlights the fact that in daily life she would not have gone barefoot, as she subverts representations of rural Mayan poverty. The themes of domesticity and natural abundance were also repeated in her speech, but they were accompanied by celebrations of economic modernization, which placed the untouched landscape in the past. Alta Verapaz was "a place that only yesterday," Armenia explained, "was sleeping in the silence of the mountains, only now and again interrupted by the beacon of the woodcutter and the melodies of the birds." Nowhere in her speech, however, did Armenia place indigenous culture in that past. And here, her words mark Mayas as natural inhabitants, but also agents of modernization: "We give a thousand applauses to he who makes a wave of progress and adapts to the greatness of this beloved soil that we had the luck of being born in.... Glory to progress, Glory to great men."[136] Strategically appropriating

---

[136] "Discurso de la india bonita," *El Norte*, August 15, 1936.

Maya folklorization, the Q'eqchi' patriarchs represented themselves as both indigenous and modern and unsettled modernities that saw them as anachronisms.

Q'eqchi' patriarchs also utilized Ubico's sanctioned indigenismo to reinforce Maya spaces of autonomy and culture and restrengthen the bonds between Q'eqchi' patriarchs and rural Mayas. Because Ubico's government repressed the new brand of Q'eqchi' political intermediaries, embodied in figures like José Angel Icó, and Q'eqchi's were marginalized on town councils, Q'eqchi' patriarchs looked to cofradías as a mechanism to recreate their authority as representatives of Mayas. The number of cofradías grew dramatically in the 1930s, as did their celebrations of saints. As a counterpart to the state fair, held every August on Cobán's patron saint day, Altaverapacence *cofrades* organized a massive department-wide processional, honoring all the saints from each of the region's towns. Some fifty-six cofradías, celebrating twenty-nine saints, participated. Cofrades carried the statues of patron saints for considerable distances in order to meet at Cobán's hermitage, located on the mountain of a powerful Tzuultaq'a. When they met at the hermitage, the cofrades bowed to each other three times in a choreographed pattern. The region-wide processions were new, as were many of the cofradías themselves. Symbolically, the most important celebrations took place in Cobán in front of the arch and tower built by Ubico when he was departmental governor. The spectacle drew the region's coffee planters as well as state officials. Everyone was invited to a feast prepared by the cofradías, who served the famous Verapaz caq iq (garlic chile turkey stew).[137] Through cofradía events, Q'eqchi' patriarchs sought to reinforce autonomy from the state where Maya culture could flourish under their guidance.

The perpetual movement between the veneration of indigenous culture and the policing of indigenous customs, the exaltation of Q'eqchi' nobility and an undermining of the local power of Q'eqchi' elites, enthusiasm for indigenous medicinal knowledge and the persecution of Maya shamans – all were slippery temporal discourses that shifted Mayas from the present to the past and allowed the simultaneous inclusion and exclusion of Mayas in the nation.[138] A similar sliding between German nationalism

---

[137] Goubaud Carrera, "Notes on San Juan Chamelco, Alta Verapaz," 90; see also Abigail E. Adams, "The Transformation of the Tzuultaq'a: Jorge Ubico, Protestants and Other Verapaz Maya at the Crossroads of Community, State and Transnational Interests," *Journal of Latin American Anthropology* 6, no. 2 (2001): 198–233.

[138] See Earle, *The Return of the Native*.

and presence in Guatemala likewise allowed Germans, and especially their Maya–German children, to defy territorial boundaries and be included in both nations. Ubico's populist regime was founded by making the boundaries between being inside and outside the nation fluid and unstable. By including Mayas via regional and national celebrations and occasionally celebrating German achievements, Ubico created a sphere that allowed for the momentary ethnicization and Europeanization of nationality that did not undermine the place of racially whitened ladinos in the nation as the standard of progressive citizens. Yet the tensions and contradictions between a sanctioned indigenismo that placed Mayas within the nation as representatives of an "authentic culture" and a racialization of indigeneity that placed Mayas outside the nation as vagrants and criminals made the definition of inclusion contingent on being both indigenous and not indigenous. By assigning Mayas to the past, the state made it almost impossible to recognize Maya political ontologies in the present.

As they had in the past, Maya cultural celebrations erupted into indigenista critiques of coffee planters' treatment of workers. Ubico's calls for justice and morality also easily translated into condemnations of exploitation. Like the choreographed speeches dedicated to Manuel Estrada Cabrera, Ubico's state fairs revealed the contradictions of his own dictatorship and his failure to end the purgatory of postponement. Cobán's annual state fair magazine printed an homage to the india bonita Armenia Macz written by Jorge Rubio Muñoz. Entitled "Amor Cobanero," the poem began with a romantic celebration of indigenous beauty and ended with themes of domination and sexual violence:

> I held you in my arms, india bonita
> of beautiful hair, color of champagne
> of red skin, small mouth,
> and of intentions as genuine as those of San Juan.
> Content and merry, fresh and cleanly
> You make me tortillas, atole and pepián[139]
> until, yesterday afternoon, you remorsefully told me,
> That you were going to your pueblo ...
> Oh, flower of Cobán;
> You are so beautiful
> that today I feel infinite regret
> of having lost you; but you must return ... !

[139] The latter two are traditional Cobanero dishes: a thick, warm corn drink and a chile-spiced turkey stew.

> You promised me, and if you do not comply,
> I will look for you, and rip out your life
> and sully the soul of your womanhood!

The poem demonstrates the ever-present threat of violence hanging over indigenous women, who were sexualized and racialized objects of lust and domination. Perhaps Rubio Muñoz referenced Guatemala's sexual labor economy, and especially German administrators who notoriously made Q'eqchi' cooks into their concubines. The poem also reveals, however, how indigenous mobility threatened the authority of coffee planters and drew out violence. One particularly prolific editorialist signed his name "Bartolomé de las Chozas" or Bartolomé of the Shacks.[140] Indigenismo, in other words, provided a common language to contest Maya treatment and demand a different kind of modernity. In Alta Verapaz, indigenismo emerging alongside German nationalism deepened, rather than ameliorated, the building tensions between Mayas, ladinos, and German settlers.

CONCLUSION

After the rise of Hitler in 1933, Alta Verapaz's German Club, as well as its newly operating German school, turned to virulent racist nationalism that clashed with sexual and social practices, and enlivened latent anti-German nationalism among ladinos and Q'eqchi's. Germans, ladinos, and Q'eqchi's struggled over national boundaries and political affiliations by debating history and appropriating the region's special history of peaceful conquest to their own ends. To further legitimize their possession of lands and their presence, Altaverapacence ladinos, Germans, and Q'eqchi's all sought to possess a folklorized and sanctioned version of Maya culture through ethnographic writings and beauty contests. These practices squared neatly with Ubico's sanctioned indigenismo, which – unlike indigenismo in Mexico – relegated Maya culture to the past as an authentic tradition, while criminalizing Maya culture in the present.

Ubico's populism rested not simply in presidential sojourns to the countryside, and personal interventions in domestic affairs, but in a temporal strategy of containing, ordering, and managing difference. More than at any point in Guatemalan history, Ubico drew on time to dispossess, disenfranchise, and exclude those deemed to be nonmodern, while

---

[140] "Comentarios verídicos IV," *El Norte*, May 28, 1938.

also empowering, uplifting, and celebrating those deemed to be modernizers. Ubico split national time by strategically celebrating Maya language and dress as authentic traditions, while he rabidly persecuted Maya cultural practices that helped produce Maya political ontologies and time. Through Ubico's expanding police state, upwardly mobile ladinos and Q'eqchi'–Germans were empowered as agents of a new modernizing progress. Downtrodden mothers who fought for their children's welfare likewise recuperated their honor and claimed a positive place in Ubico's eugenics-oriented state policies. These same individuals helped render Mayas as aliens to modernity as they policed the very practices by which Mayas had long reproduced solidarity and reciprocity, as well as Maya calendars and mountain spirits. In the 1970s and 1980s, at the height of state terror, Mayas were also made into dangerous others of modernity that had to be eradicated, even as the military appropriated aspects of Maya culture including imagery of the mountain spirits, Tzuultaq'as.

As Ubico policed modernity and brought the state into plantations, he also upended liberalism's emphasis on private initiative and will and made the state central to social justice and morality. For the first time, Guatemalan state officials entered plantations without the authorization of the coffee planter in the name of the health and welfare of the population. Ubico's biopolitical state policies and his rhetoric of social justice and morality, however, only highlighted the bankruptcy of dictatorship. Rumors and popular memories speak to Ubico's populism and his betrayal of the promise of modernity as social justice. Many Altaverapacences remember Jorge Ubico as a Q'eqchi'. Some recount that Ubico's real name was Tiburcio Icó.[141] According to these stories, Ubico was adopted as a young boy from the Alta Verapaz military base; he then left the region, the place where his umbilical cord was buried, and turned against his people. Others, however, have recounted that Ubico was born in the capital and was the son of a Q'eqchi' servant, who was adopted by his father as a legitimate son. Altaverapacence rumors metaphorically speak of Ubico's populism: he was of the people. Yet these alternative tales also give voice to Q'eqchi' unsettlings of Ubico's modernity. They reveal the feelings of betrayal arising from state promises made but not fulfilled, and the act of turning against one's own people and disavowing

---

[141] Abigail E. Adams, "Antonio Goubaud Carrera: Between the Contradictions of the Generación de 1920 and U.S. Anthropology," in *After the Coup: An Ethnographic Reframing of Guatemala, 1954,* ed. Timothy J. Smith and Abigail E. Adams (Urbana: University of Illinois Press, 2011).

one's origins. For as much as Ubico promised modernization and progress, he failed to fulfill Q'eqchi' desires for a different kind of social
justice, that is, one that rectified past injustices. Ubico's disavowal of his
Maya origins speaks to how the dictator repudiated Maya political
ontologies and policed Maya practices. These rumors speak to Ubico's
virulent politics of postponement, which sought to eradicate Maya practices as alien threats to modernity.

World War II's onset crystallized Altaverapacences' frustrated aspirations, and Guatemala once again found itself isolated from European
markets, resulting in a fall in export prices and a shift of markets to the
United States. The increasing appeals to democracy and anti-fascism
invigorated Guatemalans, who had grown frustrated by the repression
of political alternatives, the foreclosure of democracy, and the centralization of power in the hands of a ruthless dictator. In Alta Verapaz, latent
anti-German nationalism bled into anti-fascism and reinvigorated calls to
expropriate German properties and deport German citizens. By 1941,
when Guatemala entered the war on the side of the Allied powers, there
was no turning back the tide that would unleash new expectations for
state-driven social justice.

8

Now Owners of Our Land

Nationalism, History, and Memory in Revolution, 1939–1954

The original task of a genuine revolution ... is never merely to "change the world," but also – and first of all – to "change time."
—Giorgio Agamben, *Time and History*

In August 1944, Guatemalan newspapers erupted with astonishing news: the Guatemalan government had nationalized German properties. Headlines filled the front pages with titles such as "Nationalization of Nazis Properties," "Guatemala Ceases to Be an Economic Slave," and "Guatemala for Guatemalans."[1] Alta Verapaz's conservative regional newspaper *El Norte* proclaimed: "Long Live Guatemala! Now Owner of Its Land!" Declaring the dawn of a new era, the Altaverapacense editorialist J. J. Palma rejoiced that the time had arrived "to recuperate the heirlooms of our ancestors." The nationalization, he avowed, would do nothing less than "ensure the peace and tranquility of the Nation that for so many

---

[1] See "Expropiación de bienes alemanes," *La Nación*, August 14, 1944; "El decreto de expropiación en la Asamblea," *La Nación*, August 15, 1944; "Opiniones de candidatos de la presidencia," *La Nación*, August 15, 1944; "Unidad nacional frente a las expropiaciones," *La Nación*, August 16, 1944; "Convocatoria de sesiones de la legislativa para conocer el decreto de expropiación," *La Nación*, August 16, 1944; "Guatemala deja de ser una esclava económica" *La Nación*, August 17, 1944; "Las tierras expropiadas deberían quedar en manos de guatemaltecos," *La Nación*, August 21, 1944; "Sobre el decreto 3134," *Nuestro Diario*, August 17, 1944; "Expropiación, nacionalización efectiva de nuestro bienes," *Nuestro Diario*, August 24, 1944; "Confiscación total de bienes alemanes en la lista negra," *El Imparcial*, August 14, 1944; "Solo a favor de los guatemaltecos," *El Imparcial*, August 21, 1944; "Nacionalización de la tierra," *El Imparcial*, August 22, 1944; "Redención del suelo patrio," *El Imparcial*, August 22, 1944; "Tierras para guatemaltecos," *El Imparcial*, August 24, 1944.

years has suffered the disgrace of a race that has acquired almost half of Guatemala. This great step will guarantee the future of a new Guatemala."[2] German properties producing nearly 400,000 quintales of coffee per year were transferred to the newly established Department of National Plantations.[3] The dramatic nationalization emerged from a series of political and social convulsions sweeping the nation. Less than two months earlier, a burgeoning coalition of anti-fascist university students, teachers, and middle-class people in Guatemala City forced Ubico's resignation by reading aloud the Atlantic Charter, signed by the Allied powers in August 1941.[4] "Being the ideological light of humanity's war against international fascism (that reached even Jorge Ubico and Federico Ponce Vaides)," one student activist declared, "it was the Atlantic Charter that guided the revolutionaries in Guatemala in the decisive battle against dictators."[5] In the chaotic aftermath of Ubico's resignation, General Federico Ponce Vaides of Alta Verapaz, Ubico's interim successor, quickly consolidated power, despite growing demands for democracy. As part of his effort to rally mass support, Ponce nationalized German properties – not because Germans represented an international military threat but because German properties were of "public utility and need."[6] Ponce's nationalization of German-owned properties thus looked more like Mexico's nationalization of oil in 1938 than the expropriations of Axis-owned properties and assets in the name of war.

In Alta Verapaz, the nationalization ruptured German economic and social power and deepened latent anti-German nationalism. Editorialists in Guatemala's major newspapers folded the nationalization of German properties into new, grand narratives of Guatemalan history, including the history of the conquest and independence. In the process, they inverted both the civilizing and liberal metanarratives. Guatemala, they claimed, would cast off the shackles of feudalism and imperialism by confiscating the properties of the perpetrators of Guatemala's status as colonial nation vis-à-vis Europe. In August 1944, newspaper editorialists

[2] J. J. Palma, "¡Viva Guatemala! ¡Dueña ya de sus tierras!," *El Norte*, August 19, 1944.
[3] Regina Wagner, *Los alemanes en Guatemala, 1828–1944*, 2nd ed. (Guatemala: Editorial IDEA, Universidad en su Casa, Universidad Francisco Marroquín, 2007), 391.
[4] "Decreto No. 3115," *Diario de Centro América*, June 22, 1944; and "Decreto 3138," *Diario de Centro América*, June 27, 1944.
[5] Medardo Mejía, *El movimiento obrero en la Revolución de Octubre* (Guatemala: n.p., 1949), 5.
[6] See AGCA AA Leg. 621 and Leg. 622; *Recopilación de las leyes de Guatemala, 1944–1945*, vol. 63 (Guatemala: Tipografía Nacional, 1945), 418–19.

rendered German settlers, once the central agents of history and progress, as imperialists and feudalist lords. Ponce's appeals to rural Mayas and nationalism, however, ignited rather than pacified the burgeoning anti-fascist movement in Guatemala City, which sought not the redistribution of foreign-owned land, but democracy and social reforms.

While few historians have recognized the importance of Guatemala's nationalization of German properties, the social and economic rupture it produced paved the way for a more well-known political rupture: the Guatemalan Revolution of October 20, 1944. For the next decade, under two democratically elected presidents – Juan José Arévalo (1945–50) and Jacobo Árbenz (1951–4) – Guatemalans propelled a series of social reforms, ranging from rural education to labor laws and social security, that were designed to limit planter sovereignty, deepen local democracy, and modernize Guatemala. The revolution's reforms meant profoundly different things to Guatemala City elites and middle classes, German settlers, and rural Mayas. As Cindy Forster has explored, rural peasants and workers consistently radicalized the revolution, pushing it into broader definitions of democracy and social equality than previously conceived.[7] Far from simply adapting new metanarratives that mixed Marxism and social democracy, Mayas in Alta Verapaz were often guided by another logic entirely: a Maya ontology grounded in historic justice and the ethics of solidarity and reciprocity. In making the past politically relevant in the present, Mayas refused modern temporalities that envisioned time as linear, abstract, and progressive. In enacting solidarity and reciprocity, they also deepened democracy in unexpected ways. Disinherited Q'eqchi'–German sons – filled with memories of betrayal and desires for recognition as legitimate heirs – petitioned for their fathers' lands. In this sense, the most important piece of the 1944-54 revolution – Guatemala's 1952 agrarian reform – condensed nineteenth- and early twentieth-century histories of landownership and use, violent dispossessions, and struggles over inheritance and illegitimacy into bureaucratic struggles over what counted as productive or unproductive land use.

This chapter traces the origins of Guatemala's famed revolution in the political and economic realignments of World War II and illustrates how the 1944 revolution then unleashed struggles over the revolution's meaning and limits. German–Guatemalans, after the war, complicated subaltern struggles over access to political power. The 1952–4 agrarian reform expanded local

---

[7] Cindy Forster, *The Time of Freedom: Campesino Workers in Guatemala's October Revolution* (Pittsburgh, PA: University of Pittsburgh Press, 2001).

democracy and empowered rural Mayas in ways that fundamentally under-mined planter sovereignty and state power. The reform, thus, was deeply imbricated in redefining the spatial and territorial boundaries of plantations and the organization of rural space. Rural Mayas, however, also pressed Guatemala's agrarian reform forward in unexpected ways.

As a result of its strong German presence and Maya political action, Guatemala's famed 1952 agrarian reform, embodied in Decree 900, was most profoundly expressed in Alta Verapaz. If United Fruit Company properties are excluded, the state redistributed more land in Alta Verapaz than any other department in Guatemala. A total of 152,633 manzanas of land was awarded in 74 expropriations. The next closest department was Escuintla, which redistributed 8,444 manzanas across 105 expropri-ations.[8] Alta Verapaz's disproportionate share of redistributed properties is a result of the prior nationalization of German properties, which had mobilized rural Mayas around land redistribution much earlier. The state awarded more land on nationalized plantations through Decree 900 than historians have usually recognized. In Cobán and Carchá alone, the state distributed eleven nationalized plantations among 1,015 resident labor-ers.[9] Historians, however, have largely failed to acknowledge the signifi-cance of the nationalization of properties that occurred during World War II and how it shaped the course of Guatemala's famed Revolutionary Spring.

GLOBAL WAR ON THE EVE OF THE GUATEMALAN REVOLUTION

World War II generated a broad sentiment against dictatorship across Latin America. Military dictatorships that had come to power through coups during the Great Depression met their demise or were forced to change tactics to appease popular demands for democracy and reform.[10] By the time Guatemala followed the United States into World War II in December 1941, Guatemala's social and political order had already begun to change. Ubico no longer professed unwavering admiration for the German diaspora; intellectuals ceased their celebration of German–Maya mestizaje; and Guatemalans recoiled at outward displays of

---

[8] Jim Handy, *Revolution in the Countryside: Rural Conflict and Agrarian Reform in Guatemala, 1944–1954* (Chapel Hill: University of North Carolina Press, 1994), 94.

[9] These statistics are based on the Decree 900 records. See AGCA DAN-AV Paq. 17.

[10] See, for example, Leslie Bethell and Ian Roxborough, *Latin America between the Second World War and the Cold War: Crisis and Containment, 1944–1948* (Cambridge: Cambridge University Press, 1997).

German nationalism. When Ubico declared war on Germany and the Axis powers, Guatemalans celebrated in the streets.[11] Ubico attempted to navigate the new era not by halting dissident repression or enacting agrarian reform but by invoking anti-German nationalism to bolster and extend his own dictatorship. Ubico's efforts to appease the United States, however, enlivened anti-German nationalism and, by validating anti-fascism, hastened his own demise.

In Guatemala City, intellectuals, students, and teachers rallied around the banner of anti-fascism and prodemocracy, and thus inserted their local concerns about Ubico's dictatorship into the wider global dynamics.[12] Only two months after Ubico announced his intentions to renew his term, *El Liberal Progresista*, the official newspaper, published telegrams streaming from Washington and London outlining the principles of the Atlantic Charter, and the *Diario Oficial* published articles from London to Buenos Aires, Mexico to Berlin.[13] For students, teachers, and intellectuals, the global war against fascism not only inspired resistance, but gave the opposition a language to describe their own experiences. In the clandestine newspaper *Senderos*, Alfonso Bauer Paiz published a play entitled "Canciller Cadejo," which infused a story about Hitler with references to classical Guatemalan literature and folklore, ridiculing Ubico and comparing his police state to that of Hitler's Germany.[14] Political organizing in Central America also bolstered Guatemalans, especially exiles, students, disaffected army men, and professionals. News of political reforms in neighboring Mexico spread through various established networks among cross-border migrant workers and the professional middle class.[15]

In addition to burgeoning domestic dissent, Ubico also faced new U.S. diplomatic pressure to address Guatemala's "German threat." Washington naively believed the Nazi Party AO's exaggerated claims regarding the

[11] Kenneth J. Grieb, *Guatemalan Caudillo: Guatemalan Caudillo, the Regime of Jorge Ubico: Guatemala, 1931–1944* (Athens: Ohio University Press, 1979).
[12] Grieb, *Guatemalan Caudillo*, 269–74. [13] Mejía, *El movimiento obrero*, 5.
[14] Cadejo is a supernatural character in Central American folklore. See *El Liberal Progresista*, August 14 and 15, 1941, and *El Diario Oficial* for the same dates. See also Mejía, *El movimiento obrero*, 23–6, 54–5; Alfonso Bauer Paiz, *Memorias de Alfonso Bauer Paiz: Historia no oficial de Guatemala* (Guatemala: Rusticatio Ediciones, 1996), 65; Manuel Galich, *Del pánico al ataque* (Guatemala: Tipografía Nacional, 1949), 287–326; and Paul J. Dosal, *Power in Transition: The Rise of Guatemala's Industrial Oligarchy, 1871–1994* (Westport, CT: Praeger, 1995), 80.
[15] See Forster, *The Time of Freedom*, 30.

extent of their infiltration and support in the Guatemalan countryside.[16] Between July and November 1941, the Guatemalan government published a US-elaborated Proclaimed List, or blacklist, that named 254 German businesses and plantations, as well as schools and clubs, operating in Guatemala.[17] The Proclaimed List included a large part of the German population, even those who were naturalized Guatemalan citizens, because the principal security threat for Washington at this time was the sale of coffee produced by Germans. In Guatemala, Germans produced 40 percent of the coffee and exported another 30 percent of the total crop from smaller farmers for a 70 percent share of the country's total product. The US embassy was particularly concerned about Alta Verapaz, since Germans held title to 80 percent of the land there.[18] Like Erna Fergusson a few years earlier, the embassy dubbed the region "Little Sudetenland."

After Japan attacked Pearl Harbor on December 7, 1941, President Ubico convened the National Legislative Assembly to address the "German threat." On December 11, Ubico declared war on both Germany and Japan. That evening university students dramatically took to the streets to declare Guatemala an anti-fascist nation.[19] On December 23, 1941, Guatemala limited constitutional guarantees, froze German assets, and deported Germans in Guatemala whose names appeared on the Proclaimed List. Initially, only German men were listed for deportation, as women were assumed to be nondangerous by nature.[20]

Many Germans named on the Proclaimed List, however, had never joined or sympathized with the Nazi Party. Cross-checking the list of all Guatemalan deportees against the membership list of the AO, Max Paul

---

[16] Over 1938 and 1939, the Guatemalan government had passed a series of decrees banning the NSDAP and political activities of foreigners. The government also passed legislation on the naturalization of foreigners and the children of foreign men born on Guatemalan soil. See "Decreto No. 2153," *Recopilación de leyes de la República de Guatemala,* vol. 57, 215–16. Stefan Karlen, *Paz, progreso, justicia y honradez: Das Ubico-Regime in Guatemala 1931–1944* (Stuttgart: Franz Steiner Verlag, 1991), 212–17; Grieb, *Guatemalan Caudillo,* 248–51; Wagner, *Los alemanes;* and Max Paul Friedman, *Nazis and Good Neighbors: The United States Campaign against the Germans of Latin America in World War II* (Cambridge: Cambridge University Press, 2003).

[17] See AGCA AA Leg. 704 and Leg. 716; Wagner, *Los alemanes,* 372; Friedman, *Nazis and Good Neighbors,* 88.

[18] Regina Wagner, *Historia del café de Guatemala* (Bogotá, Colombia: Villegas Editores, 2001), 173–4.

[19] Mejía, *El movimiento obrero,* 30.

[20] Regina Wagner, "Los alemanes en Guatemala" (PhD diss., Tulane University, 1992), 763–5.

Friedman demonstrated that of the 558 Germans brought to Germany from Guatemala between 1942 and 1945, only 120 were party members.[21] More than half of the local Nazis remained in Guatemala. Those deported ranged from flag-waving patriots who hoped for a German victory in the war to coffee administrators with little connection with German social life to Jewish refugees, social democrats, or other opponents of Hitler's regime. The Proclaimed List, Friedman has argued, was based not only on hearsay, denunciation, and inadequate intelligence but also on the assumption that the German national identity could sufficiently predict probable dangerousness and that Nazi Party organizers' claims that they successfully aroused the transnational allegiance of all German expatriates were correct.[22] Many German coffee planters believe that internment most reflected Guatemalan and US desires to expropriate German properties and reorient trade, rather than neutralize the German threat. "They used to have a joke," explained Hugo Droege's Q'eqchi–German son Gustavo, that "after learning about the plight of deported German citizens in Guatemala, Hitler peered over the map of the world, puzzled 'where *is* this Guatemala.' But Guatemala was hidden under a few ashes from his cigar."[23]

Germans in Alta Verapaz were not unprepared, however, for what transpired after the United States entered World War II. With vivid memories of World War I, Germans in Alta Verapaz braced for intervention and expropriation. Erwin Paul Dieseldorff began preparations early on by solidifying his ties with his Guatemalan daughter, Matilde, immediately after World War I. Most Germans in Alta Verapaz prepared only after war seemed all but inevitable. Some readied themselves by acquiring Guatemalan citizenship, while others cemented their Guatemalan familial ties by legally recognizing mixed-race children. Beginning in 1938, Germans in Alta Verapaz officially acknowledged their children who were born years, if not decades, earlier at an unprecedented rate. Of all the legal recognitions of Guatemalan–German children, 69 percent occurred between 1938 and 1945.[24] This took place alongside Nazi Party concerns about mixed-race families, and the ongoing practice of first (German) and second (Q'eqchi' or ladino) families.

---

[21] See Friedman, *Nazis and Good Neighbors*, 119.
[22] See Friedman, *Nazis and Good Neighbors*.
[23] Gustavo Droege Winter, interview with the author, June 25, 2008.
[24] CM Libros de Reconocimiento and King, *Cobán and the Verapaz: History and Cultural Process in Northern Guatemala* (New Orleans: Tulane University Press, 1974), 86.

Germans' efforts to avert landing on the Proclaimed List via their Guatemalan children often proved futile; Otto Noak, Oscar Majus, and Matilde Quirin found their properties expropriated and their assets frozen.[25] This was in part because the expropriation of German assets derived as much from Guatemalan's searing anti-German nationalism as US officials' desire to reorient trade toward US markets.[26] The German–Guatemalan William Dieseldorff, son of coffee magnate and archaeologist Erwin Paul Dieseldorff, was the exception that illustrates this point. William Dieseldorff was of Jewish heritage, was married to a US woman, and vocally disapproved of Nazism. Yet, like his half-sister Matilde, he appeared on the Proclaimed List. Rather than shoring up familial ties, Dieseldorff proved his loyalty to Guatemala via political patronage and charity. Drawing on a staple of Manuel Estrada Cabrera's regime, William made donations to the Child Protection Society (Sociedad Protectora del Niño) as well as the Red Cross and the Sports Club, and he regularly provided money for the downtrodden. He also funded a new maternity wing in Cobán's hospital and donated his deceased father's archaeological collection to the National Museum.[27] According to one newspaper, Dieseldorff pledged "not to increase his material wealth during the war, but to liberally invest his commercial earnings in public works."[28] Dieseldorff also wrote to the secretary for foreign affairs, noting his prodemocratic stance and desire to support the "great inter-American movement of continental defense."[29] Unlike many wealthy German coffee planters in Alta Verapaz (including his half-sister), William Dieseldorff was never deported, nor were his assets confiscated. In 1945, when the new revolutionary government sought to expropriate German descendants' properties, William reminded the governor of his "social labor" to demonstrate his "quality as a neighbor perfectly identified with the social problems of these towns and [his] democratic faith."[30]

[25] See AGCA AA Leg. 207, 742, and 1282.

[26] Friedman, *Nazis and Good Neighbors*, 184–7.

[27] Information on his charitable acts comes from a series of letters and newspaper clippings found in TULAL DC, Box 9 Personal Correspondence, as well as CM Est. 1 Paq. 16, "W. E. Dieseldorff al intendente municipal sobre donación a la Cruz Roja," August 18, 1942.

[28] "Generosas donaciones hizo en Cobán el Sr. Willi Dieseldorff," *Nuestro Diario*, August 2, 1943.

[29] TULAL DC Box 9 Personal Correspondence, Fol. 1, "William E. Dieseldorff al JP de Alta Verapaz," February 5, 1942.

[30] AGCA JP-AV 1945 Paq. 4, "Sr. Gobernador de Guiellermo Dieseldorff," Cobán, October 16, 1945.

Most wealthy German families in Alta Verapaz were not as fortunate. For the wives and children of deported Germans, moreover, the processes of deportation and intervention of assets inaugurated an era of poverty and social marginalization. Germans found their companies blacklisted or ruined by war, their savings frozen and property confiscated, and employers unwilling to hire Germans and their Guatemalan families for fear of landing on the Proclaimed List themselves. Many German families relied on relief funds financed by the German government through the Spanish and Swiss embassies, and a network of supportive friends.[31] A variety of women were ineligible for German relief payments, including women in nonlegal unions, women who were not German citizens, or women expatriated by Nazi anti-Jewish laws. Disqualified women were left to fend for themselves, sometimes blacklisted by the remnant pro-Nazi German community as racially impure or by the US embassy and local governments as politically unreliable. Q'eqchi' wives and concubines took advantage of Ubico's populist focus on motherhood to gain financial support from the state. In November 1943, Modesta Paau demanded a government allowance since she had "procreated several children with the German Alfredo Christ, who was deported and whose properties ... in this Cabecera have been totally lost, having been intervened."[32] Likewise, Dorotea Winter Tot, the Q'eqchi'–German concubine of Hugo Droege, appealed to Ubico as a vulnerable woman who had been exploited by a German coffee planter.[33]

When the state expropriated Germans' assets and deported them, many perceived these actions as an unthinkable rupture and betrayal. Guatemala had seemingly forsaken its loyal and hardworking immigrants. For Maya plantation laborers, abandoned Q'eqchi–German children, and ladinos who envisioned Alta Verapaz as an anti-imperialist Tezulutlán, the state's actions validated their growing anti-German nationalism and their demands for justice. [34] To complete their feeling

---

[31] See Friedman, *Nazis and Good Neighbors*, 151.

[32] AGCA B Leg. 32234 Exp. 34 1943, CM Libros de Reconocimiento Número 3, Partido No. 17, Fols. 11–19. By 1956 Modesta Paau utilized the postrevolutionary government to petition for ownership of the plantation house, which had been expropriated during the intervention of German properties; see AGCA AA Leg. 307.

[33] AGCA AA Leg. 505.

[34] This burgeoning anti-German nationalism was likely heightened by wartime restrictions on coffee exports that worsened local economic conditions. See Kenneth J. Grieb, "Guatemala and the Second World War," *Ibero-Amerikanisches Archiv* 3, no. 4 (1977): 377–94.

320 Our Time Is Now

that the world had been set right, Mayas sought justice on intervened German plantations. Laborers demanded that the state rent unused portions of German properties to them.[35] Artisans in an intervened German shoe factory demanded better working conditions and increased pay.[36] While anti-German nationalism erupted when cracks in the social and political order became visible, after 1941 Mayas and lower-class ladinos believed a new and more just world was opening up and they demanded that the state realize these promises and end their exploitation.

In addition to domestic pressure, Ubico also faced new demands from the US ambassador in Guatemala City, Boaz Long. The US government threatened to suspend coffee purchases from the German plantations unless the government nationalized the properties and brought them fully under its control.[37] A spontaneous general strike on May 22, 1944, in neighboring El Salvador worsened the situation for Ubico. Drawing on the language of anti-fascism, Salvadorans toppled the dictatorship of Maximiliano Hernández Martínez, further animating Guatemalan middle-class teachers, military officers, and especially university students. In response, Ubico suspended constitutional guarantees.[38] On June 22, 1944, Guillermo Toriello, a key member of the Guatemalan oligarchy, condemned the dictator and called for his resignation, and students declared a general strike.[39] Together, they brought Guatemala City's daily routine to a standstill and crowded the streets in a massive uproar. Opening fire on the demonstrators, Ubico's army units broke up the crowds, leaving martyrs rather than defeated masses in their wake. As negotiations stalled, Ubico abruptly resigned on June 30.

Two weeks later, Guatemala's Legislative Assembly, held at gunpoint, appointed a military general from Alta Verapaz, Federico Ponce Vaides, provisional president. Elections were scheduled for mid-December. Students, teachers, and middle-class professionals, however, believed that

[35] AGCA JP-AV 1942 Paq. 1, "Al JP de Juan Oxom, Pedro Xol y otros," March 26, 1942; AGCA JP-AV 1942 Paq. 2, "Al JP de Francisco Macz y Ramon Coc por arrendamiento de 7 caballerías de tierra," April 8, 1942; and SPCM 1944, "Al Alcalde 1 de síndico municipal sobre los vecinos de Chixtun y arrendamiento de tierras," August 16, 1944.

[36] AGCA JP-AV 1944 Paq. 3, "Señor intendente municipal de los vecinos de esta localidad y trabajadores de la fabrica calzado de Cobán," August 18, 1944.

[37] Friedman, Nazis and Good Neighbors, 185.   [38] Grieb, Guatemalan Caudillo, 273

[39.] See El Liberal Progresista, August 14 and 15, 1941, and El Diario Oficial for the same dates. See also Mejia, El movimiento obrero, 23–6, 54–5; Bauer Paiz, Memorias de Alfonso Bauer Paiz, 65; Manuel Galich, Del pánico al ataque, 287–326; and Dosal, Power in Transition, 80.

Ponce intended to establish a new dictatorship.[40] The aftermath of Ubico's resignation thus emboldened the resistance. Ponce also faced competition in the upcoming presidential elections from two new parties: the National Renovation Party (Partido Renovación Nacional, PNR), which fielded the distinguished professor and doctor of education Juan José Arévalo Bermejo as its candidate, and the Popular Liberation Front (Frente Popular Libertador, FPL), which put forward the student leader Julio César Méndez Montenegro as its candidate.

Seeking to bolster his tenuous hold on power, Ponce gave voice to anti-German nationalism, likely drawn from his experience in Alta Verapaz. Distinguishing himself from fascism and validating popular demands, Ponce created the Department of National and Intervened Plantations under the direction of the secretary of treasury and public credit. On August 14, he then nationalized German plantations and expropriated all German assets, including German businesses, bonds, and shares.[41] The combined Guatemalan nationalized plantations constituted the largest economic enterprise in Central America with some 50,000 employees, 150,000 field workers, and over 30 percent of the country's best coffee plantations.[42] Many Guatemalans regarded Ubico's intervention of German properties as a desperate man's last-ditch effort to appease the anti-fascist masses. An editorialist for *El Imparcial*, for example, argued that Ubico's intervention of German properties was undertaken merely "to satisfy the aspirations of the Guatemalan pueblo in its fight alongside democratic nations against the totalitarian axis, but the majority of the public interpreted it with the classic expression 'kicking a dead horse' or rather the final effort to revive the exhausted prestige of the Ubico regime."[43] Ponce's nationalization, however, was understood as something different. Some regarded it as a nationalist effort to free Guatemala from the colonial shackles of German imperialism, while others interpreted it as a populist effort to demonstrate that Nazis, including many of Ubico's followers, no longer had any influence over the government.

For the following month, public debate and exuberance rocked the nation. *La Nación*, a left-leaning nationalist publication, narrated the expropriation of German properties as the final achievement of

---

[40] See, for example, Heather Vrana, *This City Belongs to You: A History of Student Activism in Guatemala, 1944–1996* (Berkeley: University of California Press, 2017), 36–42.

[41] See AGCA AA Leg. 621 and Leg. 622.　　[42] Handy, *Revolution in the Countryside*, 69.

[43] See "Guatemala para los guatemaltecos," *El Imparcial*, August 15, 1944.

Guatemala's long movement for independence, beginning in 1821 with its separation from Spain. In an editorial entitled "The Nationalization of Nazi Assets," a writer for *La Nación* argued that "foreign colonies ... had established great latifundios and a feudal regime that was damaging to the rights of Guatemalans." Drawing on the long-standing liberal-democratic metanarrative, the editorialist lamented that "riches remained in the hands of foreigners, which was made worse by the fact that the owners were citizens of a despotic country."[44] *La Nación* followed up with several articles detailing the sordid history of Germans in Guatemala. *El Imparcial* lauded the nationalization of German plantations as a step toward "our economic emancipation."[45] Likewise, Ponce's decree was explicitly linked to the heroic nationalization of the oil industry in Mexico six years earlier.[46] *La Nación* and newspapers like *El Imparcial* concluded that all Guatemalans were united to support nationalizing German properties and assets.[47] *Nuestro Diario*, however, clearly disagreed, pointing out how German–Guatemalans were embedded not just politically and economically, but also socially within the nation. *Nuestro Diario* gave examples of the Guatemalan wives and children of German immigrations whose properties had been intervened and asked what would become of them without these assets.[48] The editorialists of *Nuestro Diario* also questioned the automatic association between German nationality and affiliation with the Nazi Party, arguing that some Germans "qualify as faithful friends."[49] *Nuestro Diario*'s opposing voice, however, was quickly drowned out by appeals to anti-fascism and anti-imperialism that reduced German settlers to agents of empire. These editorialists inverted the liberal–democratic metanarrative for a Guatemalan context: German settlement, once a harbinger of a future nation, had actually launched the nation into the past of colonialism and dependency. Germans, rather than Mayas, were the nation's feudal, colonial holdover that prevented the nation's progress and emancipation.

Within two weeks, the national press and the National Assembly lauded Guatemala's having expropriated Nazi properties and vigorously debated how these assets could best serve the national interest. *La Nación* proposed that German properties be distributed among rural workers and

[44] "El decreto de expropiación en la Asamblea," *La Nación*, August 15, 1944.
[45] "Nacionalización de la tierra," *El Imparcial*, August 22, 1944.
[46] "Unidad nacional frente a las expropiaciones," *La Nación*, August 16, 1944.
[47] "Manifiesto de carácter nacional," *La Nación*, August 17, 1944.
[48] "Sobre el decreto número 3134," *Nuestro Diario*, August 17, 1944.   [49] Ibid.

peasants, since "nothing would be more noble and patriotic than the provision of parcels of land, giving the natives their own land, which would make them economically independent."[50] Others argued that the properties should be given to worker unions. Some thought German properties should be distributed to Guatemalans "qualified to work them," by which they clearly meant successful, large-scale Guatemalan coffee planters.[51] Students and medical doctors, on the other hand, reasoned that the properties should be donated to support a system of public health and welfare. By the end of August, nearly everyone agreed that the nationalized property must remain in Guatemalan hands to avoid "falling once again into the economic tutelage of the great foreign capitalists."[52] The National Assembly ruled that only children of Guatemalan fathers could receive nationalized properties.[53] Q'eqchi'–German children and the wives and concubines of German settlers were definitively removed from the possibility of ever possessing these properties.

Despite his populist decree nationalizing German properties and assets, Ponce faced growing urban opposition, since many viewed him as an illegitimate extension of Ubico's dictatorship. In early September, public protests continued in the capital city. Ubico's exiled critics also began to return from Mexico City and Paris. Ponce cracked down on the freedom of the press and jailed and harassed his opponents. One Mexican diplomatic cable noted: "The political situation in Guatemala continues beneath the same tyranny [and] persecutions."[54] Ponce's nationalization of German properties likewise fanned the flames of racial anxieties as Mayas mobilized in favor of land redistribution. Newspapers reported threats of Maya attacks on those preventing access to lands promised by

---

[50] "El dictamen conjunto de hacienda y relaciones: Al margen de la expropiación," *La Nación*, August 21, 1944; see also "Las tierras expropiadas deberían quedar en manos de guatemaltecos," *La Nación*, August 21, 1944.

[51] "Tierras para favorecer guatemaltecos," *La Nación*, August 26, 1944; "Sesiones de la asamblea para discutir exclusivamente un decreto complementario sobre expropiaciones," *La Nación*, August 23, 1944; "Solo a favor de los guatemaltecos," *El Imparcial*, August 21, 1944; "Tierras para guatemaltecos," *El Imparcial*, August 24, 1944; "Destino de los bienes expropiados," *El Imparcial*, August 25, 1944; "Tres mociones sobre la manera de proceder con los bienes nacionalizados en la Asamblea," *El Imparcial*, August 26, 1944; "Fincas a quienes sepan trabajarlas," *El Imparcial*, August 26, 1944.

[52] "Nacionalización de la tierra," *El Imparcial*, August 22, 1944.

[53] "Destino de los bienes expropiados," *El Imparcial*, August 25, 1944.

[54] Telegram from Mexican embassy in Guatemala, August 29, 1944, cited in Guadalupe Rodríguez de Ita, *La participación política en la primavera guatemalteca: Una aproximación a la historia de los partidos durante el período 1944–1954* (Mexico: UNAM, 2003), 120.

Ponce. On September 15, Guatemala's Independence Day, machete-wielding Maya peasants demonstrated in the Guatemala City neighborhood of La Aurora, proclaiming their allegiance to Ponce's Liberal Party. The press speculated that the president had bribed the poor Mayas in an attempt to intimidate urban ladinos.[55] Where newspaper editorialists had earlier celebrated Ponce's nationalization of German properties, by mid-September they denounced "Ponce's terrorist regime."[56]

Unrest and racial tensions flourished in the countryside as urban teachers, students, and military officers organized to oppose the regime, while rural Mayas and peasants led uprisings in Ostuncalso, Chichicastenango, and El Quiché.[57] In September, state officials warned teachers to stop spreading propaganda in their classrooms.[58] As during other moments of tense political mobilization, Cobaneros expressed their anxieties about social and political disorder by complaining about unsanitary dwellings and dirty people lurking in the city's streets. To rein in unsavory elements, local taverns were forced to close, and then the sale of liquor was prohibited altogether.[59]

On October 20, 1944, a group of young, idealistic ladinos from Alta Verapaz joined the largely urban insurrection in Guatemala City and toppled Ubico's would-be successor. As these revolutionaries celebrated the victory of democracy and freedom over tyranny in the city, racial tensions exploded in the countryside. Against the tide of largely urban-ladino popular sentiment of freedom and democracy, Kaqchikels from the town of Patzicía, Chimaltenango, mobilized to ensure that the land Ponce Vaides had promised them would be recognized. Led by Trinidad Esquit Morales, a lieutenant in the army, about twenty-five Kaqchikels armed with machetes, axes, and stones gathered to support Ponce and to protest ladino control of rural property. In response, twenty-two ladinos armed with guns from the neighboring ladino town of Zaragoza arrived in Patzicía to put down the rebellion. The Kaqchikels' machetes were no

---

[55] Piero Gleijeses, *Shattered Hope Shattered Hope: The Guatemalan Revolution and the United States, 1944–1954* (Princeton, NJ: Princeton University Press, 1992), 28.

[56] Ibid.

[57] Richard N. Adams, "Ethnic Images and Strategies in 1944," in *Guatemalan Indians and the State: 1540 to 1988*, ed. Carol Smith (Austin: University of Texas Press, 1990), 144–5. See also Jim Handy, "'A Sea of Indians': Ethnic Conflict and the Guatemalan Revolution, 1944–1952," *The Americas* 46, no. 2 (1989): 189–204.

[58] CM Est. 1 Paq. 3, "Circular a los maestros," September 23, 1944.

[59] AGCA JP-AV Paq. 2 1944, "Circular No. 4275: Proceda cierre establecimientos y ventas de licores," Cobán, October 13, 1944. Another circular followed on October 20.

match for ladino guns. More ladinos from Zaragoza and other towns quickly followed. By the time the national army arrived a few days later, 12–14 ladinos and 60–900 Kaqchikels had been killed.[60] News spread of flaring caste wars as the question of what to do with Guatemala's newly nationalized plantations remained unanswered.[61]

The violence of Patzicía weighed heavily on the revolutionaries, especially as their young leaders deliberated over Maya citizenship, agrarian reform, and the nationalized plantations. By the time the spiritual socialist Juan José Arévalo was elected in 1945, Altaverapacence Mayas already expected the new revolutionary government to deliver justice – the redistribution of the 130 plantations confiscated from the German community. Anti-German nationalism, however, had never been straightforward. The social and political boundaries dividing Germans and Guatemalans had been blurred over decades of sexual unions and marital relations, along with the German diaspora's social and political investments in the region.

REVOLUTION FROM ABOVE, REVOLUTION FROM BELOW

At the outset, revolutionary leaders aspired to modernize Guatemala by definitively separating it from its supposedly dark and outmoded past – from the legacies of colonialism and its enduring feudalism to the more recent histories of dictatorship. Shaped by World War II, the revolution overturned the civilizing metanarratives that had guided celebrations of German settlement in Guatemala. Whereas once Germans and other European foreigners were understood to be historical agents of progress, they were now rendered as anachronistic agents of a feudal order that held Guatemala in a colonial past. Consequently, nationalizing German properties in August and the revolution on October 20 unsettled the foundations of planter sovereignty and coerced labor in Alta Verapaz and Guatemala more generally. While Maya peasant activists like José Ángel Icó seized the opportunity to end vagrancy laws and unpaid labor, and redistribute German farms, embedded local ladino elites and their national allies held debates nationally over the pace of change and the

---

[60] David Carey, Jr., "A Democracy Born in Violence: Maya Perceptions of the 1944 Patzicía Massacre and the 1954 Coup," in *After the Coup: An Ethnographic Reframing of Guatemala 1954*, ed. Timothy J. Smith and Abigail E. Adams (Urbana: University of Illinois Press, 2011), 73–98; Richard N. Adams, "Las matanzas de Patzicía en 1944: Una reflexión," in *Etnias en evolución social: Estudios de Guatemala y Centroamérica* (Mexico: Universidad Autónoma Metropolitana, 1995).

[61] Adams, "Ethnic Images and Strategies in 1944," 144–5.

limits of citizenship. During the first years of the revolution, the contours of the new social and political order – from the meaning of democracy and citizenship to the boundaries of free wage labor and the distribution of nationalized plantations – remained largely unresolved. While the revolution emphasized overturning the old feudal order, the new revolutionaries still largely relegated Mayas to the past, and, like Ubico, they posited that the state's duty was to civilize the poor, indigenous masses. The state was thus given the role of managing the revolution from above. Rural Mayas in Alta Verapaz, however, pushed for a revolution from below as they sought to make real the promises of the revolution, including land redistribution and the end of coerced labor.

Guatemala's revolutionaries required a new constitution to execute their desired social and political reality. Immediately following Juan José Arévalo's election in December 1944, a Constitutional Assembly was elected and set to work under a leadership that included both youthful student leaders and more senior members of the Generation of 20. By the time Juan José Arévalo assumed power on March 15, 1945, the Constitutional Assembly had agreed on the need to decentralize the state's executive power, reorganize the military, and ensure both municipal and judicial autonomy. The 1945 constitution also laid the basis for the revolution's progressive legislation, including the 1947 labor code, the 1948 social security legislation, and the 1952 agrarian reform. Like other social constitutions that emerged in Latin America during the mid-twentieth century, Guatemala's 1945 constitution was the product of revolution and concessions among competing factions and across generations. As Heather Vrana has shown, the constitutional process also reflected the class and ethnic position of the members of the ruling junta, who were from largely literate and increasingly middle-class Guatemala City.[62] The constitutional process thus revealed deep-seated fears about Maya preparedness for participation in civil life, which had defined the politics of postponement for decades. However, it also reflected a hopeful exuberance for a new future and great optimism in the top-down, state-directed change of high modernism.

As the revolutionary leaders sought to define the meaning of the new era, the political and racial violence unleashed by Ponce's nationalization of German properties and his appeals to Maya demands for land weighed heavily on the architects of the 1945 constitution. Patzicía's violent legacy

---

[62] Vrana, *This City Belongs to You.*

most dramatically revealed itself during the Constitutional Assembly's debates over the boundaries of citizenship and the nationalized properties of German–Guatemalans. The ruling junta opposed enfranchising illiterate men and women, not only because they were understood to be backward and uncivilized, and thus unprepared for the responsibilities of citizenship, but also because they believed limited citizenship would secure the nation against fascism and dictatorship.[63] Just as Conservatives in the 1850s and 1860s argued for limiting citizenship because the masses were too easily swayed by demagogues and false promises, the junta, too, argued for limiting citizenship because they believed Mayas were easily exploited by politicians with totalitarian intentions. The revolutionaries established the recognition of political parties and obligatory suffrage and secret ballots for literates (including women), and obligatory and public ballots for illiterate men. Illiterate men were allowed to vote only in municipal elections.[64]

Despite the vociferous conflict over the nationalized plantations, the assembly astonishingly passed Article 152. The article went well beyond what Ponce or the US government had ever intended. Instead, it ratified the expropriation of properties for public need or social uses and opened the door for the expropriation of Guatemalan properties, rather than just those of the foreign nationals of an enemy nation.[65] The 1945 constitution also included a progressive chapter on labor providing for a minimum salary, eight-hour workday, days of rest and vacations, freedom to form unions and to strike, indemnification for wrongful dismissal, and social security. The new constitution, however, also retained a clause on labor as an individual right and social obligation, while vagrancy was a punishable offense.[66] The 1945 constitution thus set the basis for a revolution from above that sought to manage and direct the population to new heights via education and social and cultural reform.

Despite the constitution's limitations, it frightened many landowners and local officials and helped unleash a revolution from below. Moreover,

---

[63] Guatemala Asamblea Nacional Constituyente, *Diario de sesiones de la Asamblea Nacional Constituyente de 1945: Año 1 de la revolución* (Guatemala: Tipografía Nacional, Ministerio de Gobernación, 2006), 124.

[64] Jorge Mario García Laguardia, *Constituciones iberoamericanas: Guatemala* (Mexico: Universidad Nacional Autónoma de México, 2006), 37–8.

[65] Ibid., 41–2.

[66] See 1945 congressional decree 118, which defines vagrants and sets a prison term of thirty days. In *Recopilación de leyes de la República de Guatemala*, vol. 66 (Guatemala: Tipografía Nacional, 1947).

while the new constitution generated rural expectations for agrarian reform and labor rights, no existing legislation put these new norms into practice. In the wake of the 1945 constitution, rural laborers and peasants continuously demanded that the government divide the nationalized plantations among workers.[67] Administrators on nationalized plantations also reported that workers demanded higher wages, neighbors requested the right to plant or rent property, and some laborers refused to work altogether.[68] By mid-1946 Sanpedranos had already taken up the charge of seeking access to intervened plantations. Martin Xi Chub requested that the state grant him a part of Sacatiji since the land "had been abandoned for at least 40 years."[69] Likewise, rural laborers attacked the remaining forms of obligatory and unpaid labor for public works and demanded the implementation of new labor rights. In the first months of the revolution, a group of Sanpedrano Q'eqchi's, aided by a local lawyer, requested that the departmental governor halt the "commissions that come to our properties to remove us and take us to el pueblo to do diverse and forced labor without remuneration."[70] Within a month, Alta Verapaz's municipal councils wrote to the president about the change in labor relations, asking whether colonos, who resided on plantations, counted as laborers under the new law and thus should enjoy eight-hour workdays and vacation pay; whether seasonal wage laborers needed to have a contract, since they worked only one or two days at a time and moved between coffee plantations; and, if so, whether they could continue to run contracts collectively to expedite the process.[71] Coffee planters were deeply troubled. "Cobán's wealth," as one planter put it, resided not "in the soil but in the low wages of our laborers."[72]

As confusion reigned about what the changes in labor law meant on the ground, Arévalo's administration feared communism and believed in gradually "dignifying the workers" through educational reform, rather than material changes.[73] In the president's words, the revolution would be one of "spiritual socialism," rather than the material socialism of

---

[67] Handy, *Revolution in the Countryside*, 81; see also *El Imparcial*, June 21, 1945, August 26, 1947, May 3, 1948; *Diario de Centro-América*, October 3, 1949, and May 21, 1951.

[68] AGCA JP-AV 1944 P1, "Al JP de Dept. de Fincas Intervenidas," September 19, 1945.

[69] AGCA, Ministerio de Gobernación-Alta Verapaz (hereafter MG-AV) B Leg. 32744 Exp. 28 1946.

[70] AGCA, JP-AV 1945 Paq. 6, "Sr. Gobernador Dept. de Francisco Pop, Nicolas Caal, Agustin Caal, Vicente Tec, Reyes Cholom, Nicolas Pan y comp.," August 10, 1945; and SPCM 1945, "JP al intendente municipal," August 24, 1945

[71] CM Est. 8 Paq. 15, "Del Alcalde 1° al Gobernador Departamental," April 2, 1945.

[72] Cited in Handy, *Revolution in the Countryside*, 10.

[73] Forster, *The Time of Freedom*, 88.

redistribution and reform. Avoiding the constitutional amendments on agrarian reform, Arévalo aimed to resolve land inequality and subsistence problems with schemes to colonize the northern jungles.[74] In part, he sought to calm the landed elite's fears, but he also perceived the need for gradual change. Arévalo prohibited rural unions on plantations with fewer than 500 workers and, in a very clear message, dispatched the army to support the coffee planters.[75] He also clarified the vagrancy law: all men, he decreed, were required to carry proof of employment or land-ownership.[76] As a result, the state furiously pursued vagrants. In Carchá, the municipality arrested more than 200 vagrants per month on average.[77] The ongoing persecution of Mayas as vagrants led fifteen Q'eqchi's from San Juan Chamelco to write to president in 1947: "We are land-owners and dedicated to ... intense cultivation. Nevertheless, the large planters of Alta Verapaz force us to abandon our crops [paying us only] a work card ... *in exchange for our free labor.*"[78]

While enforcing legislation that maintained the social and economic order, Arévalo promoted gradual cultural reforms designed to assimilate Mayas and forge a homogeneous nation.[79] Following broader global shifts in racialized discourse, revolutionary indigenismo changed from emphasizing racial degeneration and eugenics to social and structural reasons for the failure to assimilate Mayas into national life. Instead of focusing on bringing German immigrants to improve the racial stock of Mayas, reformers now advocated for increased state intervention in order to protect and assimilate Mayas. In September 1945, Guatemala's Instituto Indigenista Nacional, modeled on its Mexican counterpart the Mexican Instituto Nacional Indigenista, was inaugurated. The institute was designed to bring legal aid, replace corrupted tinterillos and Maya patriarchs, and create bilingual education projects to incorporate Mayas into the nation.[80] A year later, Arévalo founded the famous Mobile Basic

[74] Tony Andersson, "Arévalo's Tomorrowland on the Petén Frontier," in *Out of the Shadow: Revisiting the Revolution from Post-Peace Guatemala*, ed. Julie Gibbings and Heather Vrana (Austin: University of Texas Press, 2020).

[75] Forster, *The Time of Freedom*, 139.

[76] Recopilación de leyes de la República de Guatemala, vol. 66 (Guatemala: Tipografía Nacional, 1947)

[77] Grandin, *The Last Colonial Massacre*, 38.

[78] Cited in Grandin, *The Last Colonial Massacre*, 39. See also AGCA Ministerio de Trabajo (hereafter MT) Leg. 48750, April 11, 1947.

[79] Cited in Dennis Floyd Casey, "Indigenismo: The Guatemalan Experience" (PhD diss., University of Kansas, 1979), chapter 6.

[80] Abigail E. Adams, "Anonio Goubaud Carrera: Between the Contradictions of the Generación de 1920 and U.S. Anthropology," in *After the Coup: An Ethnographic Reframing*

Cultural Missions (Misiones Ambulantes de Cultura Inicial), which were responsible for teaching peasants in the farthest reaches of the country about their civic duties and civil rights, and the revolution's social and moral bases. Coffee planters and state officials who hindered efforts to educate and uplift Mayas were deemed to be anti-patriotic. When one coffee planter, Rafael Casasola, wrote that it was not possible to establish a school on his plantation, because of its distance from Cobán, the rural education inspector lambasted him as an "enemy of the nation."[81] Despite loud critiques of worker exploitation and efforts to discipline planters who opposed rural education efforts, state officials' emphasis on cultural assimilation via education again rendered Mayas as temporal anomalies in the nation, who could be included as agents and actors in the march of progress only once they had ceased to be Maya.

In Alta Verapaz, Q'eqchi' patriarchs sought to represent rural Mayas and civilize the lower classes by participating in efforts to uplift the rural masses. Just as Q'eqchi' patriarchs appointed themselves representatives of indigenous culture in Cobán's department fair, Maya patriarchs made themselves crucial intermediaries in indigenista efforts to implement social and education programs in the countryside.[82] Such efforts often explicitly aimed to inculcate good civic behavior and undermine Maya peasant activists, pejoratively termed *líders*. In 1946 an assembly of governors and mayors warned that "the rise of [campesino] leaders and agitators had served only to take to the countryside and as such to instill campesinos with ideas of labor unionism," which required "counter-propaganda with the purpose of

---

of Guatemala, 1954, ed. Timothy J. Smith and Abigail E. Adams (Urbana: University of Illinois Press, 2011), 17–48.

[81] CM Est. 3 Paq. 7, "Sr. Inspector Técnico de Educación Pública al Rafael Casasola," April 4, 1949.

[82] On the formation of the Instituto Indigenista, see Antonio Goubaud Carrera, *Indigenismo en Guatemala*, prologue by Vela David (Guatemala: Centro Editorial "José de Pineda Ibarra," Ministerio de Educación Pública, 1964), and Jorge Ramón González-Ponciano, "*De la Patria del Criollo a la Patria del Shumo*: Whiteness and the Criminalization of the Dark Plebeian in Modern Guatemala" (PhD diss., University of Texas-Austin, 2005), especially chapter 2. On the misiones ambulantes, see publications by the Institution Indigenista Nacional, especially, "Informe del Instituto Indigenista Nacional," *Boletín del Instituto Indigenista* 3, no. 1 (March 1948): 40, and the *Boletín* published by the Misiones beginning in April 1949. For the link between democracy, cooperativism, and indigeneity, see, especially, J. Fernando Juárez Muñoz, "El indigenismo y la democracia," *Academia Sociedad de Geografía e Historia de Guatemala* 18, no. 2 (1942): 135–8. The Ministry of Education organized a national convention of indigenous teachers in Cobán in June of 1945; see "Incorporación indígena, convención de maestros indígenas en Cobán," *Boletín del Instituto Indigenista Nacional* 1, no. 1 (October–December 1945)

demonstrating to the campesinos the errors sustained by the leaders." One way to halt politicization, the mayors and governors argued, was through the "promotion of sport as a method of removing political ideas."[83] Revolutionary indigenismo thus critiqued exploitation, but like sanctioned indigenismo under Ubico, it also sought to rein in Maya political agitation and promote permissible civic behavior and the ideal of hard work.[84]

Even as Arévalo and state officials, along with Maya and ladino allies, sought to limit and direct reform from above, some Maya peasants pushed for revolution from below by joining political parties that pressed for change. Formal democracy and political parties, as they had in the earlier democratic experiments, presented challenges for Q'eqchi' patriarchs, who had relied on the civil–religious hierarchy, rather than political parties, to seek representation and mediation with the state. The emergence of multiparty competition once again allowed for another kind of intermediary, like José Ángel Icó, to reemerge, alongside a new generation of activists and reformers. These new ladino reformers included Manuel Chavarría Flores and Oscar Narcisco Reyes, who, like Icó and his great-nephew Alfredo Cucul, had familial and personal genealogies dating back to the Unionistas.[85] Some of the most vehement reformers, however, were Q'eqchi'–Germans, whose German fathers had betrayed their familial obligations during the war.

Beyond promoting political organization through party structures, José Ángel Icó also promoted agrarian communities and, later, rural labor unions as means to mobilize Maya peasants and laborers and press for change, particularly the redistribution of nationalized plantations, and an end to vagrancy laws and unpaid labor. Following the 1945 Constitution, José Ángel Icó traveled across the countryside meeting with Maya peasants, requesting contributions for the creation of the Indigenous

---

[83] CM Box. 1946, "Segunda Asamblea de Gobernadores y Alcaldes de Cabeceras Correspondientes a las zonas Norte y Oriente de la República," March 5, 1946. See also CM Est. 1 Paq. 19, "Al Sr. Intendente Municipal del Prof. de Ed. Física," June 14, 1945.

[84] See SPCM 1946, "La revolución," October 20, 1946.

[85] On José Ángel Icó, see, especially, AGCA B Leg. 32578 Exp. 37 1945; AGCA B Leg. 32578 Exp. 52 1945; AGCA B Leg. 32578 Exp. 37; and Grandin, *The Last Colonial Massacre*, 37–45. On Manuel Chavarría, see Manuel Chavarría Flores, *Política educacional de Guatemala* (Guatemala: Imprenta Universitaria, 1951); and Medardo Mejia, *El movimiento obrero*, 45–6. On teachers in the revolution more generally, see Simona Violetta Yagenova, *Los maestros de la Revolución de octubre de 1944–54: Una recuperación de la memoria histórica del Sindicato de Trabajadores de la Educación de Guatemala (STEG)* (Guatemala: Editorial de Ciencias Sociales, 2006). On Oscar Narcisco Reyes, see personal archive held by his daughter.

Agricultural Community of San Pedro Carchá (Comunidad Agraria de Indígenas de San Pedro Carchá, CAISP). The agricultural union's purpose was "to fight for the rights of each and every person before those who always try to exploit the indigenous race."[86] Legalized by the Arévalo administration, agrarian communities were like a combination of union and mutual aid society and were often affiliated with the newly formed national labor federation, the Confederation of Guatemalan Laborers (Confederación de Trabajadores Guatemaltecos, CTG).[87] According to the dozens of court testimonies from rural Mayas, Icó supported the distribution of nationalized plantations among the region's Mayas, so they would no longer be required to work on coffee plantations.[88] Despite opposition in Carchá, Icó used the Comunidad Agraria to halt the persecution of Maya peasants for vagrancy. He wrote personal letters for all members of his Indigenous Agricultural Community, noting that they met the property requirements for exemption from the state's vagrancy laws. These moves infuriated local officials, who had used bureaucratic inefficiencies to round up Maya peasants as vagrants, despite meeting the property requirements.[89]

Together, but often with competing interests, new Q'eqchi' s and ladino political leaders pushed for change and responded to the expectations of free wage labor and land reform from below. By early 1946, the governor of Alta Verapaz, Miguel Ángel Recinos, warned that Maya campesino leaders had "gathered donations with promises to buy land" and urged alcaldes to "oblige coffee planters to pay better salaries and give better living conditions to the campesinos and workers." Most importantly, the governor cautioned that "the leaders and political agitators of the masses must be energetically combated, since these are only thieves who cheat the *indios* with threats, offering them great amounts of land and freedom from labor. As a result, this propaganda must be combated, first with good manners and then with force, since we have just entered an era of true democracy and the leaders have jumped up to discredit it, which goes against the revolution and it must be combated by all means."[90] Likewise, coffee planters and even the governor insisted that, given the department's labor shortage, granting exemptions to all

---

[86] AGACA J-AV 106 Leg. 47 G Exp. 17 1946.
[87] Handy, *Revolution in the Countryside*, 149–50; and Grandin, *The Last Colonial Massacre*, 39.
[88] AGCA J-AV 106 Leg. 47 G Exp. 17 1946.   [89] Ibid.
[90] CM Box 1946, "Segunda Asamblea de Gobernadores y Alcaldes de Cabeceras Correspondientes a las zonas norte y oriente de la República," March 5, 1946.

peasants, as per the law, would cause great "harm to agricultural production."[91] Angered by the disregard for the law, Icó distributed his own
certifications. By November 1946, Carchá's Agricultural Association
charged Icó with extortion, noting that he threatened the region's peace
and tranquility, but also its important agricultural enterprises. Once
again, the Q'eqchi' leader was arrested. His arrest signaled the resurfacing
of Q'eqchi' political mobilization through the alternative channels of local
versions of political parties, which, much like it had in the 1920s, challenged ladino and elite boundaries for social and political reform. Beginning in 1947, German settlers' return from the war furthered polarized
social and political relations.

REVOLUTIONARY TRANSFORMATIONS: GERMANS, NATIONALIZED PLANTATIONS, AND GUATEMALA'S LABOR CODE

In 1949 the Guatemalan anthropologist Antonio Goubaud Carrera
recorded a Q'eqchi' woman's dream in his field notes. According to
Goubaud, the Q'eqchi' woman had encountered a pale, blond German,
who turned out to be the hill's owner – a Tzuultaq'a. Instead of treating
the foreigner kindly, the Q'eqchi' woman was frightened and screamed.
As a result of her disrespect, she would never receive the fortune carried
on the German's mule.[92] Anthropologists highlight deep symbolic similarities between the German settlers and the Tzuultaq'a mountain deities,
which continue today. Tzuultaq'as appear in dreams, like the one
described above, as tall figures, robed in white cotton, with white skin
and hair and, if male, beards. Both the Tzuultaq'as and the Germans are
called bosses, and both are said to have eaten workers. Germans and
Tzuultaq'as are kin to Q'eqchi' communities, related both biologically
and ritually, and each is paid with the fruits of Q'eqchi' labor.[93] Both

[91] Cited in Grandin, *The Last Colonial Massacre*, 42.

[92] Antonio Goubaud Carrera, "Notes on San Juan Chamelco, Alta Verapaz," Microfilm Collection of Manuscripts on Middle American Cultural Anthropology, University of Chicago Library (Chicago, 1949).

[93] Wilson, *Maya Resurgence in Guatemala*, 57–8, 136, 243; Hilary E. Kahn, *Seeing and Being Seen: The Q'eqchi' Maya of Livingston, Guatemala and Beyond* (Austin: University of Texas Press, 2006), especially chapter 4. Karl Sapper argued that the Q'eqchi' understood the Christian God as a white person, and that "they suspect he runs a ranch in the afterlife similar to those that the Europeans own in the Alta Verapaz." See Karl

Germans and Tzuultaq'as are volatile forces in the lives of Q'eqchi'
mozos, capable of extending protection and provisions, but also capable
of retributive violence and denial. For Tzuultaq'as and German planters,
a Q'eqchi' must request permission to use resources and demonstrate
personal discipline, sacrifice, and loyalty in order to elicit the patrón's
goodwill. In this instance, the Q'eqchi' woman's dream can also be seen
as a window into Alta Verapaz's post–World War II historical context.
During the prior two years, deported Germans had begun the arduous
journey back to Guatemala. These Germans, however, returned to discover a revolutionary government that was unwilling to reinstate confiscated assets and properties. As this Q'eqchi' woman's dream suggests,
Q'eqchi's might have worried about how the state and Guatemalans had
betrayed the formidable German settlers and their consequently shifting
economic and historical fortunes. Like the mercurial Tzuultaq'as, the
dream expressed anxiety about retribution for disloyalty and the consequences for the nation's material and economic future. Uncertainties and
tensions about the national future, the return or redistribution of German
properties, and historical justice for Maya laborers played out with
greatest force on the region's nationalized plantations.

As the dust settled following the war's end, Germans interned in the
United States were repatriated to Germany. Some of them, especially
those with few connections to the fatherland, began to make the long
and difficult return to Guatemala. Germans who had been interned as
dangerous Nazis faced great difficulty in obtaining visas from Allied
occupation forces, leading to long and difficult journeys. Hugo Droege,
for example, trekked by foot across the French border, hitchhiked to
Paris, and eventually obtained passage on a series of steamers and small
planes to reach Guatemalan soil in 1948.[94] Having made the onerous trip
to Guatemala, many Germans, like Droege, naively hoped the state would
return their properties and assets. The revolutionary government, however, had little interest in returning German properties, which provided
sources of political patronage and state income. The Q'eqchi–German
children whose German fathers did not return to Guatemala after the war
also faced new hardships and frequently sought their fathers' land and

---

Sapper, "Religious Customs and Beliefs of the Q'eqchi' Indians," in *Early Scholars' Visits
to Central America: Reports by Karl Sapper, Walter Lehmann, and Franz Termer*, ed.
Marilyn Beaudry-Corbett and Ellen T. Hardy (Los Angeles: Costen Institute of Archaeology, University of California, 2000), 37.
[94] Friedman, *Nazis and Good Neighbors*, 225.

possessions. Rodolfo and Francisco Coy Büschel – the sons of Manuela Coy and Gerardo Büschel – petitioned the state for their father's property in 1947. Seeking redress for their poverty, Rodolfo and Francisco explained: "While he was poor and an employee, Sr. Gerardo Büchsel procreated us. But after he had properties and was the owner of plantations, he married another woman, leaving us abandoned, not even recognizing us with a small allowance." "Since we are poor and our mother helped him get rich," they explained, "we come to beg you, Señor Minister, that you grant us this property." The revolutionary government, however, refused to grant Rodolfo and Francisco's request, arguing that personal effects could only be given directly to the owners or their legal representatives.[95]

More generally, the revolutionary governments of Arévalo and Árbenz had no interest in returning nationalized German properties. Instead, the nationalized plantations became a crucial source of patronage politics. In 1947 the nationalized plantation Chimax, which bordered on the expanding city of Cobán, had become home to "the proletariat," and then to a sports stadium to promote the population's health and bodily discipline.[96] The revolutionary government also used positions as administrators on nationalized plantations to reward loyal supporters of the regime, especially after Mariano Arévalo, the president's brother, became director.[97] After Arévalo's election, hundreds of supporters wrote to the new president requesting employment on nationalized plantations, sometimes citing their experience or family obligations, but more frequently their political allegiance and support.[98] As a result, local state officials sometimes gave away portions of nationalized plantations to compensate political allies or rally voters. A 1947 Ministry of the Interior circular to the alcaldes warned against the unauthorized redistribution of nationalized properties in Alta Verapaz.[99] According to the inspector for nationalized plantations, Arturo Laguardia, the resident laborers on the plantation Actela refused to work for an entire year as Cahabón's alcalde promised workers that the plantation would be distributed among them.[100]

---

[95] On his Nazi sympathies, see Terga, *Almas gemelas*, 214–15; on his children's claims, see AGCA AA Leg. 1023.

[96] CM 1947 Est. 6, "Finca intervenida Chimax," and CM 1947 Est. 9.

[97] Handy, *Revolution in the Countryside*, 69

[98] AGCA Ministerio de Agricultura (hereafter MA) Leg. 525.

[99] CM Box 1, "Al Sr. Alcalde Municipal del Gobernador del Ministerio de Gobernación," April 15, 1947.

[100] AGCA MT Leg. 17 Exp. 67.

When the National Assembly finally passed a new labor code in 1948, conflict escalated on nationalized plantations. The moderate labor code was a crucial watershed in Guatemalan history: it inaugurated the forty-eight-hour workweek, regulated the labor of children, set basic health and safety guidelines for the workplace, and introduced a court under the Ministry of Labor to specifically address labor disputes.[101] For the first time, the state offered an official avenue of redress for labor grievances. In practice, however, the Ministry of Labor focused its efforts principally on Guatemala City and the plantations of the southern and Atlantic coasts. In Alta Verapaz, labor disputes continued to go through the departmental governor and local judges; thus, they generated battles over planters' threatened territorial sovereignty. When workers complained that the coffee planter Edith Hesse forced them to work from 7 a.m. to 6 p.m. without a break, in violation of the law, they claimed she retorted that "she had bought this property with her money and the president could not give orders in her property." According to the workers, she had threatened to kick them off the property and to burn their milpa plants.[102] Miguel Pu, along with other residents of the plantation Mocá, complained that the plantation owner, Robert Hempstead, had held them in a makeshift jail for fifteen days.[103] The new law opened up the possibility of challenging the coffee planters' partial sovereignty, but it also generated growing expectations that, above all else, the state should finally end the unpaid and obligatory services Mayas provided in public works and on state-owned plantations.

Q'eqchi's regularly questioned the obligatory labor they provided to municipal councils. Manuel Chen and six other Q'eqchi's from Cobán wrote to the municipality, with the help of Federico Caal Stalling: "We are poor, living off our personal labor as workers who toil [on] the land of those who protect us and we repay that protection with our labor."[104] While referencing the reciprocal obligations that guided plantation labor, the workers objected not to their labor on the plantations but to the municipality's unjust practices, which required residents to provide a week of free labor, since the new labor code required that "all labor must

[101] Forster, *The Time of Freedom*, 156.

[102] AGCA MT Leg. 13 Exp. 168; for another case of workers being removed from the property, see AGCA MT Leg. 25 Exp. 16; and for one in which workers lost their source of water, AGCA MT Leg. 35 Exp. 69.

[103] AGCA MT Leg. 25 Exp. 45.

[104] CM Est. 1 Paq. 6, "Al Señor Ministerio de Gobernación de Manuel Chen Col y comp.," April 1, 1947.

be remunerated."[105] Others challenged Q'eqchi' patriarchs and ladinos who utilized their authority on municipal councils to mobilize indigenous labor for their private plantations. On April 6, 1951, Marco Pop, along with other residents of Cahabón, complained to the president that Francisco Curley Garcia, the alcalde, had required them to plant large extensions of milpa on his plantation without paying a centavo. The Cahaboners recounted that Garcia had emphasized that the workers were providing their service to the state.[106] By questioning the unpaid labor they provided for public works, Q'eqchi's highlighted not only their belief in wage labor, but the fact that Q'eqchi's' reciprocal obligation in the form of unpaid labor to the state was decisively corrupt.

Despite protestations over unpaid labor to municipal councils, rural Mayas exerted power over the councils through long-established channels and mechanisms. Shortly after the passage of the labor code, rural Mayas played municipalities off against each other, as they had in the nineteenth century, to avoid providing their unpaid labor. As a result, conflicts among municipalities over labor for public works projects grew so great that the departmental governor called for redrawing the dividing lines between Alta Verapaz's municipalities.[107] Likewise, Q'eqchi's challenged the vagrancy laws and work cards imposed on them. Mateo Cuhuec Cu and sixty-nine other Mayas wrote to the Ministry of Labor on February 6, 1947, complaining that the indigenous alcalde of Purulhá had forced them to buy work cards and to labor for ten centavos per day on his private plantations on the presumption that they were vagrants.[108] They argued that such a meager salary "was not just or legal" and would recreate "slavery." When the inspector from the Department of National and Intervened Plantations informed the minister that work cards created opportunities for local officials to abuse Mayas, he retorted that such cards were necessary "especially in the frontier zones of the Republic, where there are many illicit means to live."[109]

Revolutionary ideals and old patriarchal politics also clashed with great force on nationalized plantations. While laborers believed that nationalized plantations should have been a vanguard for good labor practices, administrators were unwilling to implement the law or promote

[105] Ibid.   [106] AGCA MT Leg. 35 Exp. 30.
[107] CM Est. 3 Paq. 17 Leg. 8, "Municipalidad de Cobán a Gobernador," April 31, 1947; CM Est. 3 Paq. 17 Leg. 8, "Del Municipalidad de Carchá al Alcalde 1° de Cobán," April 24, 1947.
[108] AGCA MT Leg. 11 Exp. 26, "Mateo Cahuec Cu y compañeros."   [109] Ibid.

laborers' well-being and social uplift. Rather, nationalized plantations operated much as they had when German–Guatemalans owned and operated them. Indeed, shortly after the passage of the labor code, the director of nationalized plantations wrote to the Ministry of Labor to inquire whether laborers employed by the nationalized plantations were even considered to be workers under the new law.[110] National plantation administrators frequently violated the labor code. On the nationalized plantation Xicacao, the administrator Miguel Ángel Roca Barrillas gave tasks that were impossible to complete, provoking the rebellion of workers, who demanded an eight-hour workday.[111] Some denied stipulated rations for workers, while others gave excessive tasks or stole workers' wages through manipulative bookkeeping. Both inspectors and national labor leaders reported that "the greater part of the management-level employees of the National Plantations deny benefits to the workers."[112] Laborers deemed lazy or drunk were kicked off plantations, their crops sold, and their land given to others.[113] Violent physical punishment remained part of daily life. On the nationalized plantation Pantic in Tamahú, Francisco Poou, along with other laborers, requested that the Ministry of Labor intervene so that the plantation's majordomo would stop whipping them.[114] Less than a year later, the same laborers wrote again to the Ministry of Labor, claiming that the plantation administrator did not pay wages and insulted them.[115] When increases to the minimum wage were finally passed in 1950, again the national plantations failed to comply.[116] Despite having broken German–Guatemalan power, the nationalized plantations operated with much the same kind of planter sovereignty as in the past, even though rural laborers pressed the state to uphold its own laws.

As labor and administration diverged on nationalized plantations, labor strikes were common affairs.[117] At times, national plantation strikes went well beyond simply requesting better treatment and adherence to the law. Mayas also articulated their long-standing desire for land ownership and the redistribution of nationalized plantations. Located north of Cobán in the hot lowlands, Chama had been a classic finca de mozos with a large resident population who worked principally

---

[110] AGCA MT Leg. 16 Exp. 105.   [111] AGCA J-AV 107 Leg. 55 G Exp. 4222.
[112] Forster, *The Time of Freedom*, 160.   [113] AGCA MT Leg. 25 Exp. 150.
[114] AGCA MT Leg. 27 Exp. 5.   [115] AGCA MT Leg. 27 Exp. 148.
[116] Forster, *The Time of Freedom*, 175.
[117] See, for example, discussions in Forster, *The Time of Freedom*, 88–9; Handy, *Revolution in the Countryside*, 65–71.

on milpas producing food for their own consumption and for the consumption of workers on the plantations. In the early twentieth century, the German coffee planter Juan von Turkheim owned Chama, but lost the highly indebted plantation, and it subsequently became nationalized. After the revolution, Turkheim's Q'eqchi–German son Jesús Pacay Turkheim became a radical advocate for Q'eqchi' laborers on Chama and a "perennial troublemaker." Shortly following the passage of the 1947 labor code, Jesús Pacay Turkheim led the villagers of Chama to strike, but far from simply demanding better working conditions and adherence to the labor code, they demanded that the government award them ownership.[118] Instead, the Department of National Plantations donated it to the Ministry of Public Health and Social Assistance, so that the plantation would supply corn and beans to local hospitals.[119] In 1950 Jesús Pacay Turkheim once again led resident laborers to demand the distribution of the land among them. As the alcalde auxiliar, Ricardo Yaxcal, noted, the residents were required to plant milpa for the hospital, but "they were very abandoned by the state and have never received any medicine."[120] If the state provided for the health and welfare of other Guatemalans through the backbreaking labor of the villagers of Chama, then why could it not provide land or even medicine to the villagers of Chama?

On the eve of the 1950 presidential election, two forces dramatically deepened political polarization. On the one hand, new rural labor unions channeled the burgeoning pressures for reform from below and quickly injected them into electoral and party politics. On the other hand, nationalized plantations had become central sources of conservative politics that sought to limit reform, particularly agrarian reform, and to direct voting and political participation. After 1948 rural unions spread like wildfire. In 1944 hardly any unions existed in the country. By 1954, 300,000 members of 2,000 rural and urban unions brought together coffee, banana, railroad, and factory workers.[121] As Icó's Comunidad Agraria had demonstrated only a few years earlier, local organizations were potent vehicles for mobilizing rural Mayas in formal electoral politics. Guatemala's nationalized plantations were also highly coordinated mechanisms for limiting and directing votes, and coffee planters mounted obstacles to Maya political participation. While coffee

---

[118] CM Est. 1 Paq. 6, "Ministerio de Gobernación de Jesús Turkheim," April 1, 1947.
[119] AGCA J-AV 107 Leg. 56 D Exp. 214.   [120] Ibid.
[121] Grandin, *The Last Colonial Massacre*, 51.

planters from the Regional Planters Association campaigned against Árbenz, others sought to prevent rural Q'eqchi's from voting by blocking roads and bringing transportation to a halt, forcing Q'eqchi's to make the sixty-kilometer trek to Cobán to vote.[122] Miguel Morales, the general administrator of nationalized plantations in Alta Verapaz, attempted to coerce all the administrators and laborers on the nationalized plantations to vote for the PNR, which did not back agrarian reform.[123] Despite their efforts, Árbenz won in a landslide victory, garnering 258,987 votes out of 404,739 ballots cast. Miguel Ydígoras Fuentes, a general linked to various coup attempts against Arévalo, came in second with 72,796 votes.[124]

Fierce political competition and voter suppression, however, deepened following Árbenz's victory as national political parties also recognized the need to control municipal politics.[125] Likewise, partisan politics and rural labor unions challenged the Maya civil–religious hierarchy and the principles of reciprocity that governed municipal politics. Instead, Maya peasant leaders rallied votes for municipal councils based not only on the patriarchal politics of the civil–religious hierarchy but also on political platforms of agrarian reform, wage increases, and better working conditions. Indeed, San Pedro Carchá's Q'eqchi' elders continue to discuss Ubico's system of intendentes and the subsequent rise of partisan politics during the revolution as the two forces that ruptured the civil–religious hierarchy.[126] Indeed, not since Jorge Yat's attempted revolution in local politics, nearly a century earlier, had rural Mayas mounted such sustained opposition to the local power of both Q'eqchi' patriarchs and ladinos. These cracks in the political order were not, however, without backlash from local power brokers. In the aftermath of Árbenz's victory, municipal elections were highly contested. In Alta Verapaz, Justo Winter Tot, a Q'eqchi–German national plantation administrator, confiscated Q'eqchi' citizenship cards in an effort to prevent voting.[127] In 1951 the Ministry of the Interior circulated a report calling for the preservation of democracy and imploring municipalities to "sustain essential liberties" and "fight for the unaltered maintenance of public order."[128] Despite their efforts, the rural tide of demand for agrarian reform could not be stopped. By 1953, the

[122] Ibid., 44.   [123] AGCA J-AV 107 Leg. 56 Exp. 10 1950.
[124] Gleijeses, *Shattered Hope*, 83.   [125] Forster, *The Time of Freedom*, 73.
[126] Carlos Avilno, interview with the author, September 13, 2007.
[127] AGCA J-AV 107 Leg. 57 K Exp. 834 1951.
[128] CM Est. 3 Paq. 18, "Circular No. 2112 del Ministerio de Gobernación," May 4, 1951.

Revolutionary Action Party (Partido Acción Revolucionaria, PAR), which backed Árbenz, controlled all but one of the region's municipalities.[129]

Árbenz's electoral promise of agrarian reform sharpened social and political tensions in Alta Verapaz. Cobaneros expressed their anxiety about ruptures in social and racial hierarchies, as they had in the past, through renewed fears about the spread of disease, insecurity, and the health of the body politic. Beginning in 1951, Cobaneros lodged complaints about the city's hygiene and drew up new plans to renovate the market.[130] In 1952 Cobán's public health officials once again complained about the city's indigenous landscape: "There are many buildings and homes without adequate fences, [which] is a considerable danger ... since these places frequently become public garbage pits and refuges for vagrants and delinquents."[131] Concerned with the lack of Spanish-style walls surrounding homes and businesses, Cobanero ladinos read urban patios as indigenous vectors of disease and insecurity.

In the countryside, coffee planters' anxieties also rapidly escalated as they prepared for agrarian reform. Among the first legislations Árbenz passed was a modification of the 1949 forced rental law, Decree 853. The General Association of Agriculturalists in Alta Verapaz was up in arms. The agriculturalists complained of an "agitation developing among rural workers" that was "provoked by irresponsible leaders." Altaverapacence coffee planters decried the "situation of anarchy" and "illegal strikes" that were disrupting the national economy and asked for immediate intervention.[132] As rural workers pushed for land, and Árbenz moved forward with the reform legislations, coffee planters turned to traditional mechanisms for instilling fear and discipline. Some kicked troublesome workers off plantations; others squared off with neighbors over plantation boundaries.[133] Nothing, however, deepened the emergent local democracy and challenged both planter sovereignty and Maya patriarchy

---

[129] Grandin, *The Last Colonial Massacre*, 59.

[130] CM Est. 3 Paq. 17 Leg. 3 1952, "Al Alcalde Municipal del Inspector de Sanidad, 'El deterioro casi de los edificios nacionales y malas condiciones higiénicas'"; CM Est. 3 Paq. 12, "Al Alcalde Municipal del Inspector de Sanidad, acumulación de basura enfrente del mercado municipal"; and CM Est. 3 Paq. 19 1955, "Al Alcalde Municipal del Inspector de Sanidad, trasladar al mercado municipal."

[131] CM Box 1952, "Dirección General de Estadísticas 1952."

[132] AGCA MT Leg. 35 Exp. 91

[133] AGCA MT Leg. 41 Exp. 1; see also AGCA MT Leg. 41 Exp. 2; AGCA MT Leg. 41 Exp. 30. On May 31, Enrique Villela Rosa threatened to kick all of his laborers off his plantation. AGCA MT Leg. 41 Exp. 50; see also AGCA MT Leg. 41 Exp. 78; AGCA J-AV 107 1951 Leg. 57 D Exp. 564.

more than Decree 900. Mayas petitioned for land under Decree 900 not simply to hasten Guatemala's transition to modern capitalism as the revolutionaries had hoped, but rather for reasons, including historical justice and memory, that belonged to another logic entirely.

INSURGENT TEMPORALITIES AND CITIZENSHIPS DURING GUATEMALA'S AGRARIAN REFORM

After Árbenz's election, Maya expectations that the state would award workers the national plantations reached startlingly new heights. While the chorus of agrarian reform began among Mayas in the countryside, it was also echoed through the CTG and the PAR. The push for agrarian reforms also reflected the midcentury belief among developmental economists, many of them associated with the United Nation's Comisión Económica para América Latina, that economic and political modernization could best be achieved by a strong activist state. Commissioned by the Food and Agricultural Organization of the United Nations for a global study of food production and landownership, the 1950 census revealed, for the first time, the extent of land concentration in Guatemala, among the highest in Latin America.[134] Seventy-two percent of the agricultural land in the country was controlled by slightly more than 2 percent of farming units, while 88 percent of the farming units controlled only 14 percent of the land. In a country where close to 70 percent of the population depended on agriculture for a living, Guatemala's land concentration meant that almost half of the farming units, representing 165,850 families, had fewer than two manzanas each, a figure suggested as the bare minimum needed for subsistence. On the other hand, 22 planters controlled 13 percent of the agricultural land of the country.[135] Alta Verapaz had the largest concentrations of landed property in Guatemala with 17 plantations of more than 100 caballerías, and another 16 plantations between 50 and 100 caballerías.[136] These statistics, however, are probably inaccurate, as the largest coffee planters put up continual barriers to the collection of statistics, refusing to let state officials enter their property, underestimating the size or value of their properties, or

---

[134] See Handy, *Revolution in the Countryside*, 83.   [135] Ibid., 82–3.
[136] The next closest department was Escuintla with nine plantations over 100 caballerías, and 25 plantations between 50 and 100 caballerías in extension. See *Censo agropecuario, 1950*, 1: 2–24.

simply submitting incomplete records.[137] The 1950 agricultural census was further reinforced by growing international consensus on the need for agrarian reform. That year, a United Nations special council on agrarian reform contended that "economic progress and political stability are closely related to the systems of agricultural economics in force," and called for measures to reduce the causes of "agrarian agitation, political instability, and to foment an elevation in the living standards of workers."[138] Agrarian reform, in other words, was understood as crucial to stemming the tide of rural unrest, blocking the appeal of communism, and ensuring democracy.

Guatemalan revolutionaries also connected the need for agrarian reform with a modified liberal–democratic metanarrative. Rather than blaming Guatemala's backward status on recalcitrant rural Mayas, who refused to labor for wages, they blamed a feudal bourgeoisie that maintained their power and wealth through excessive landholdings and exploited Maya laborers. Guatemala's revolutionaries believed that land and labor reform would curb the power of the bourgeoisie, reduce reliance on coffee exports, increase national production of subsistence products, and gradually turn Mayas into consumers of nationalized manufactures. In short, land reform would support the transition to modern capitalism in Guatemala and, for some, was even the backbone for consolidating Guatemala as a democracy. *El Libertador*, the PAR newspaper, stated in 1951 that "the realization of agrarian reform through the abolition of latifundia and the distribution of land to the campesinos who work it … is the fundamental prerequisite for all the October Revolution's economic, political, and social reforms. No democratic conquest will be stable or permanent without the previous achievement of agrarian reform."[139] For Mayas, however, agrarian reform symbolized something different altogether: the possibility of historic justice and the restitution of lands. For them, access to land was not about charting the way forward in the liberal–democratic metanarrative of progress and emancipation from colonialism and medieval feudalism, but rather about recognizing the presence of the past. They refused to march forward and leave behind the violent politics that had defined plantation life and land dispossession.

---

[137] Forster, *Time of Freedom*, 185.
[138] Cited in Handy, *Revolution in the Countryside*, 83.
[139] *El Libertador*, June 30, 1951, cited in Handy, *Revolution in the Countryside*, 85.

In June 1952, the Guatemalan National Congress passed Decree 900, the agrarian reform law, which allowed individuals or peasant organizations to claim uncultivated land on farms larger than two caballerías, unused municipal property, and national plantations. Rather than managing the revolution from above, Decree 900 also extended democracy into the countryside, empowered Maya peasants, and weakened the power that coffee planters held on agrarian life.[140] Further, land redistribution opened the door to petitioning both nationalized properties and those of Guatemalan landowners. As a series of corruption scandals rocked the Nationalized Plantations Department, a Guatemalan tribunal ruled to liquidate the department and transfer 110 nationalized plantations to the National Agricultural Department (Departamento Agrario Nacional, DAN) for distribution among workers and peasants.[141] By March 1953, seventy-three of those plantations were set to be allocated to peasants and workers.[142] According to newspaper reports, rural smallholders and workers had invaded the nationalized plantations.[143] The reform challenged planter sovereignty not only by expropriating unused land, but also through a series of laws that empowered rural peasants and activists.

First, the agrarian reform undermined planter sovereignty by reordering the territorial basis of the plantation itself and helping foster local leadership. The Decree 900 law established plantation communities of more than fifteen families as their own legal jurisdictions, which significantly undermined coffee planters' power over resident laborers. The reform also promoted the spread of campesino unions. These unions were designed to help rural laborers demand higher salaries, which reformers hoped would both turn rural laborers into consumers of nationally produced manufactured goods and force planters to invest in technology and rationalize production. Likewise, campesino unions sought to facilitate direct relationships between the state and rural laborers and empower the workers to manage everything from social assistance to literacy and health programs. Guided by a mixture of idealism, nationalism, and resentment of the power wielded by coffee planters, Alfredo Cucul, José Ángel Icó's great-nephew, along with a cadre of Maya and ladino activists, fostered the agrarian reform and campesino unions. Within two

---

[140] See Greg Grandin, "Everyday Forms of State Decomposition: Quetzaltenango, Guatemala, 1954," *Bulletin of Latin American Research* 19, no. 3 (2000): 303–20.

[141] "Presupuesto a discusión del congreso" *El Imparcial*, November 3, 1952.

[142] "73 fincas nacionales prestas a parcelarse," *El Imparcial*, March 17, 1953.　　　[143] Ibid.

months of passage of the reform law, these activists had established 185 unions in Alta Verapaz.[144]

Second, the agrarian reform law's bottom-up implementation also undermined planter sovereignty. The agrarian reform was driven by the Local Agrarian Committees (Comites Agrarios Locales, CALs), which were designed to bypass institutions controlled by ladinos and Maya patriarchs, such as municipal councils and their local alcaldes auxiliares and local courts, which planters had historically controlled. The CALs also empowered Maya peasants to invert local hierarchies. Local CALs received the initial land claim, reviewed the documentation, conducted a survey of the land, and passed their recommendation to the Departmental Agrarian Committees (Comites Agrarios Departmentales, CADs), which ruled on the expropriation. Planters could appeal decisions first to the agrarian reform's national oversight board and then to the president, who was the ultimate arbiter of disputes. The agrarian reform law also stipulated the composition of the CALs, which helped shift power in the countryside. Each CAL had five members: campesino unions appointed three and the municipality and departmental governor named the remaining two. In practice, the presidents of the Campesino Union and of the CAL were often the same person. Consequently, the leader of the campesino union petitioning for the land was often also the state representative charged with initially ruling on the petition. The operation of the agrarian reform thus fundamentally challenged coffee planters' version of modernity, which had required partial sovereignty in the space of the plantations. While coffee planters fretted over its meaning, kicked workers off the plantation, and burned milpas, Decree 900, by deepening local democracy and empowering campesino unions, had more far-reaching consequences than anyone had likely anticipated.

For rural Q'eqchi's in Alta Verapaz, Decree 900 went beyond increasing economic efficiency and promoting capitalist development to fortify local democracy, empowering them to once again challenge the authority of both Q'eqchi' patriarchs and ladinos. Even more, the agrarian reform symbolized the historic justice of reclaiming lands unscrupulously acquired by coffee planters and finally ending the violence that marked plantation life. For rural Q'eqchi's, then, agrarian reform did not symbolize a future capitalist modernization. It represented a different time

---

[144] Grandin, *The Last Colonial Massacre*, 56.

altogether: one grounded in Maya histories and practices that had frequently been disavowed by the state. For rural Mayas, Decree 900 opened up an undeferred revolutionary time that countered the politics of postponement with the euphoria of acting in historical time and creating history. For the illegitimate and unrecognized sons and daughters of German coffee planters, the agrarian reform elicited claims to inheritance and familial origin. Altaverapacences, in fact, argue that it was the disinherited sons of German coffee planters who claimed the most land under Decree 900. These rumors of Q'eqchi'–Germans' personal revenge for their loss of inheritance speak to the historical genealogy of patriarchal politics on coffee plantations in Alta Verapaz, and operate in yet another temporality of historical justice that indelibly shaped the implementation of Decree 900.

The agrarian reform came with opportunities and risks for Mayas, along with new conflicts over land rights and boundaries. Coffee plantation life, while far from perfect, offered a known security. The benefits of plantation patriarchy and life were many: planters had historically offered loyal workers protection from the state's worst abuses, paid taxes and fees, obtained exemptions from military service and public work obligations, and defended workers in court. The revolution, however, offered promises that often seemed much less tangible.[145] As a result, divisions among rural Mayas proliferated, as evidenced by the alarming explosion of local conflicts that left burned-out houses and lost harvests in its wake.

The decree also reignited old divisions among Mayas over competing historic ties to land. Maya migration and usufruct land practices had made territorial boundaries movable; while land surveying and titling in the nineteenth century had sought to fix these boundaries, they largely failed. Thus, old divisions, claims, and efforts to recover ancestral lands erupted. In the process, enduring memories of land use were condensed into heated conflicts. For example, Chimo residents petitioned for the neighboring plantation Raxaha on May 24, 1953. Across the first decades of the twentieth century, Erwin Paul Dieseldorff had gradually built the plantation Raxaha from the privatized individual plots of Tanchi-Raxaha, a communal plantation that the Q'eqchi' patriarchs Pedro Coc and Fabian Tiul had sought to turn into a coffee plantation (see Chapters 2 and 3). Chimo's residents had been co-owners of the larger

---

[145] See ibid., 60.

communal property Tanchi-Raxaha, but unlike their neighbors they had not sold off their individual plots to Dieseldorff. In effect, Chimo was the Q'eqchi'-owned remainder of the great Tanchi-Raxaha. Chimo's residents had also sided with the upstart patriarch Fabian Tiul against Pedro Coc, when the latter attempted to make the plantation his own personal property. When Chimo residents petitioned for Raxaha in 1953, they likely did so by evoking memories of and historic claims to Tanchi-Raxaha. Yet the agrarian reform only permitted them to petition for uncultivated or underused property, which sparked a back-and-forth over defining the boundaries of the property and what counted as productive land use. When Erwin Paul Dieseldorff's son William, however, heard of Chimo's petition, he notified the residents of Tanchi-Raxaha, who then submitted their own request under Decree 900.[146] Here, the archival record goes silent and the conflicts that may or may not have erupted between Chimo and the resident laborers of Tanchi-Raxaha remain untold. For the Q'eqchi's of Chimo and Tanchi-Raxaha, Decree 900 did not speak only to the temporality of agricultural modernization. Rather, the Q'eqchi's of Chimo were oriented toward the temporality of belonging to a place and of historic conflicts over land privatization in the late nineteenth century that had divided their community.

Q'eqchi' memories of communal landownership and occupation sometimes united Q'eqchi's in petitioning land under Decree 900. When Andrés Catún and forty other Mayas petitioned for the unused portion of Federico Schleehauf's plantation Aquil in April 1954, their petition included the original land titling measurements to demonstrate both the accurate mojones (boundary markers) of the property and their historic ties to the property as the descendants of its original inhabitants, as if those could be found in some fixed and stable location in the past.[147] State officials, rural Q'eqchi's, and plantation owners, of course, had long struggled to define the fluid boundaries of plantations and their complex social and legal histories of purchase and sale, dismemberment and reconstitution. The state officials had not succeeded, either in the nineteenth or the twentieth century, in fixing land boundaries to the neatly drawn lines of an abstract map. Despite the impossibility of ever recovering fixed boundaries, one might also wonder if these Q'eqchi's did not also recall, despite decades of changing land use, the deeply meaningful markers of identity and belonging of the Tzuultaq'as.

---

[146] AGCA DAN-AV Paq. 6 Exp. 6.   [147] AGCA DAN-AV Paq. 3 Exp. 8.

When Q'eqchi's included historic titles and maps, they also exceeded Decree 900's requirements. As a mid-twentieth-century bureaucratic practice, the Decree 900 petitions were intended to be highly formulaic documents, which left no physical space for presenting local memories and histories of land use. Thus, when Andrés Catún petitioned for Aquil, he must have felt strong in his conviction that such memories were central to the agrarian reform's meaning and aims. Catún's violation of these formal bureaucratic norms with communal memories of land use was common. When Tiburcio Poou and four other Mayas petitioned the state through Decree 900 to award them the plantation San Antonio Tontem, they carefully detailed their right to the land through their father and grandfather. The current owner, Ricardo Garcia, the petitioners claimed, had taken advantage of a Poou family illness to obtain the title to the land: "it rightfully belongs to us and all of this time the señor [Garcia] has denied us the right to plant our milpa on this land."[148] Like Chimo's residents, Aquil residents explicitly based their claim on longer memories of land use and belonging and sought historic justice. Such memories validated the historic justice of the agrarian reform for rural Mayas, even as it was part of a set of Maya temporalities. In disrupting a staid bureaucratic procedure with socially dense memories of land inheritance, Q'eqchi's transcended and violated the norms of bureaucratic records, which required Maya petitioners to frame their desires and demands in terms of the state's own criteria: the plantation's size and the productive use of the land. In doing so, they demonstrate the multiple meanings and times associated with the reform.

The agrarian reform also symbolized familial genealogies and rights to the Q'eqchi–German children of German planters. In August 1953, Eduardo Kurtzel's four Q'eqchi–German children petitioned for their father's nationalized land under Decree 900.[149] After Benjamin Champney Caal lost his father's plantation to his siblings, he petitioned through Decree 900 for his father's land.[150] Some Q'eqchi–German children, like the Winter Tot brothers, also worked alongside their German fathers and uncles seeking the return of German property confiscated during the war.[151]

[148] AGCA DAN-AV Paq. 5 Exp. 9.
[149] AGCA DAN-AV Paq. 17 Exp 3; Juan Kurtzel, interview with the author, April 7, 2008.
[150] AGCA DAN-AV Paq. 1 Exp. 11; also Edgar Champeny, interview with the author December 15, 2007.
[151] AGCA J-AV Leg. 59 M Exp. 1770 1953.

Rumors circulate in Alta Verapaz that the illegitimate children of Q'eqchi–Germans also petitioned for their fathers' land. Spoken through the temporal register of rumor, tales of unrecognized and illegitimate Q'eqchi–German children seeking their inheritance speak to deeper social truths that transcend dichotomies between fact and fiction. In part, these tales emerge only through rumor, because, as the products of plantation rape and exploitation, these children are living evidence of the bitter sexual and racial violence of plantation sovereignty and Eurocentric modernism. As one Guatemalan coffee planter explained: "The only solution for Guatemala is to improve the race, to bring in Aryan seed to improve it. On my plantation, I had a German administrator for many years, and for every Indian he got pregnant I would pay him an extra fifty dollars."[152] The German coffee planter Hugo Droege's son-in-law noted that Hugo cultivated an "improved" and "loyal workforce" through interracial sex, supposedly having fathered more than a hundred children.[153] Through Decree 900, the 277 resident laborers of San Vicente petitioned for and received the plantation that Hugo Droege had owned before the war. If the rumors of interracial union are true, then as least some of the residents would have been Hugo Droege's unrecognized children. [154]

Coffee planters and nationalized plantation administrators fought viciously against the reform.[155] In the nationalized plantation Sacoyou, the administrators, Rafael Alvarado and Benjamin Valdez, spread reports that the plantation would become a cooperative if workers petitioned the land. One witness remarked, "We will never form a cooperative with them, since this will just be a new vehicle for our exploitation and for this we have formed a Campesino Union and petitioned for this plantation in individual parcels." The administrators Alvarado and Valdez, the witness continued, only wanted "to make a joke of our only desire and Coronel Árbenz's proposal to liberate the campesino with the correct application of Decree 900 of the National Congress."[156] As the workers persisted, Alvarado and Valdez aggressively sought to prevent state officials from measuring the land. According to workers, administrators also threatened

[152] Marta Elena Casaús Arzú, *Guatemala: Linaje y racismo*, 3rd ed. (Guatemala: F&G Editores, 2007), 251.
[153] Eduardo Rosales Rulet, interview with the author, April 15, 2008.
[154] AGCA DAN-AV Paq. 17 Exp. 11.
[155] AGCA DAN-AV Paq. 17 Exp. 3; AGCA DAN-AV Paq. 17 Exp. 4.
[156] AGCA DAN-AV Paq. 17 Exp. 4.

to incarcerate peasants who petitioned for land.[157] Coffee planters fired workers who made claims under Decree 900. Other planters torched grazing lands, killed cattle, or burned laborers' homes.[158] William Dieseldorff, long known for co-opting peasants, sought to make personal deals with laborers. First, he offered laborers title to their existing plots in the finca de mozos; when this plan failed, he offered them additional property on an adjacent plantation.[159] What Dieseldorff presented as a planter's generous offerings were actually law: the agrarian reform required that all communities of fifteen families or more be granted title to the plot of land they occupied.[160] As his father had before him, Dieseldorff recognized the power of keeping the state out, reaffirming his own sovereignty and patriarchal power.

As the agrarian reform emboldened Maya peasants to upset racial and social hierarchies, Decree 900 also heightened the association between race and politics. Racial ascriptions in Alta Verapaz had long relied on effective performances as markers of difference, just as space and time had been used to discipline and postpone poor Mayas. Maya performances existed within a political and widely contested discursive field. During Guatemala's October Revolution, the term *líder* (leader) became a pejorative accusation. It was used as a synonym for trouble-maker and attributed to Maya activists, as Boshevik agitators had been in the 1920s. The term racially darkened those who were labeled with it. Few associated the Q'eqchi–German Maya leaders Eliseo Ax Burmester, Jesús Pacay Turkheim, or Federico Caal Stalling with the racial white-ness of their German fathers. On the other hand, anti-communism took on a racial-whitening flair and, by 1954, became associated with order, progress, and modernity. The most virulent anti-communists were the Q'eqchi'–German Winter Tot family and the Chinese Guay family. The Guay family, in particular, worked hard to distinguish themselves as racially white, and had been labeled and policed by the state in the 1930s as the "yellow race." Together, the Guay and Winter Tot families harassed and violently attacked activists such as Eliseo Ax Burmester and Federico Caal Stalling in the streets of Carchá.[161] Belen Guay, along with her sisters and aunts, was one of the principal anti-communists in the town of Carchá, and Belen's daughter proudly recalled in an

---

[157] AGCA DAN-AV Paq. 17 Exp. 20.   [158] Foster, *The Time of Freedom*, 183.
[159] AGCA DAN-AV Paq. 1 Exp. 1; AGAC DAN-AV Paq. 6 Exp. 8; AGCA DAN-AV Paq. 5 Exp. 11.
[160] Forster, *The Time of Freedom*, 178.   [161] AGCA J-AV 107 Leg. 56 Exp. 238 1950.

interview how they distributed anti-communist leaflets and badgered Communist organizers.[162] By participating in local party politics, women like Belen Guay effectively entered the world of politics and claimed racial whiteness.

Alta Verapaz's racialized politics reached a crescendo during the CIA-supported coup on June 17, 1954. When news reached Alta Verapaz of bombings in the capital, hundreds of Altaverapacence students and peasants headed to Guatemala City. The military intercepted them on the way. When the revolutionaries arrived at a local military base, the organizers suddenly realized that they were not being transported to defend the revolution, but had become political prisoners.[163] Gustavo Droege Winter, the Q'eqchi'-German son of the German planter Hugo Droege, was among the resisters. Politics, while seemingly riven along racial lines, crossed and divided families. From the rumors of illegitimate children petitioning for their father's land to planter's children defending the revolution, intimate tales of sexual excess, betrayals, and revenge permeate the memories of Guatemala's 1952 agrarian reform and the 1954 coup. These rumors speak to how rural Mayas and Q'eqchi–Germans troubled racial and political boundaries as they sought different futures.

HISTORY INTERRUPTED: THE 1954 COUP

If the revolution ignited local democracy and inspired Maya peasants to end the historical purgatory of postponed citizenship, then, as Greg Grandin argues, the counterrevolution that followed also generated particular understandings of time that demobilized and depoliticized people, turning them into spectators rather than political agents.[164] While the events of 1920 and 1944 had given rise to the feeling that people were living and acting in revolutionary time, 1954 removed this sense of historical and political agency, rendering people as passive bystanders. [165] But it was also a shared historical event experienced in profoundly different ways. While some like Gustavo Droege Winter joined the resistance, others like the North American Hempstead family provided intelligence to the CIA, as they had during World War II, and celebrated the coup.[166]

---

[162] Isle Paredes Sánchez, interview with the author, September 14, 2007.
[163] Grandin, *The Last Colonial Massacre*, 66.   [164] Ibid.   [165] Ibid.
[166] Leslie Hempstead, interview with the author, September 19, 2007.

In the coup's aftermath, politicians hostile to the revolution's direction transformed political party affiliates into provisional anti-communist defense committees and took charge of municipal and departmental offices. The new provincial government set up the National Defense Committee Against Communism, granting it both judicial and executive power to investigate, arrest, and try suspected subversives. The Preventive and Penal Law Against Communism empowered the committee to create a register of all the people who had participated in Communist activities. While some individuals accused of being Communists had been affiliated at one time with either the PNR or Guatemala's Communist Party (Partido General de Trabajadores, PGT), others were more clearly victims of retribution. Carlos Winter Tot, for example, had twelve Q'eqchi' members of the CAL in San Vicente arrested as suspected Communists in July 1954.[167] Francisco Curley, a peasant organizer, was arrested with ten others and accused by Belen Guay's friends in Carchá. Their interrogation consisted of being asked whether they had ever been members of the PGT, whether they believed in Marxism, and whether they had ever "agitated the campesino masses."[168] The son of the indigenista Celso Reyes, who had advocated for indigenous citizenship in the 1920s, declared that his only crime was having "worked to teach people to read."[169] Another prisoner, Guillermo Wagner Weikert, from the Czech Republic, admitted only to having "made propaganda during the elections in the finca Chinasayub."[170] A local anti-communist newspaper, *El Sulfato*, celebrated the persecution of Communists in Alta Verapaz. Yet even *El Sulfato* published editorials that began to critique the state violation of the constitutional guarantees to a fair trial. Arturo Morales Cruz, William Dieseldorff's principal manager and lawyer, penned a powerful editorial calling for justice and liberty – the rule of law and democracy. He called for "ideological toleration" so that "no one is persecuted for the expression of their loyal and well-intentioned thought." These were necessary conditions, he argued, so that "the barbarians never again arrive at the ports of the Nation."[171]

As local Maya and ladino peasant leaders were beaten, tortured, and imprisoned, fear spread across the countryside, enabling the near-complete reversal of the agrarian reform. Q'eqchi's who had only recently been granted usufructal rights to land under the decree reversed course by

---

[167] AGCA J-AV 107 Leg. 60 H Exp. 2108 1954.
[168] AGCA J-AV 107 Leg. 60 H Exp. 2111 1954.   [169] Ibid.   [170] Ibid.
[171] Arturo Morales Cruz, "Del actual momento político-social," *El Sulfato*, June 4, 1955, 2.

arguing that they had been coerced by peasant leaders like Cucul into petitioning for land. Pedro Caal, Sebastian Icó, and others who had received usufructal title to Chapultepeque in San Pedro Carchá on January 15, 1954, relinquished their claim one year later on January 27, 1955. That day, the Sanpedranos announced that "they were working in harmony with their patrona and that she provided them with the plots of land they wanted for their own crops and that they had made the petition because one day three campesino leaders arrived at the plantation and they had forced them to do it or others would and they would be forced from their homes."[172] These Q'eqchi's may simply have been drawing on the outside agitator trope to assert their innocence and limit the possibility of backlash. While June 1954 represented the violent closure of an era, for many others, history remained the fervent promise of a different future. In December 1954, Victoriano Tiul, Alberto Tiul, and Juan Tiul – residents of the plantation Chitocan – allegedly resisted arrest on charges of vagrancy. According to their captors, the Tiul brothers had charged at the local alcaldes auxiliares with their machetes and yelled, "You will not remain long in the post that you occupy, because soon the government will fall, because it is worthless and the only good president was Árbenz and when the current government falls they would be in charge." When Federico Caal Stalling, their patrón, arrived at the court, he verified that the Tiul brothers had not completed their work obligations. While Caal Stalling had once supported the agrarian reform, he now sealed his workers' fate as vagrants and political agitators. The Q'eqchi's' testimony highlights the enduring legacies of the sovereignty of plantation politics, the racial order, and coerced labor as they collided with the hope that a different era was on the horizon.

When the agrarian reform came to a sudden halt with the overthrow of Árbenz in 1954, Q'eqchi–Germans petitioned the state to return their fathers' plantations. Individuals who had been on opposite sides of the political struggle over agrarian reform during the revolution – the rabid anti-communists Doratea Winter Tot and Carlos Winter Tot; the participant in the Hitler Youth, Otto Schleehauf Pacay; the advocates of agrarian reform and Maya peasants, Jesús Pacay Turkheim, Frederico Caal Stalling, and Lorenza Sapper – united under the banner of the Authentic Liberal Party (Partido Liberal Auténtico, PLA) to claim their fathers' properties. Asserting their German heritage and rights to their fathers'

[172] AGCA DAN-AV Paq. 7 Exp. 2.

properties, none of the petitioners included their mother's Q'eqchi' name in the petition. Referring to Guatemala's place in the global hierarchy, the Altaverapacence Q'eqchi–Germans wrote, "The Authentic Liberal Party is working toward the return of German properties that are still found intervened and nationalized in order to place our beloved Guatemala on par with other nations of our continent, who are providing a beautiful example of returning what legally does not belong to them."[173] They would not, however, be among those who received nationalized properties in the counterrevolution.

The right-wing, anti-communist administrations that followed in the wake of Árbenz's overthrow did return some German properties. General Miguel Ydígoras Fuentes had befriended many Germans while serving as Guatemala's ambassador to Great Britain in the 1940s. He had visited Guatemala's deported Germans held in camps in occupied Germany after the war and pledged to help them.[174] When Ydígoras Fuentes took power in 1958, he claimed that the confiscation of German properties had been a "national shame" and returned some of the properties to their original owners. But his administration also used the plantations for patronage politics, and some of the nationalized plantations were to be redistributed. Two hundred military officers were the first buyers.[175]

CONCLUSION

Guatemala's famed revolutionary spring was a defining event in the Latin American Cold War. The revolution also has longer historical genealogies that date from the rise of coffee production, with its practices of coerced labor, and German settlement across the nineteenth and early twentieth centuries. The revolution cannot be reduced to the 1947 labor code and the 1952 agrarian reform, although they were indelibly important. The revolution was also a historic moment that foregrounded Maya historical memories of struggles over land use and a different kind of democracy rooted in reciprocal obligations and solidarity that took place over the course of the nineteenth century. In the more immediate context, the

---

[173] Marta Elena Casaús Arzú, *Guatemala: Linaje y racismo*, 251, Eduardo Rosales Rulet, interview with the author, April 15, 2008; AGCA AA Leg. 775.

[174] Friedman, *Nazis and Good Neighbors*, 186.

[175] Thomas Melville and Marjorie Melville, *Guatemala: The Politics of Land Ownership* (New York: Free Press, 1971), 122–33; and Christiane Berth, *Biografien und Netzwerke im Kaffeehandel zwischen Deutschland und Zentralamerika 1920–1959* (Hamburg: Hamburg University Press, 2014), 424–43.

revolution was also defined by the rise of fascism and anti-fascism in both Germany and Guatemala, and pushes us to move beyond the national frame of traditional historiography to place Guatemala's famed revolution in the broader global context.[176] While historians have rarely considered either World War II or the nationalization of German properties, these processes are crucial to understanding the revolution's origins, processes, and legacies. In the longer duration, the revolution bore the imprint of the legacies of German settlement: interracial unions that generated hierarchies among first and second families, and between mixed-race children and their German counterparts. The feelings of intimate betrayal and rightful inheritance played a central role in mobilizing some to petition for their fathers' land. Even more centrally, the mobilization of Maya peasants for land, along with their ladino allies, was generated by unfulfilled expectations for democracy and equality, citizenship and inclusion within the nation. The agrarian reform in Alta Verapaz, where more land was awarded than anywhere else, cannot be separated from these longer and global histories, even as it was, as Greg Grandin has argued, a central place where the more typical story of the Cold War also played out.

As this chapter has demonstrated, Guatemala's revolution was also neither singular nor unified. Q'eqchi's, ladinos, and German– Guatemalans also struggled over the boundaries and meanings of the revolution. These many revolutions also shifted over time as the initial euphoria of democratic eruption in 1944 gave way to doubts and disagreements among the revolutionary leaders over the extent of reform. Ultimately, however, the burgeoning demands from below pushed the revolution to deeper political, social, and economic changes with the election of Árbenz and the 1952 agrarian reform.

Historical time was at the heart of the revolution, not just in the teleological notion that the state should direct the nation toward a modernist capitalism, but in another time altogether that cannot be easily subsumed into the time of modernity and the state. For some, like Q'eqchi' laborers on nationalized plantations, the past was present because it held memories of land use and ownership, with their norms of reciprocity and solidarity, and promised a historical reckoning in the present. For Mayas and ladinos who sought to break with the past and forge new futures, however, history also offered them a way to think of

[176] See also Weld, "The Other Door."

their ability to act and influence the world around them in contingent circumstances. The revolution invited them to think of it and their own lives as historical, and therefore politically relevant, and to challenge Mayas' relegated location in the past of modern nations and civilized peoples. At the heart of these struggles were efforts to unsettle or reaffirm the legacies of nineteenth-century capitalist development in Guatemala: the racialized distribution of labor and capital, the postponement of Maya citizenship, and the privileging of northern Europeans as the pinnacle of modernity.

Conclusion

Colonial pasts, the narratives recounted about them, the unspoken distinctions they continue to "cue," the affective charges they reactivate, and the implicit "lessons" they are mobilized to impart are sometimes so ineffably threaded through the fabric of contemporary life forms they seem indiscernible as distinct effects, as if everywhere and nowhere at all.

—Ann Stoler, *Duress: Imperial Durabilities in Our Times*

For nearly a century, Altaverapacences fought over time: they evoked and challenged the historical times of liberal–democratic and civilizing metanarratives, they debated who and what counted as agents of history, they contested which nations and peoples were civilized or uncivilized, they fought over the commodification of labor time, and they sometimes created cyclical and spirit times embedded in the agency of days and mountain spirits. Time mattered. Q'eqchi's and others wrestled over temporal categorization and metanarratives because time was central to political contests over potently distinct visions of the future. Mobilizing the disciplining power of periodization, Guatemalan elites and state officials argued that backward and uncivilized Mayas were *not yet* ready for citizenship and free wage labor. Mayas then became objects of state and nonstate management and intervention, ranging from vagrancy laws and sanitation campaigns to whipping posts and regulation of subsistence production. Through references to liberal–democratic and civilizing metanarratives, state officials and coffee planters used periodization to give political weight to racialized differences and to define who counted as citizens. Temporal categorization converted people who were culturally different into dangerous others who imperiled the nation and progress.

Time could also liberate. Q'eqchi's sought to forge new and unsettling modernities grounded equally in universal aspirations for prosperity and self-determination and locally specific practices of solidarity and reciprocity. Time also mattered because the histories of Q'eqchi' political struggles left indelible debris in memories, institutions, and landscapes. The remnants of subaltern struggles formed time-knots: those disruptive moments such as Jorge Yat's attempted 1865 revolution and the 1952 agrarian reform. During these moments, Q'eqchi's made the past present and thus opened their worlds to historical reckoning and justice. In both instances, these revolutionary time-knots required a violent overthrow that dramatically ended one era and launched a new and more vicious one: the 1871 Liberal Revolution and Guatemala's post-1954 civil war.

The time-knot of Jorge Yat's 1865 rebellion wove together enduring colonial pasts, liberal–democratic ideologies, and emergent futures based on coffee production and racial capitalism. Yat's rebellion brought together forms of native mediation and indigenous practices of reciprocity and solidarity built over several centuries of colonial rule, democratic ideas of popular sovereignty founded in the age of Atlantic revolutions, and the violent and racialized dispossessions of nineteenth-century capitalism. Because these pasts, presents, and futures were so contested and potent, state officials, ladinos, and rural Mayas also interpreted the short-lived rebellion's causes and consequences differently. As state officials and ladinos sought to control the meaning of the rural Q'eqchi' uprising that took control over San Pedro Carchá's municipal council and jailed Q'eqchi' patriarchs, they inscribed their own explanations of the events as a race war by Mayas against ladinos and coffee production into the archive itself. Yet, even that archive revealed, through the words and actions of those who stood trial for sedition, that rural Q'eqchi's fought not against ladinos but against Q'eqchi' patriarchs. They were inspired to act not out of fear of coffee production and land alienation, but by the liberal–democratic promise of popular sovereignty and in response to the state's encroachment into their largely autonomous rural spaces. Historians, however, have often been far too willing to view Guatemalan history as defined by a binary conflict between Mayas and ladinos, rather than to discover more complex stories that cross racial, gender, and class divides. These multiple axes of conflict over power help us to better understand the 1871 Liberal Revolution led by upwardly mobile ladinos from Guatemala's western highlands.

After 1871, some Q'eqchi' patriarchs in Alta Verapaz navigated the new Liberal era by strategically embracing new Liberal principles of land privatization, coffee capitalism, and state expansion. These Q'eq-chi' patriarchs titled communally owned properties often as their own private plantations and planted coffee trees in the place of milpa. In the process, they translated Q'eqchi' principles of labor reciprocity on communal properties into the labor obligations of resident workers on coffee plantations. Further, if we speculatively read the land titling process for its unintended principles, we can also see how Q'eqchi's sought to fix spiritual markers of the Tzuultaq'as to the boundary markers of new private properties. Q'eqchi' patriarchs likely sought not only to enrich themselves and bolster their class positions but also to protect rural Q'eqchi's from the vagaries of mandamiento labor. Despite Q'eqchi' patriarchs' efforts, however, state officials rarely recognized Q'eqchi' coffee plantations. As a result, the lower-class Q'eq-chi's from Q'eqchi' plantations were still required to provide their labor to non-Maya planters through mandamientos. In their responses to Q'eqchi' efforts to forge plantations, land surveyors and state officials often revealed their racism with a startling frankness. They were also willing to bend the law to support non-Maya planters over their Q'eq-chi' counterparts. Unable to protect rural Mayas from coffee planters' seemingly insatiable demands for labor, Q'eqchi' patriarchs soon faced a growing crisis of native mediation.

As coffee production devoured Q'eqchi' land and labor during the mid-1880s coffee boom, rural Q'eqchi's also faced increasingly precarious conditions and found their communal bonds of reciprocity and solidarity strained. When a massive frost destroyed coffee harvests in January 1886, many rural Mayas, as well as local ladinos, interpreted the frost as the revenge of the mountain spirit Xucaneb against the evils of coffee production. Since the agency of the mountain spirit Xucaneb was so central to Q'eqchi' and non-Maya responses to the frost, these events reveal the limits of writing disenchanted histories that refuse to account for nonhuman agency and spirit worlds in the making of history. As the region descended into a moral and economic crisis, coffee planters, Q'eq-chi' patriarchs and their ladino allies, and state officials made historical time and metanarratives central to the debate over mandamiento labor's place in a modern nation. While coffee planters and state officials frequently deployed the politics of postponement to argue that rural Mayas were not yet civilized enough for free wage labor, other Q'eqchi's and their ladino allies argued that there was no place for slavery in a modern nation. The dramatic nature of the 1886 frost and responses to it became etched deeply in popular historical memory, and references to Xucaneb's revenge repeatedly resurfaced during moments of subaltern resistance to forced labor.

Alta Verapaz's late nineteenth-century crisis of native mediation and coerced labor, as well as the post-1898 global coffee crisis, gave rise to new modalities of coffee production based on fincas de mozos. A small handful of German settlers with access to foreign capital were particularly well placed to take advantage of spiraling inflation and indebted planters who could not pay their loans. These well-positioned planters, especially Erwin Paul Dieseldorff and Richard Sapper, could rapidly expand their holdings by purchasing the highly indebted properties of Guatemalans as well as other settlers who lacked such ready access to foreign capital. As they expanded their land ownership, some German coffee planters reshaped Alta Verapaz's plantation economy around fincas de mozos or plantations whose primary purpose was to ensure a stable labor force for coffee plantations. Modeled on colonial haciendas, German and other coffee planters not only secured steady access to labor for coffee production, but also forged a kind of limited territorial sovereignty in the space of the plantation, complete with whipping posts and jail cells. Likewise, a sexual economy emerged alongside coffee planting, as some Q'eqchi' women became both domestic servants and concubines to German and other coffee planters. These fincas de mozos also marked Alta Verapaz as significantly different from other coffee-producing regions in Guatemala, where fincas de mozos existed but were not the norm. Examining fincas de mozos also helps us to better understand why Guatemalan state expansion in the nineteenth century was circumscribed, why planter power was so pervasive, and why Maya patriarchs' power did not, as Greg Grandin has claimed, grow directly in relation to the expansion of the state.[1] Indeed, Guatemalan state expansion was much more uneven and the role of Q'eqchi' patriarchs far more circumscribed than previously thought. Coffee plantations constrained state expansion and helped define racial, sexual, and class relations in Guatemala. Despite planter sovereignty, Q'eqchi' resident laborers used the means at their disposal, including petitioning to state authorities and clandestinely producing goods for local markets, to increase their autonomy and limit planter power.

While fincas de mozos marked the limits of state expansion and generated racial, gendered, and class hierarchies, Q'eqchi' laborers have

---

[1] Grandin, *The Blood of Guatemala.*

also offered us trenchant critiques of Guatemala's racial capitalism as it functioned on fincas de mozos through the figure of El Q'eq. Reading oral histories for their philosophical content, El Q'eq – a half-man, half-cow who steals from poor laborers to enrich coffee planters – reveals Guatemala's racial capitalism to be a perversion of Q'eqchi' norms of solidarity and reciprocity. A voracious consumer of eggs, symbols of new life, El Q'eq represents the kind of social death that occurred on coffee plantations. Policing the boundaries of the plantation under the cover of darkness and terrifying those it encounters, El Q'eq also discloses the coffee planter's territorial sovereignty as an integral dimension of the disciplinary regime of coffee capitalism. As the product of sexual perversion, El Q'eq also underscores the centrality of the sexual labor economy in plantation politics. Unlike Marx's metonymic chain of commodities, El Q'eq operates through metaphor and allegory, revealing the multiple layers of material and symbolic power central to racial capitalism. Q'eqchi's reveal that racial capitalism was morally bankrupt and could impoverish, discipline, and terrify in addition to subjecting Mayas to class alienation.

By the end of World War I, the contours of Alta Verapaz's plantation economy had been largely established around a few prominent German coffee planters and a preponderance of fincas de mozos, which housed rural Q'eqchi' laborers. The politics of postponement represented a central component of this racialized plantation economy, in which racial difference was intimately tied to Mayas' purported inability to participate effectively in either a modern capitalist economy or democratic political life. The solution to this racialized dilemma was to foster racial improvement under the careful tutelage of a coffee planter, who would require Mayas to labor for the advancement of the nation. The politics of postponement, however, ensured that many Guatemalans perceived their own modernity as circumscribed and postponed. This sense of waiting was further aggravated by the growing class of urban plebeians, who crowded urban streets and confounded racial categorizations. Urban, middle-class anxieties about unfulfilled modernities set the stage for the common Latin American drama of populism, revolution, and counter-revolution. While dramatically different, these different modalities of governance all promised to end the waiting of the lower and middle classes and inaugurate a more inclusive society. For example, while historians have often interpreted Manuel Estrada Cabrera's twenty-two-year dictatorship through the lens of nineteenth-century liberal caudillismo, these interpretations largely overshadow the protopopulist dimensions of his rule. In particular, President Estrada Cabrera made exceptional use of urban associations and workers' clubs, as well as the spectacular Minerva festivals, to offer Guatemalans of all social classes a means to access the highest forms of Western civilization and participate actively in their cities' modernization and beautification. Through urban associations, many Guatemalans actively adopted Manuel Estrada Cabrera's anti-aristocratic and anti-immigrant discourses and celebrated the ladino artisan as the basis of a new Guatemalan society.

The Mexican and Russian Revolutions, alongside World War I and the 1919 influenza pandemic, created the context for dictator Manuel Estrada Cabrera's overthrow. As in other populist dictatorships, the very tools that had once been instruments of popular incorporation, including the Minerva festivals, became popular symbols of the regime's decay and corruption. By 1920, a broad coalition led by the Unionist Party over-threw Estrada Cabrera and inaugurated a short-lived experiment in democratic and social reform. Rural Q'eqchi's, including leaders such as José Angel Icó, took advantage of the political opening to push far more radical reforms than the Guatemala City–based Unionist party leaders had ever imagined. The democratic opening offered Q'eqchi' patriarchs the opportunity to pursue new forms of native mediation through polit-ical parties instead of municipal councils and Q'eqchi' patriarchal politics. Rural Q'eqchi's engaged in labor strikes and land invasions that upended plantation sovereignty and politics of postponement that loomed so large in Guatemala's racial capitalism. For Guatemalan elites, these radical actions fostered renewed alliances with German immigrants to quell popular rural dissent. This alliance was most dramatically symbolized in an incipient national mestizaje project built around German–Maya racial mixing.

The political opening of the 1920s came to a dramatic close with the stock market crash of 1929 and the Central American Red Scare of 1932. Under the guidance of President Jorge Ubico, the self-proclaimed chief of sanitation, the Guatemalan state expanded rapidly into the countryside through a new corpus of state employees charged with policing vagrancy and boj production as well as promoting rural education and sanitation. These new state workers also effectively challenged plantation sover-eignty, although they did not end it. Ubico also sought to resolve the temporal predicament of Guatemala's nationalism by allowing for the nation's temporary ethnicization through folklore and indigenous beauty pageants that celebrated Maya ethnicity. At the same time, however, he rabidly persecuted certain aspects of Maya culture, including shamanism and boj production, as anti-modern forces that needed to be eradicated. By the mid-1930s, the rise of German National Socialism fostered an anti-imperialist, anti-German, and, ultimately, anti-fascist nationalism, symbolized most profoundly in the adoption of a new regional identity based on Tezultzán. For their part, German–Guatemalans responded with their own versions of Tezultlzán and the peaceful conquest, which continued to grant German immigrants a special place in the nation. After 1942, however, Guatemalans increasingly participated in a growing tide of global anti-fascism that spurred Ubico's downfall and gave rise to a new era of social and political reforms.

While historians have long acknowledged the centrality of Guatemala's 1944 revolution to Latin America's Cold War, they have been much slower to place the revolution in a broader and more global context, including World War II and anti-fascism. The history of Alta Verapaz, however, illustrates how Ponce Vaides's decision to nationalize German properties on the eve of the October 1944 revolution emboldened both revolutionaries and rural Mayas and indelibly shaped the course of the revolution itself. Following new revisionist accounts of the October revolution, this book has sought to attend to the many revolutions from above and below that also took place from 1944 to 1954.[2] These many revolutions became most dramatically evident during the 1952–4 agrarian reform, when Q'eqchi's took up the long-held promise of agrarian reform to demand not simply the redistribution of land, but historical justice and reckoning. As with Yat's 1865 rebellion, the agrarian reform brought together both nineteenth-century histories of land dispossession and labor exploitation and mid-twentieth-century bureaucratic processes in pursuit of capitalist modernity. Similar to Yat's rebellion, the agrarian reform also stood on the precipice of a future to come, in this case one defined by Guatemala's descent into Cold War terror after the military coup of 1954.

The 1954 CIA-supported coup dramatically suspended time, evacuated agency, and restored the violence and fear at the heart of the politics of postponement. It also foretold an ominous future. For Guatemala's upper class, the Guatemalan Revolution was a brief interlude that confirmed the lessons that democracy was dangerous, and reformers were Communists. The "Liberation," for these elites, signaled the end of history: the death of the liberal-democratic metanarrative. When Francis

---

[2] See Julie Gibbings and Heather Vrana, eds., *Out from the Shadow: Revisiting the Revolution from Post-Peace Guatemala* (Austin: University of Texas Press, 2020).

Fukuyama imprudently declared the victory of liberal democracy and the end of history after the collapse of the USSR, he inverted Guatemalan elites' overwhelming sense of the dangers of liberal democracy in 1954.[3] In 1966, when Guatemalan reformers and revolutionaries hoped to recreate the alliances of the Ten Years of Spring and elect Julio César Méndez Montenegro as their leader, they faced a new set of internationalized repressive capabilities that made sure that the revolution would never be replicated. In the face of the resurgent and militant national and continental left and haunted by the legacies of Juan José Arévalo and Jacobo Árbenz, counterrevolutionaries embraced terror with unthinkable zeal. Although the CIA-supported coup and military repression of the 1960s foreclosed the possibility of a more inclusionary nation-state, they did not extinguish Maya and ladino desires for a modernity premised on social and historical justice.

In the aftermath of the military coup, the United States also poured funds into Guatemala's economic development. In March 1955, less than a year after the coup, the vice president of the United States, Richard M. Nixon, announced to the National Security Council that "the United States was now provided with an opportunity to accomplish in two years in Guatemala what the Communists had completely failed to accomplish in ten years."[4] Funding rural and urban infrastructure and championing free trade and private enterprise, the United States sought to turn Guatemala into a showcase for liberal development in Latin America. However, these efforts to manage the counterrevolution and promote economic development worsened Guatemalan poverty and socioeconomic inequality instead of alleviating them.[5] If we take the US officials at their word, new development-oriented foreign aid officers believed they could radically transform Guatemala in as little as two years. Beyond this rhetoric, however, the economic development promoted by the United States and Guatemala's new counterrevolutionary government principally benefited Guatemalan elites, military officers, and foreign investors. In Alta Verapaz, the growth of cattle ranches and coffee plantations, and the ongoing

---

[3] Francis Fukuyama, *The End of History and the Last Man* (New York: Simon and Schuster, 2006 [1992]).

[4] Cited in Stephen M. Streeter, "The Failure of 'Liberal Developmentalism'?: The United States's Anti-Communist Showcase in Guatemala, 1954–1960," *The International History Review* 21, no. 2 (1999): 386.

[5] Stephen M. Streeter, *Managing the Counterrevolution: The United States and Guatemala, 1954–1961*, 34 (Athens: Ohio University Press, 2000); Streeter, "The Failure of 'Liberal Developmentalism.'"

alienation of Q'eqchi' lands, heightened land scarcity and propelled a new round of migration into the northern lowlands of Petén.[6]

This US-backed liberal developmentalism also nullified the democratic promise of the liberal–democratic metanarrative, while at the same time assuring that it would make prosperity and consumption available to all, regardless of class or race.[7] Thus, even while liberal developmentalism downplayed popular sovereignty, this form of economic development marked a significant shift from explanatory models for differences between nations based on race to ones based on resources, industry, and technology.[8] Alongside these novel explanatory models, a cadre of newly minted development experts espoused the belief that a change in external conditions could accelerate cultural and racial improvement.[9] However, this new anti-communist developmentalism, just like the revolution it sought to displace, rested on the historical rubble of nineteenth-century modernity. For revolutionaries and developmentalists alike, the world still consisted of two principal kinds of subjects – the modern and the non-modern – and nonmodern subjects required intervention and guidance to achieve modernity, whether conceived in liberal or Marxist terms.[10]

Q'eqchi' beliefs that another society was possible, alongside ongoing political repression, led many Q'eqchi's in Alta Verapaz to seek new alternatives built on creative translations between universalist Marxist philosophies and Maya political ontologies based on Tzuultaq'as.[11] Even as the countryside militarized, repression grew, and the war escalated, Q'eqchi' leaders worked to end forced labor and redistribute land. These leaders built on the legacies of generations of Q'eqchi' political struggles and were deeply embedded within community structures. Similar to José Angel Icó, new Q'eqchi' leaders worked to be good fathers who supported their villages' interests. To that end, they joined different clandestine movements, including Guatemala's Communist Party (Partido

---

[6] See, especially, Liza Grandia, *Enclosed: Conservation, Cattle, and Commerce among the Q'eqchi' Maya Lowlanders* (Seattle: University of Washington Press, 2012).

[7] For this history, see Gilbert Rist, *The History of Development: From Western Origins to Global Faith* (New York: Zed Books, 2003), 69–70.

[8] On development as a depoliticizing force, see James Ferguson, *The Anti-Politics Machine: "Development," Depoliticization, and Bureaucratic Power in Lesotho* (Cambridge: Cambridge University Press, 1990).

[9] On the cultural racism of developmentalism, see, for example, De la Cadena, *Indigenous Mestizos*.

[10] María Josefina Saldaña-Portillo, *The Revolutionary Imagination in the Americas and the Age of Development* (Durham, NC: Duke University Press, 2003).

[11] See, for example, Grandin, *The Last Colonial Massacre*.

General de Trabajadores, PGT), the Peasant Unity Committee (Comité de Unidad Campesina, CUC), and the Guerrilla Army of the Poor (Ejército de Guerrilla de los Pobres, EGP). Over generations, the networks and practices for these patriarchal politics changed, and sometimes individuals shifted political allegiances, as they had over decades in Alta Verapaz when legal norms surrounding municipal councils and party politics changed. In the 1970s, whole extended families and, at times, whole communities joined their leaders in the PGT, CUC, and EGP, thus reflecting the enduring power of patriarchal bonds. Facing increased mobilization and demands for reform, the state and ruling class, through police, the military, and death squads, responded with untold violence and repression. By the 1980s, the military unleashed a wave of terror that severed alliances, destroyed organizations, and decimated rebels. The counterinsurgent campaign was designed to destroy Maya relations of power and authority, as well as the distinct visions of political modernity that Mayas had fought to create.

In Alta Verapaz, this new age of state terror was announced most dramatically on May 29, 1978. In the town of Panzós, located in Alta Verapaz's Polochic valley, between 500 and 700 Q'eqchi' men, women, and children arrived to present a letter to the mayor announcing the impending visit of a union delegation from the capital to discuss long-standing peasant complaints against local planters and a nickel mining company. As Q'eqchi's had done on countless other occasions, they assembled in the town square to press for their demands for land and justice. On this occasion, however, the military had gathered nearby and opened fire on the protestors. At least thirty-five Q'eqchi's were murdered and dozens wounded, although survivors suggest the number of dead reached into the hundreds. While death squads had been targeting activist leaders well before the Panzós massacre, the 1978 killing prefigured Guatemala's dramatic descent into Cold War state terror and gave state violence a decidedly ethnic cast.[12]

At the same time, in the department of Alta Verapaz, the Guatemalan government continued to celebrate Maya traditions and culture, most visibly in the region's national folklore festival held each July in Cobán.[13] Since 1971 festival organizers had brought together regional indigenous beauty queens from across the nation to compete for the title of Daughter of the King (*Rabín Ahua*). Building on the legacies of Ubico's sanctioned

---

[12] Grandin, *The Last Colonial Massacre.*
[13] Betsy Konefal, "Subverting Authenticity: Reinas Indigenas and the Guatemalan State, 1978," *Hispanic American Historical Review* 89, no. 1 (February 1, 2009): 41–72.

indigenismo, the folklore festival was designed to celebrate and "keep watch over" Maya authenticity.[14] In the aftermath of the Panzós massacre of Q'eqchi's, Maya beauty queens condemned the state-sponsored folk festival and called on supporters to boycott it. Drawing on the gendered symbolism of Maya culture and dress, they protested army violence against indigenous communities. Other Maya elites, however, aligned themselves more closely with the military. For instance, Marta Elena "Nana" Winter, a Q'eqchi'–German, who was crowned Cobán's 1961 india bonita, was the common-law spouse of the brutal Altaverapacence military general, Manuel Benedicto Lucas García. Nana Winter quickly became the anti-communist counterpart to Rigoberta Menchú. During the 1980s and 1990s, she traveled to Europe and the United States representing the Maya people of Guatemala.[15]

The Panzós massacre, then, marked a crucial historical watershed in Guatemala's descent into genocidal violence that marked the early 1980s. As Greg Grandin has argued, it is tempting to understand the Panzós massacre as "a third-world perversion of the fall of the Bastille, ushering in not liberty, equality, and fraternity but a kind of postcolonial modernity based on subjugation, exclusion, and terror."[16] As Grandin rightly notes, it is far too simplistic to blame this kind of violence on a largely fictive Enlightenment that generated discourses of racial hierarchy and rationalized the use of repressive state apparatuses. Instead, Grandin maintains that such violence was rooted in the political struggles of the Cold War. Modernity, however, should not be dismissed so lightly. For more than a century, Altaverapacences' political struggles pertained to different modernities and the promised futures they foretold. Given these histories, we can see how the violence of Panzós was itself a time-knot that braided together the historical debris of Guatemala's racial capitalism and the contemporary brutality of the Cold War, presaging the prodigious political violence yet to come. Only three years later, the military launched a genocidal scorched-earth campaign that murdered more than 100,000 Mayas and annihilated more than 400 indigenous Communists. In this genocidal violence, Guatemala's postcolonial modernity revealed its truly monstrous historical formation.

Guatemala's violence brought together anti-Communist zeal and a racial hatred rooted in the historical remains of more than a century of

---

[14] Folklore festival organizer, cited in ibid., 43.
[15] Interview with the author, April 5, 2008. [16] Grandin, *The Last Colonial Massacre*, 3.

understanding Mayas as dangerous anachronisms that threatened
national progress. The killings were brutal beyond imagination: the military engaged in mass rapes, extracted organs and fetuses, and burned
victims alive. These practices were deployed in a genocidal campaign that
was designed to break down what strategists deemed to be the closed,
caste-like isolation of indigenous communities and extend the state into
rural space. While late nineteenth-century Liberals identified the Maya
civil–religious hierarchy as the reason for Mayas' resistance to wage
labor, late twentieth-century anti-communists believed that isolation
explained Mayas' supposed collective susceptibility to communism. As
such, they were identified as enemies for being guerrilla sympathizers and
as enemies of the modern nation. As Jean Franco has suggested, the
military understood Mayas as aliens to modernity; they represented a
particular threat to the nation that justified the brutality of the state's
response.[17] Following the military's logic that equated indigenous culture
with subversion, army units destroyed ceremonial sites and turned sacred
places, such as village hermitages and caves, into torture chambers. As
Enrique Dussel has argued, "Since the barbarian is opposed to the civilizing process, modern praxis must in the end use violence if necessary to
destroy the obstacles to modernization."[18] When Guatemalan modernizers – from the German coffee planter Richard Sapper to Jorge Ubico and
the genocidal dictator, Efrain Ríos Montt – encountered stubbornly
heterogeneous Mayas, they denounced them as anachronisms, sometimes
with unthinkable violence.

Under the infamous dictatorship of Efrain Ríos Montt, the army's
program of pacification and development pursued the twin goals of
destroying Maya communal life and rewarding survivors with tools
and work in reorganized communities. Ultimately, this program sought
to extend the state into the countryside and root out dangerous threats
to the nation, once and for all. The first phase of this program, known as
Operation Ashes (Operación Ceniza), led to the mass slaughter of
approximately 7,500 people over eighteen months. During this stage,
the state acted not only to physically eliminate guerrillas and their real
or imagined supporters but also to symbolically conquer the national
territory. As Greg Grandin has argued, the military "coloniz[ed] the
spaces, symbols, and social relations analysts believed to be outside of

---

[17] Jean Franco, *Cruel Modernity* (Durham, NC: Duke University Press, 2013).
[18] Enrique Dussel, *El encubrimiento del otro: Hacia el origen del mito de la modernidad*
(Quito: Editorial Abya Yala, 1994), 209–10.

state control."[19] At times, these spaces were Q'eqchi' political ontologies themselves. The Guatemalan Ministry of Defense sponsored a local historian to write a history of the peaceful conquest, *El Mundo K'ekchi' de la Vera-Paz* (1979), which celebrated the virtue of the Verapaz Maya "kings" who brokered peace with the Spanish friars.[20] The army also appropriated the figure of Tzuultaq'a, erecting a sign that said, "Cobán's Military Base, Home of the Tzuultaq'a Soldier."[21] The second phase took place through the reorganization of indigenous life around model villages and development poles, which subjected people to barracks-like conditions under military surveillance. While the first phase articulated Mayas as dangerous threats to modernity, the second drew on the legacies of coerced labor and surveillance as the core of state and nonstate civilizing efforts.

Central to the military's counterinsurgency offensive in the countryside was the formation of civil defense patrols (Patrullas de Autodefensa Civil, PAC). In Alta Verapaz, the PAC were modeled on coffee planters' efforts to arm resident laborers to defend the plantation territory from subversives.[22] Officially, the PAC were set up to defend Maya villages against guerrilla attacks, and participation in the patrols was supposedly voluntary. Unofficially, however, all males between the ages of eighteen and sixty were obligated to join the PAC, on penalty of severe punishment or even death. Some of those who were forced to serve were as young as eight years old. The patrollers' workweek could be up to twenty-four hours, and they were not compensated. Besides acting as an information network for the military, they were forced to carry out military tasks, including sweeping areas for guerrillas and attacking so-called subversive villages. Their actions, in many respects, mirrored those of El Q'eq, who roamed the plantation at night, policing and disciplining workers, and

---

[19] Grandin, *The Last Colonial Massacre*, 129.

[20] Drawing on widely believed oral tradition, Estrada Monroy narrates how the Q'eqchi' caciques Don Miguel de Paz y Chun, Don Juan Rafael Ramírez Aj Sakq'um, and Don Diego de Ávila Mo y Pop, headed by the "cacique of caciques" Juan Aj Pop'o Batz, traveled to and were received in the Spanish court by Prince Felipe, regent of Carlos V. Juan Aj Pop'o Batz presented Felipe with 2,000 Quetzal feathers on behalf of the caciques of Tuzulutlán. Many even claim he was received by Felipe as an equal, as a prince. As a result of his diplomacy, it is said, Tezulutlán became known as Vera-Paz (True Peace) and was declared free from the influence of Spanish encomenderos. See Agustín Estrada Monroy, *El mundo K'ekchi' de la Vera-Paz* (Guatemala: Editorial del Ejército, 1979).

[21] Wilson, *Maya Resurgence in Guatemala*, 241–2.

[22] Grandin, *The Last Colonial Massacre*, 126–30.

questions emerge about how the PAC also violated Q'eqchi' moral norms.[23] Many civil patrollers, especially higher-ranking ones, were involved in massacres and other human rights abuses throughout the civil war.[24] Others used their power to settle old feuds and steal land or cattle. As Jennifer Schirmer argues, "Nowhere else in Latin America has an army managed to mobilize and divide an indigenous population against itself to such an extent – even to the point of forcing victims to become accomplices and kill one another."[25] Through coerced labor, the Guatemalan military sought to dismantle the basis of Q'eqchi' political ontologies; they "not only broke local solidarity but, following the primary objective of the pacification campaign, bound the perpetrators in an impious blood ritual to a larger impersonal state collective as represented by the military."[26] In a perversion of the past, the military deployed the the state's most dreaded practice – coerced labor – to defeat the most sacred principles of Q'eqchi' political life – solidarity and reciprocity.

The use of civil patrols as part of a state counterinsurgency campaign speaks to a perverse legacy of coerced labor in Guatemala. After the transition to democracy in 1985, Article 34 of the new constitution established that "no Guatemalan could be forced into servitude." Based on this provision, some civil patrollers demanded that they no longer be forced into servitude for the state.[27] Nevertheless, the civil patrols continued until the signing of the Peace Accords in 1996. Once mobilized and armed in the context of civil war, the former civil patrol now sits in uneasy relationship with past struggles against coerced labor, because patrollers, too, committed human rights violations. The civil patrols, and the military program's general logic, illustrate how enduring practices, such as coerced labor, surveillance, and state sovereignty, resurface in subsequent moments with altered meanings, contours, and effects. Struggles over modernity, and the colonial pasts they evoke, are so deeply threaded through the fabric of contemporary life that they remain present everywhere.

---

[23] Alfonso Huet, *Nos salvó la sagrada selva: la memoria de veinte comunidades Q'eqchi'es que sobrevivieron al genocidio* (Guatemala: ADICI Wakliiqo, 2008).

[24] Simone Remijnse, "Remembering Civil Patrols in Joyabaj, Guatemala," *Bulletin of Latin American Research* 20, no. 4 (December 16, 2002): 454–69.

[25] Jennifer Schirmer, *The Guatemalan Military Project: A Violence Called Democracy* (Philadelphia: University of Pennsylvania Press, 2010), 81.

[26] Grandin, *The Last Colonial Massacre*, 129.

[27] https://nvdatabase.swarthmore.edu/content/guatemalans-refuse-serve-civil-patrols-1988-1993. Last accessed 09/03/2020

These recursive and time-knotted histories are also multiple. As this book has illustrated, Guatemala's state formation and capitalist expansion were neither straightforward nor linear; these were fragmented and uneven processes that grew in fits and starts, reversals and leaps, and depended as much on private planter sovereignty as on state control. Mandamiento labor, for example, expanded rapidly across the 1870s and early 1880s, was abolished in 1892 following much regional and national debate, and then was reintroduced in the form of zapadores after 1898 and brought back during the coffee boom of the late 1920s. Likewise, capitalism expanded unevenly and drew on, rather than extinguished, Maya political ontologies and practices of subsistence production. As such, Q'eqchi's, and especially Q'eqchi' patriarchs, actively participated in the making of the nation-state and capitalism, even if they rarely attained the visions of modernity that they envisioned. Indeed, it is easy to elide Q'eqchi' political ontologies, because they exist largely in archival gaps and fissures that come to life through a careful reading along and against the archival grain. Occasionally, these political ontologies erupted through events, such as Alta Verapaz's 1886 frost, which so clearly evinced the centrality of spirit worlds to Q'eqchi' interpretations of coffee production and mandamiento labor. In those moments, another view of history – one not based on the singular and disenchanted time of Eurocentric modernity – becomes possible. Through such moments, we can grasp the multiple and competing times and views of causation that shaped historical action in the past. Indeed, history itself was often made in the clash between these competing perspectives.

Such moments also reveal that capturing the complexity of subaltern action in society must recognize that rural Mayas were not untouched by power but deeply imbricated in their own hierarchies and possessed and reproduced through their own occlusions. Just as there was no homogenous or single group of German coffee planters acting with unified interests, rural Q'eqchi's were neither unified nor unitary, and social hierarchies cut across their social relations. Attending to subaltern stories, then, necessitates that we avoid romanticizing indigenous actors as we actively seek to recuperate their often-hidden stories.

Through their many political actions, ranging from land invasions and labor strikes to allegories of plantation capitalism in El Q'eq, and millennial revolts spurred by the revenge of the mountain spirit Xucaneb, Q'eqchi's continually made the violent pasts of the nineteenth century visibly present and offered alternative routes to a more inclusive modernity. As they have repeatedly shown, history leaves debris and time accumulates.[28] The wreckage of the past weighs particularly heavily on postcolonial nations such as Guatemala, where the racialized violence of their foundations remains ever alive. Guatemala's racialized state violence, like the contemporary neoliberal era of insecurity, is thus not an aberration from the past, but the culmination of historical remnants that refuse to be vanquished. In order to overcome the legacies of racism, colonialism, and political violence, we must undertake a wide-ranging critique of racism and ideologies of difference, including history and its legacies. As Achille Mbembe writes, such a critique means *"[t]he weight of history will be there. We must learn to do a better job of carrying it, and of sharing its burden. We are condemned to live not only with what we have produced but also with what we have inherited."*[29] Mbembe's words remind me of an encounter I witnessed when Marlon García Arriaga, my research assistant, and I were helping relocate Cobán's municipal archive from a dank basement with dirt floors to drier, more secure conditions. Municipal maintenance employees aided the arduous work of carrying heavy boxes of historical records across Cobán's central plaza. One of the workers, Mateo, was loaded with heavy boxes, when he was stopped by a ladino wearing smart boots and an expensive jacket. In the shadow of a monument to Manuel Tot, the Q'eqchi' independence leader, the wealthy ladino interrupted Mateo with the sharp accusation: "What are you doing?" Barely missing a beat, Mateo responded with a proud smile: "We are carrying history, sir." It is time to share that burden.

---

[28] For this insight, see Ian Baucom, *Specters of the Atlantic: Finance Capital, Slavery, and the Philosophy of History* (Durham, NC: Duke University Press, 2005).

[29] Achille Mbembe, *Critique of Black Reason* (Durham, NC: Duke University Press, 2017), 177. Emphasis added.

Glossary

Alcalde auxiliar plantation representative before the municipal council
Alcalde primero first mayor
Aldea small village
Altaverapacenses Residents of Alta Verapaz
Awas series of prohibitions, moral values according to which the
    Tzuultaq'as regulate resources and other objects in their territories
Ayuntamiento municipal council
Barrios neighborhoods, arranged by ethnic clans
Boj maize liquor
Brazos literally arms; refers to laborers
Caballería unit of land measurement equal to approximately 45 hectares
Cabecera seat of government
Cabildo town council
Caciques indigenous political leader or boss
Caporal foreman
Cargos contributions, duties, and communal sacrifices
Castas mixed-race peoples
Caudillo strongman leader
Censo rent
Censo enfiteusis rental of municipal lands
Censo enfitéutico system of renting municipal lands
Censo de vialidad road census
Chinames elders
Ciudad letrada lettered city
Civilización civilization
Cobaneros residents of Cobán

Cofrade member of a **cofradía**
Cofradía confraternity
Colonos resident laborers
Coronel colonel
Corregidor chief magistrate
Croqui sketch
Cuerda unit of land measurement
Curanderos shamans
Ejido town common lands
Enganchados indebted contract laborers
Enganche indentured labor
Fichas plantation currency
Finca de mozos coffee plantation with resident workers obliged to work
  for the planter
Fomento development
Gobernador governor
Habilitación wage advance
Habilitador person who gives workers a **habilitación** to seal a work
  agreement
Hacienda landed estate
Indigenismo pro-indigenous reforms
Indigenista pro-indigenous reformers
Indio Indian
Intendente municipal municipal mayors in the 1930s
Jornaleros indebted contract laborers
Ladino non-Maya
Latifundio large estate
Legua league
Libreta passbook to prove working status
Lista negra blacklist
Maguey fiber for making rope
Mandamientos system of forced wage labor, a reconstitution of colonial-
  era **repartimientos**
Manzana unit of land, approximately 1.72 acres
Mayek ceremonial arrangements
Mecapal leather device for carrying heavy loads (tumpline)
Mestizaje miscegenation
Milpa planted field that combined maize and other foods, such as beans
  and squash
Mozos resident laborers

Mozos colonos resident laborers
Naturales Natives
Orejas spies
Paab'ank celebration for the patron saint
Parcialidades commonly held lands of ethnic clans
Patrones bosses
Plano plan
Préstamo loan
Principales elders
Progreso progress
Pueblo the people
El Q'eq half-man, half cow that polices German plantations
Quintal unit of weight measurement; 100 Spanish pounds, or 46
  kilograms
Reducción colonial-era settling process of congregating indigenous
  peoples
Reducciones congregations of Indians
Regidores low-level town council members
Repartimiento Spanish system of forced labor and production
Sanpedranos residents of San Pedro Carchá
Selva untamed forest or jungle
Tarea task
Teniente corregidor lieutenant magistrate
Tezulutlán Land of War
Tierras baldías unoccupied public lands owned by the state
Tinterillo unofficial lawyer
Totopaste dried tortilla meal
Tzuultaq'as Mountain deities
Vara staff of office
Viajes presidenciales president's annual inspection trips
Zapadores labor battalions organized under military discipline for work
  on roads and fortifications

Index

Cambridge Latin American Studies (*continue from page ii*)